SHONEN JUMP ADVANCED
Manga Edition

黒姫
KUROHIME

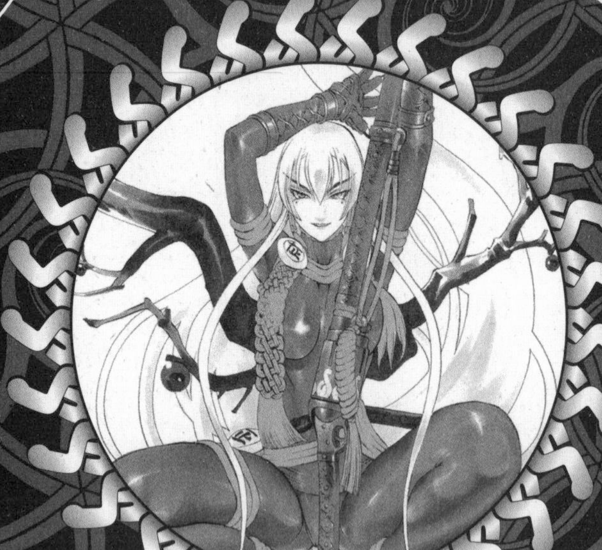

VOL. 1
GUN OF JUSTICE

Story & Art by
Masanori • Ookamigumi • Katakura

黒姫 KUROHIME™

Vol. 1
CONTENTS

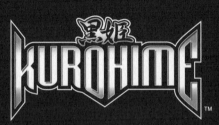

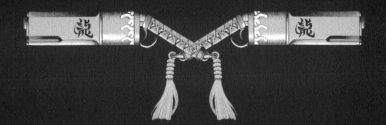

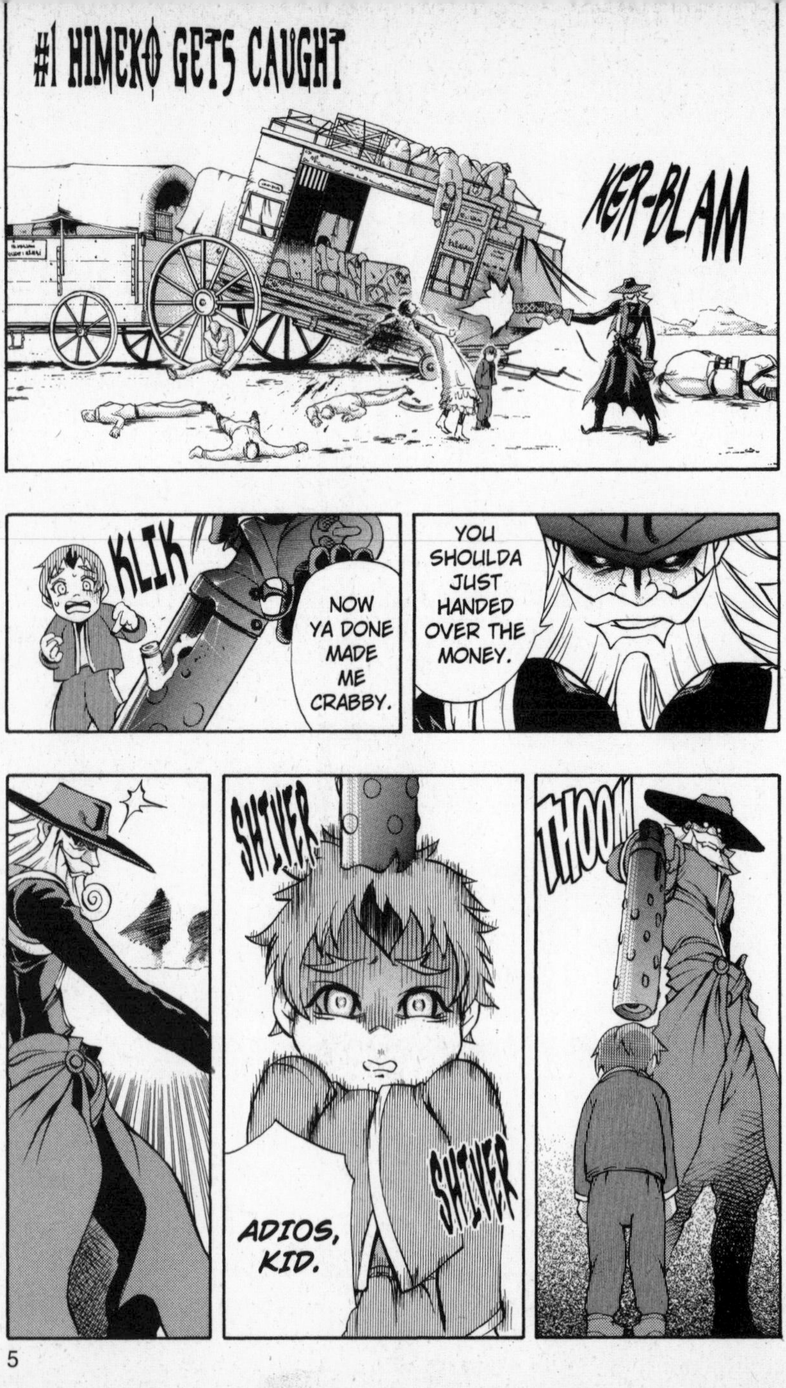
#1 HIMEKO GETS CAUGHT
KER-BLAM
YOU SHOULDA JUST HANDED OVER THE MONEY.
NOW YA DONE MADE ME CRABBY.
KLIK
THOOM
SHIVER
ADIOS, KID.
SHIVER

#1 HIMEKO GETS CAUGHT

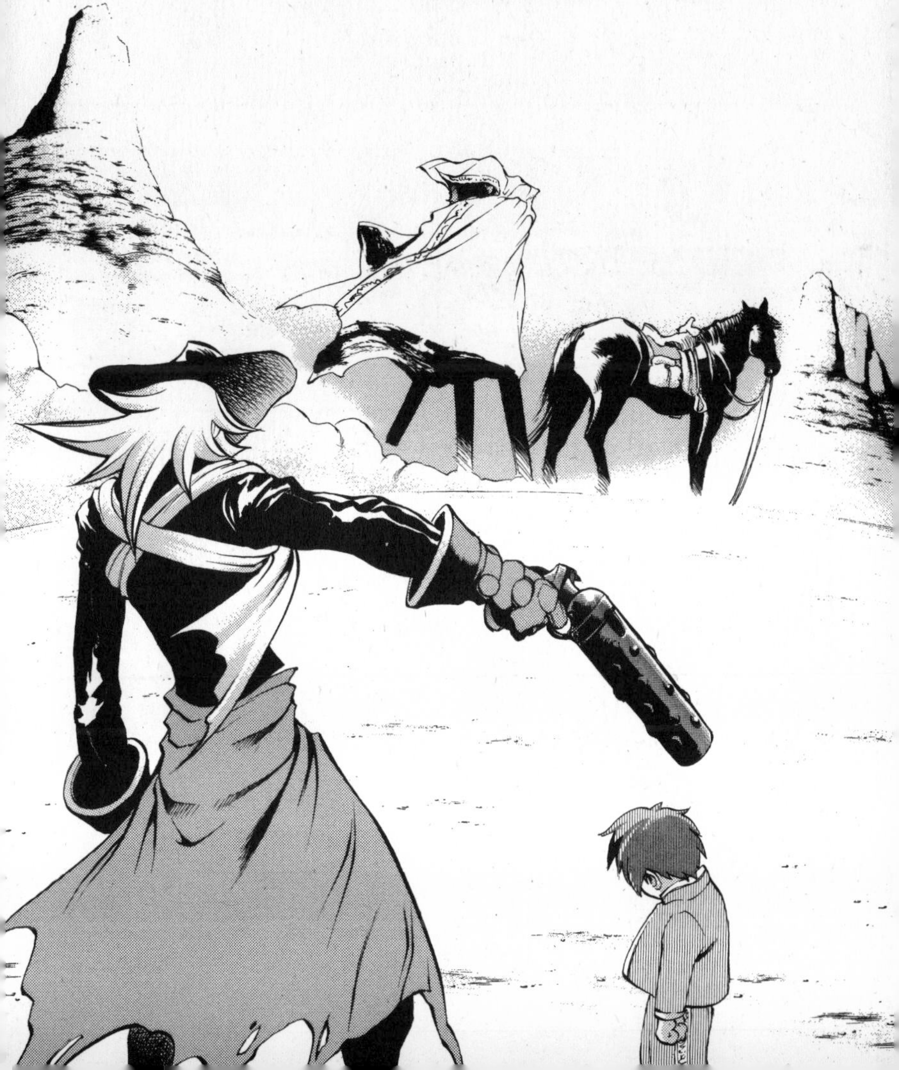

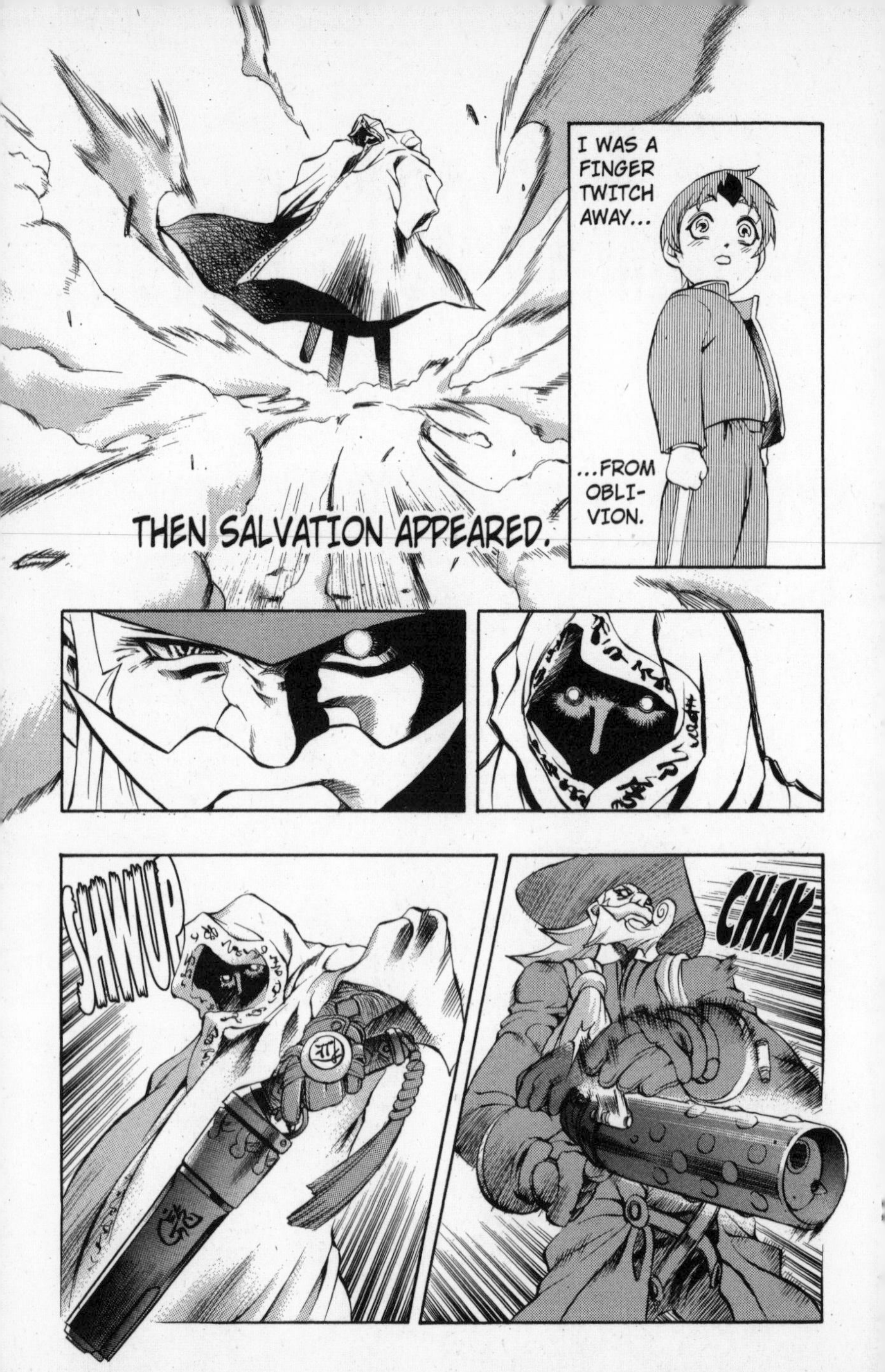
I WAS A FINGER TWITCH AWAY...
...FROM OBLIVION.
THEN SALVATION APPEARED.
CHAK
SHWUP

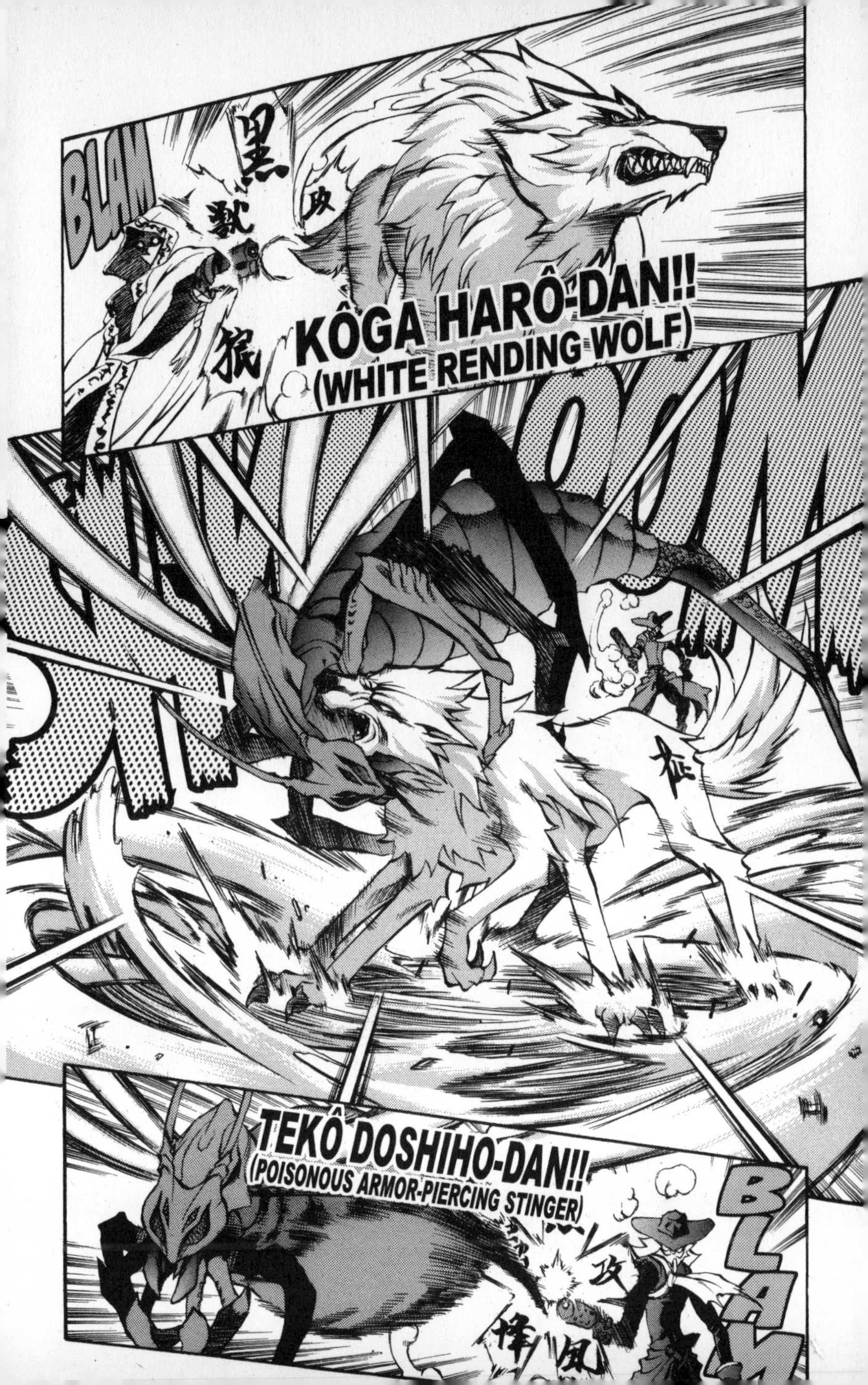
BLAM
KÔGA HARÔ-DAN!!
(WHITE RENDING WOLF)
TEKÔ DOSHIHO-DAN!!
(POISONOUS ARMOR-PIERCING STINGER)
BLAM

READ THIS WAY

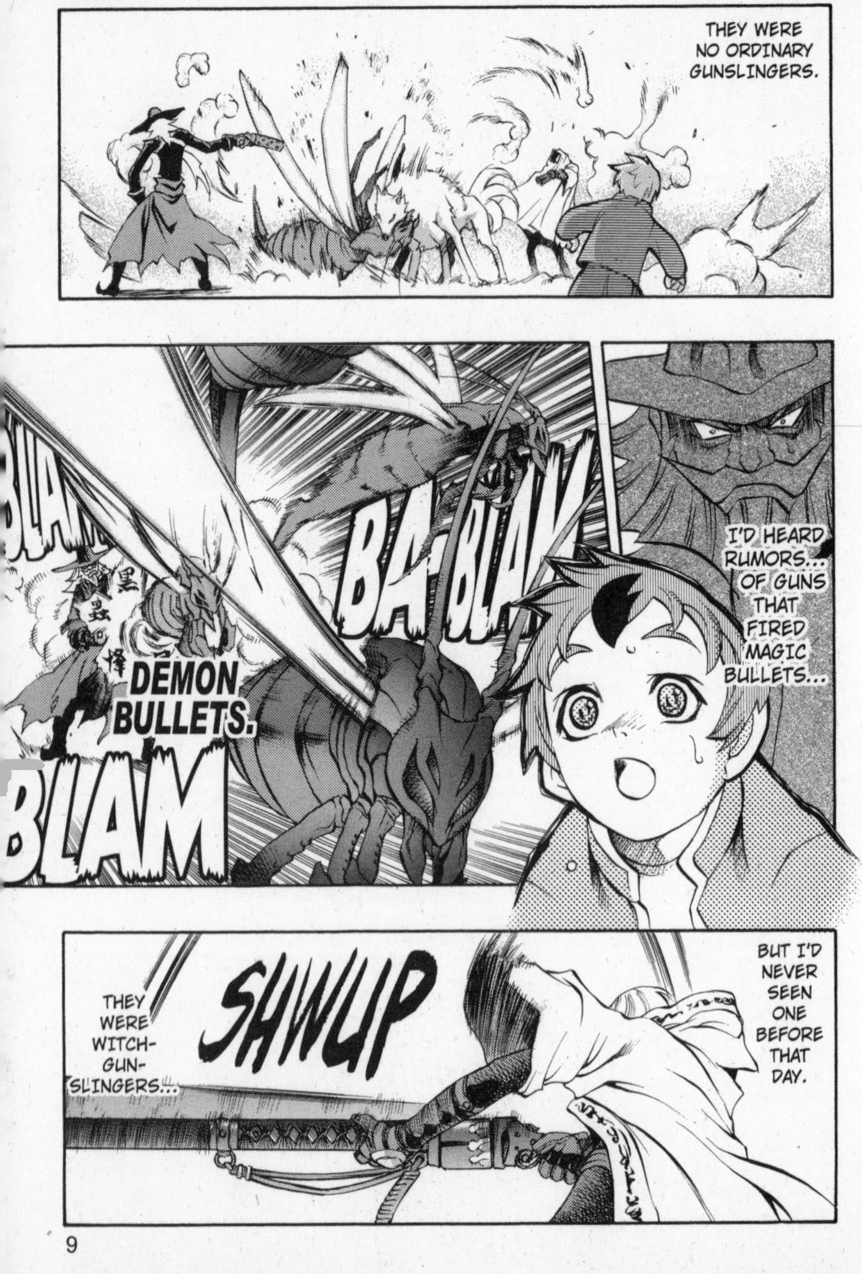

THEY WERE NO ORDINARY GUNSLINGERS.
I'D HEARD RUMORS... OF GUNS THAT FIRED MAGIC BULLETS...
BA-BLAM
DEMON BULLETS.
BLAM
BUT I'D NEVER SEEN ONE BEFORE THAT DAY.
SHWUP
THEY WERE WITCH-GUNSLINGERS...

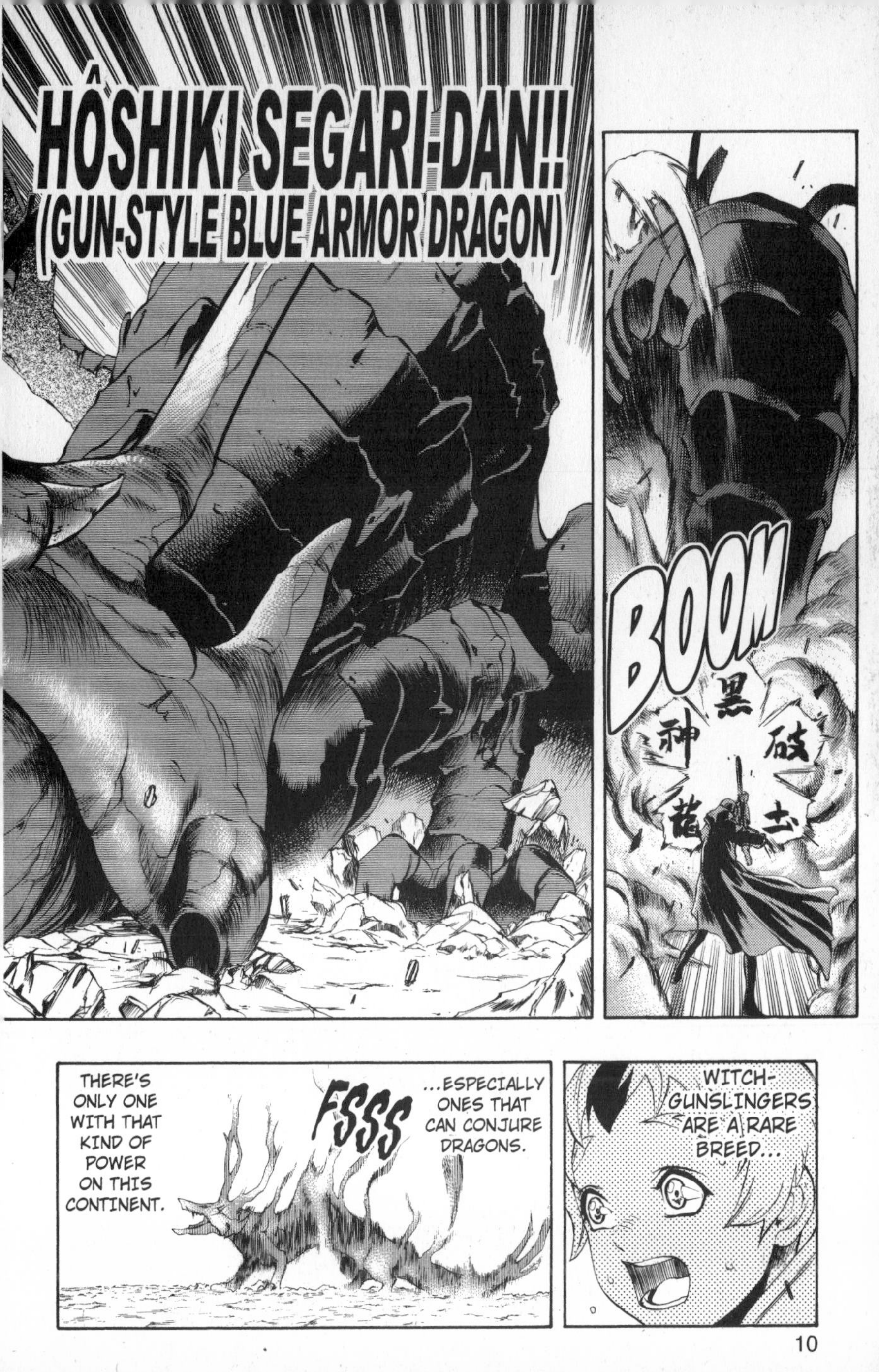
BOOM
HÔSHIKI SEGARI-DAN!!
(GUN-STYLE BLUE ARMOR DRAGON)
WITCH-GUNSLINGERS ARE A RARE BREED...
...ESPECIALLY ONES THAT CAN CONJURE DRAGONS.
FSSS
THERE'S ONLY ONE WITH THAT KIND OF POWER ON THIS CONTINENT.

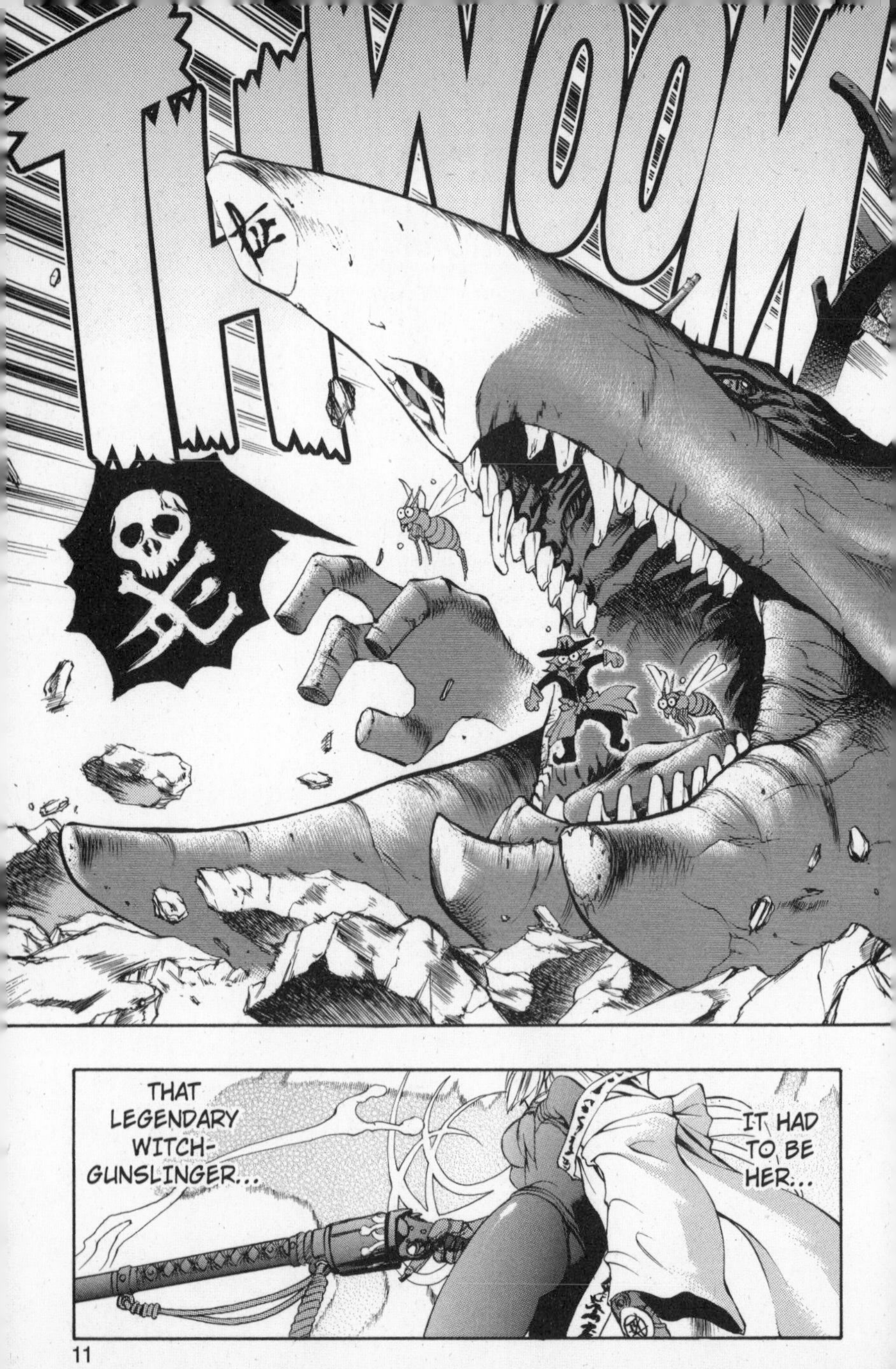
THWOOM
IT HAD TO BE HER...
THAT LEGENDARY WITCH-GUNSLINGER...

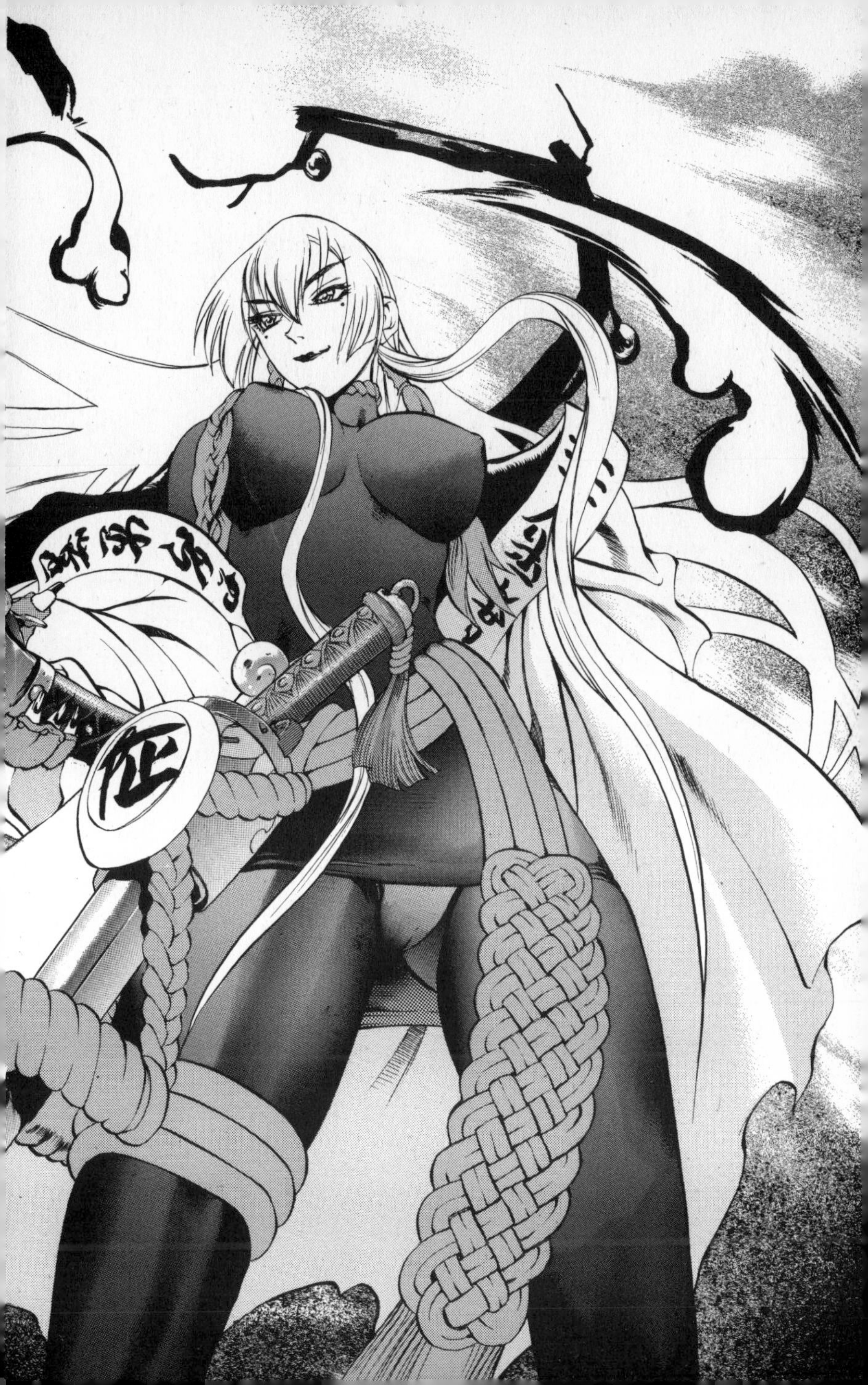

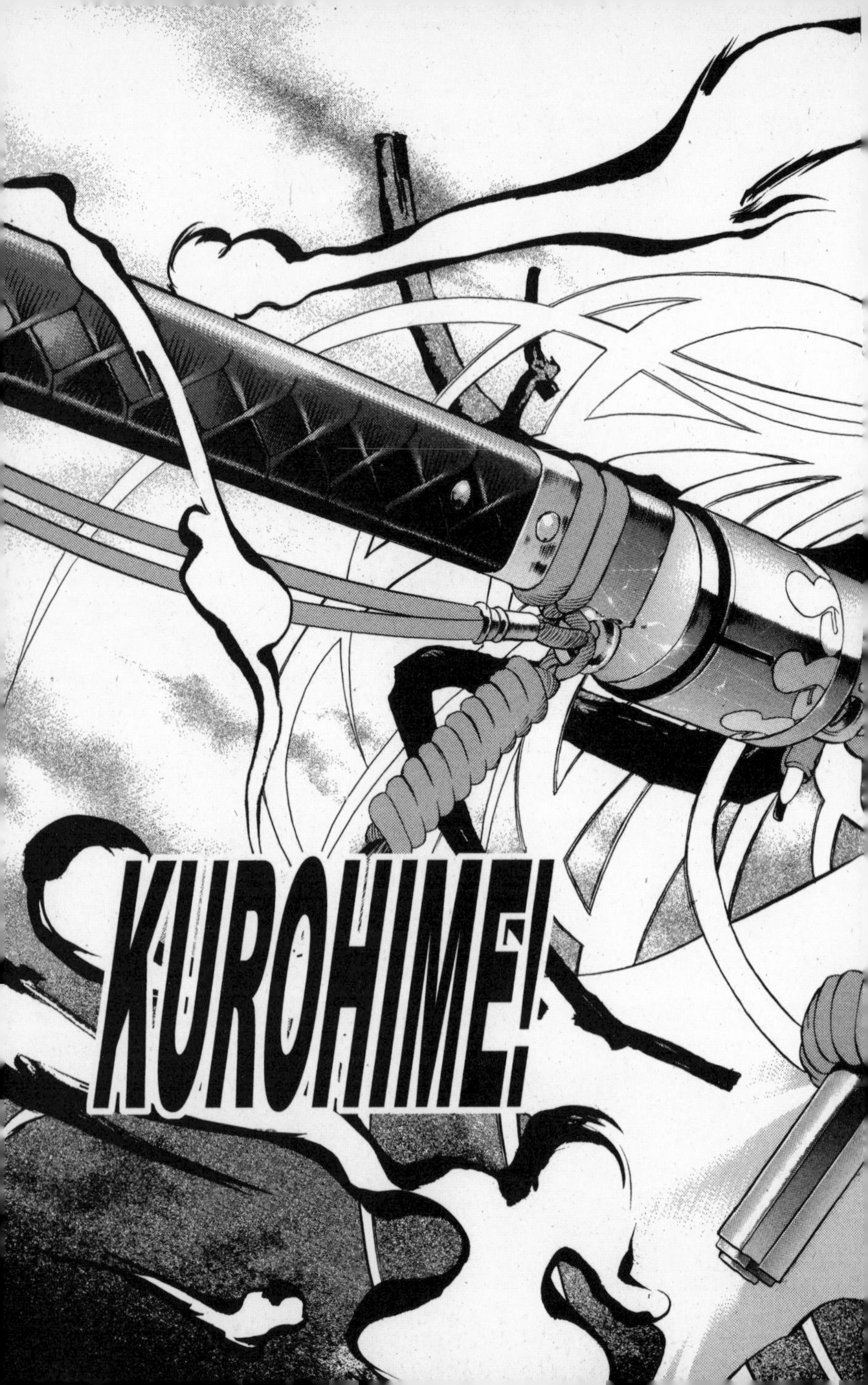
KUROHIME!

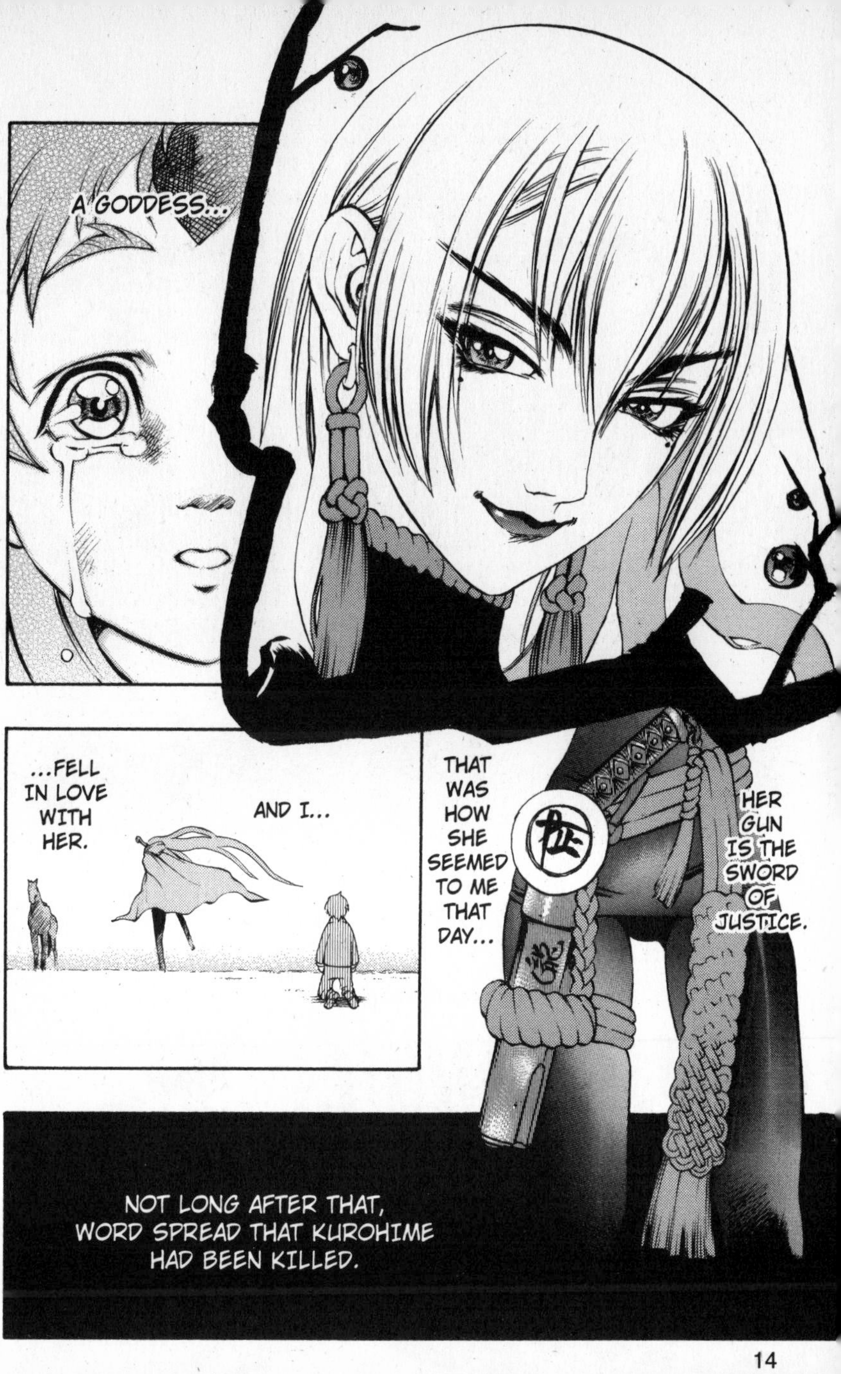
A GODDESS...
HER GUN IS THE SWORD OF JUSTICE.
THAT WAS HOW SHE SEEMED TO ME THAT DAY...
AND I...
...FELL IN LOVE WITH HER.
NOT LONG AFTER THAT, WORD SPREAD THAT KUROHIME HAD BEEN KILLED.

READ THIS WAY

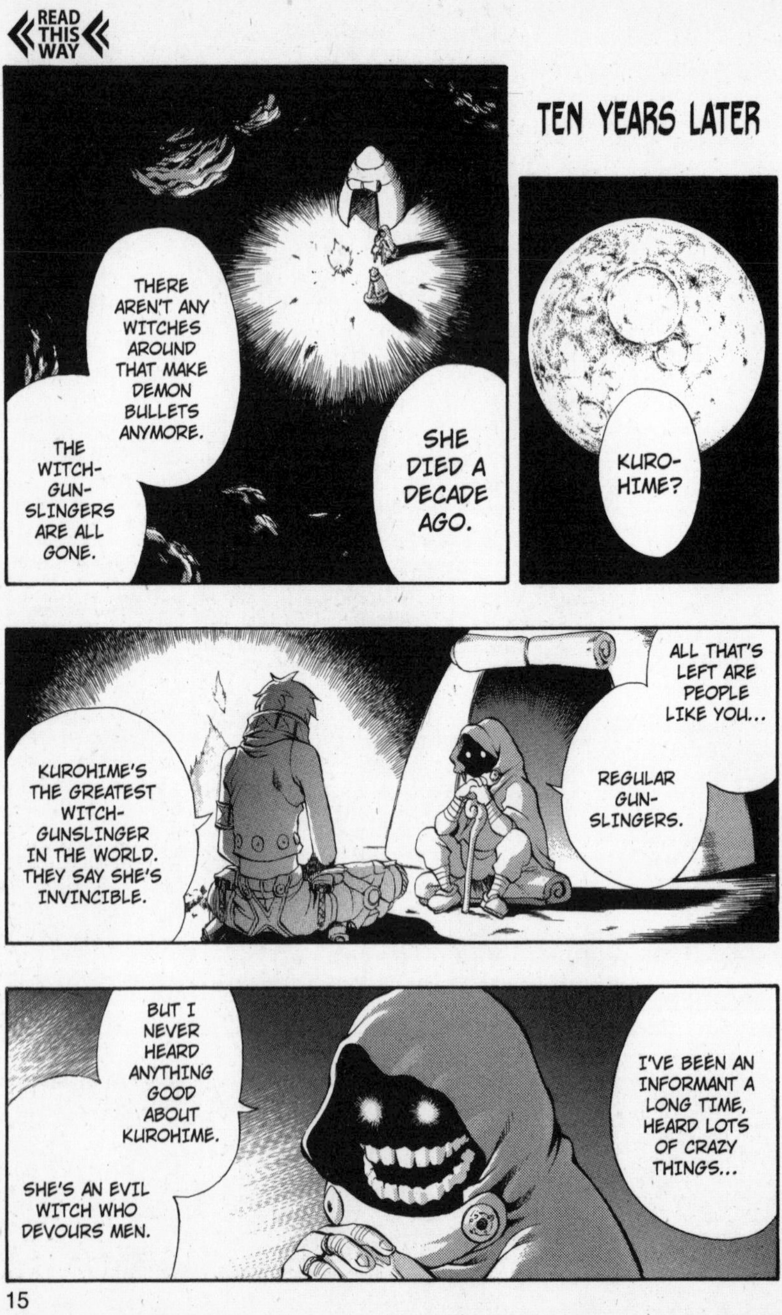
TEN YEARS LATER
KURO-HIME?
SHE DIED A DECADE AGO.
THERE AREN'T ANY WITCHES AROUND THAT MAKE DEMON BULLETS ANYMORE.
THE WITCH-GUN-SLINGERS ARE ALL GONE.
ALL THAT'S LEFT ARE PEOPLE LIKE YOU...
REGULAR GUN-SLINGERS.
KUROHIME'S THE GREATEST WITCH-GUNSLINGER IN THE WORLD. THEY SAY SHE'S INVINCIBLE.
I'VE BEEN AN INFORMANT A LONG TIME, HEARD LOTS OF CRAZY THINGS...
BUT I NEVER HEARD ANYTHING GOOD ABOUT KUROHIME.
SHE'S AN EVIL WITCH WHO DEVOURS MEN.

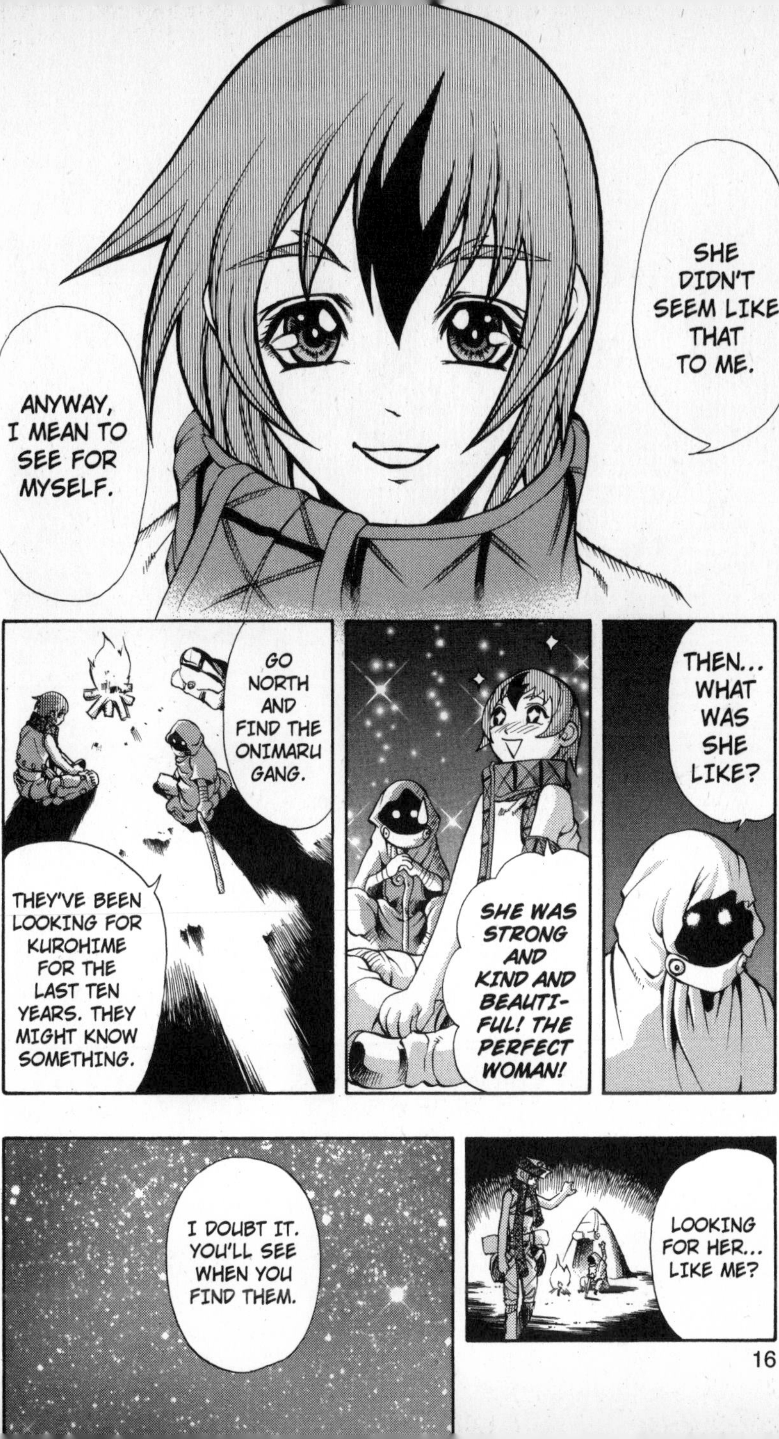
SHE DIDN'T SEEM LIKE THAT TO ME.
ANYWAY, I MEAN TO SEE FOR MYSELF.
THEN... WHAT WAS SHE LIKE?
SHE WAS STRONG AND KIND AND BEAUTIFUL! THE PERFECT WOMAN!
GO NORTH AND FIND THE ONIMARU GANG.
THEY'VE BEEN LOOKING FOR KUROHIME FOR THE LAST TEN YEARS. THEY MIGHT KNOW SOMETHING.
LOOKING FOR HER... LIKE ME?
I DOUBT IT. YOU'LL SEE WHEN YOU FIND THEM.

READ THIS WAY

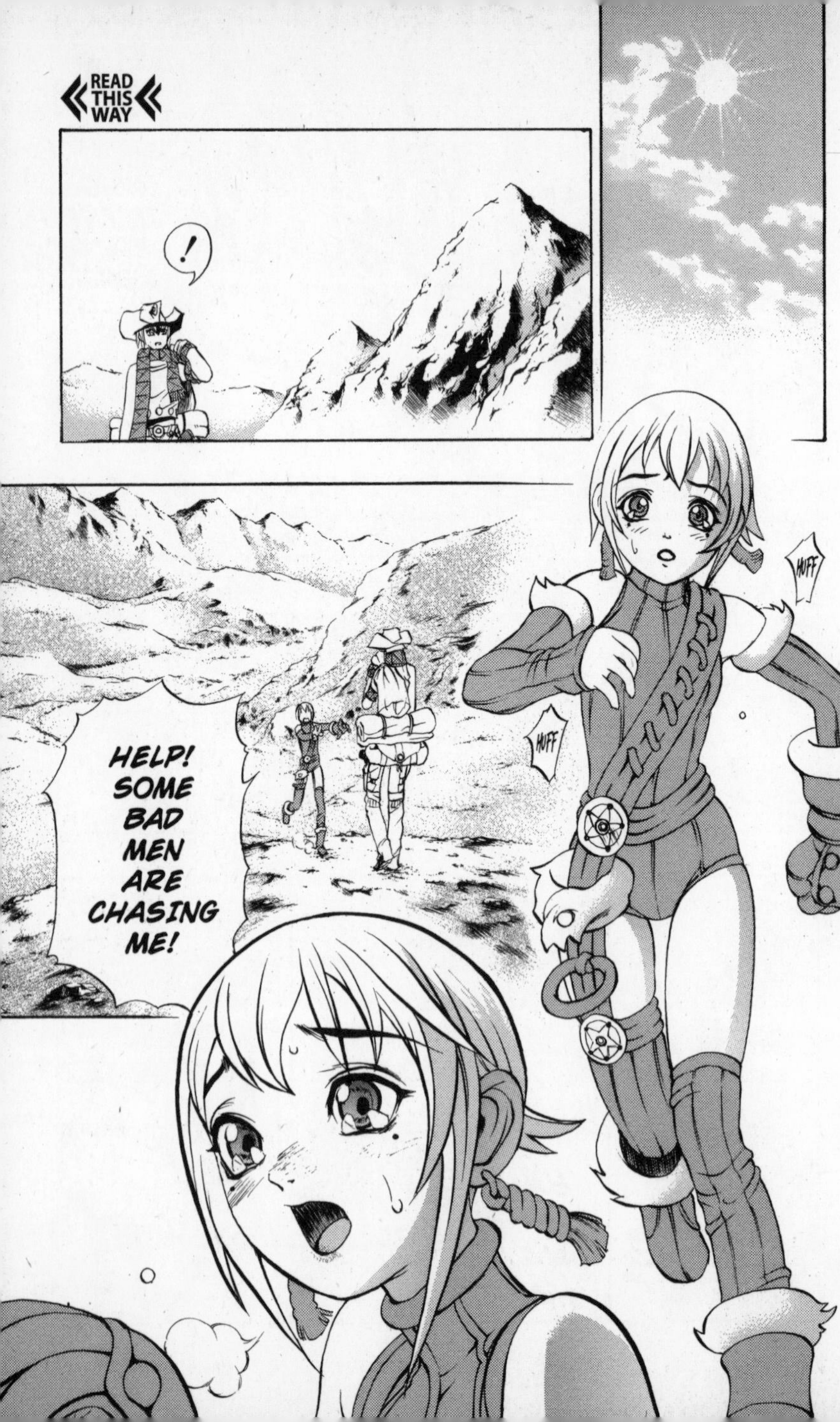
!
HUFF
HUFF
HELP! SOME BAD MEN ARE CHASING ME!

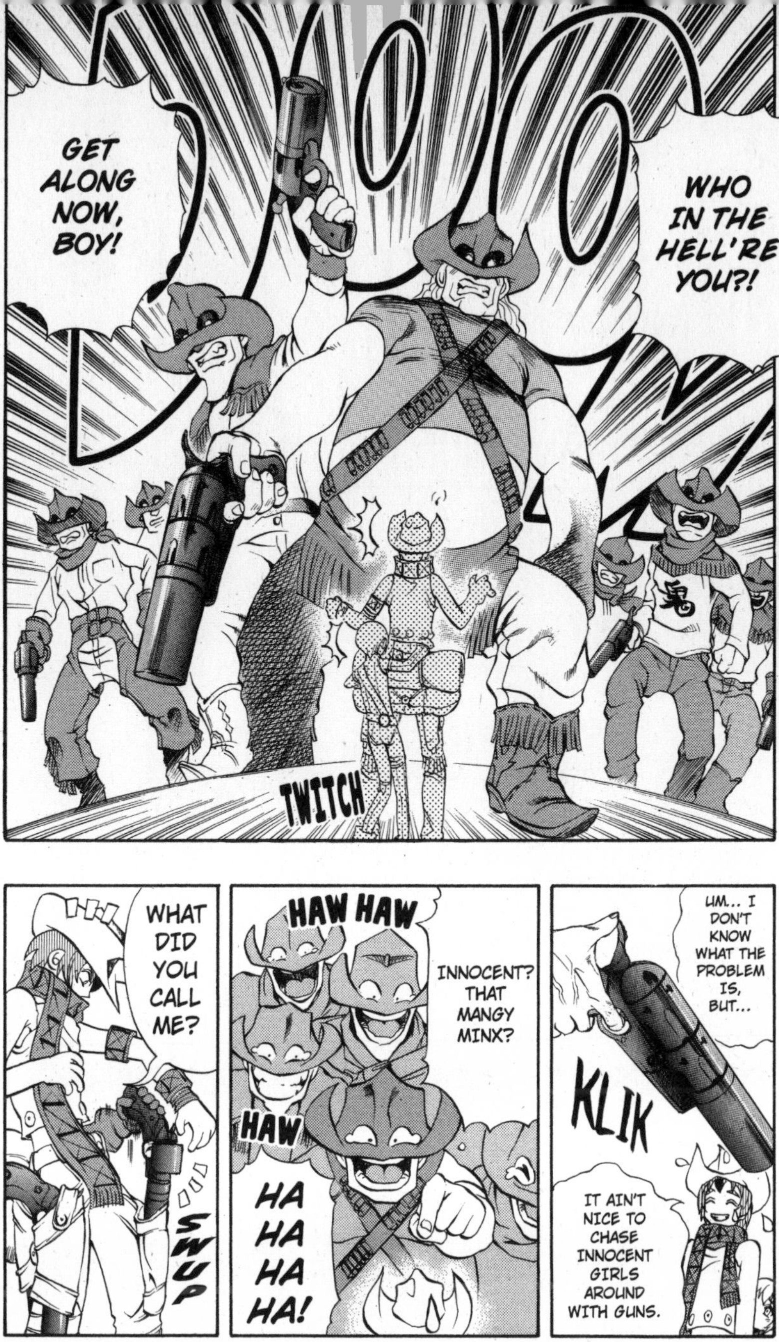
WHO IN THE HELL'RE YOU?!
GET ALONG NOW, BOY!
TWITCH
UM... I DON'T KNOW WHAT THE PROBLEM IS, BUT...
KLIK
IT AIN'T NICE TO CHASE INNOCENT GIRLS AROUND WITH GUNS.
HAW HAW
INNOCENT? THAT MANGY MINX?
HAW
HA HA HA HA!
WHAT DID YOU CALL ME?
SWUP

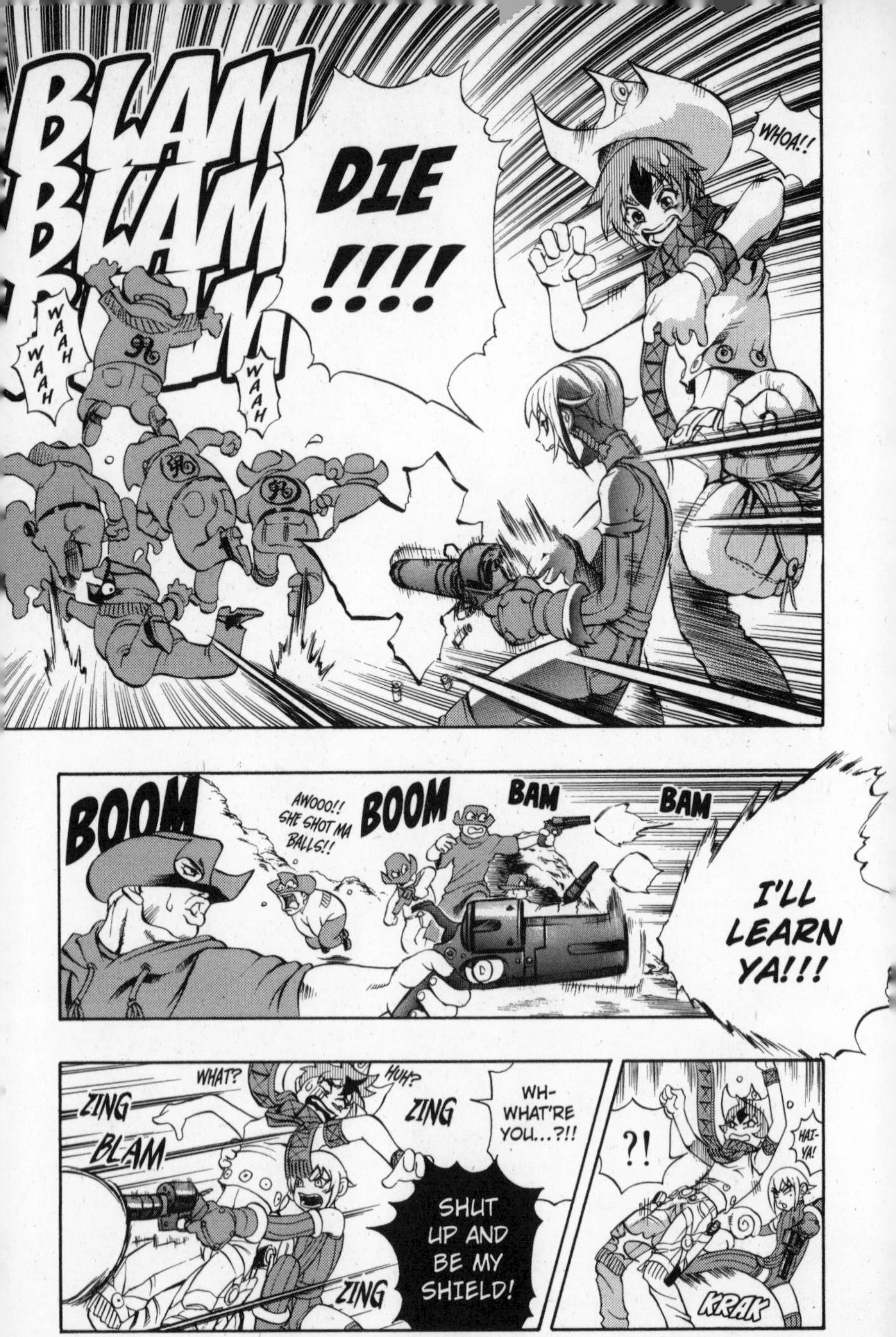
WHOA!!
BLAM
BLAM
BLAM
DIE!!!!
WAAH WAAH
WAAH
I'LL LEARN YA!!!
BAM
BAM
BOOM
AWOOO!! SHE SHOT MA BALLS!!
BOOM
HAI-YA!
?!
KRAK
WH- WHAT'RE YOU...?!!
HUH?
ZING
SHUT UP AND BE MY SHIELD!
WHAT?
ZING
BLAM
ZING

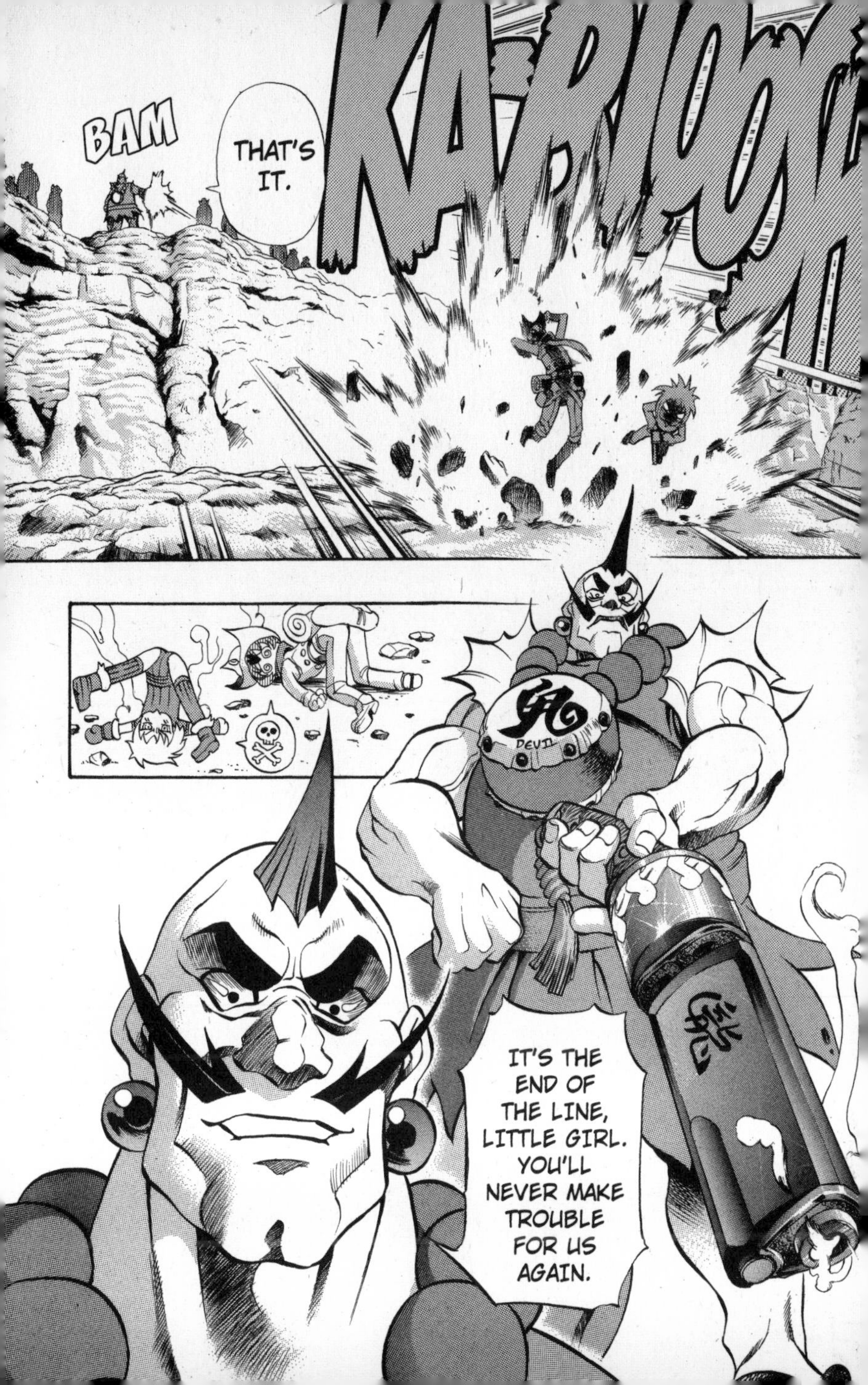
KA-BLOOO
THAT'S IT.
BAM
DEVIL
IT'S THE END OF THE LINE, LITTLE GIRL. YOU'LL NEVER MAKE TROUBLE FOR US AGAIN.

READ THIS WAY

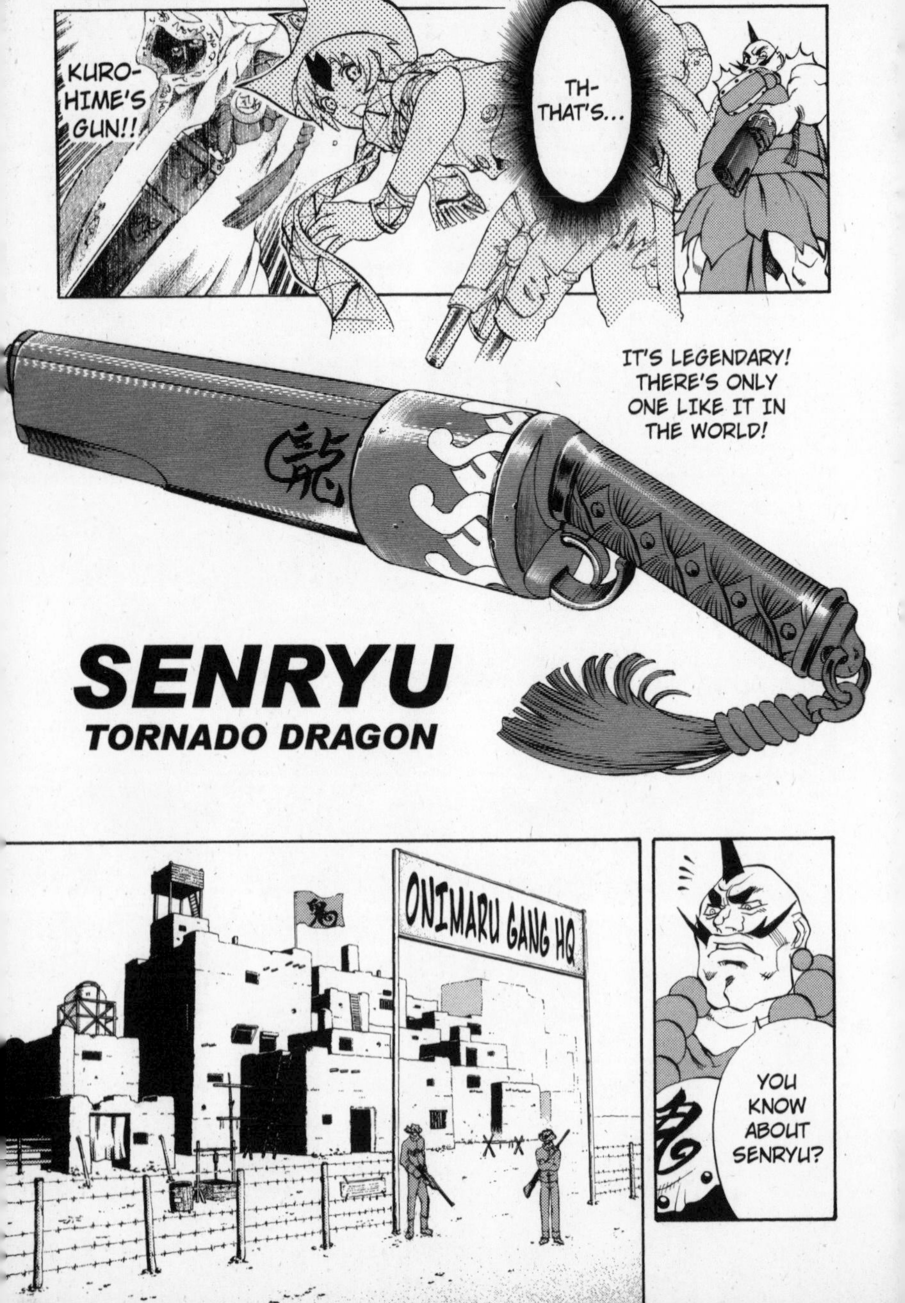
TH- THAT'S...
KURO-HIME'S GUN!!
IT'S LEGENDARY! THERE'S ONLY ONE LIKE IT IN THE WORLD!
SENRYU
TORNADO DRAGON
YOU KNOW ABOUT SENRYU?
ONIMARU GANG HQ

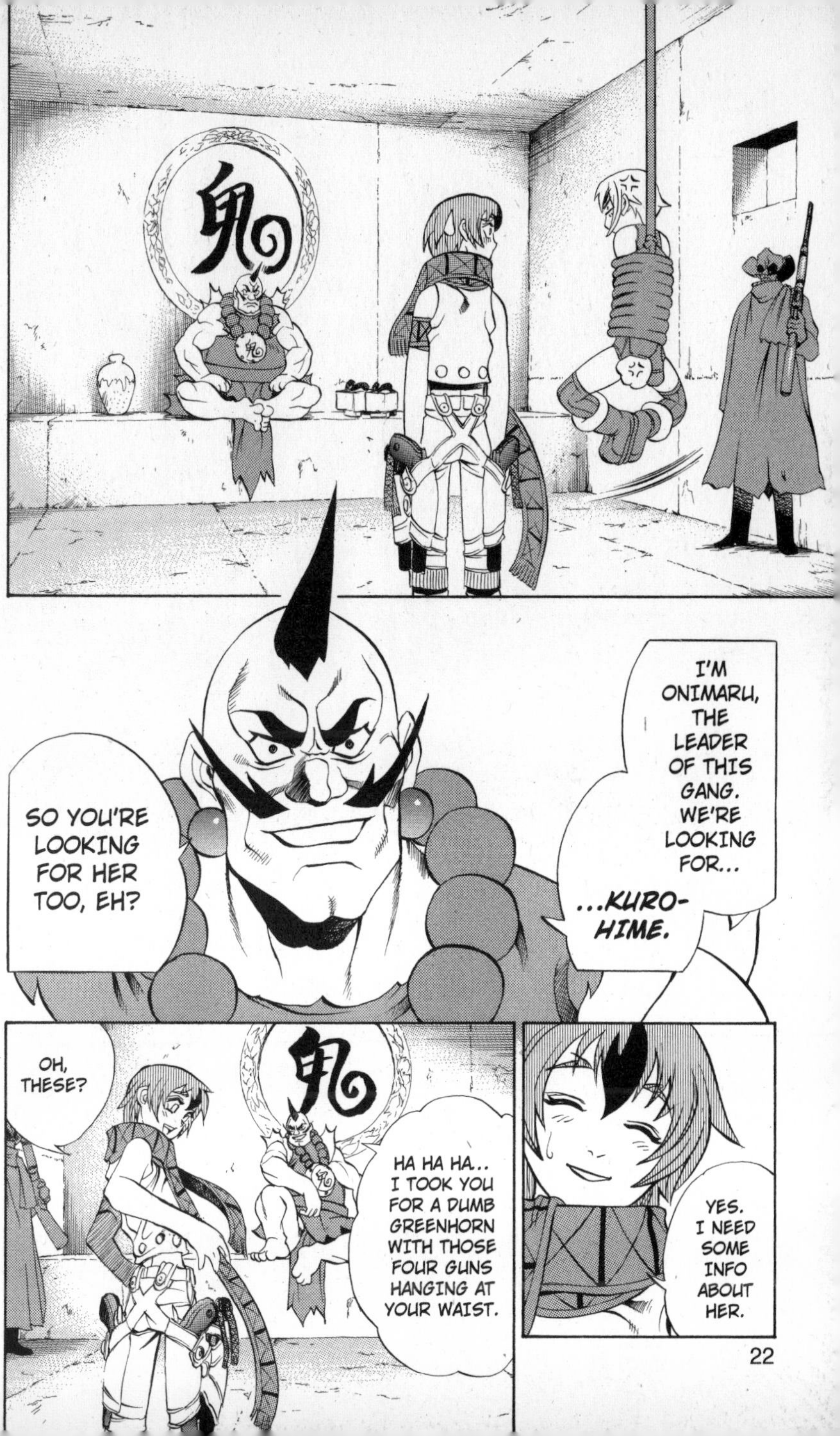
I'M ONIMARU, THE LEADER OF THIS GANG. WE'RE LOOKING FOR...
...KURO-HIME.
SO YOU'RE LOOKING FOR HER TOO, EH?
YES. I NEED SOME INFO ABOUT HER.
HA HA HA... I TOOK YOU FOR A DUMB GREENHORN WITH THOSE FOUR GUNS HANGING AT YOUR WAIST.
OH, THESE?

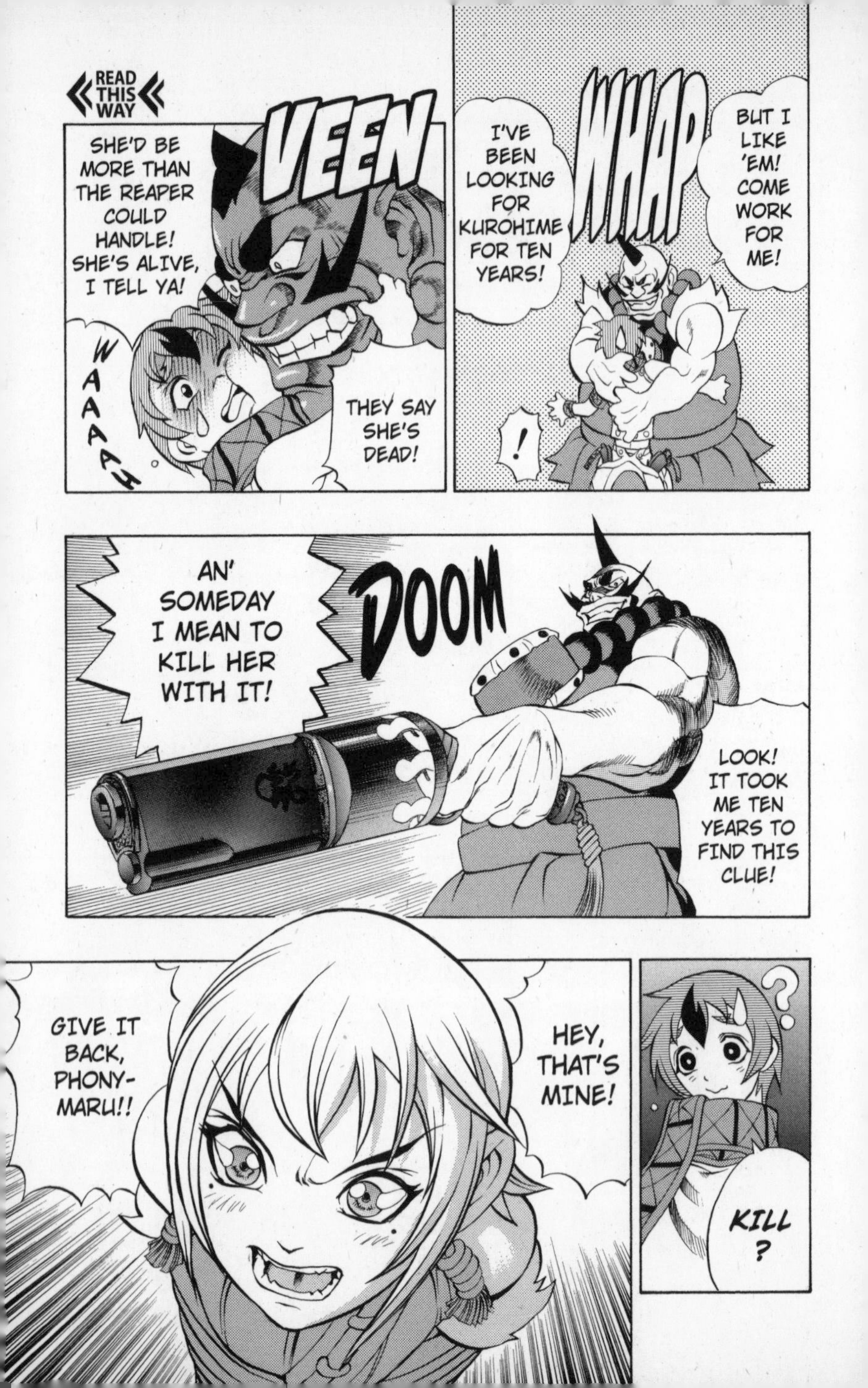
READ THIS WAY
BUT I LIKE 'EM! COME WORK FOR ME!
WHAP
I'VE BEEN LOOKING FOR KUROHIME FOR TEN YEARS!
!
VEEN
THEY SAY SHE'S DEAD!
SHE'D BE MORE THAN THE REAPER COULD HANDLE! SHE'S ALIVE, I TELL YA!
WAAAAH
LOOK! IT TOOK ME TEN YEARS TO FIND THIS CLUE!
DOOM
AN' SOMEDAY I MEAN TO KILL HER WITH IT!
?
KILL ?
HEY, THAT'S MINE!
GIVE IT BACK, PHONY-MARU!!

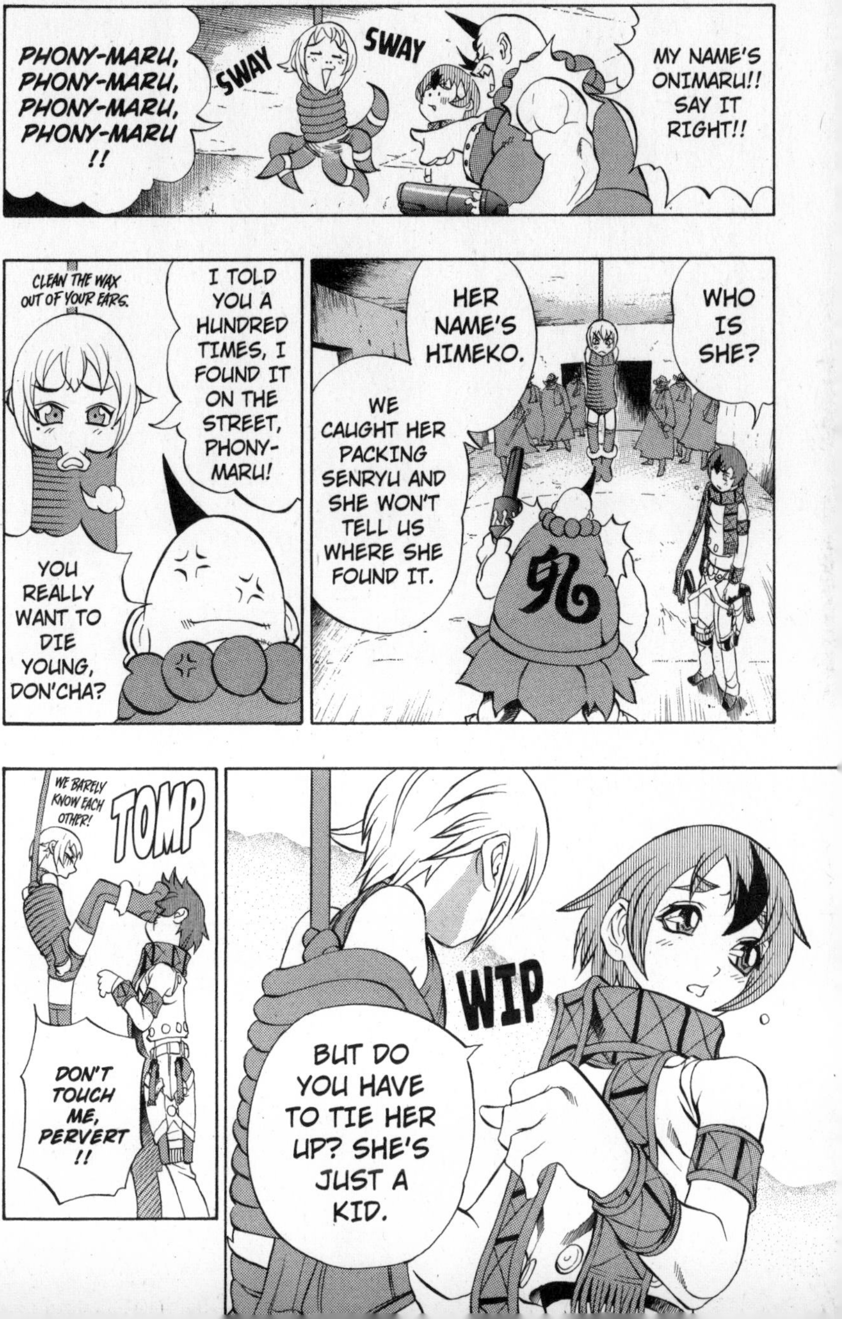
MY NAME'S ONIMARU!! SAY IT RIGHT!!
SWAY
SWAY
PHONY-MARU, PHONY-MARU, PHONY-MARU, PHONY-MARU !!
WHO IS SHE?
HER NAME'S HIMEKO.
WE CAUGHT HER PACKING SENRYU AND SHE WON'T TELL US WHERE SHE FOUND IT.
I TOLD YOU A HUNDRED TIMES, I FOUND IT ON THE STREET, PHONY-MARU!
CLEAN THE WAX OUT OF YOUR EARS.
YOU REALLY WANT TO DIE YOUNG, DON'CHA?
WIP
BUT DO YOU HAVE TO TIE HER UP? SHE'S JUST A KID.
TOMP
WE BARELY KNOW EACH OTHER!
DON'T TOUCH ME, PERVERT !!

READ THIS WAY

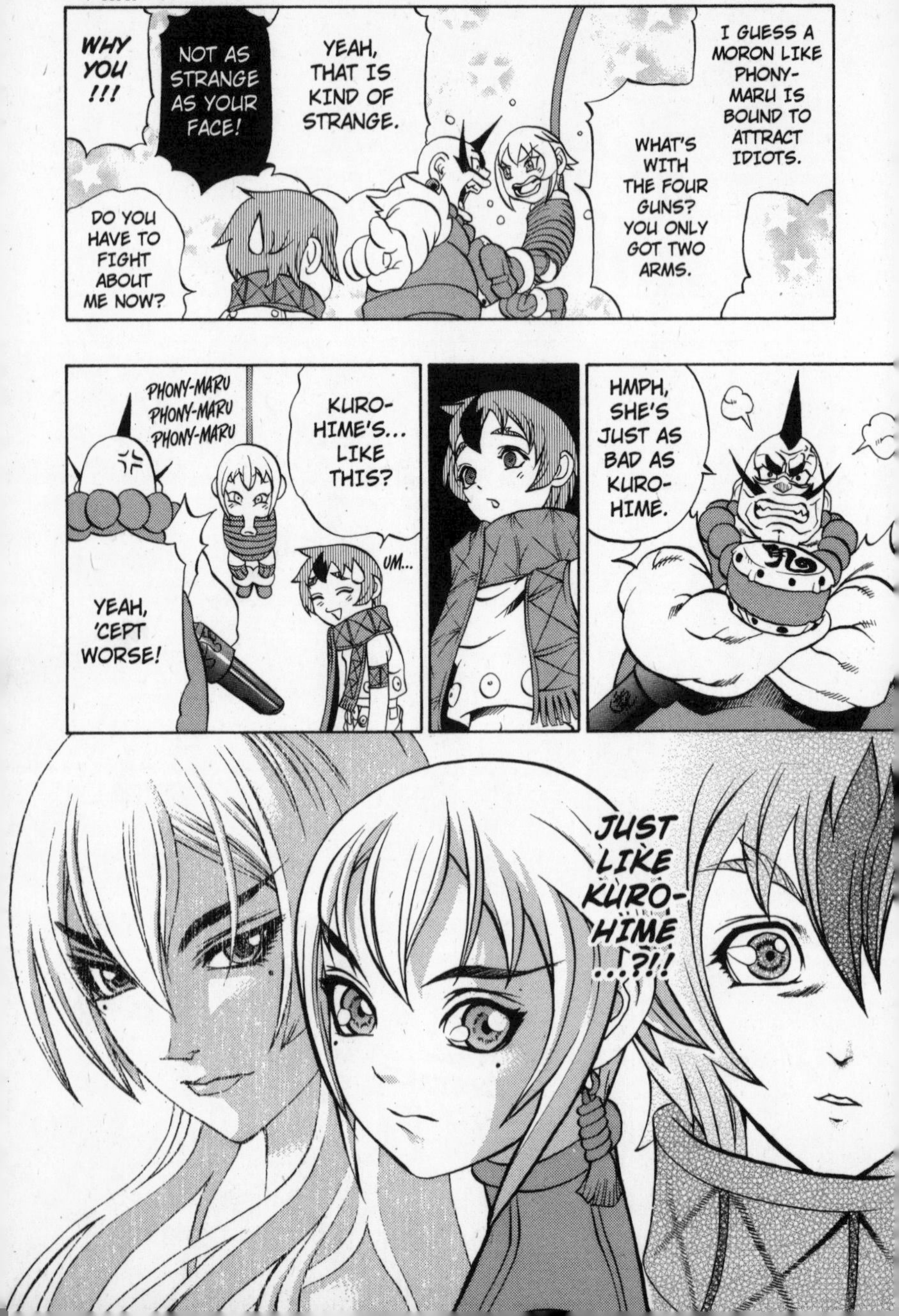
I GUESS A MORON LIKE PHONY-MARU IS BOUND TO ATTRACT IDIOTS.
WHAT'S WITH THE FOUR GUNS? YOU ONLY GOT TWO ARMS.
YEAH, THAT IS KIND OF STRANGE.
NOT AS STRANGE AS YOUR FACE!
WHY YOU!!!
DO YOU HAVE TO FIGHT ABOUT ME NOW?
HMPH, SHE'S JUST AS BAD AS KURO-HIME.
KURO-HIME'S... LIKE THIS?
UM...
PHONY-MARU PHONY-MARU PHONY-MARU
YEAH, 'CEPT WORSE!
JUST LIKE KURO-HIME...?!!

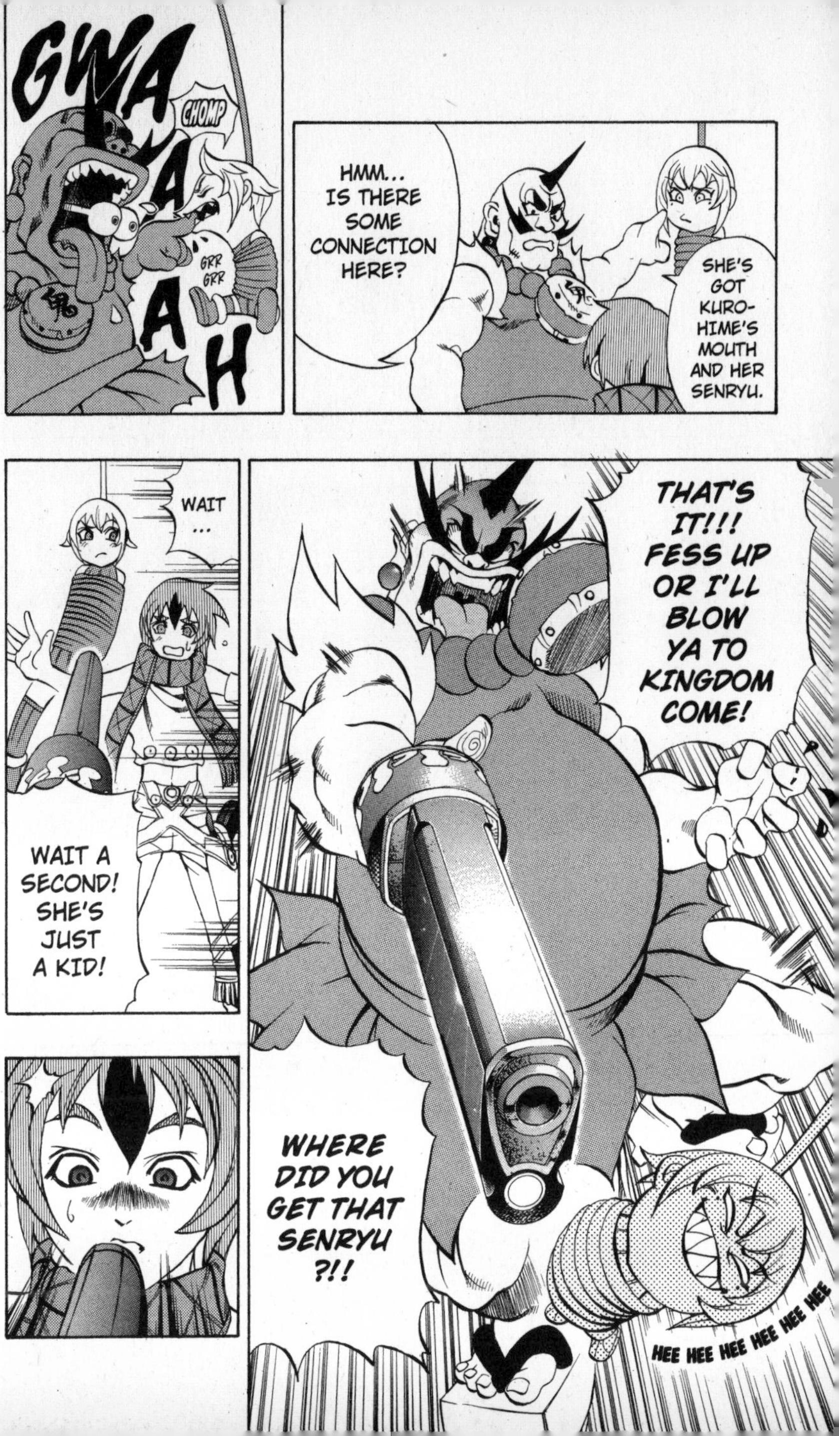
HMM... IS THERE SOME CONNECTION HERE?
SHE'S GOT KURO-HIME'S MOUTH AND HER SENRYU.
GWAAAH
CHOMP
GRR GRR
THAT'S IT!!! FESS UP OR I'LL BLOW YA TO KINGDOM COME!
WHERE DID YOU GET THAT SENRYU ?!!
HEE HEE HEE HEE HEE HEE HEE
WAIT ...
WAIT A SECOND! SHE'S JUST A KID!

READ THIS WAY

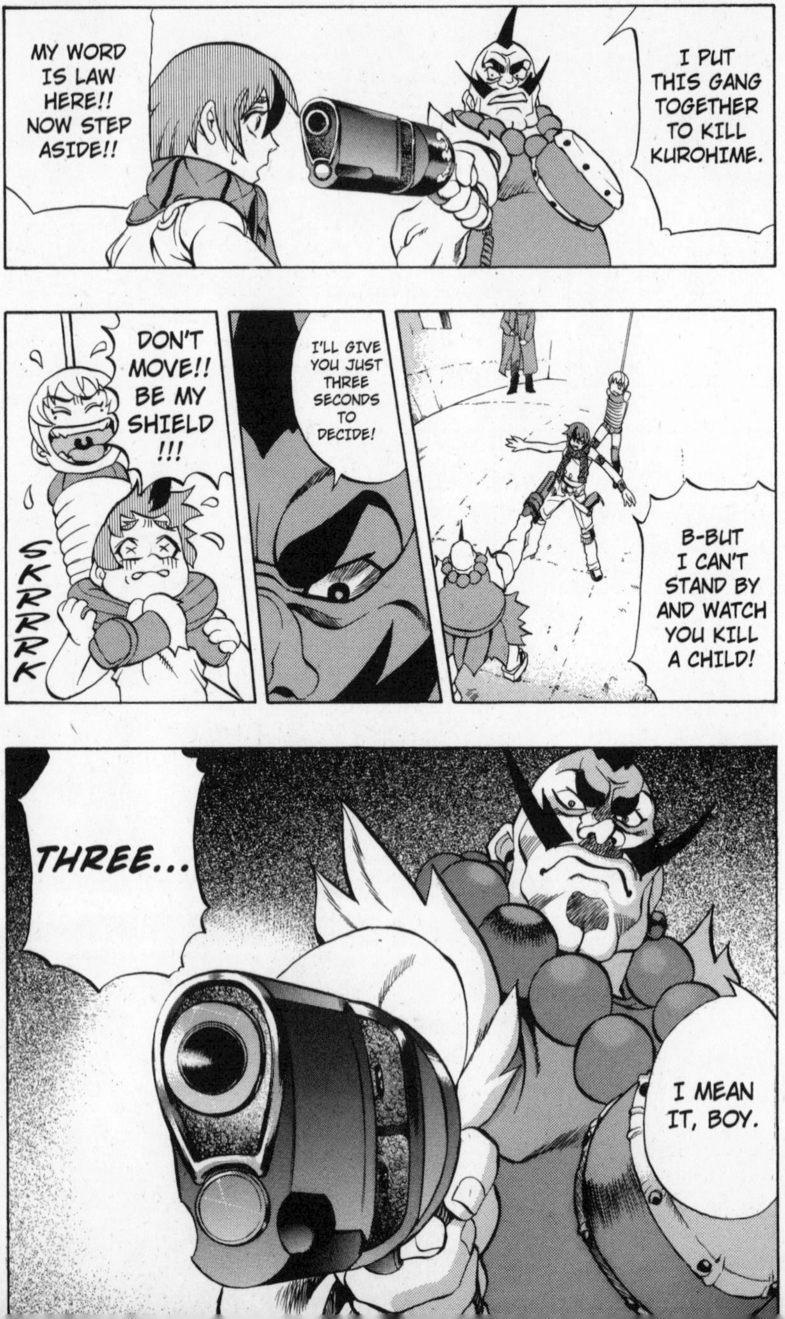

I PUT THIS GANG TOGETHER TO KILL KUROHIME.
MY WORD IS LAW HERE!! NOW STEP ASIDE!!
B-BUT I CAN'T STAND BY AND WATCH YOU KILL A CHILD!
I'LL GIVE YOU JUST THREE SECONDS TO DECIDE!
DON'T MOVE!! BE MY SHIELD!!!
SKRRRK
THREE...
I MEAN IT, BOY.

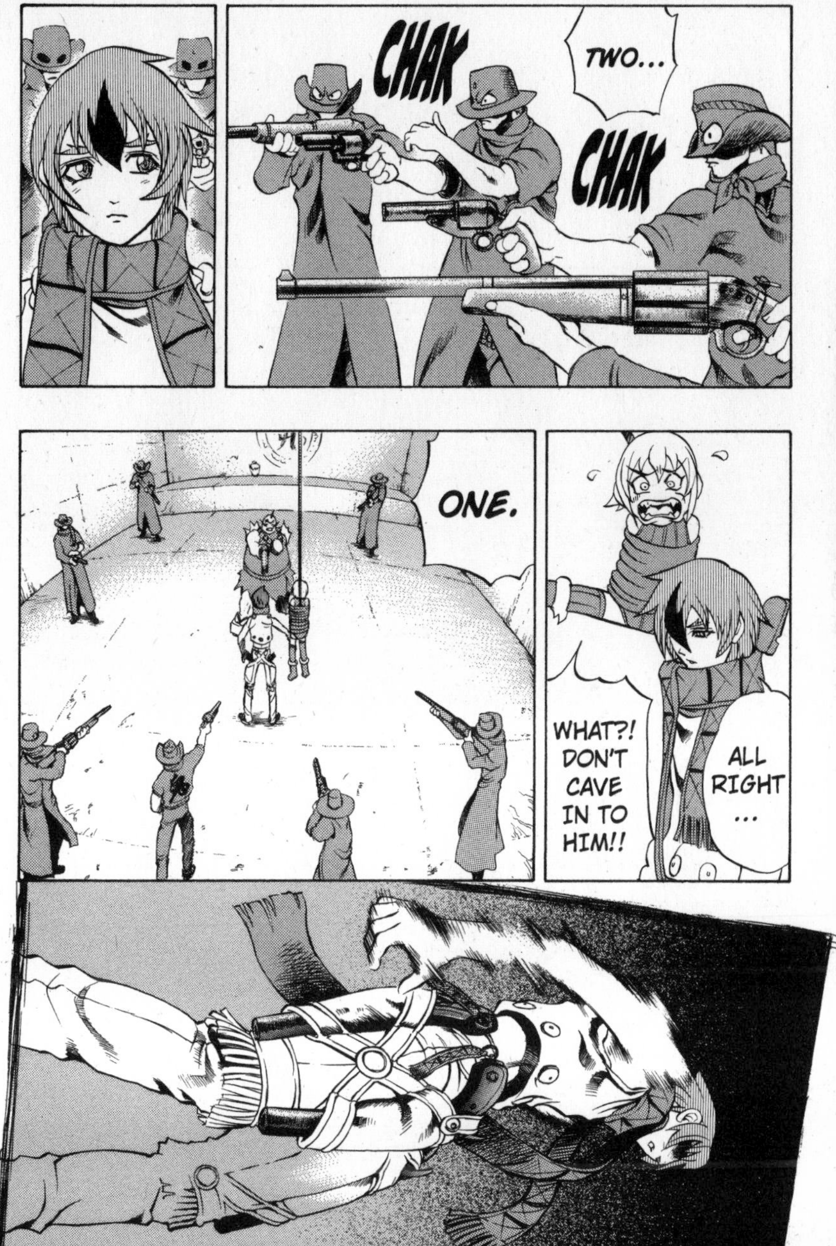
TWO...
CHAK
CHAK
ALL RIGHT...
WHAT?! DON'T CAVE IN TO HIM!!
ONE.

READ THIS WAY

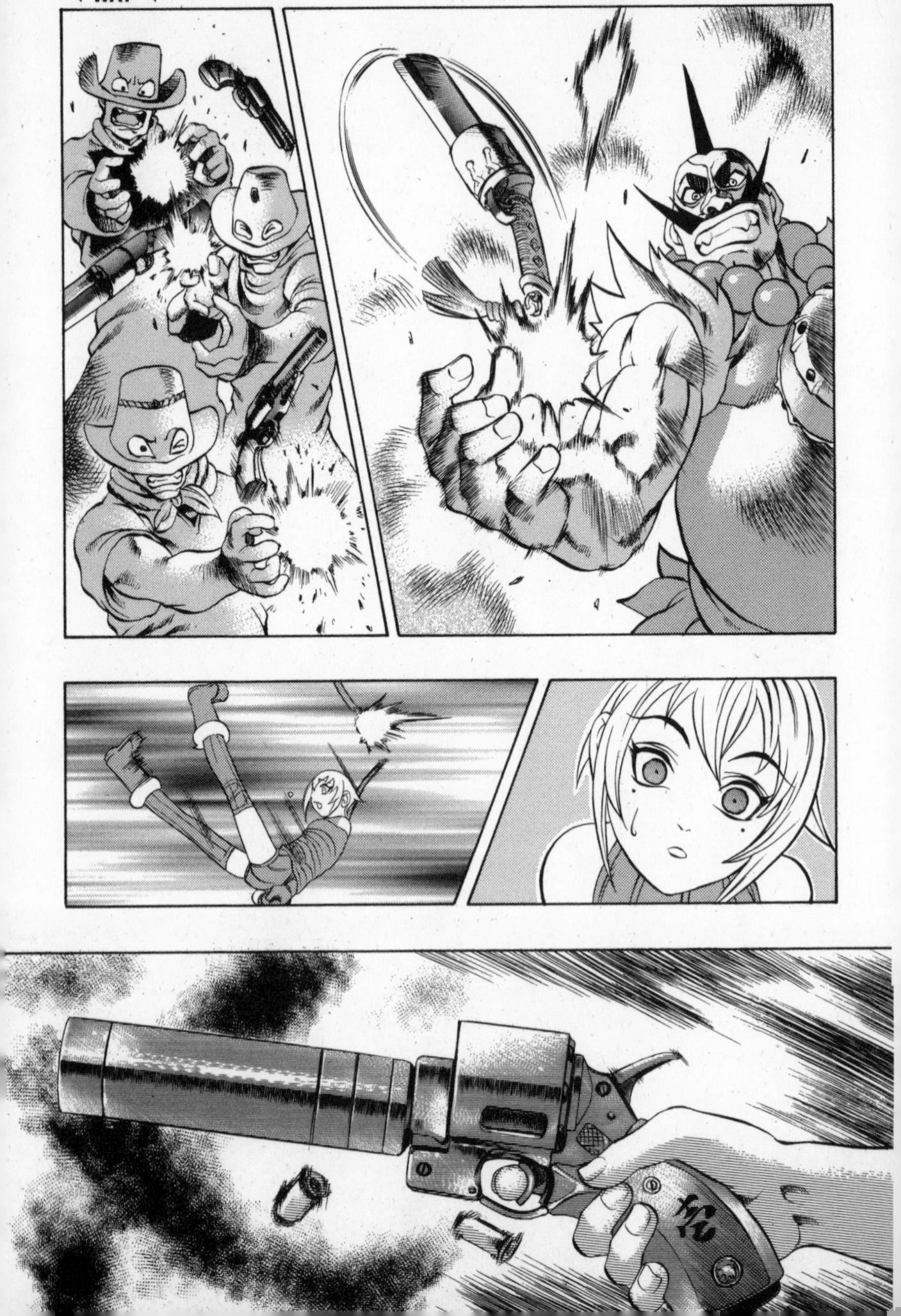

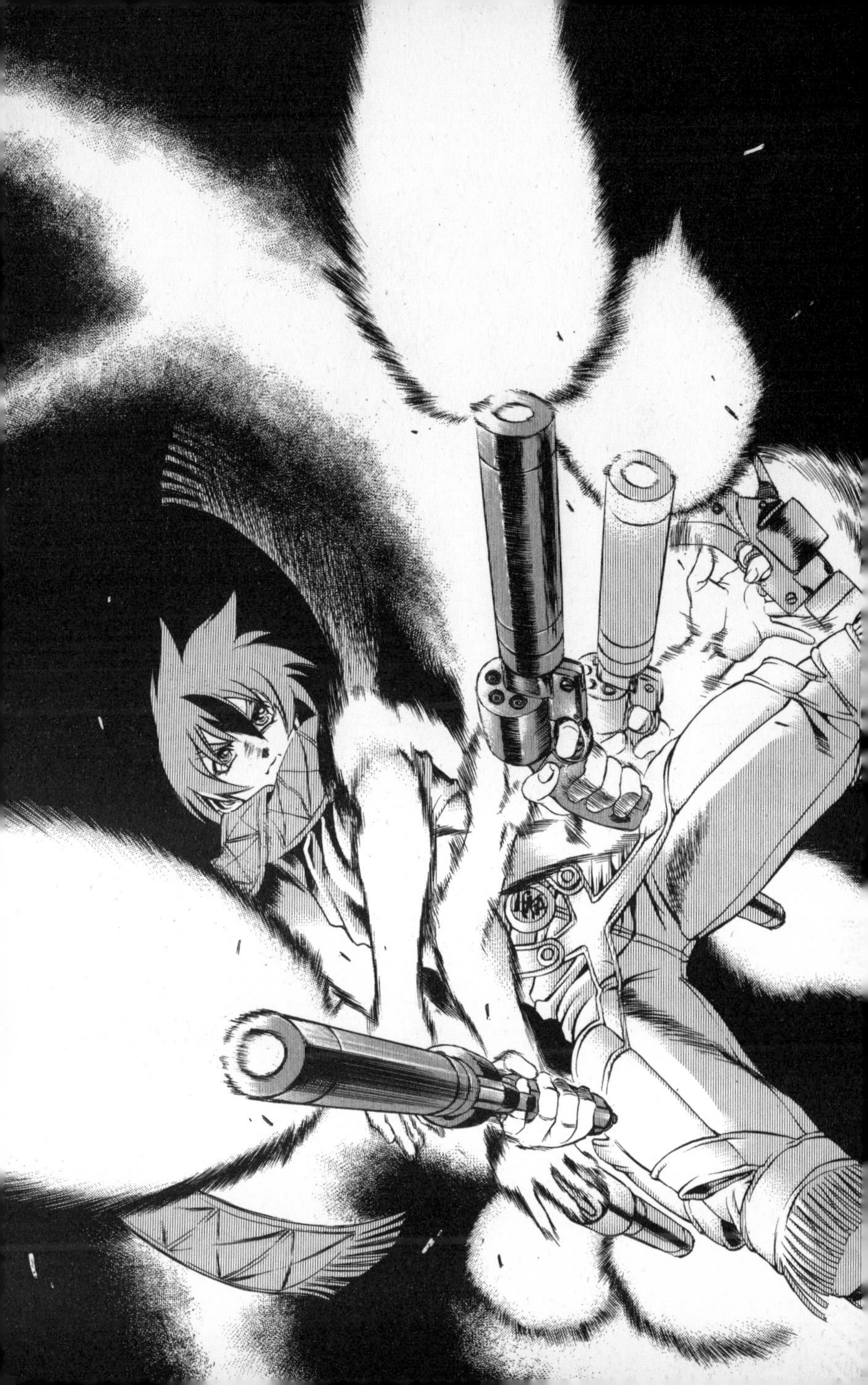

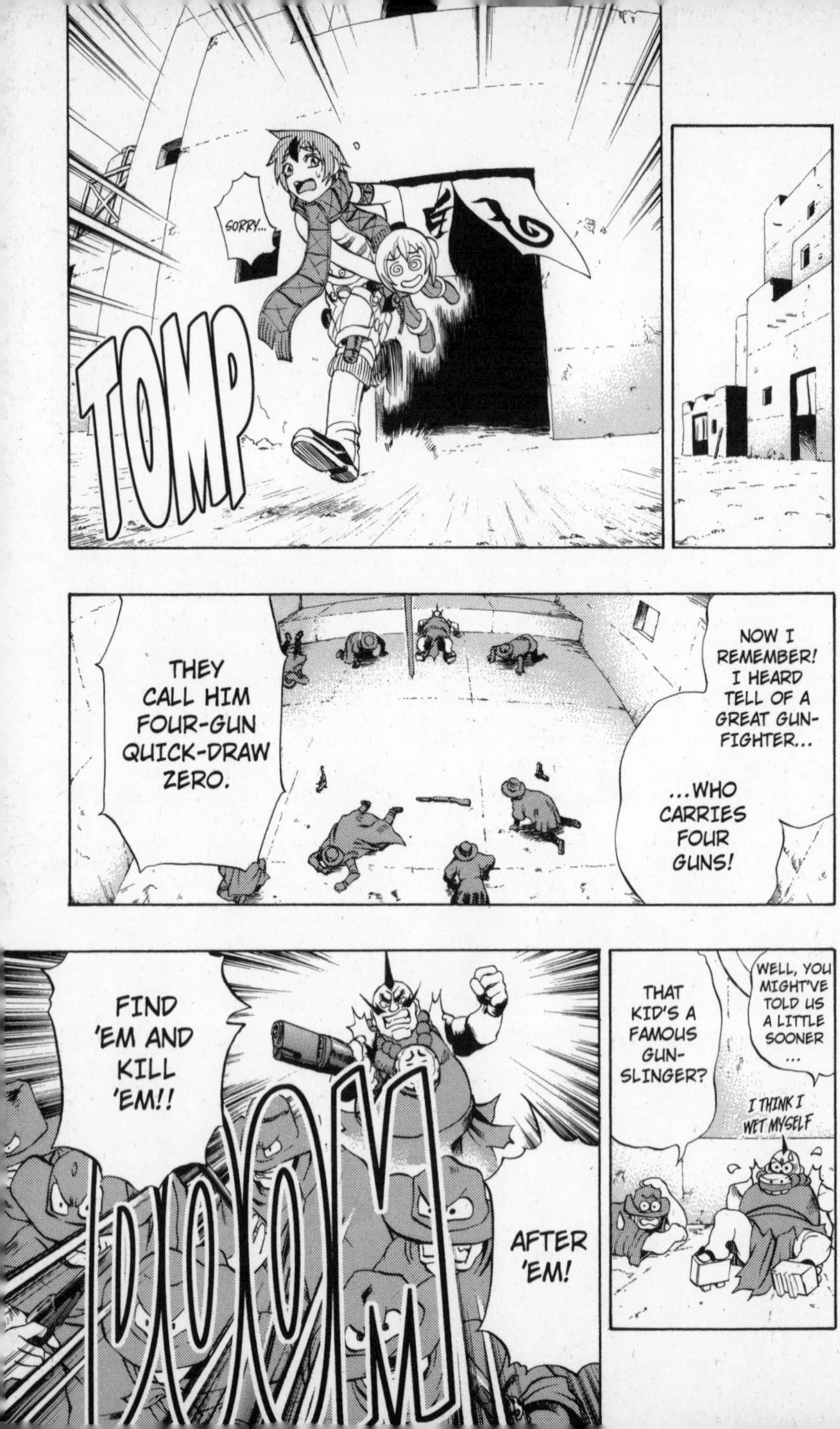
SORRY...
TOMP
NOW I REMEMBER! I HEARD TELL OF A GREAT GUN-FIGHTER...
...WHO CARRIES FOUR GUNS!
THEY CALL HIM FOUR-GUN QUICK-DRAW ZERO.
WELL, YOU MIGHT'VE TOLD US A LITTLE SOONER ...
THAT KID'S A FAMOUS GUN-SLINGER?
I THINK I WET MYSELF
FIND 'EM AND KILL 'EM!!
DOOOM
AFTER 'EM!

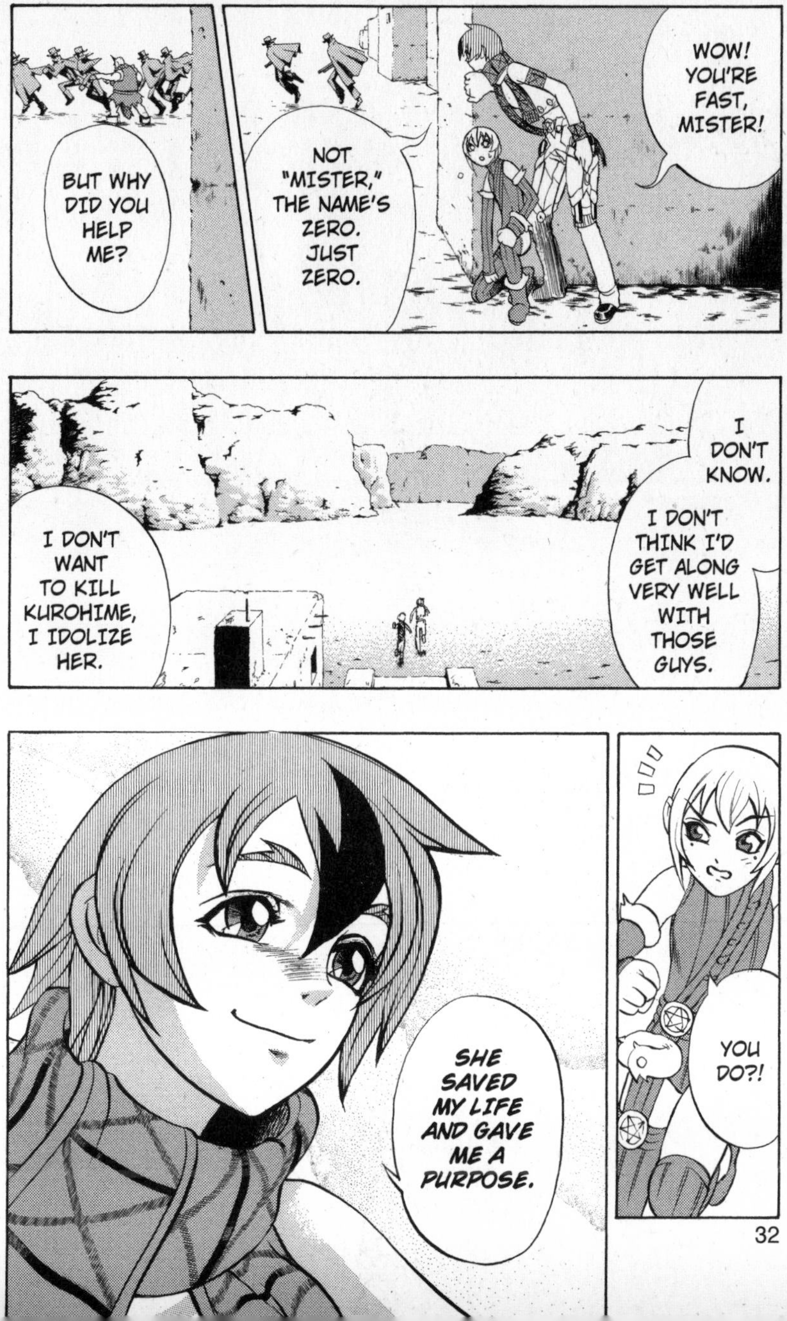
WOW! YOU'RE FAST, MISTER!
NOT "MISTER," THE NAME'S ZERO. JUST ZERO.
BUT WHY DID YOU HELP ME?
I DON'T KNOW.
I DON'T THINK I'D GET ALONG VERY WELL WITH THOSE GUYS.
I DON'T WANT TO KILL KUROHIME, I IDOLIZE HER.
YOU DO?!
SHE SAVED MY LIFE AND GAVE ME A PURPOSE.

READ THIS WAY

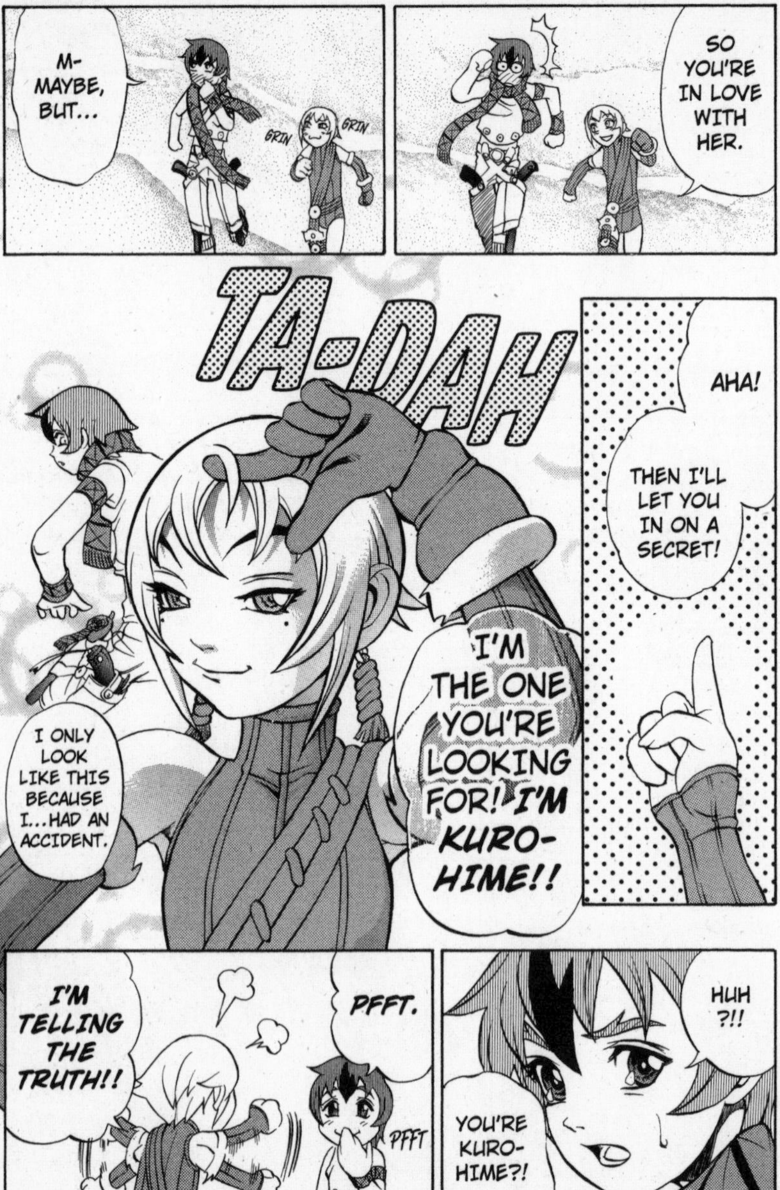

SO YOU'RE IN LOVE WITH HER.
M-MAYBE, BUT...
GRIN
GRIN
AHA!
THEN I'LL LET YOU IN ON A SECRET!
TA-DAH
I'M THE ONE YOU'RE LOOKING FOR! I'M KURO-HIME!!
I ONLY LOOK LIKE THIS BECAUSE I...HAD AN ACCIDENT.
HUH ?!!
YOU'RE KURO-HIME?!
PFFT.
PFFT
I'M TELLING THE TRUTH!!

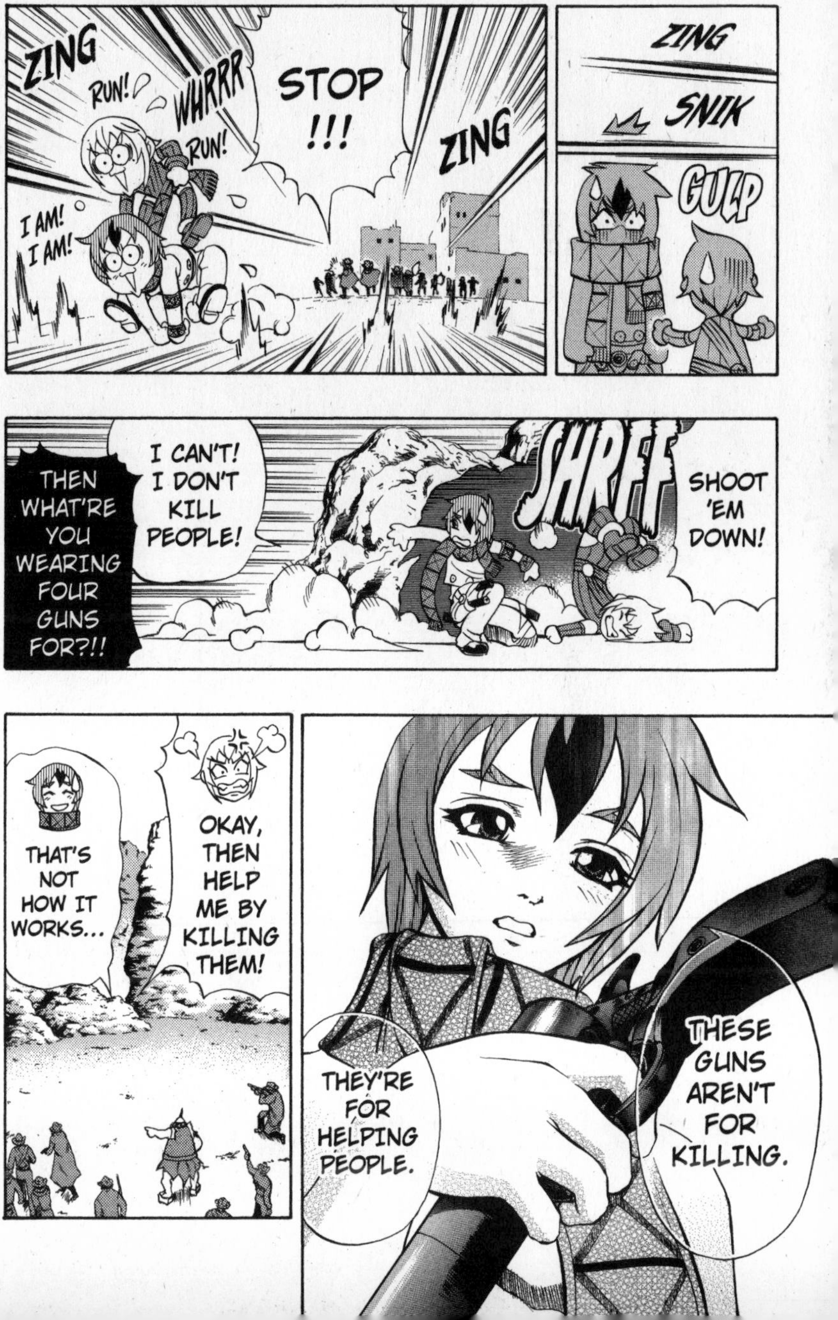
ZING
SNIK
GULP
STOP!!!
ZING
WHRRR
RUN!
ZING
RUN!
I AM! I AM!
SHOOT 'EM DOWN!
SHRFF
I CAN'T! I DON'T KILL PEOPLE!
THEN WHAT'RE YOU WEARING FOUR GUNS FOR?!!
THESE GUNS AREN'T FOR KILLING.
THEY'RE FOR HELPING PEOPLE.
OKAY, THEN HELP ME BY KILLING THEM!
THAT'S NOT HOW IT WORKS...

READ THIS WAY

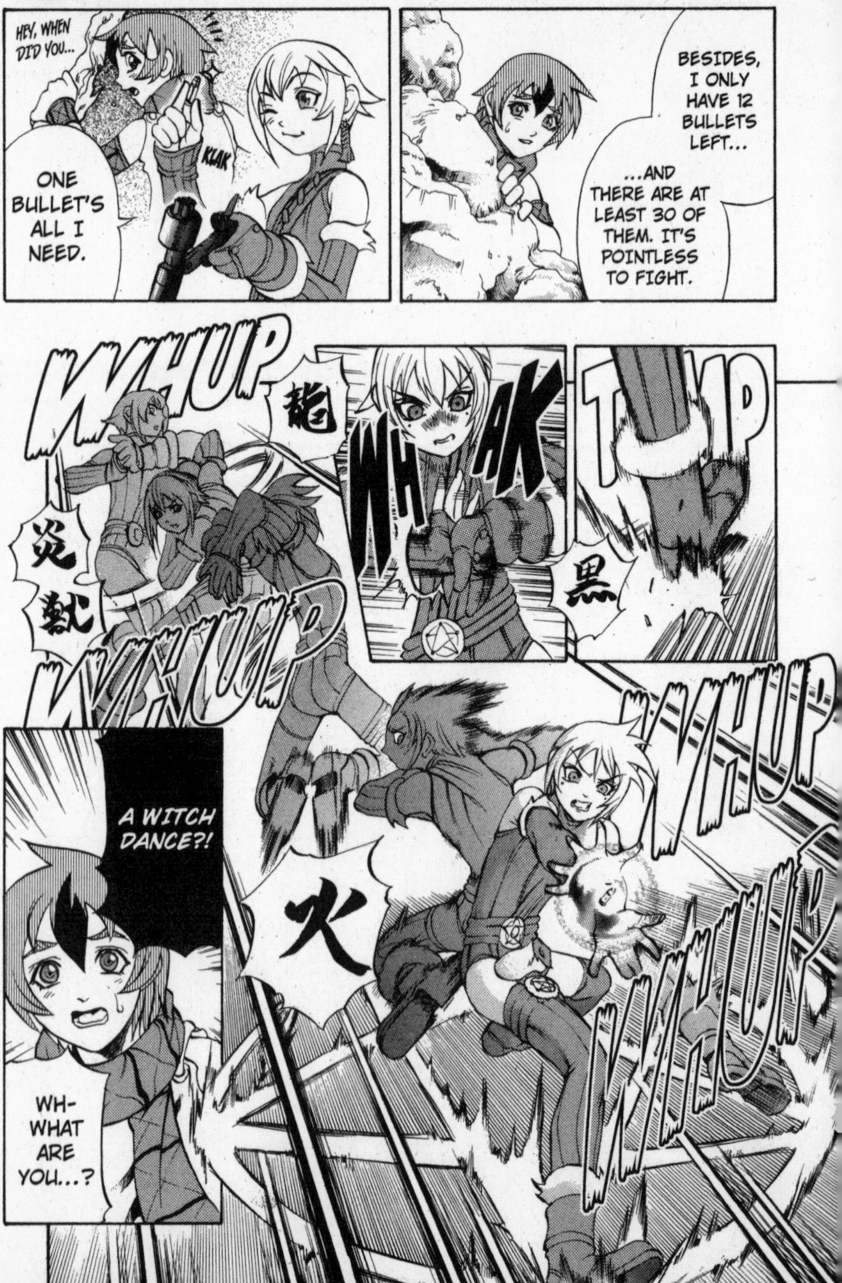
BESIDES, I ONLY HAVE 12 BULLETS LEFT...
...AND THERE ARE AT LEAST 30 OF THEM. IT'S POINTLESS TO FIGHT.
HEY, WHEN DID YOU...
KLAK
ONE BULLET'S ALL I NEED.
TMP
黒
WHAK
龍
WHUP
炎獄
WHUP
WHUP
火
WHUP
A WITCH DANCE?!
WH-WHAT ARE YOU...?

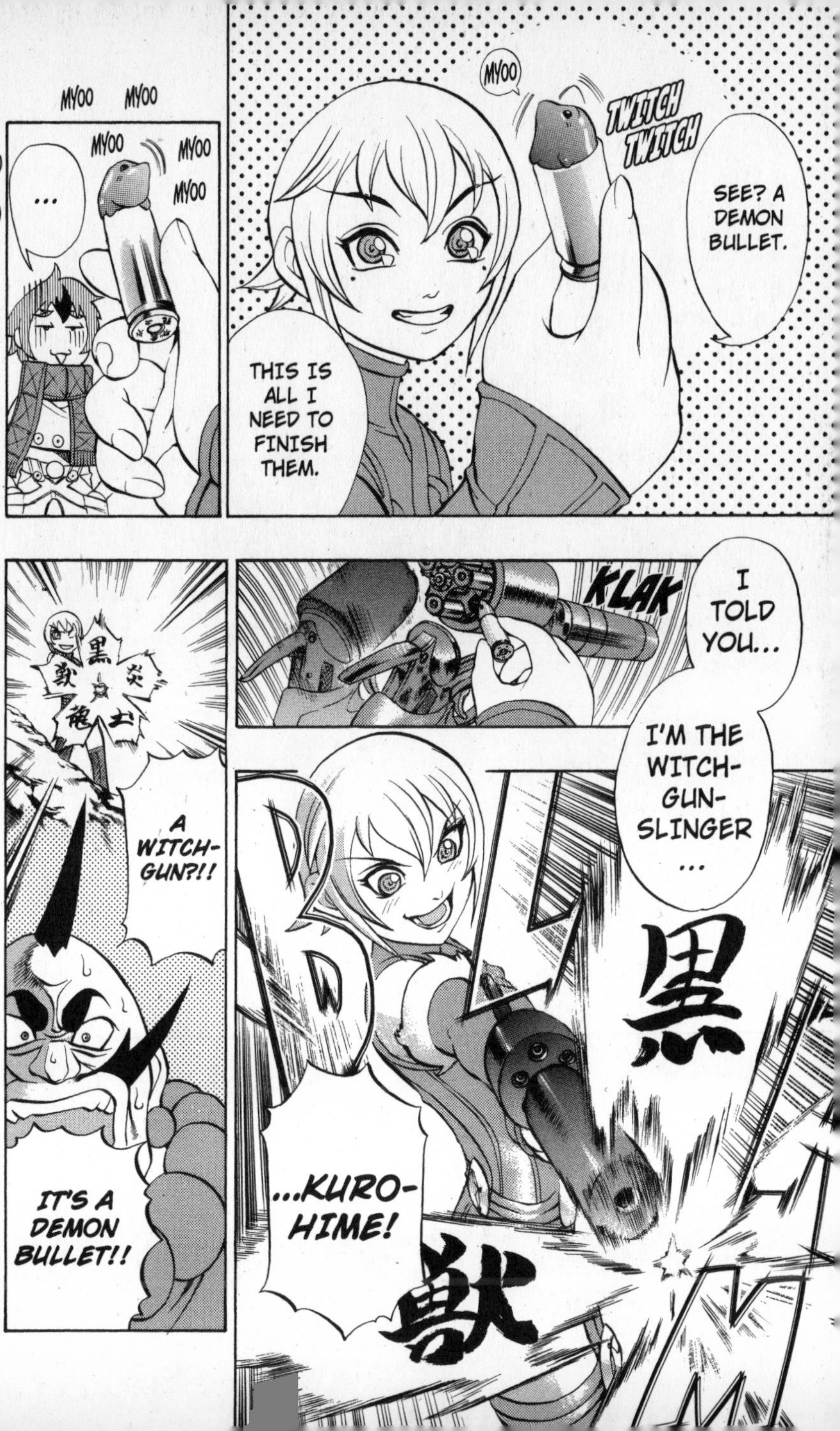
MYOO
TWITCH TWITCH
SEE? A DEMON BULLET.
THIS IS ALL I NEED TO FINISH THEM.
MYOO MYOO
MYOO
MYOO
MYOO
MYOO
MYOO
...
KLAK
I TOLD YOU...
I'M THE WITCH-GUN-SLINGER...
...KURO-HIME!
黒
獣
A WITCH-GUN?!!
IT'S A DEMON BULLET!!

READ THIS WAY

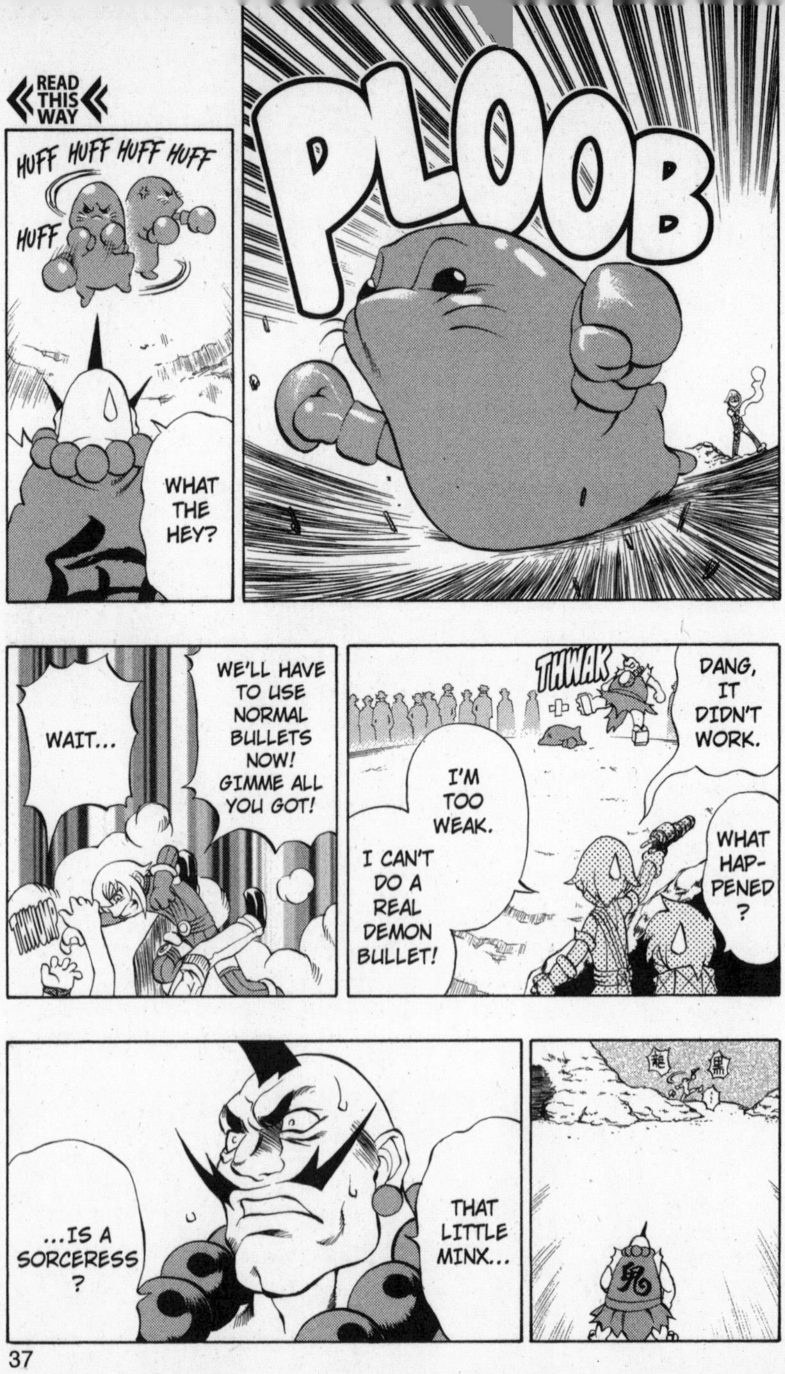
PLOOB
HUFF HUFF HUFF HUFF
HUFF
WHAT THE HEY?
THWAK
DANG, IT DIDN'T WORK.
WHAT HAP-PENED?
I'M TOO WEAK.
I CAN'T DO A REAL DEMON BULLET!
WE'LL HAVE TO USE NORMAL BULLETS NOW! GIMME ALL YOU GOT!
WAIT...
THWOMP
THAT LITTLE MINX...
...IS A SORCERESS?

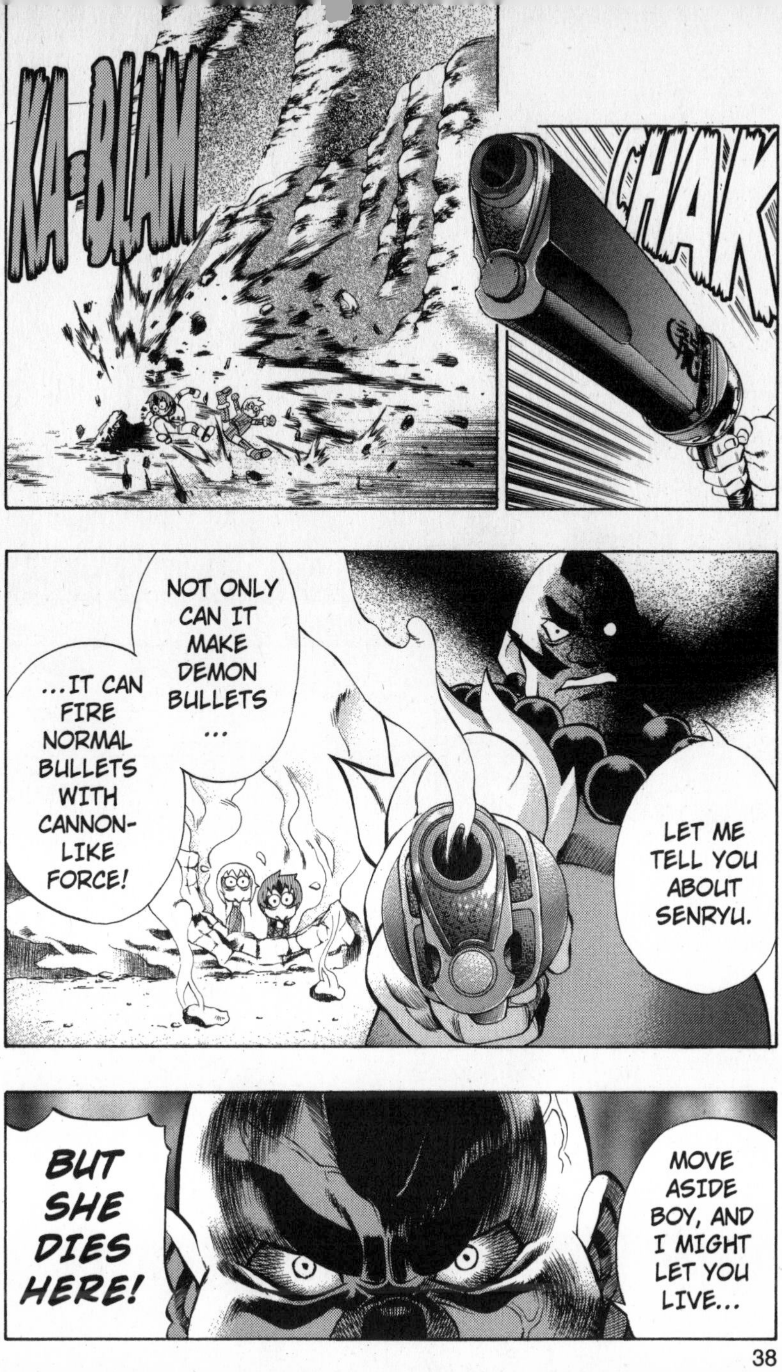
CHAK
KA-BLAM
LET ME TELL YOU ABOUT SENRYU.
NOT ONLY CAN IT MAKE DEMON BULLETS...
...IT CAN FIRE NORMAL BULLETS WITH CANNON-LIKE FORCE!
MOVE ASIDE BOY, AND I MIGHT LET YOU LIVE...
BUT SHE DIES HERE!

READ THIS WAY

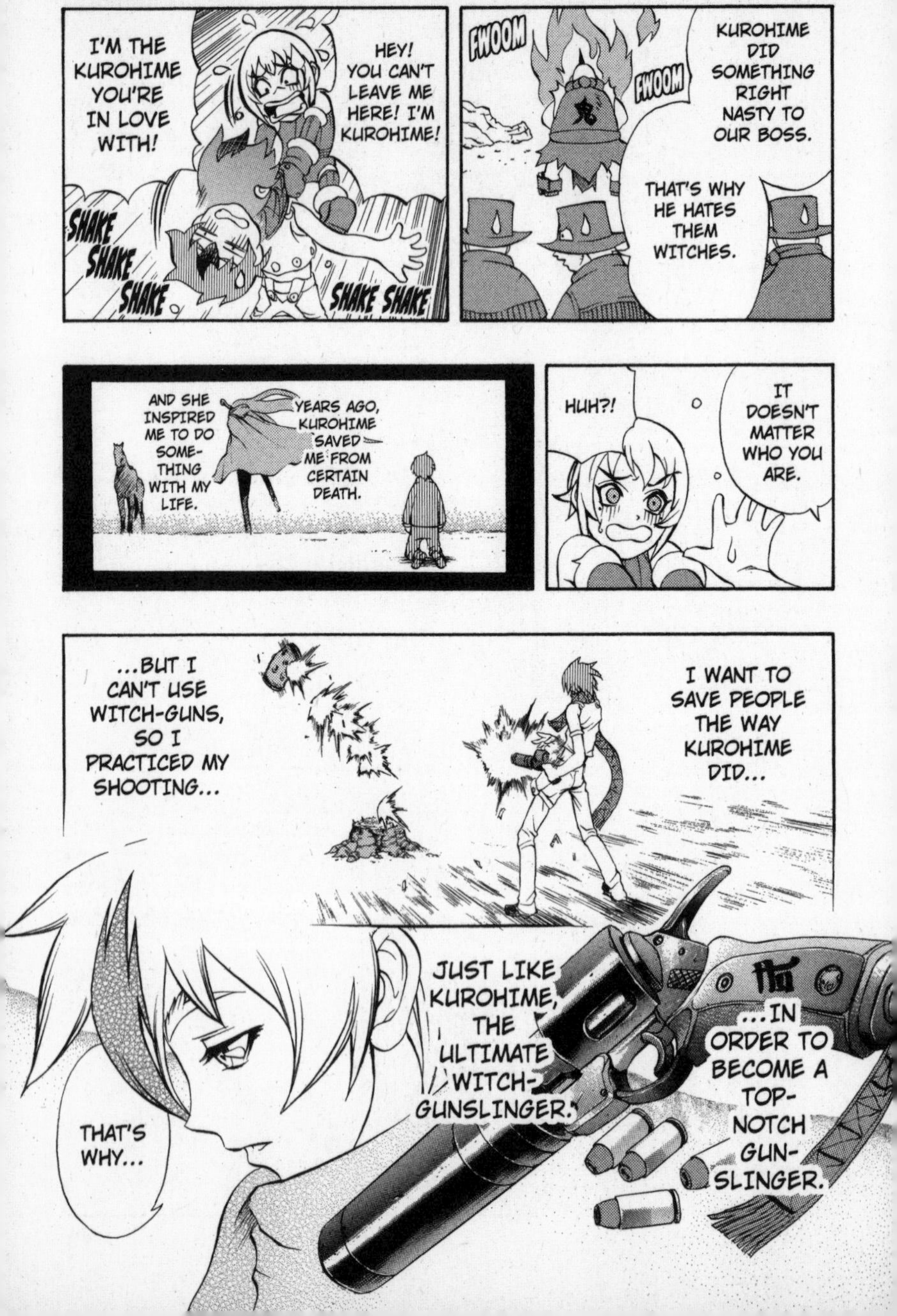
FWOOM
KUROHIME DID SOMETHING RIGHT NASTY TO OUR BOSS.
FWOOM
THAT'S WHY HE HATES THEM WITCHES.
HEY! YOU CAN'T LEAVE ME HERE! I'M KUROHIME!
I'M THE KUROHIME YOU'RE IN LOVE WITH!
SHAKE SHAKE SHAKE
SHAKE SHAKE
IT DOESN'T MATTER WHO YOU ARE.
HUH?!
YEARS AGO, KUROHIME SAVED ME FROM CERTAIN DEATH.
AND SHE INSPIRED ME TO DO SOME-THING WITH MY LIFE.
I WANT TO SAVE PEOPLE THE WAY KUROHIME DID...
...BUT I CAN'T USE WITCH-GUNS, SO I PRACTICED MY SHOOTING...
...IN ORDER TO BECOME A TOP-NOTCH GUN-SLINGER.
JUST LIKE KUROHIME, THE ULTIMATE WITCH-GUNSLINGER.
THAT'S WHY...

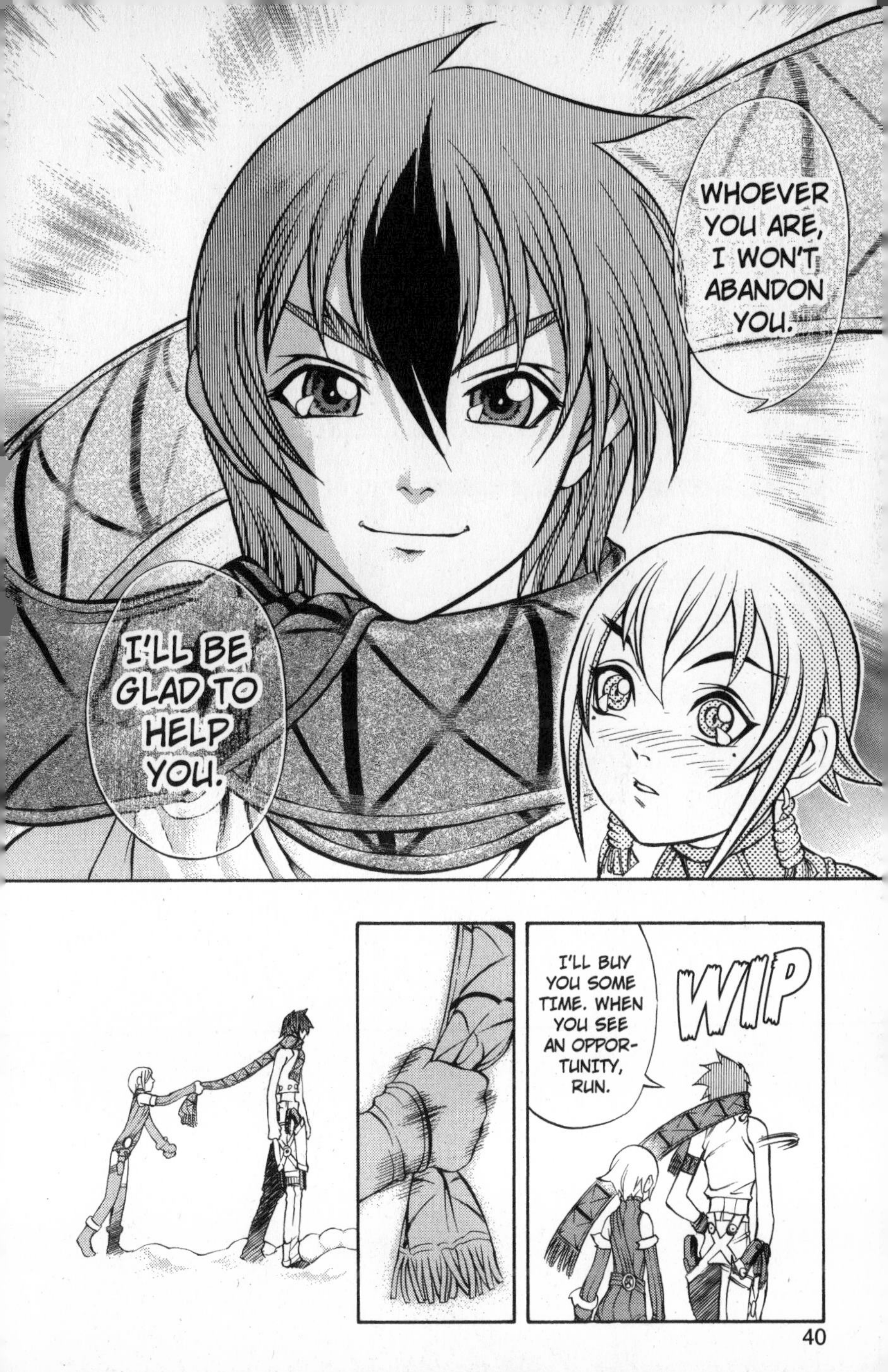
WHOEVER YOU ARE, I WON'T ABANDON YOU.
I'LL BE GLAD TO HELP YOU.
I'LL BUY YOU SOME TIME. WHEN YOU SEE AN OPPOR-TUNITY, RUN.
WIP

READ THIS WAY

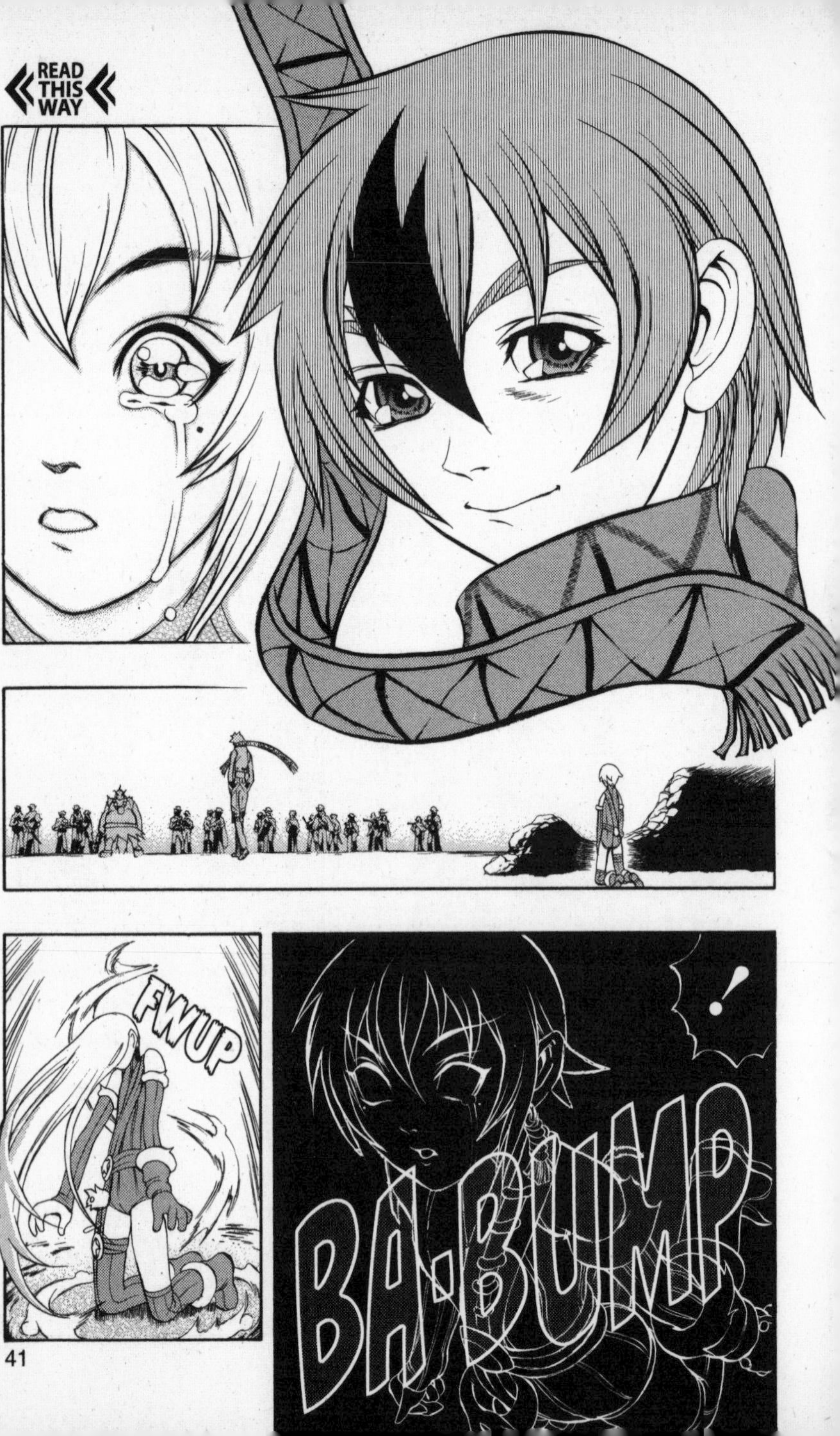
FWUP
!
BA-BUMP

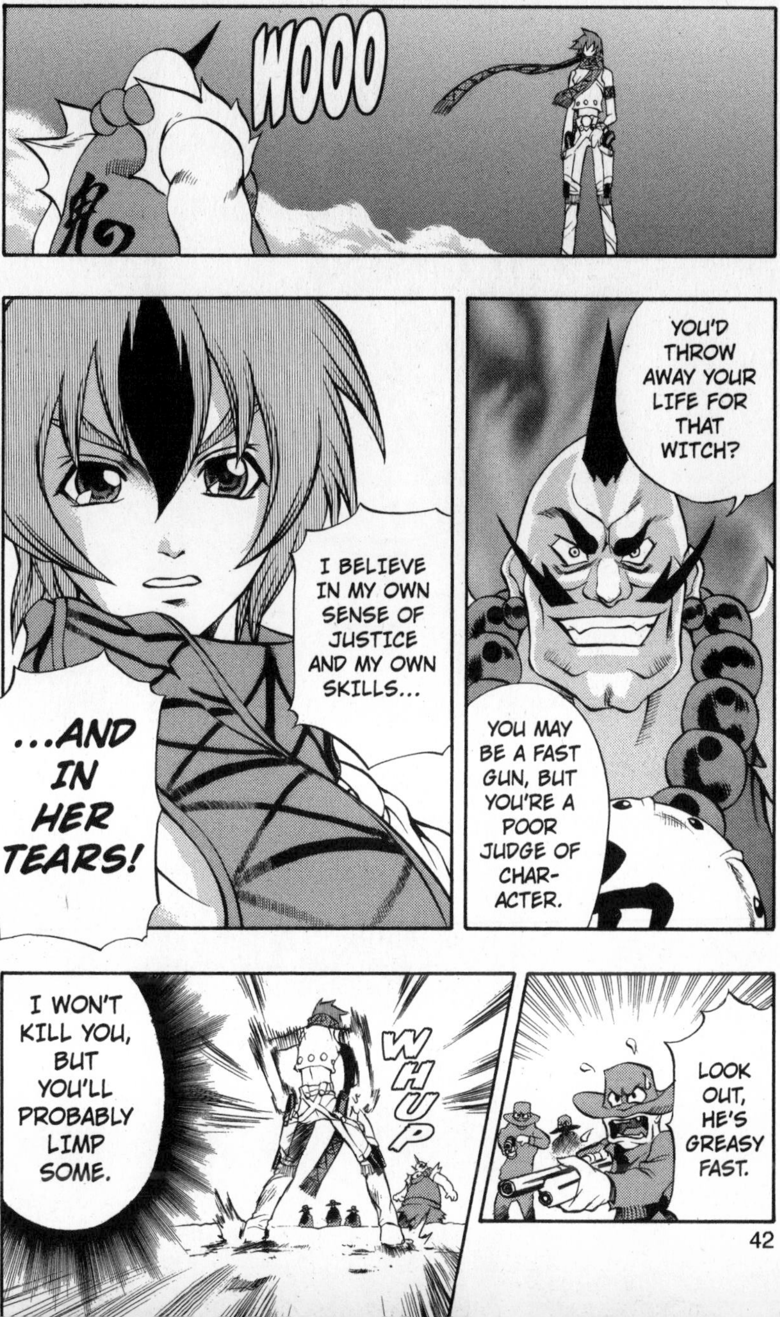
WOOO
YOU'D THROW AWAY YOUR LIFE FOR THAT WITCH?
YOU MAY BE A FAST GUN, BUT YOU'RE A POOR JUDGE OF CHAR-ACTER.
I BELIEVE IN MY OWN SENSE OF JUSTICE AND MY OWN SKILLS...
...AND IN HER TEARS!
LOOK OUT, HE'S GREASY FAST.
I WON'T KILL YOU, BUT YOU'LL PROBABLY LIMP SOME.
WHUP

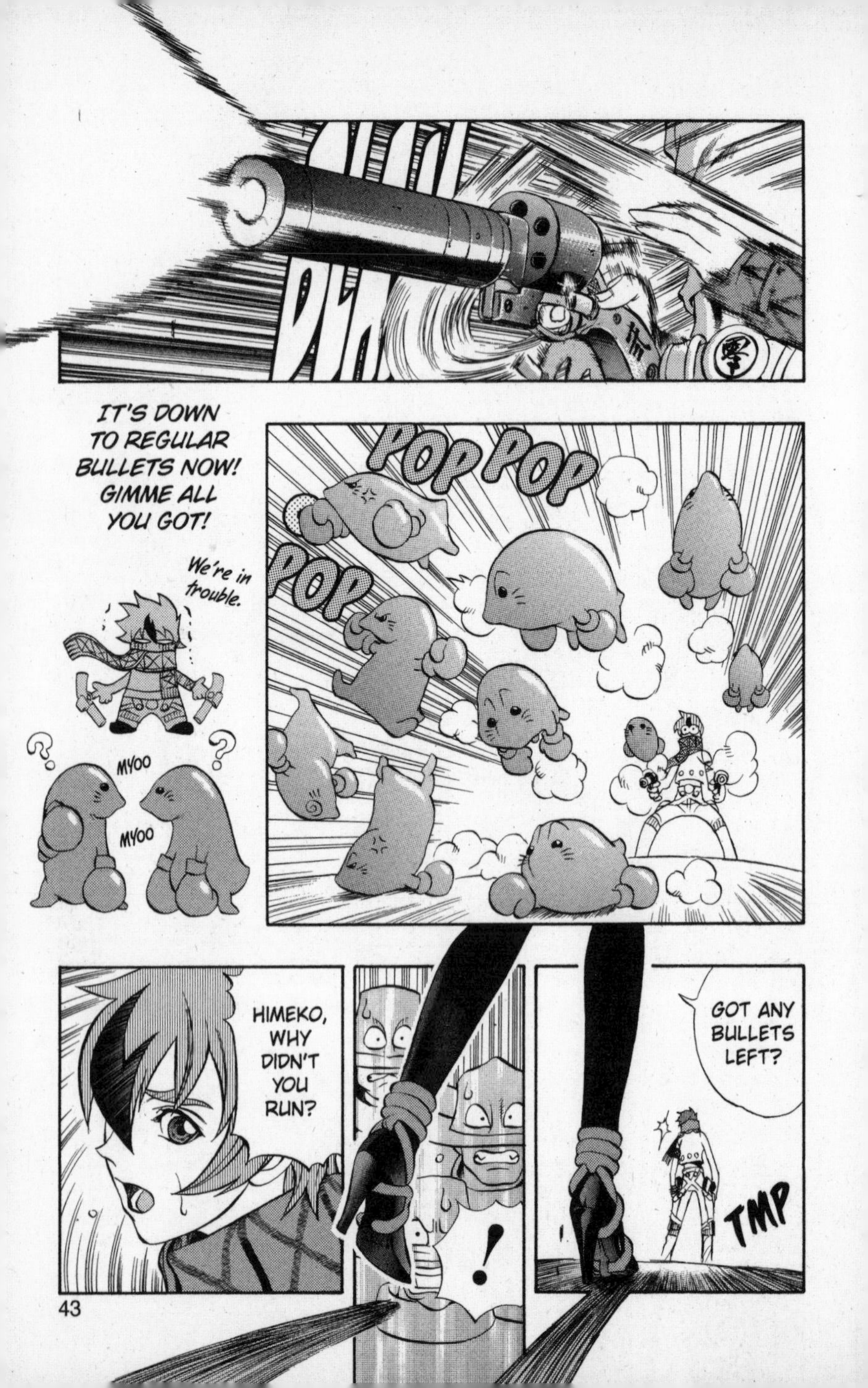
POP POP
POP
IT'S DOWN TO REGULAR BULLETS NOW! GIMME ALL YOU GOT!
We're in trouble.
MYOO
MYOO
GOT ANY BULLETS LEFT?
TMP
!
HIMEKO, WHY DIDN'T YOU RUN?

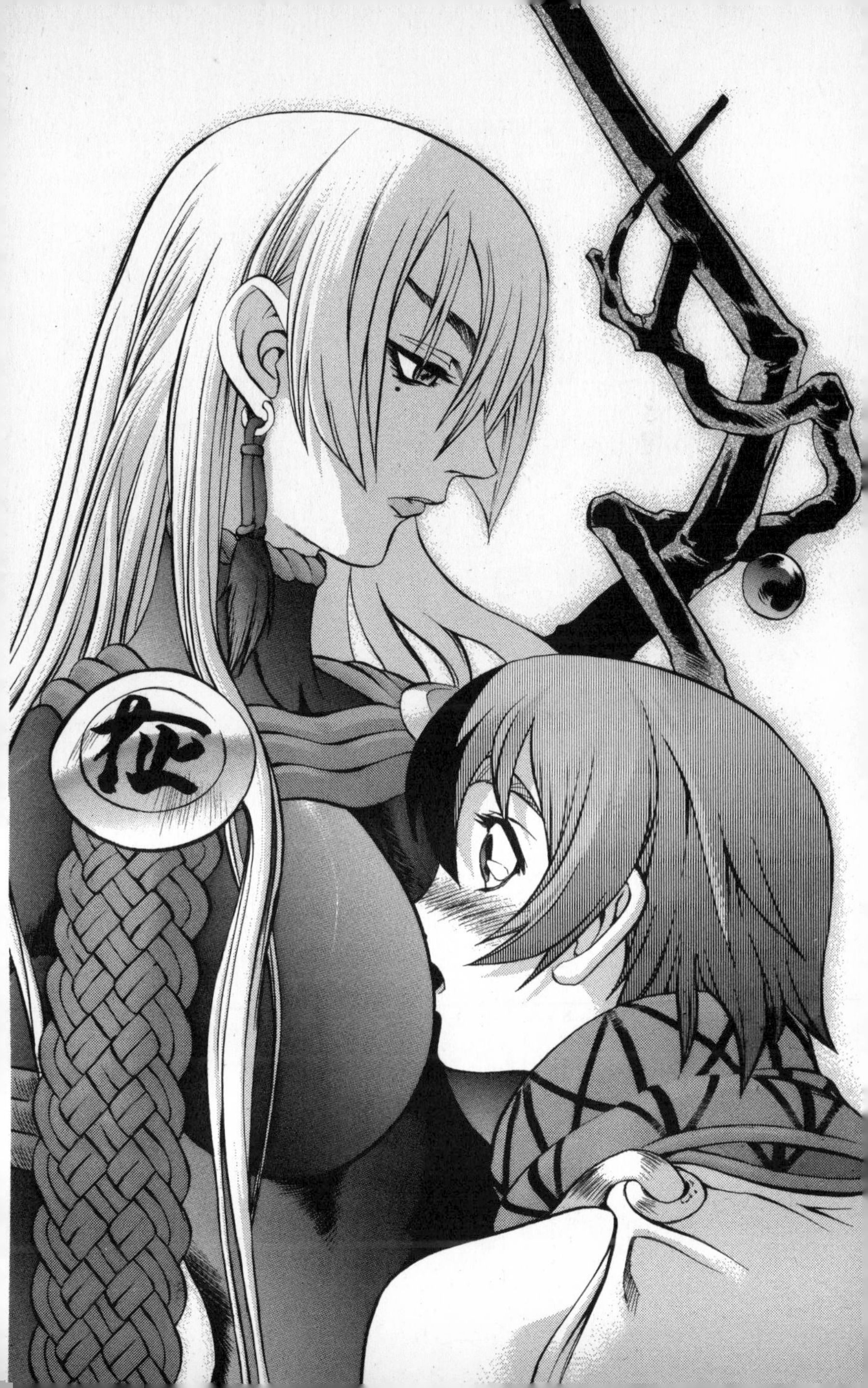

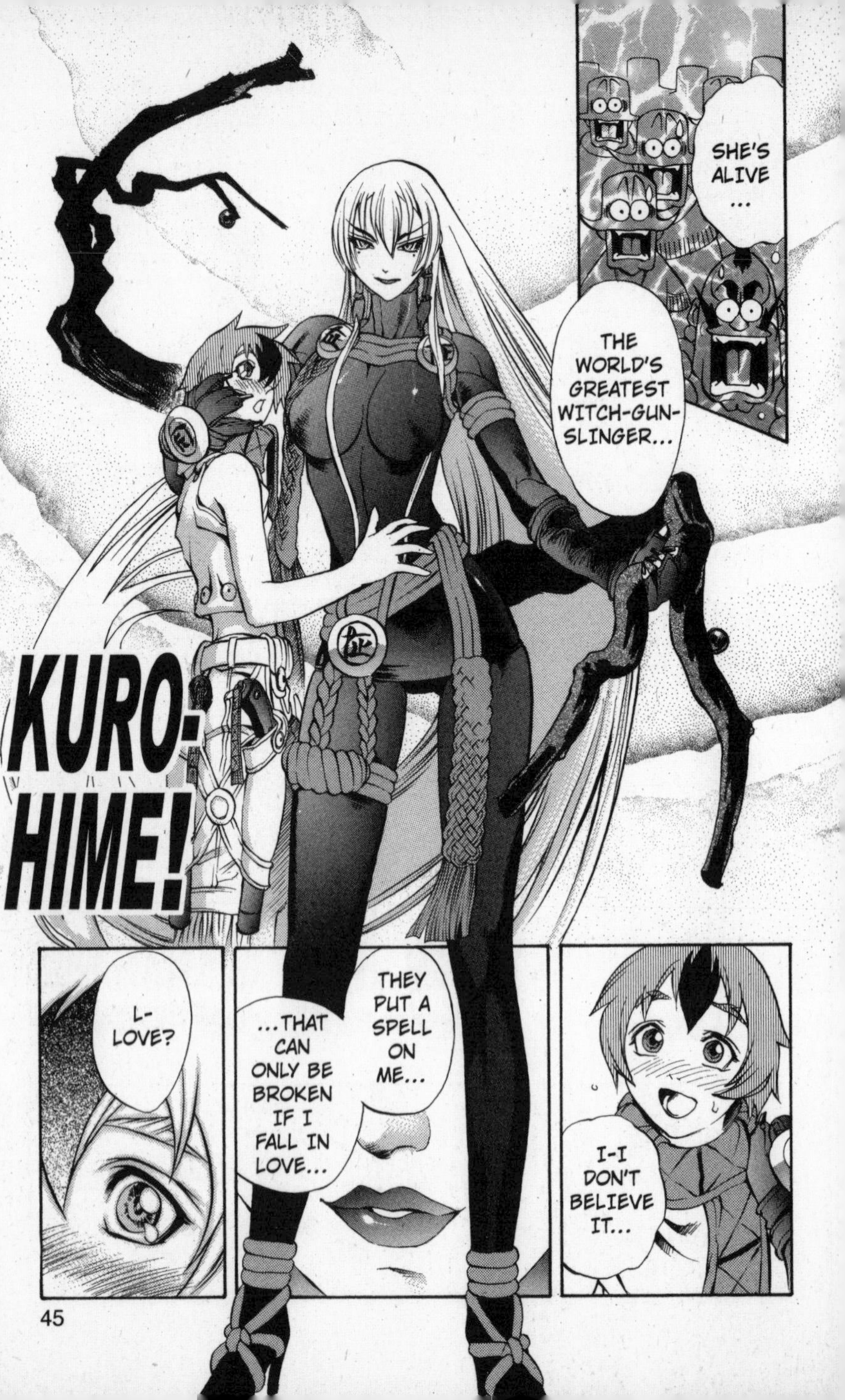
SHE'S ALIVE ...
THE WORLD'S GREATEST WITCH-GUN-SLINGER...
KURO-HIME!
I-I DON'T BELIEVE IT...
THEY PUT A SPELL ON ME...
...THAT CAN ONLY BE BROKEN IF I FALL IN LOVE...
L-LOVE?

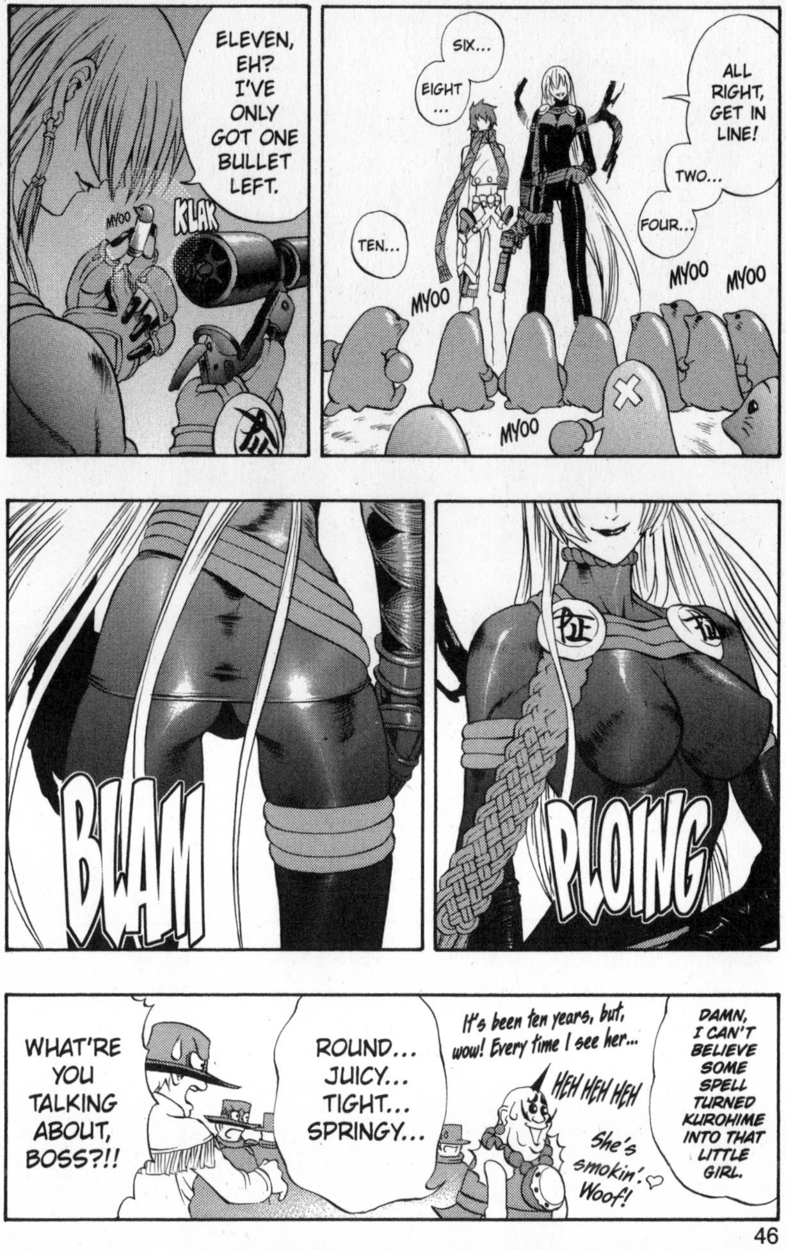
ALL RIGHT, GET IN LINE!
TWO...
FOUR...
SIX...
EIGHT...
TEN...
MYOO
MYOO
MYOO
MYOO
ELEVEN, EH? I'VE ONLY GOT ONE BULLET LEFT.
KLAK
MYOO
PLOING
BLAM
DAMN, I CAN'T BELIEVE SOME SPELL TURNED KUROHIME INTO THAT LITTLE GIRL.
It's been ten years, but, wow! Every time I see her...
HEH HEH HEH
She's smokin'! Woof!♡
ROUND... JUICY... TIGHT... SPRINGY...
WHAT'RE YOU TALKING ABOUT, BOSS?!!

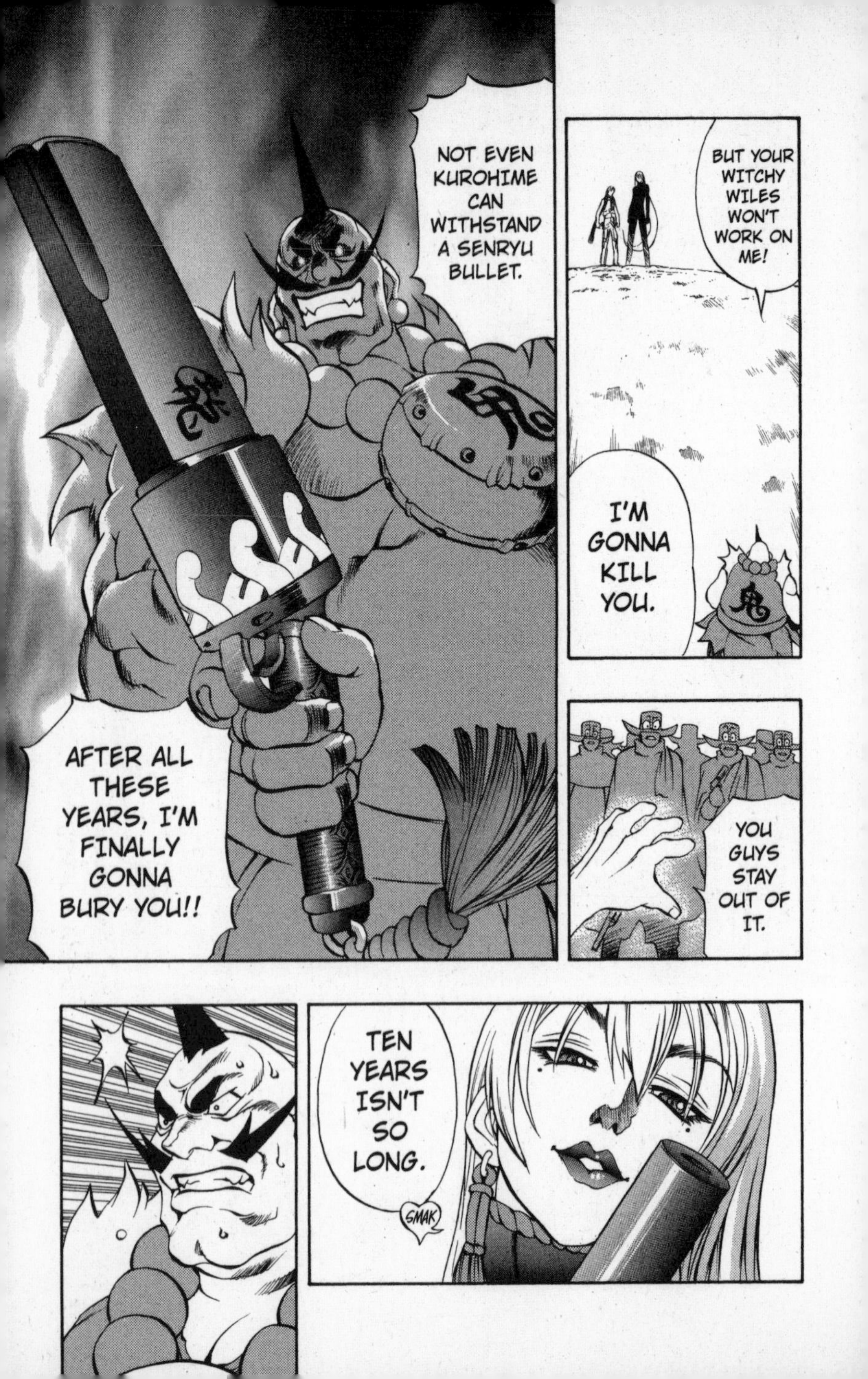
BUT YOUR WITCHY WILES WON'T WORK ON ME!
I'M GONNA KILL YOU.
YOU GUYS STAY OUT OF IT.
NOT EVEN KUROHIME CAN WITHSTAND A SENRYU BULLET.
AFTER ALL THESE YEARS, I'M FINALLY GONNA BURY YOU!!
TEN YEARS ISN'T SO LONG.
SMAK

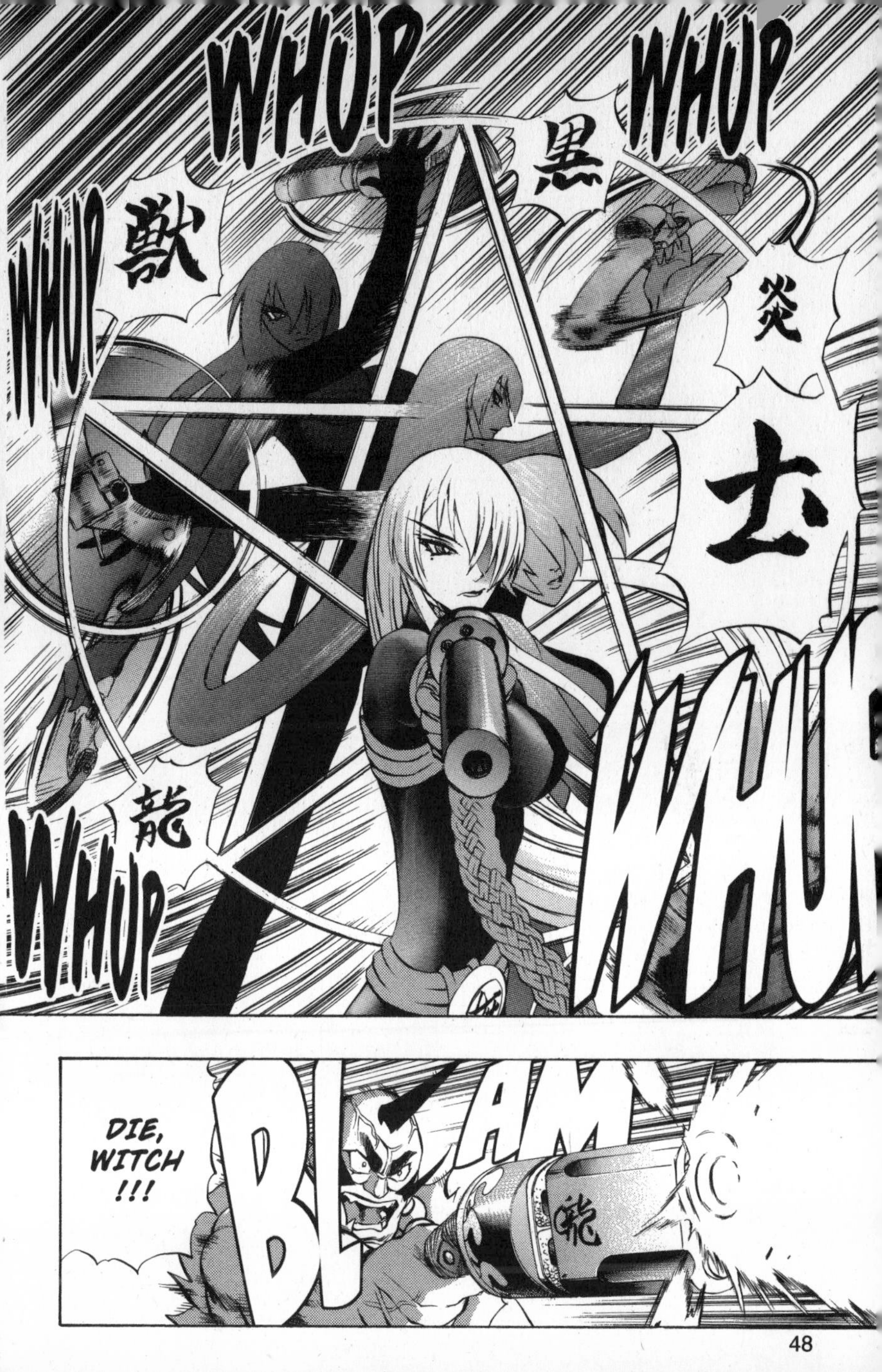
WHUP
黒
WHUP
獣
WHUP
炎
土
龍
WHUP
BLAM
DIE, WITCH !!!

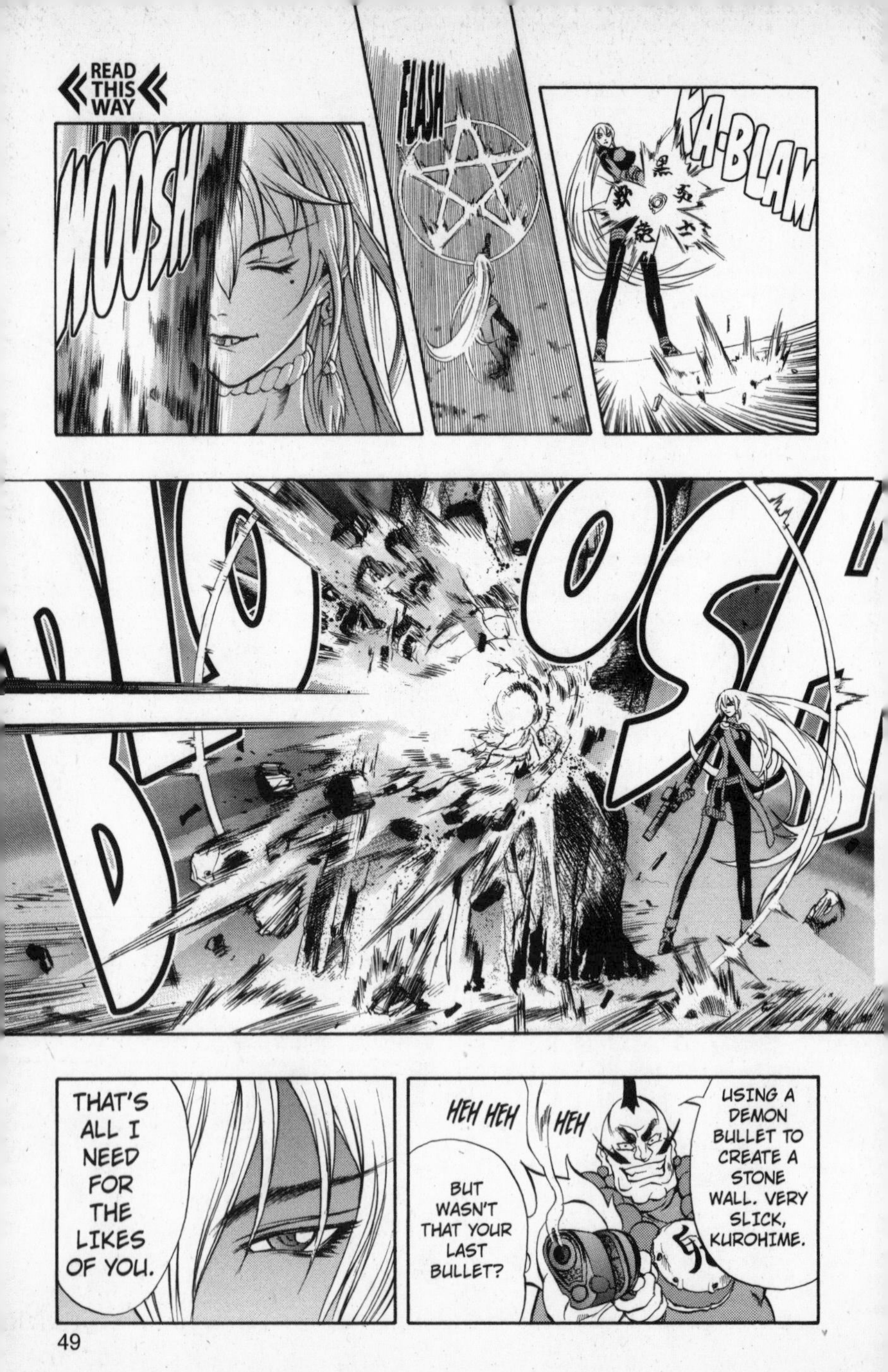
READ THIS WAY
KA-BLAM
FLASH
WOOSH
USING A DEMON BULLET TO CREATE A STONE WALL. VERY SLICK, KUROHIME.
HEH HEH HEH
BUT WASN'T THAT YOUR LAST BULLET?
THAT'S ALL I NEED FOR THE LIKES OF YOU.

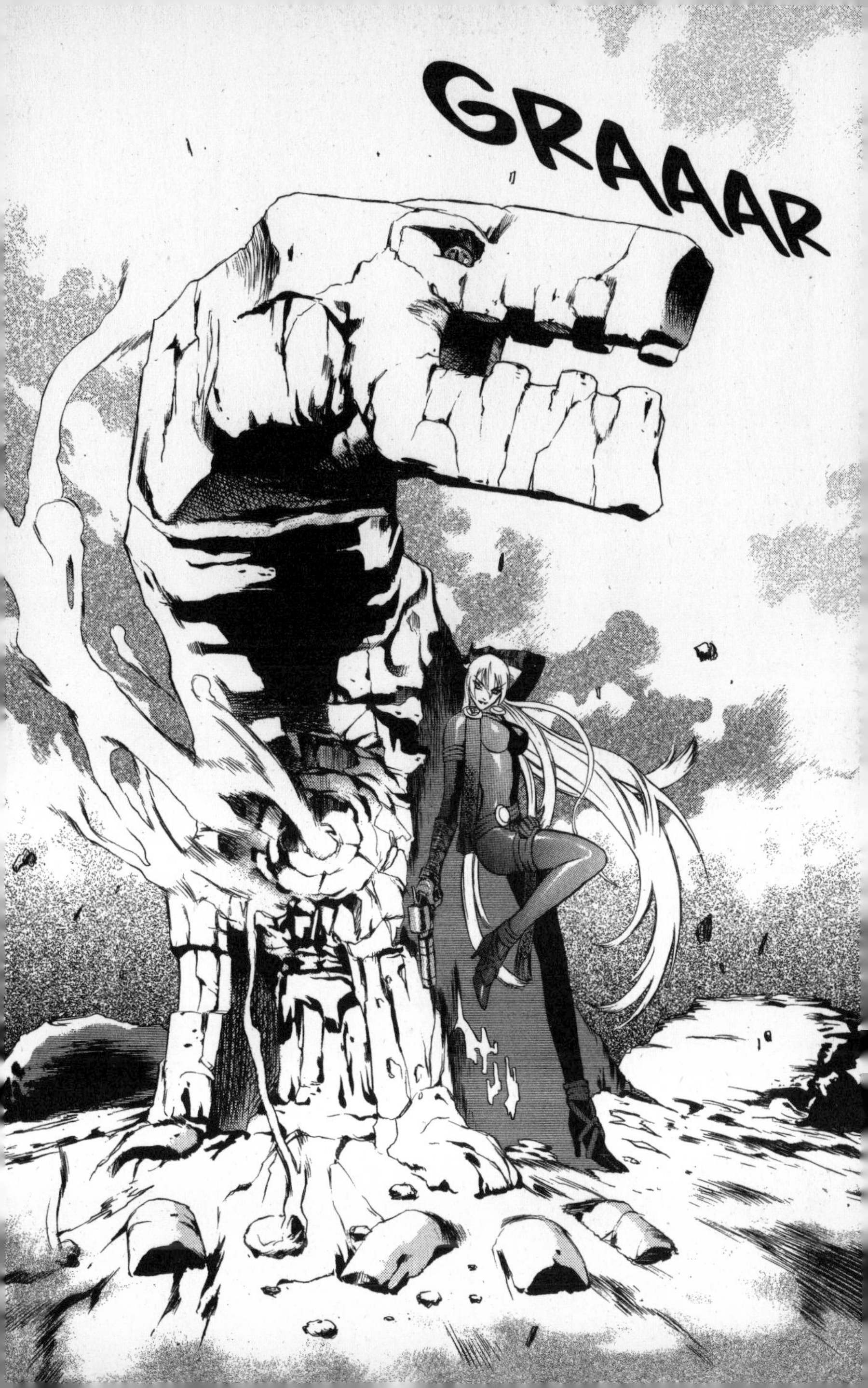
GRAAAR

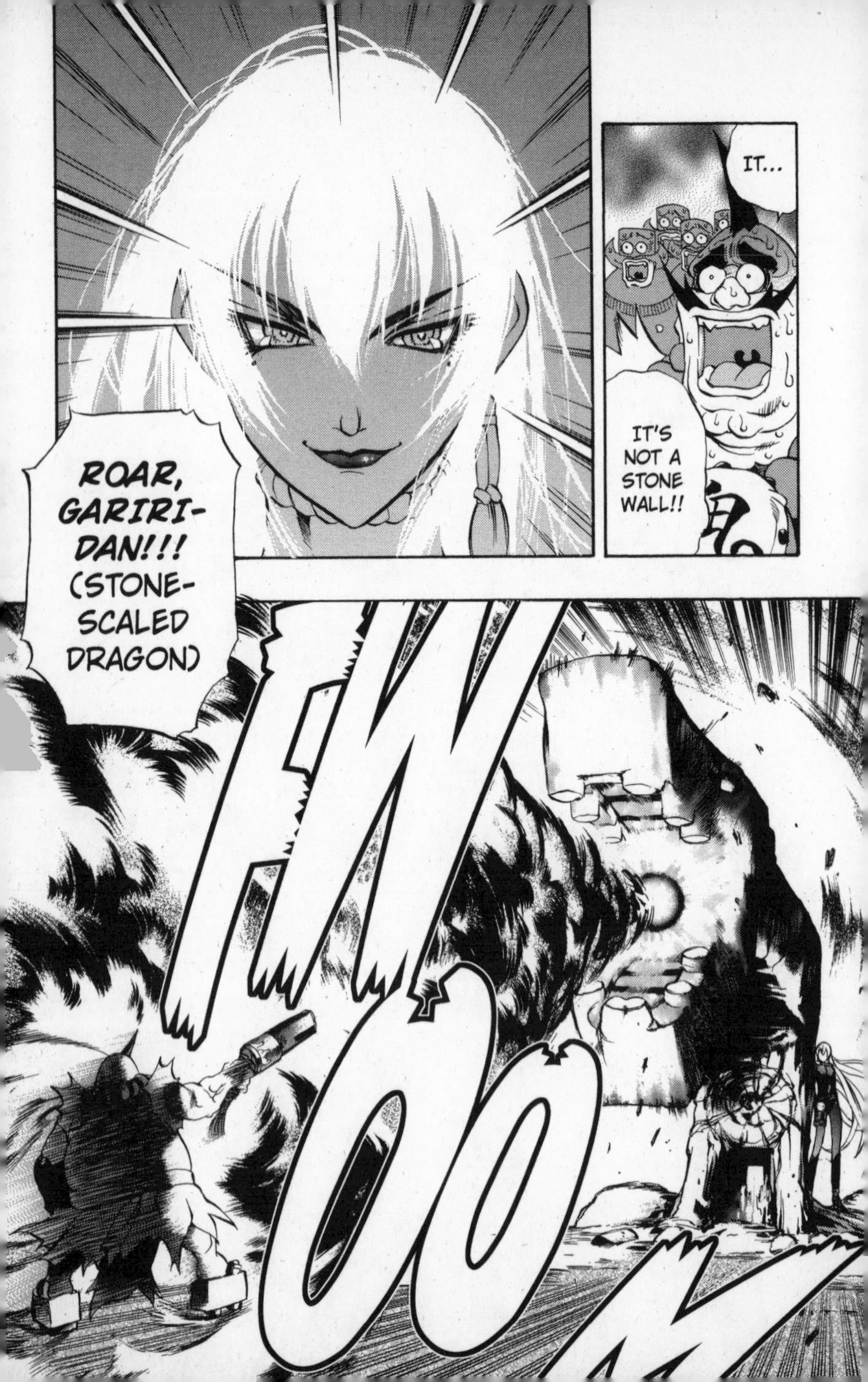
IT...
IT'S NOT A STONE WALL!!
ROAR, GARIRI-DAN!!! (STONE-SCALED DRAGON)
FWOOM

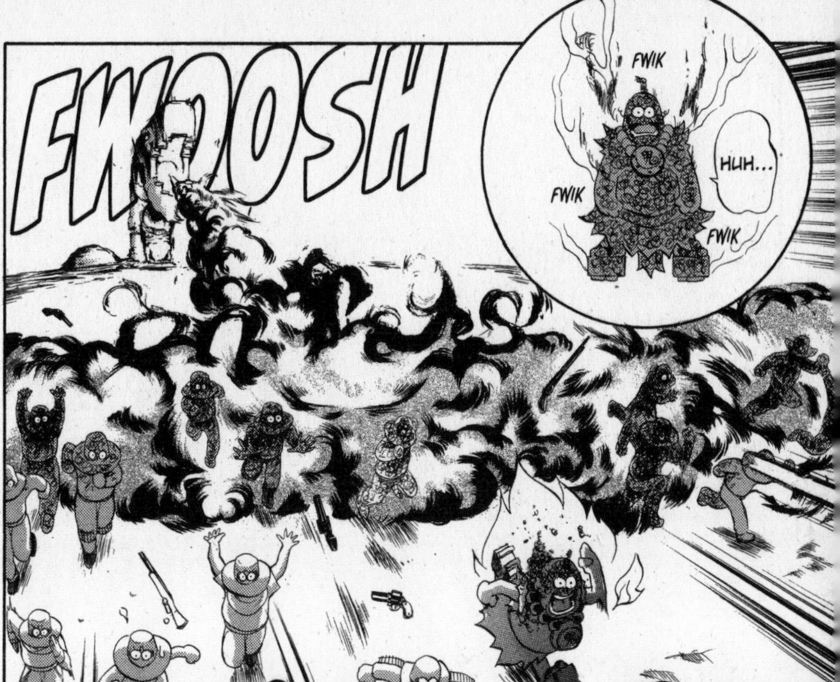
FWOOSH
FWIK
HUH...
FWIK
FWIK
WAAAH

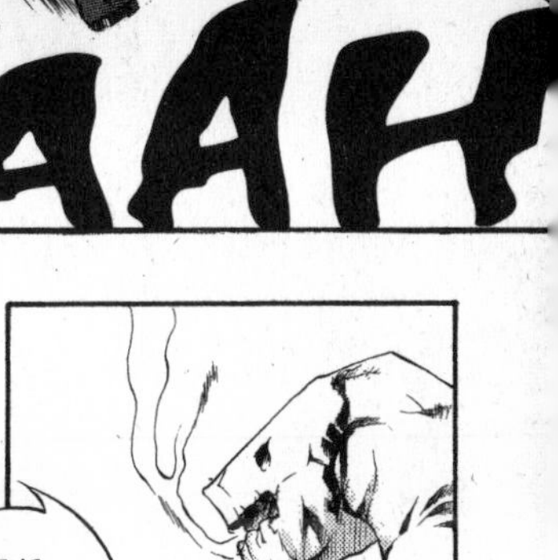
I'll get you yet!

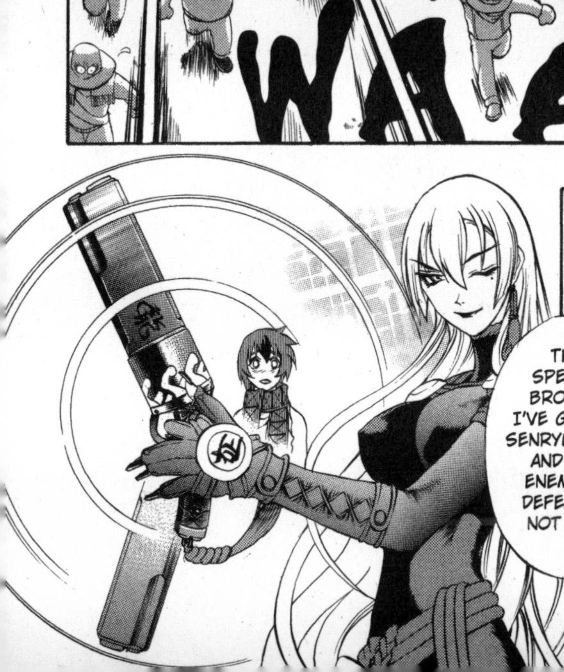
THE SPELL'S BROKEN, I'VE GOT MY SENRYU BACK, AND THE ENEMY IS DEFEATED. NOT BAD.

READ THIS WAY

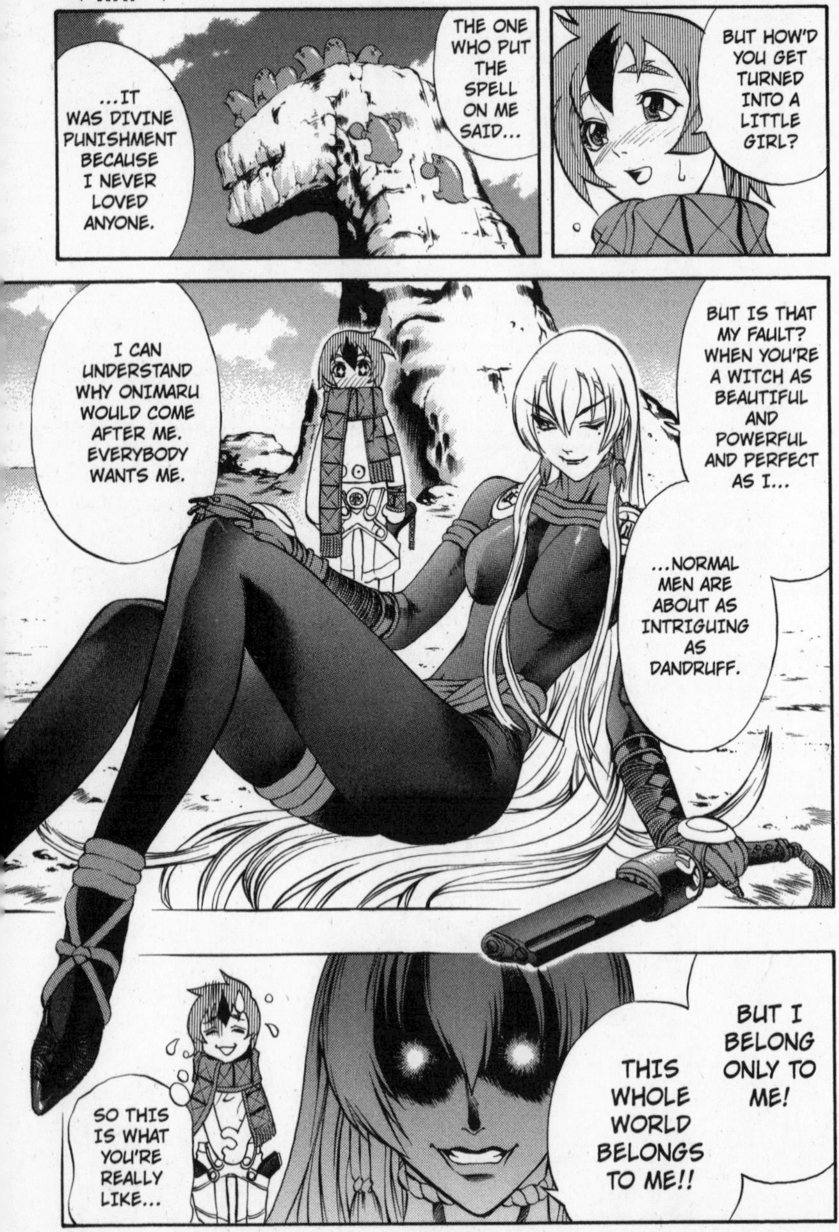
BUT HOW'D YOU GET TURNED INTO A LITTLE GIRL?
THE ONE WHO PUT THE SPELL ON ME SAID...
...IT WAS DIVINE PUNISHMENT BECAUSE I NEVER LOVED ANYONE.
I CAN UNDERSTAND WHY ONIMARU WOULD COME AFTER ME. EVERYBODY WANTS ME.
BUT IS THAT MY FAULT? WHEN YOU'RE A WITCH AS BEAUTIFUL AND POWERFUL AND PERFECT AS I...
...NORMAL MEN ARE ABOUT AS INTRIGUING AS DANDRUFF.
THIS WHOLE WORLD BELONGS TO ME!!
BUT I BELONG ONLY TO ME!
SO THIS IS WHAT YOU'RE REALLY LIKE...

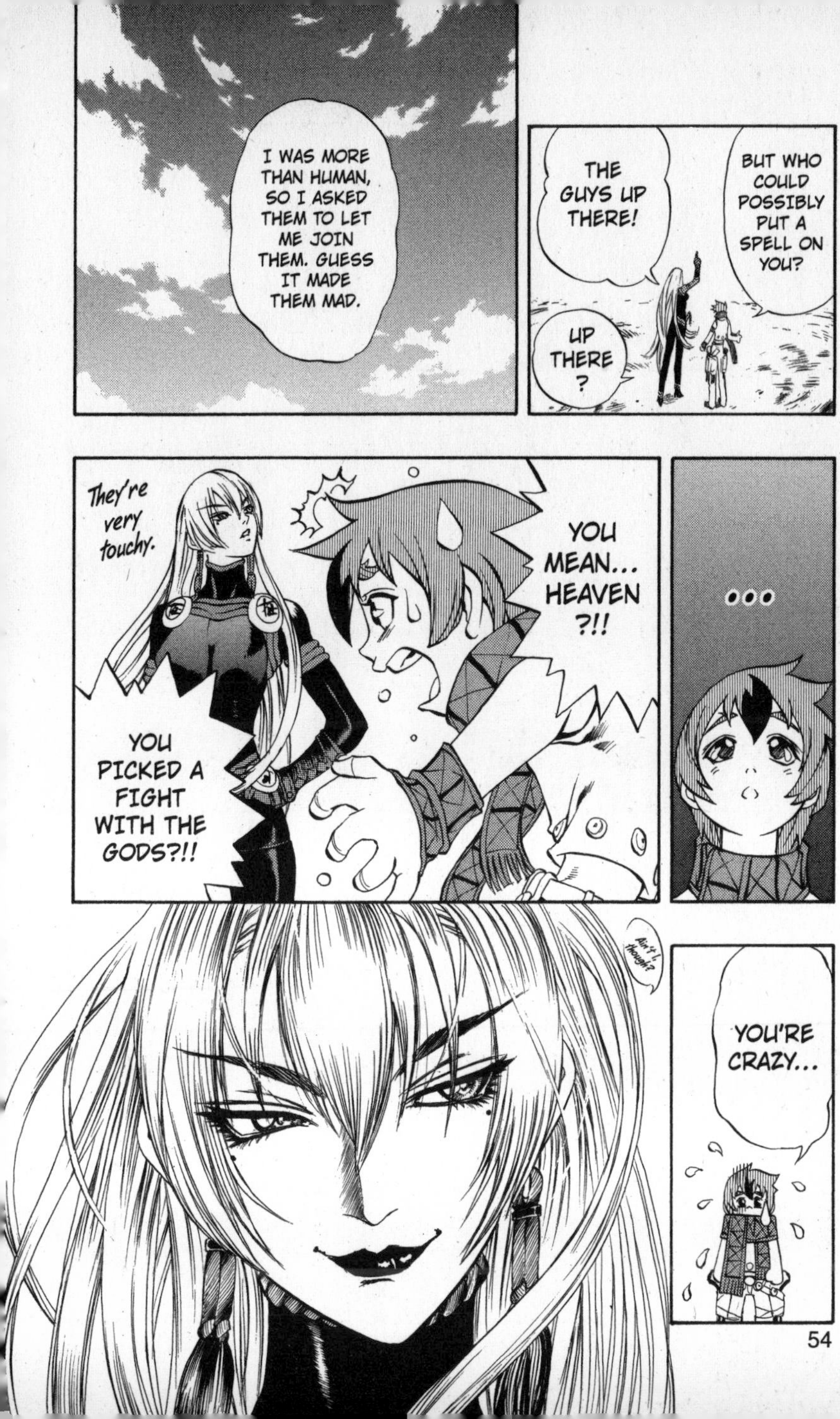
BUT WHO COULD POSSIBLY PUT A SPELL ON YOU?
THE GUYS UP THERE!
UP THERE?
I WAS MORE THAN HUMAN, SO I ASKED THEM TO LET ME JOIN THEM. GUESS IT MADE THEM MAD.
...
YOU MEAN... HEAVEN?!!
YOU PICKED A FIGHT WITH THE GODS?!!
They're very touchy.
YOU'RE CRAZY...
Ain't I, though?

READ THIS WAY

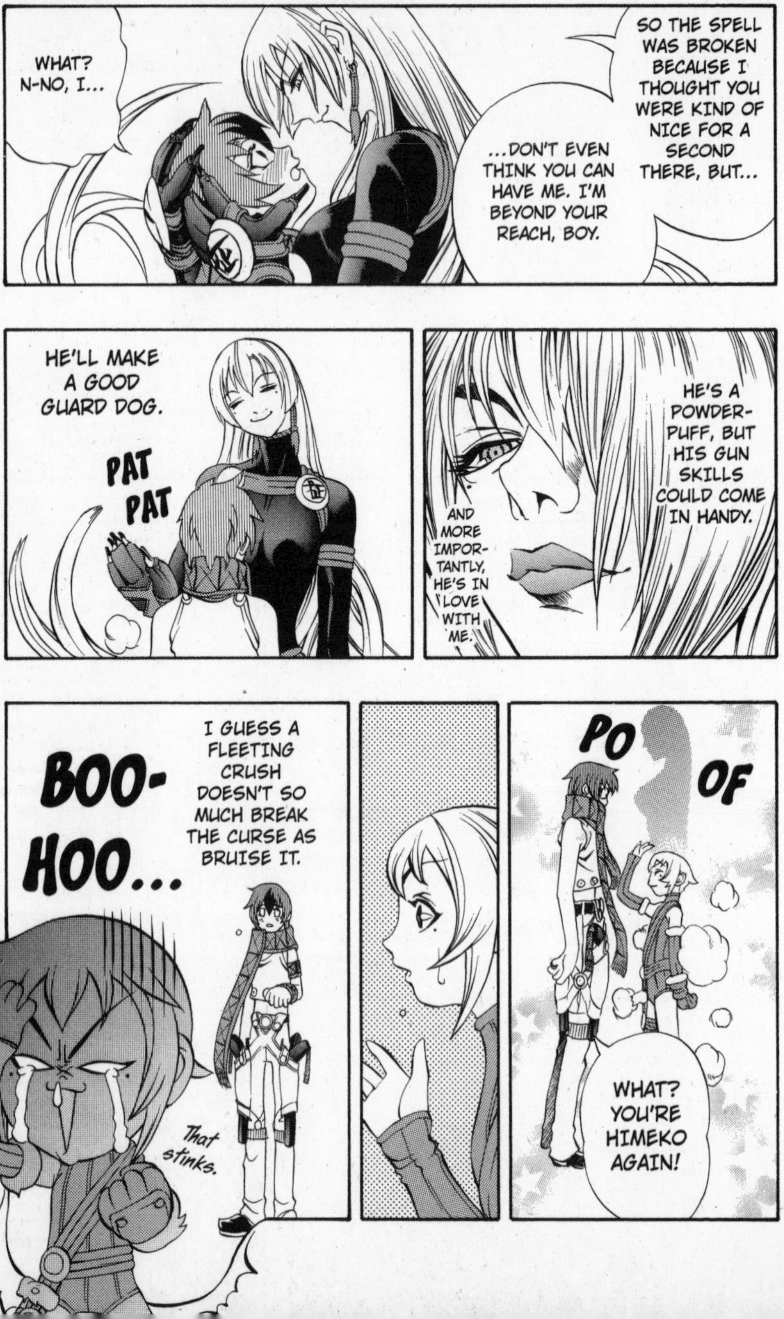

SO THE SPELL WAS BROKEN BECAUSE I THOUGHT YOU WERE KIND OF NICE FOR A SECOND THERE, BUT...
...DON'T EVEN THINK YOU CAN HAVE ME. I'M BEYOND YOUR REACH, BOY.
WHAT? N-NO, I...
HE'S A POWDER-PUFF, BUT HIS GUN SKILLS COULD COME IN HANDY.
AND MORE IMPORTANTLY, HE'S IN LOVE WITH ME.
HE'LL MAKE A GOOD GUARD DOG.
PAT PAT
PO OF
WHAT? YOU'RE HIMEKO AGAIN!
I GUESS A FLEETING CRUSH DOESN'T SO MUCH BREAK THE CURSE AS BRUISE IT.
BOO-HOO...
That stinks.

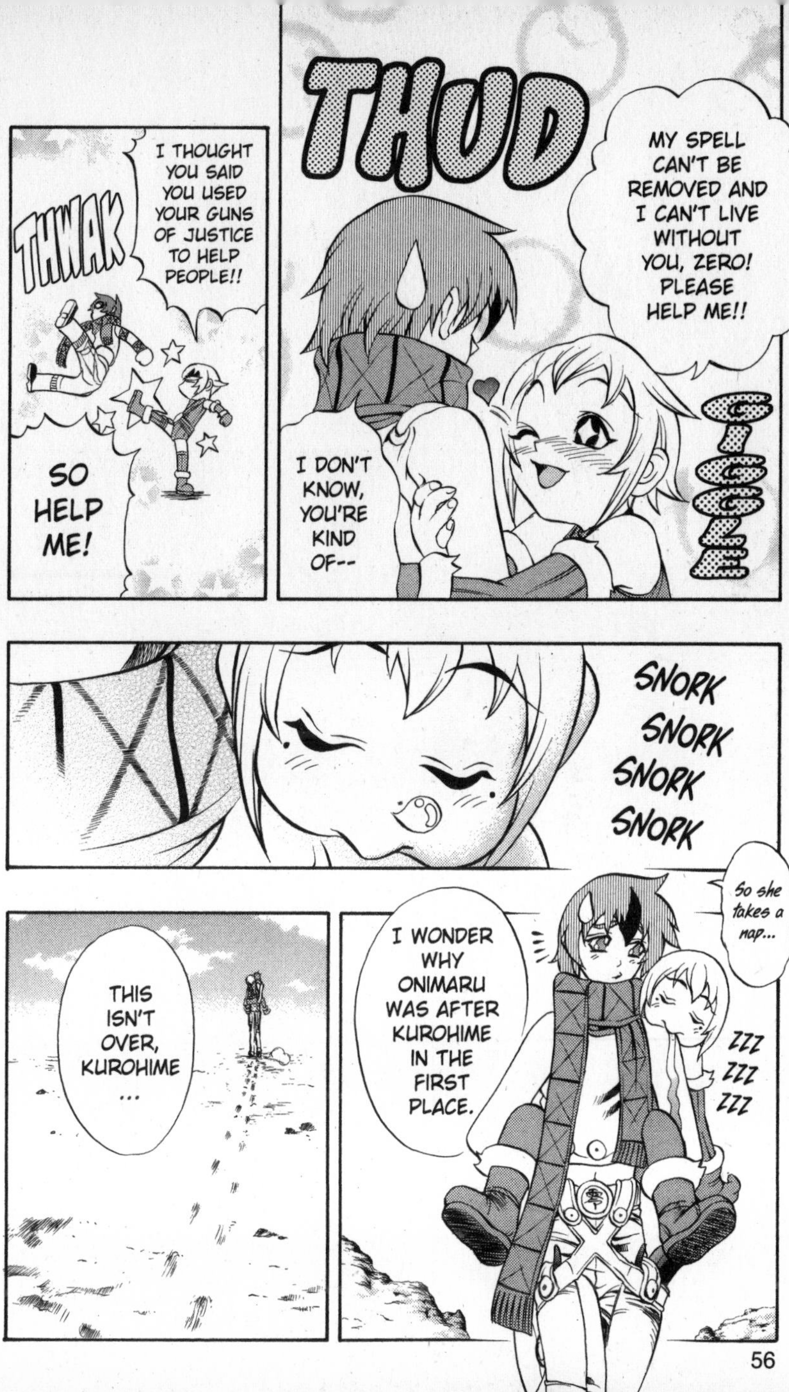
THUD
MY SPELL CAN'T BE REMOVED AND I CAN'T LIVE WITHOUT YOU, ZERO! PLEASE HELP ME!!
GIGGLE
I DON'T KNOW, YOU'RE KIND OF--
THWAK
I THOUGHT YOU SAID YOU USED YOUR GUNS OF JUSTICE TO HELP PEOPLE!!
SO HELP ME!
SNORK SNORK SNORK SNORK
So she takes a nap...
I WONDER WHY ONIMARU WAS AFTER KUROHIME IN THE FIRST PLACE.
ZZZ ZZZ ZZZ
THIS ISN'T OVER, KUROHIME...

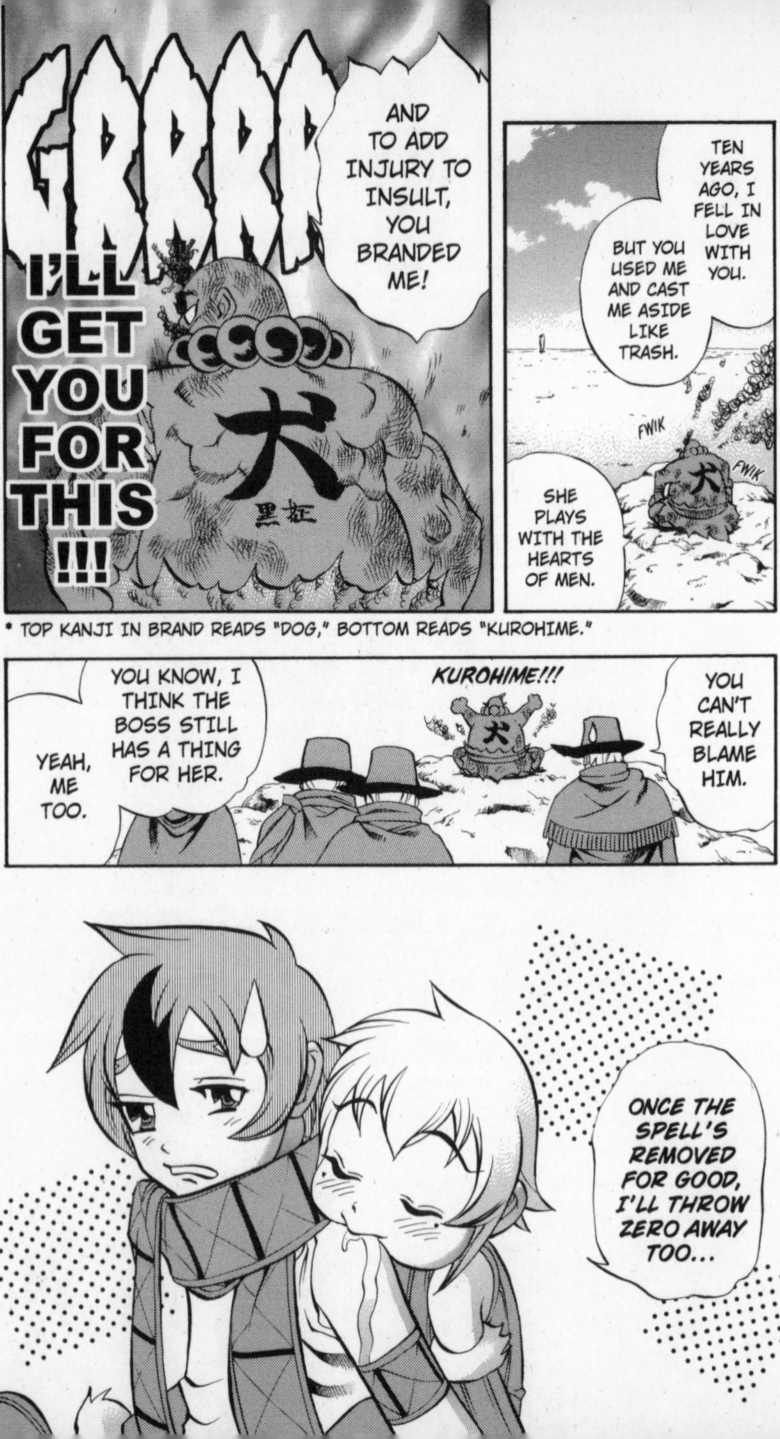
TEN YEARS AGO, I FELL IN LOVE WITH YOU.
BUT YOU USED ME AND CAST ME ASIDE LIKE TRASH.
FWIK
FWIK
SHE PLAYS WITH THE HEARTS OF MEN.
AND TO ADD INJURY TO INSULT, YOU BRANDED ME!
GRRRR
I'LL GET YOU FOR THIS!!!
YOU CAN'T REALLY BLAME HIM.
KUROHIME!!!
YOU KNOW, I THINK THE BOSS STILL HAS A THING FOR HER.
YEAH, ME TOO.
ONCE THE SPELL'S REMOVED FOR GOOD, I'LL THROW ZERO AWAY TOO...

* TOP KANJI IN BRAND READS "DOG," BOTTOM READS "KUROHIME."

#2 GUN OF JUSTICE

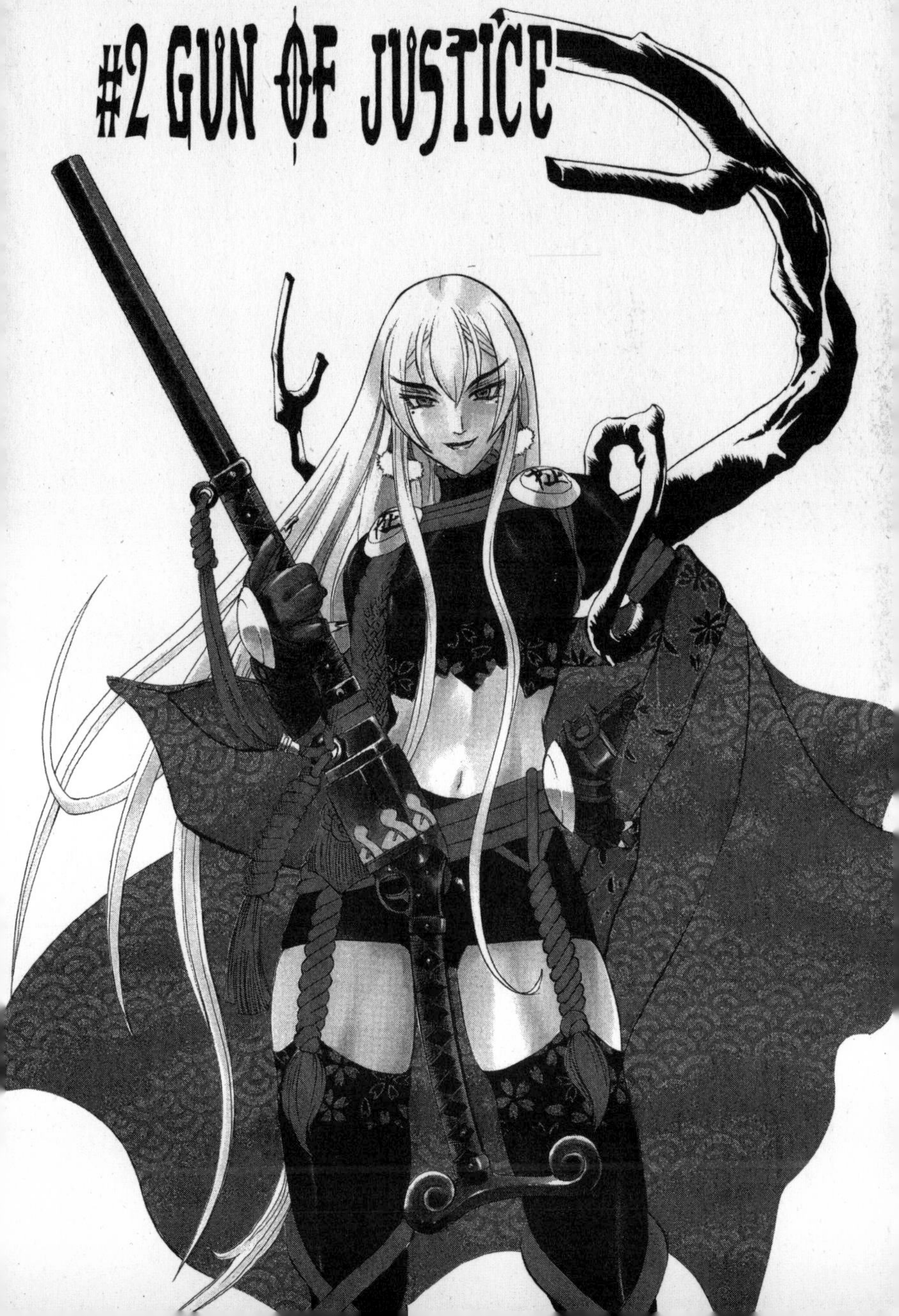

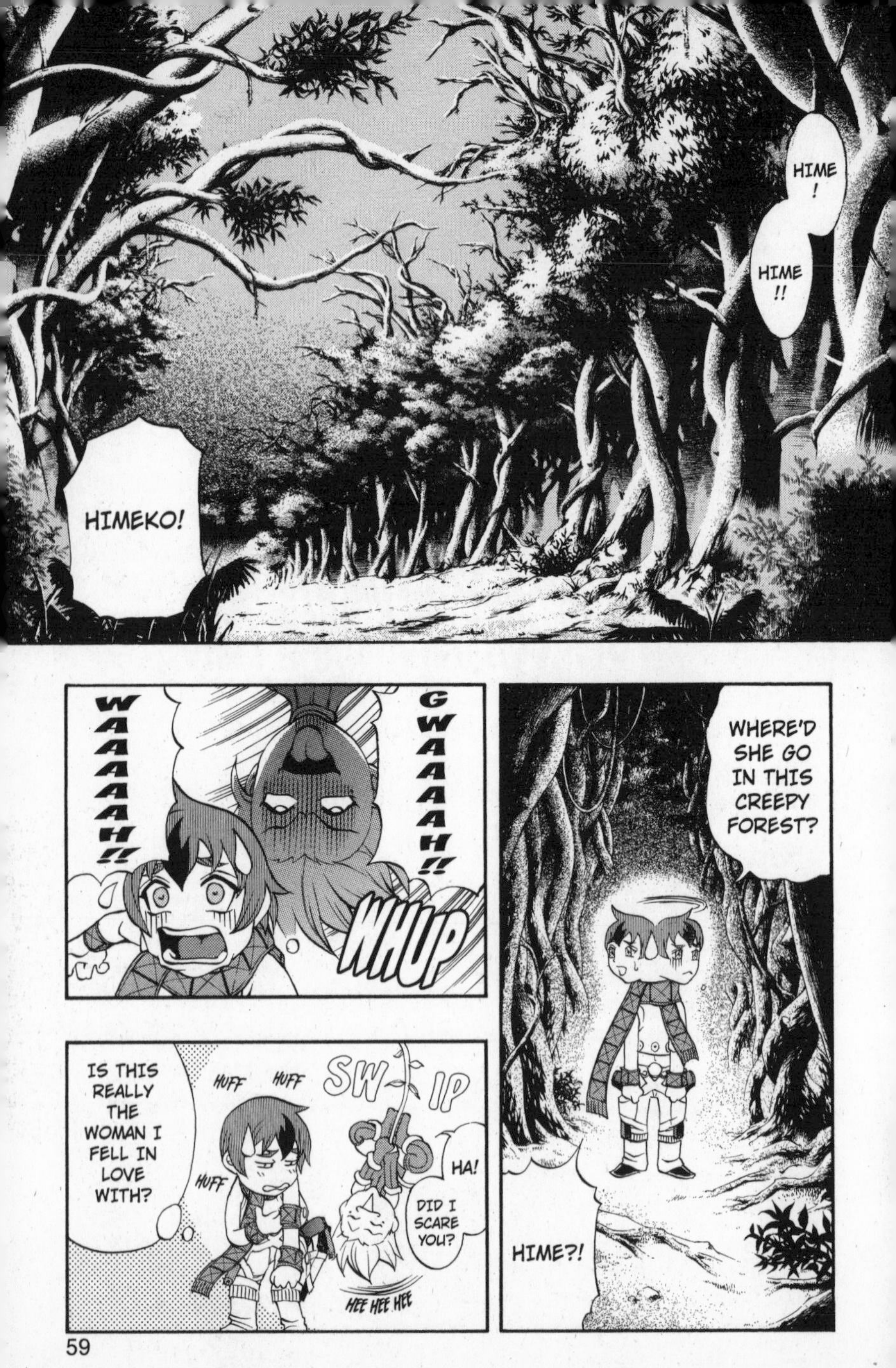
HIME!
HIME!!
HIMEKO!
WHERE'D SHE GO IN THIS CREEPY FOREST?
HIME?!
GWAAAAAH!!
WAAAAAAH!!
WHUP
SWIP
HA!
DID I SCARE YOU?
HEE HEE HEE
HUFF HUFF
HUFF
IS THIS REALLY THE WOMAN I FELL IN LOVE WITH?

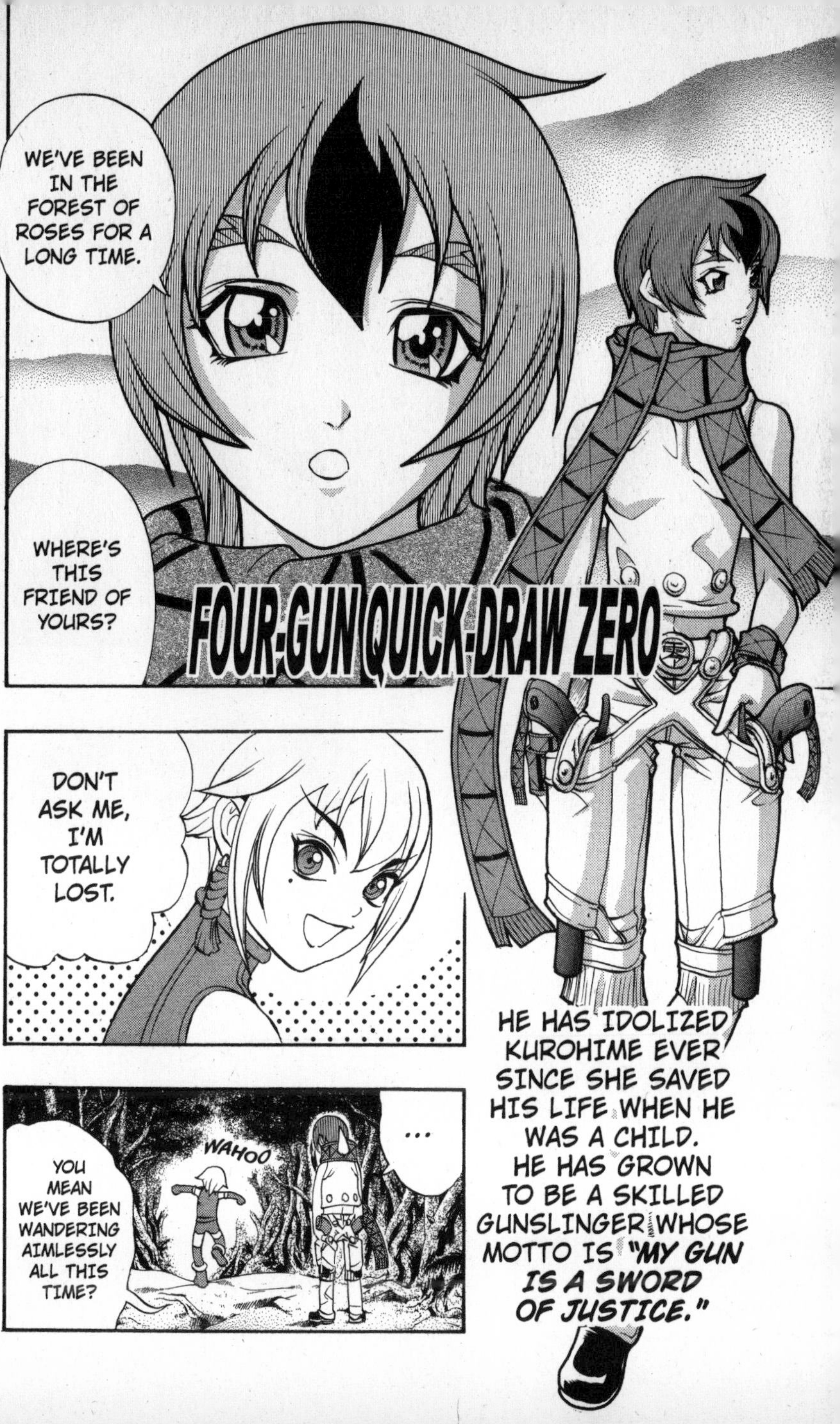
FOUR-GUN QUICK-DRAW ZERO
WE'VE BEEN IN THE FOREST OF ROSES FOR A LONG TIME.
WHERE'S THIS FRIEND OF YOURS?
DON'T ASK ME, I'M TOTALLY LOST.
...
WAHOO
YOU MEAN WE'VE BEEN WANDERING AIMLESSLY ALL THIS TIME?
HE HAS IDOLIZED KUROHIME EVER SINCE SHE SAVED HIS LIFE WHEN HE WAS A CHILD. HE HAS GROWN TO BE A SKILLED GUNSLINGER WHOSE MOTTO IS "MY GUN IS A SWORD OF JUSTICE."

HIMEKO--BAD LITTLE GIRL

SHE IS REALLY THE LEGENDARY KUROHIME, THE WORLD'S GREATEST WITCH-GUNSLINGER WHO HAS BEEN TRANSFORMED INTO A LITTLE GIRL FOR DEFYING THE GODS.

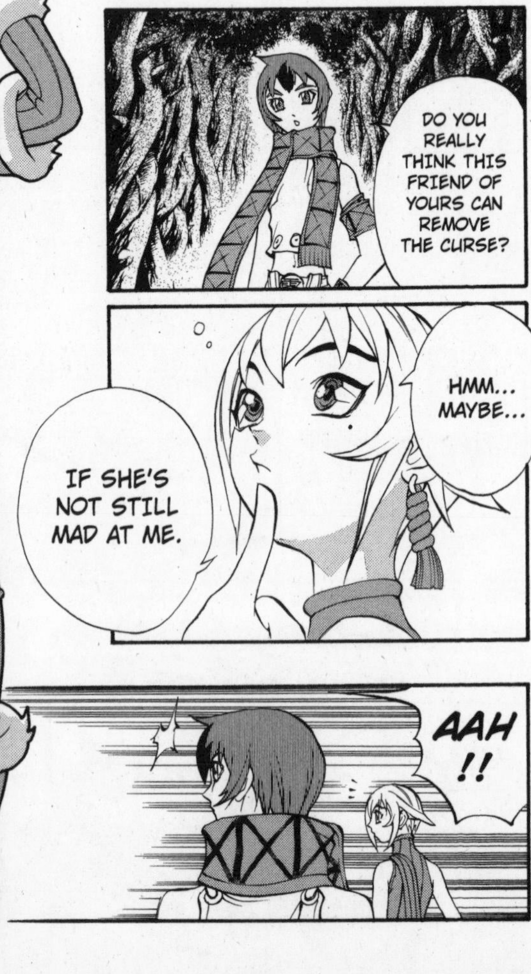
DO YOU REALLY THINK THIS FRIEND OF YOURS CAN REMOVE THE CURSE?
HMM... MAYBE...
IF SHE'S NOT STILL MAD AT ME.
AAH !!

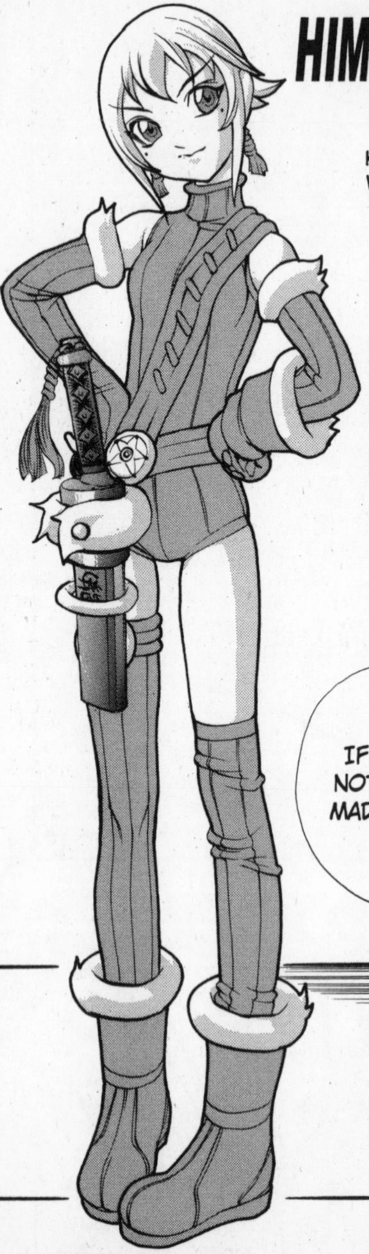

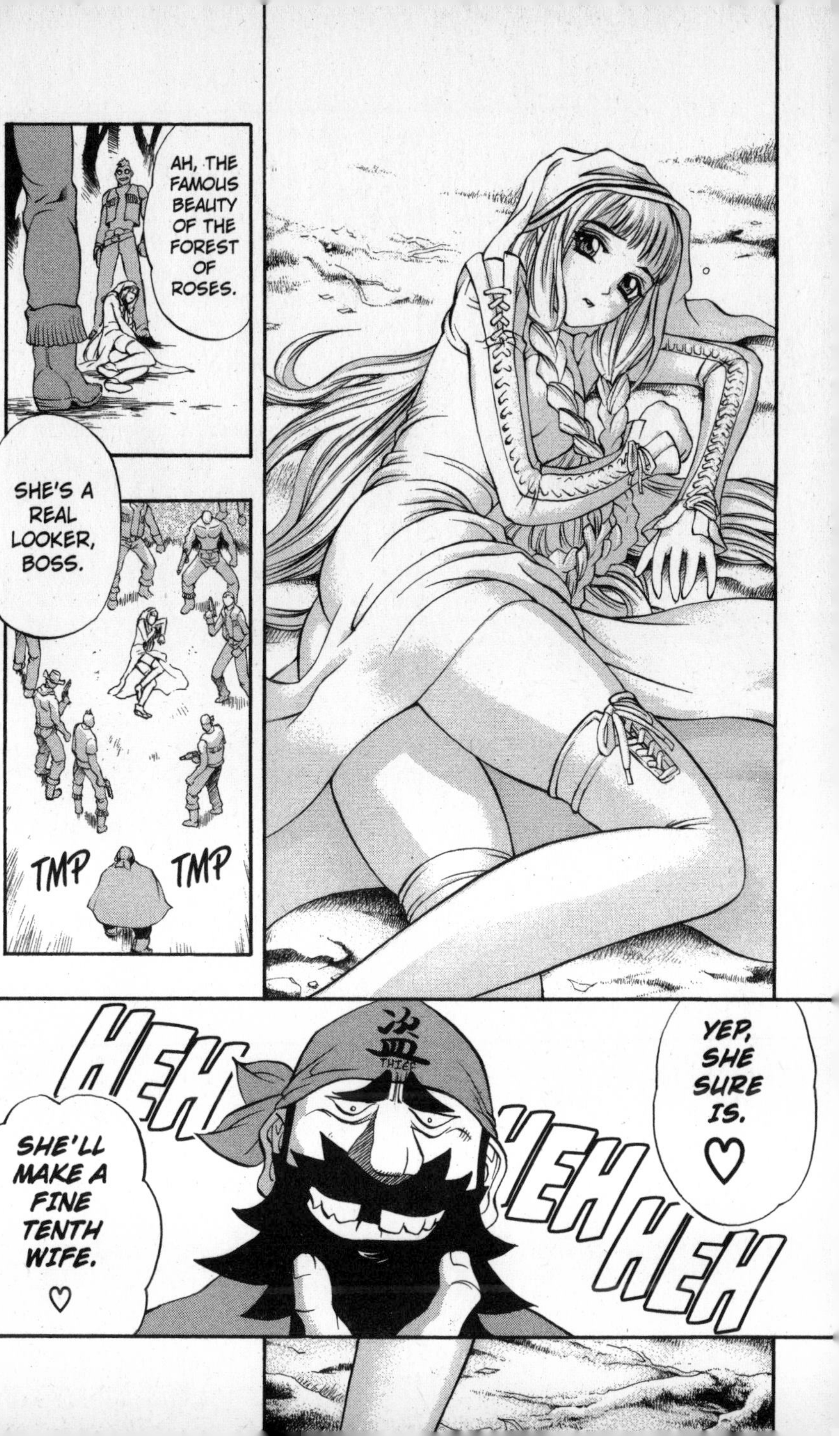
AH, THE FAMOUS BEAUTY OF THE FOREST OF ROSES.
SHE'S A REAL LOOKER, BOSS.
TMP TMP
YEP, SHE SURE IS. ♡
HEH HEH HEH HEH
SHE'LL MAKE A FINE TENTH WIFE. ♡

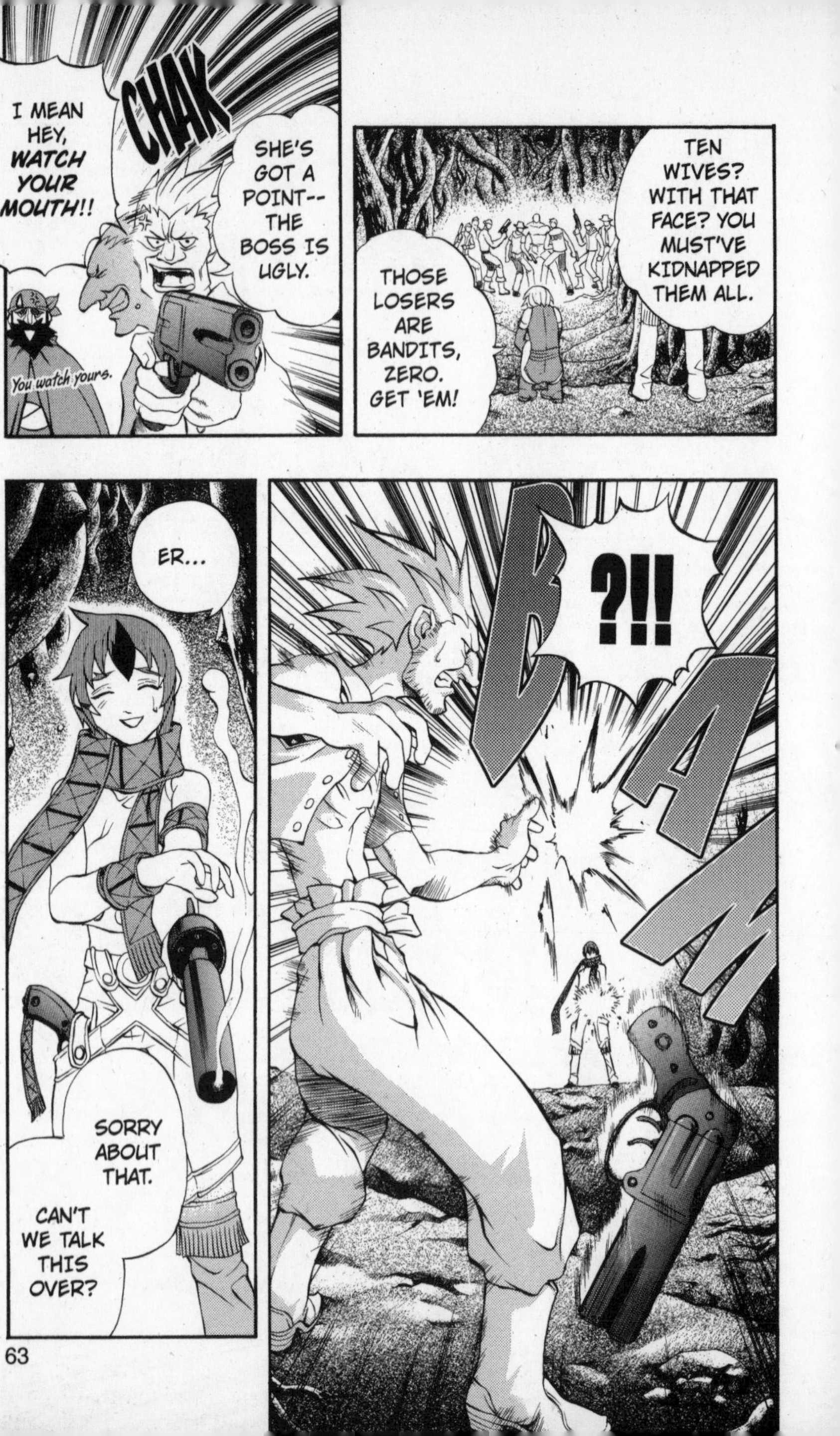
TEN WIVES? WITH THAT FACE? YOU MUST'VE KIDNAPPED THEM ALL.
THOSE LOSERS ARE BANDITS, ZERO. GET 'EM!
CHAK
SHE'S GOT A POINT-- THE BOSS IS UGLY.
I MEAN HEY, WATCH YOUR MOUTH!!
You watch yours.
BAM
?!!
ER...
SORRY ABOUT THAT.
CAN'T WE TALK THIS OVER?

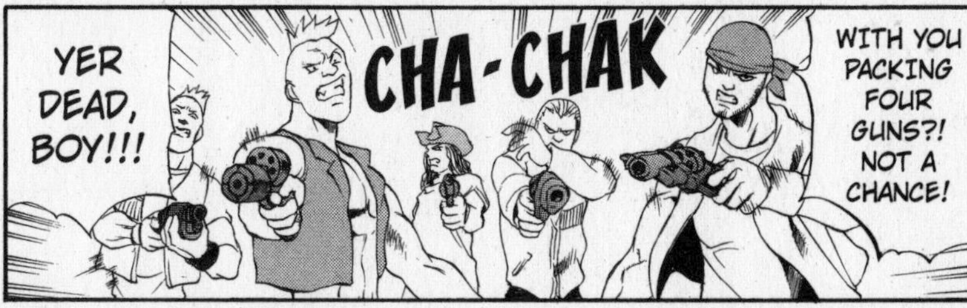
WITH YOU PACKING FOUR GUNS?! NOT A CHANCE!
CHA-CHAK
YER DEAD, BOY!!!

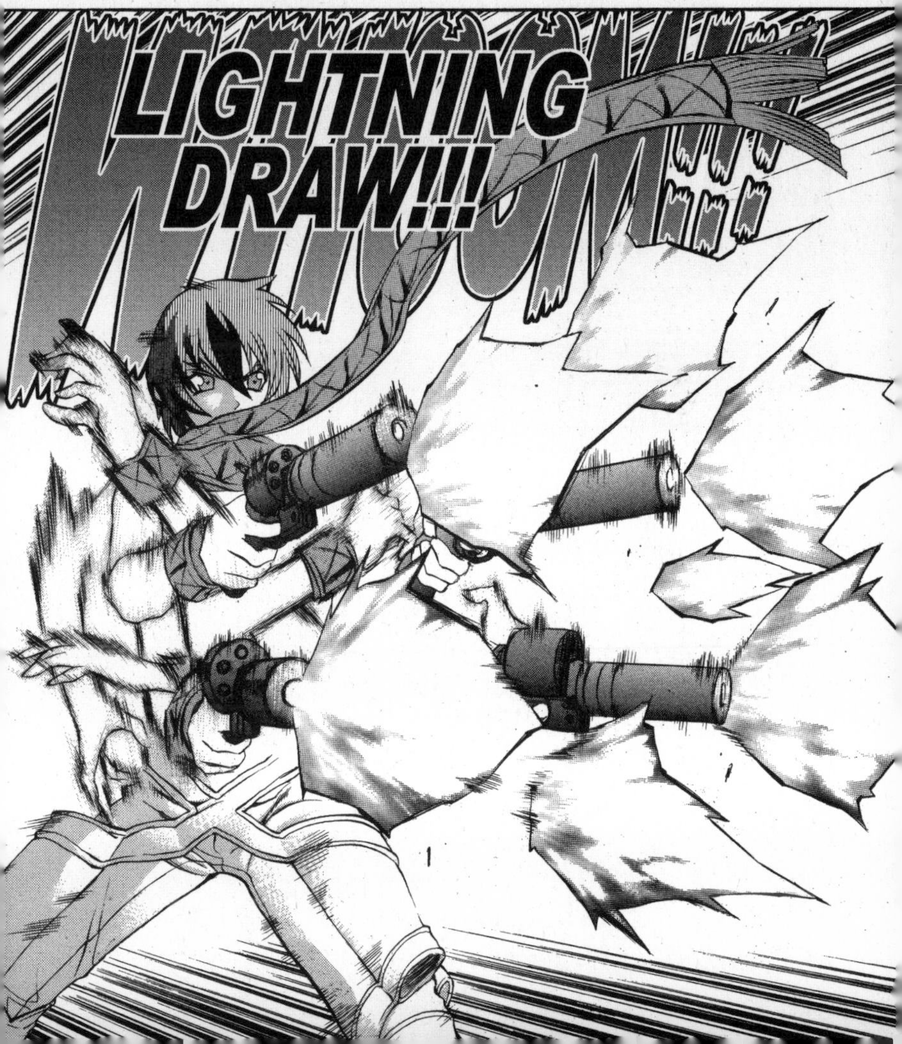
LIGHTNING DRAW!!!

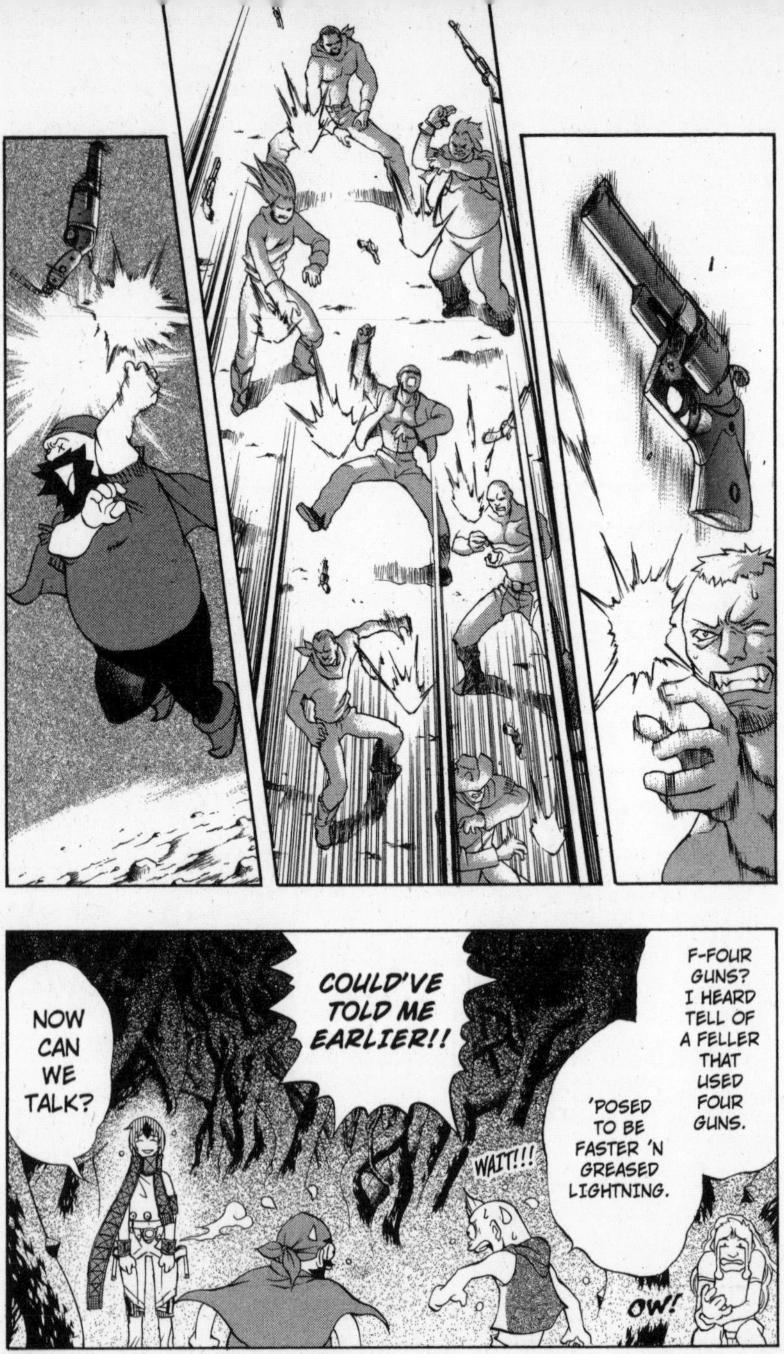
F-FOUR GUNS? I HEARD TELL OF A FELLER THAT USED FOUR GUNS.
'POSED TO BE FASTER 'N GREASED LIGHTNING.
WAIT!!!
COULD'VE TOLD ME EARLIER!!
OW!
NOW CAN WE TALK?

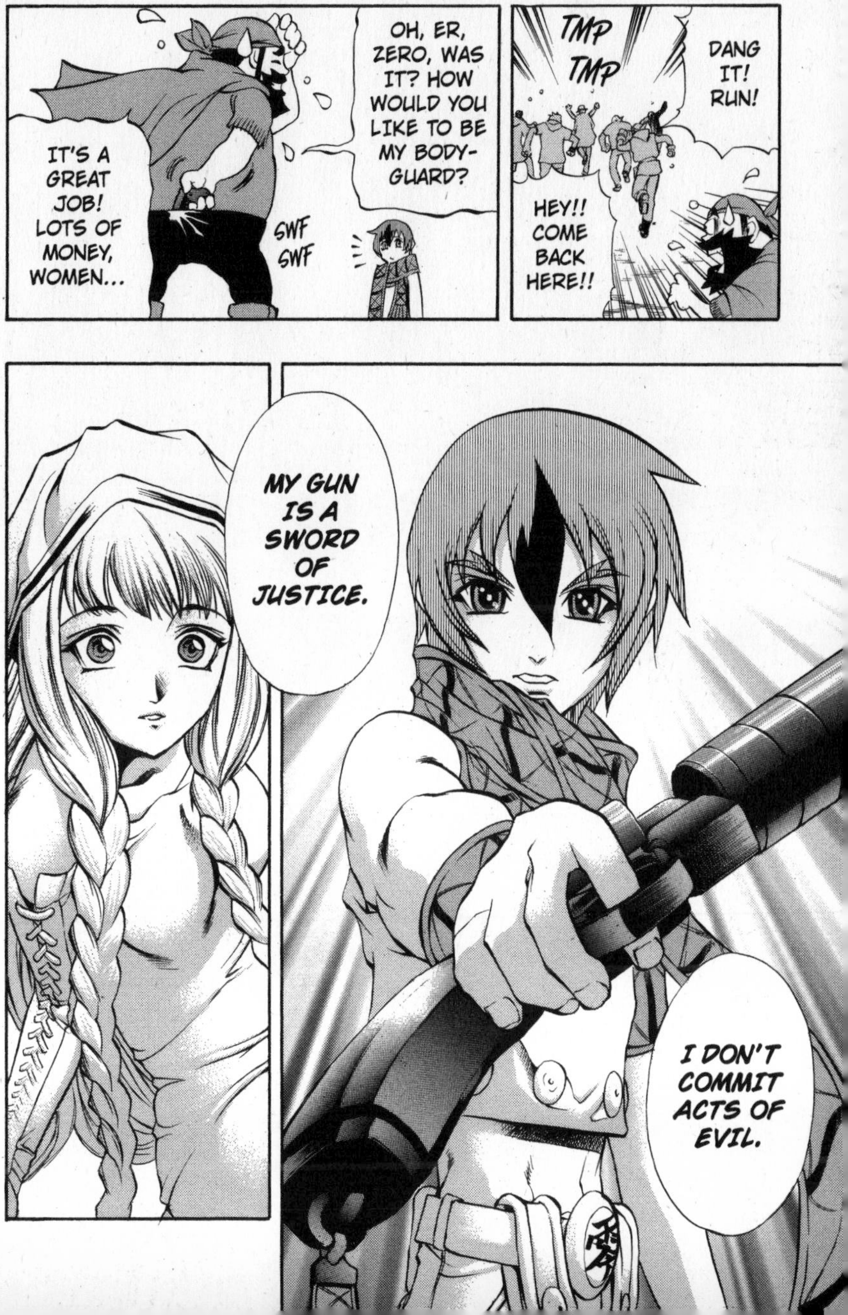
DANG IT! RUN!
TMP
TMP
HEY!! COME BACK HERE!!
OH, ER, ZERO, WAS IT? HOW WOULD YOU LIKE TO BE MY BODY-GUARD?
IT'S A GREAT JOB! LOTS OF MONEY, WOMEN...
SWF
SWF
MY GUN IS A SWORD OF JUSTICE.
I DON'T COMMIT ACTS OF EVIL.

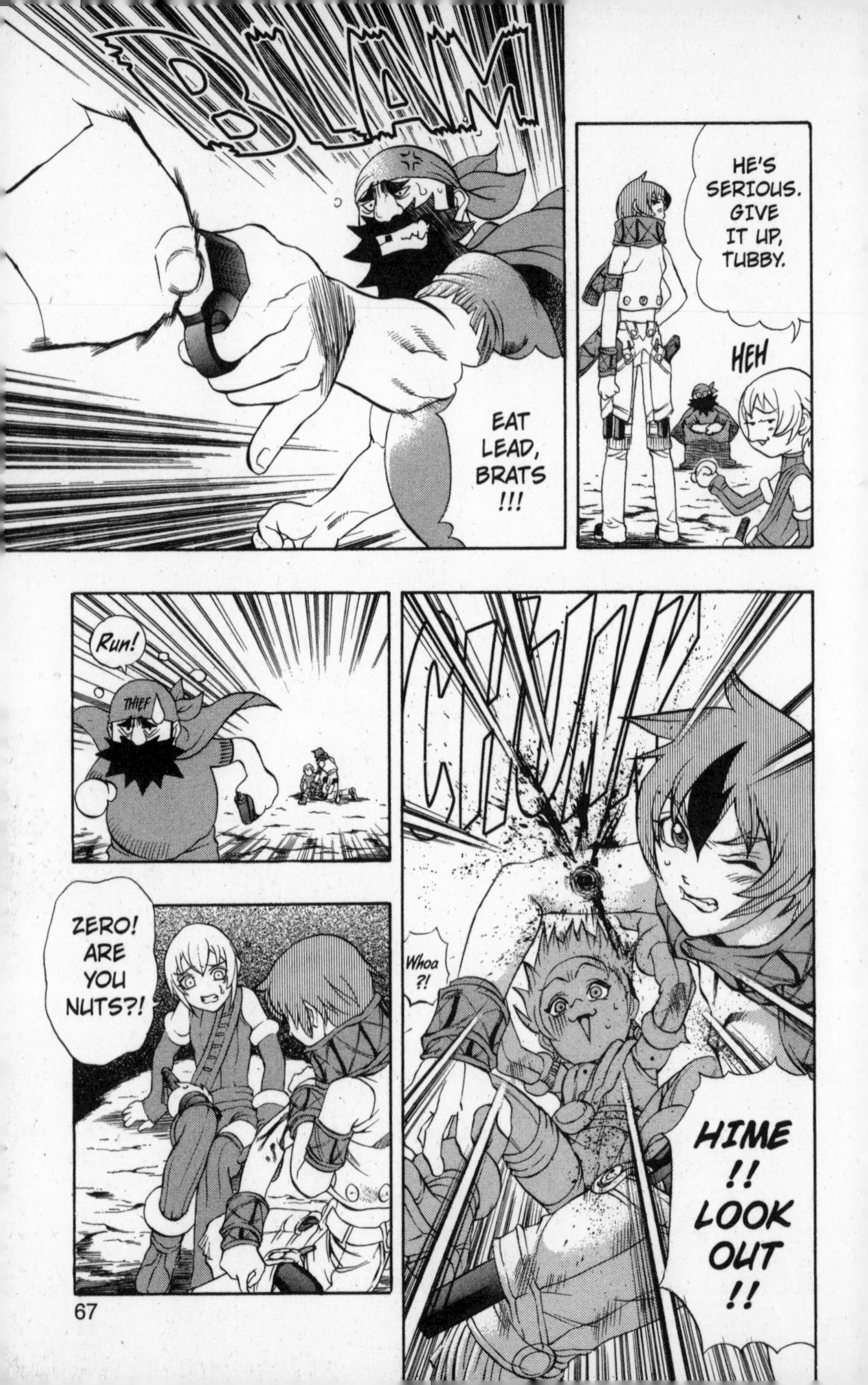
HE'S SERIOUS. GIVE IT UP, TUBBY.
HEH
BLAM
EAT LEAD, BRATS !!!
Whoa ?!
HIME !! LOOK OUT !!
Run!
THIEF
ZERO! ARE YOU NUTS?!

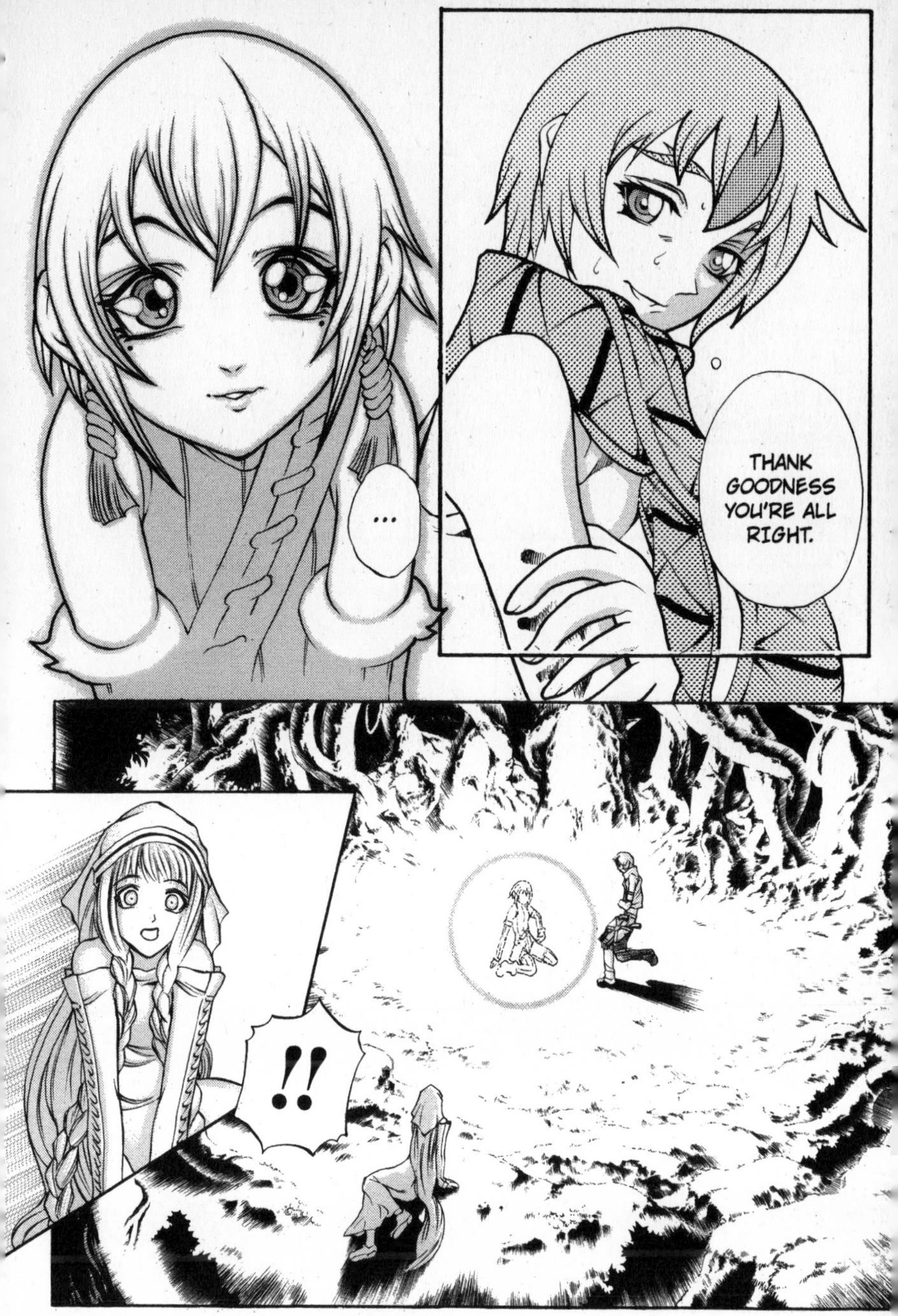
THANK GOODNESS YOU'RE ALL RIGHT.
...
!!

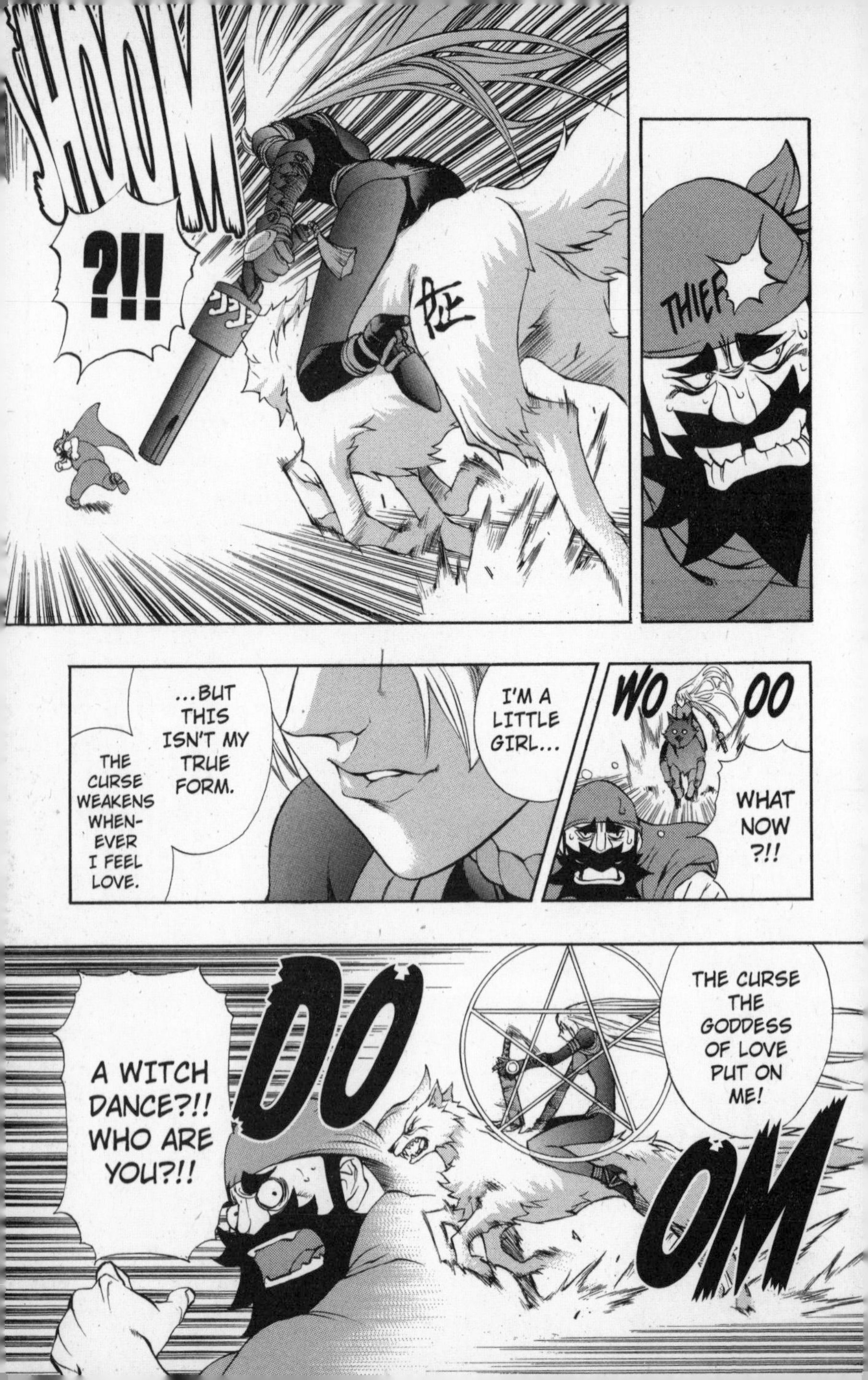
THIEF
SHOOM
?!!
WO OO
WHAT NOW ?!!
I'M A LITTLE GIRL...
...BUT THIS ISN'T MY TRUE FORM.
THE CURSE WEAKENS WHEN-EVER I FEEL LOVE.
THE CURSE THE GODDESS OF LOVE PUT ON ME!
DOOM
A WITCH DANCE?!! WHO ARE YOU?!!

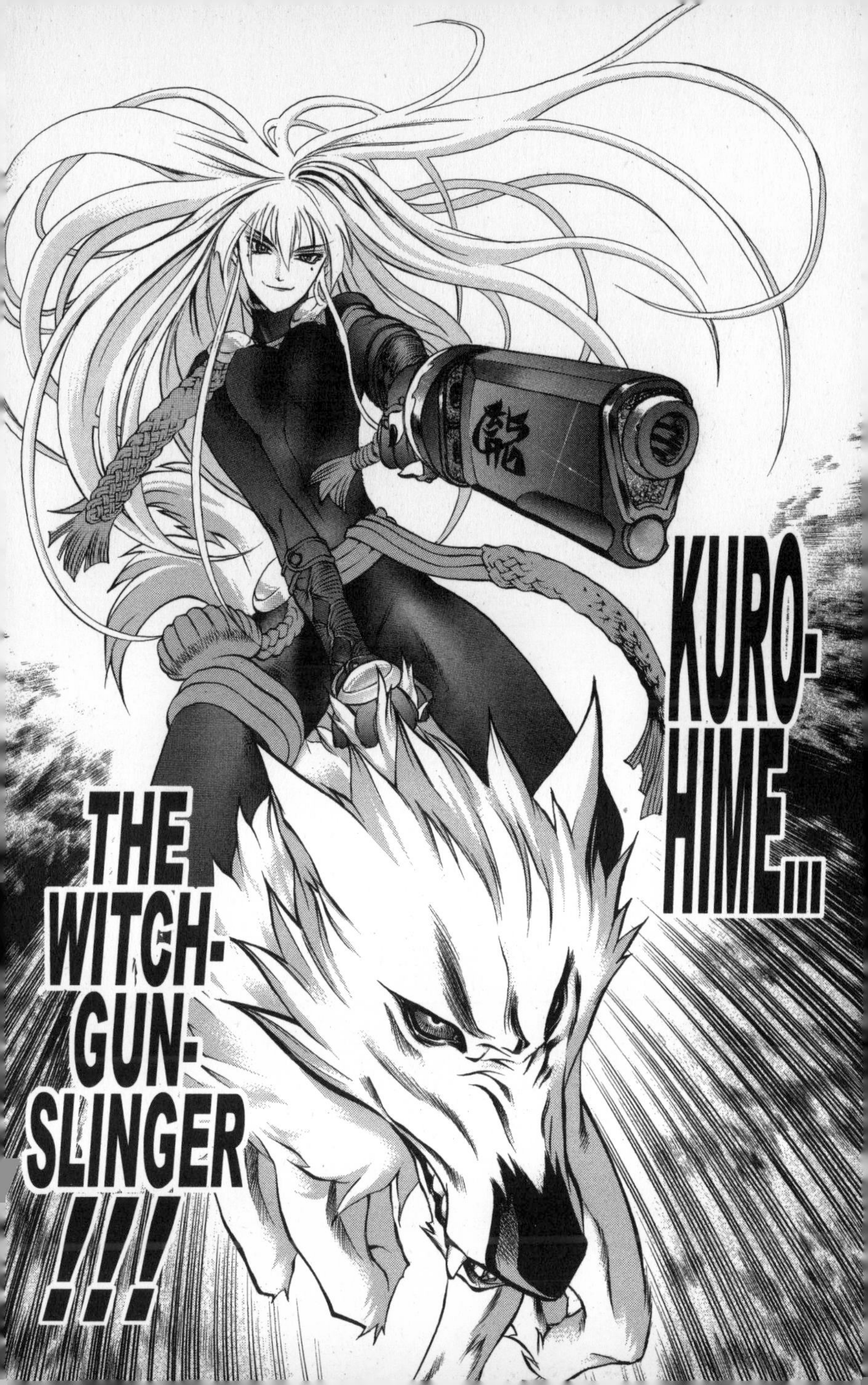
KURO-HIME...
THE WITCH-GUN-SLINGER!!!

A WITCH-GUNSLINGER IS A SORCERESS WHO CONJURES BULLETS WITH MAGIC POWERS CALLED WITCH BULLETS.

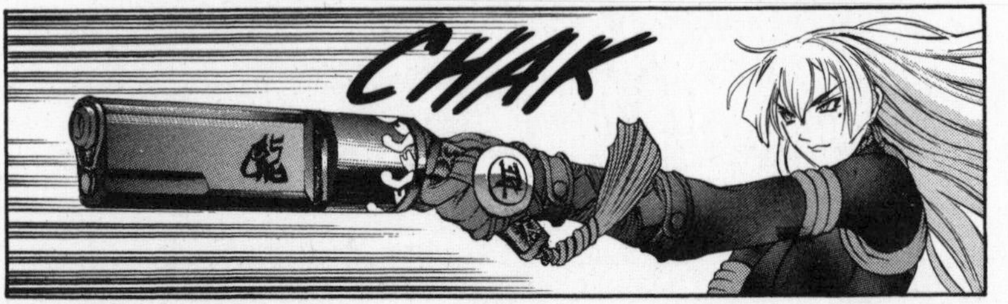
CHAK

THESE BULLETS FIRE PROJECTILES CALLED WITCH BEASTS.

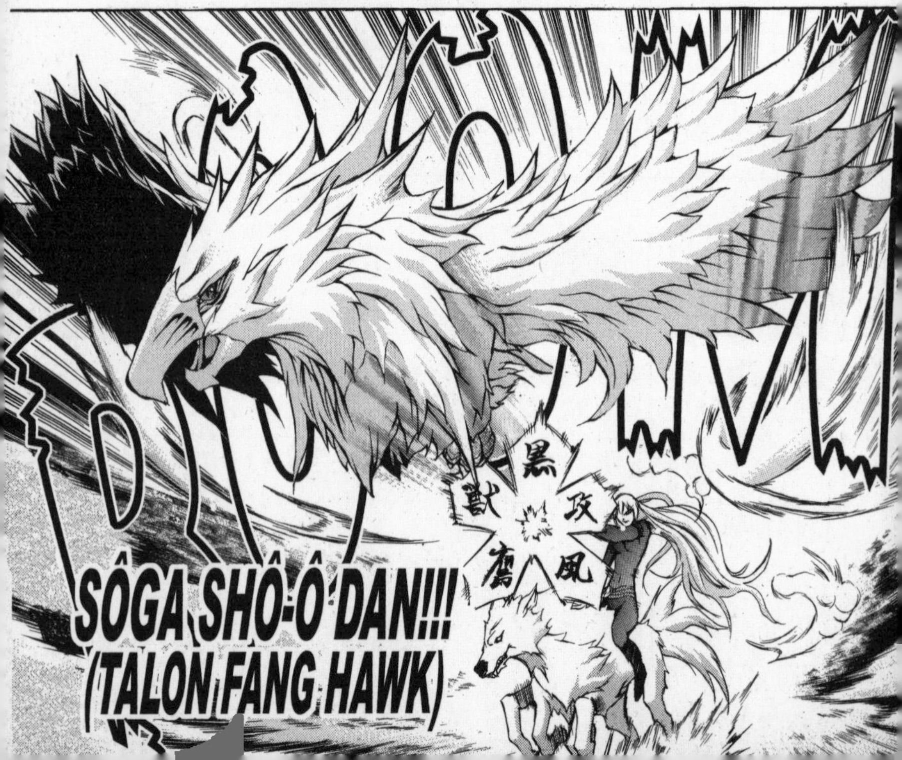
SÔGA SHÔ-Ô DAN!!!
(TALON FANG HAWK)

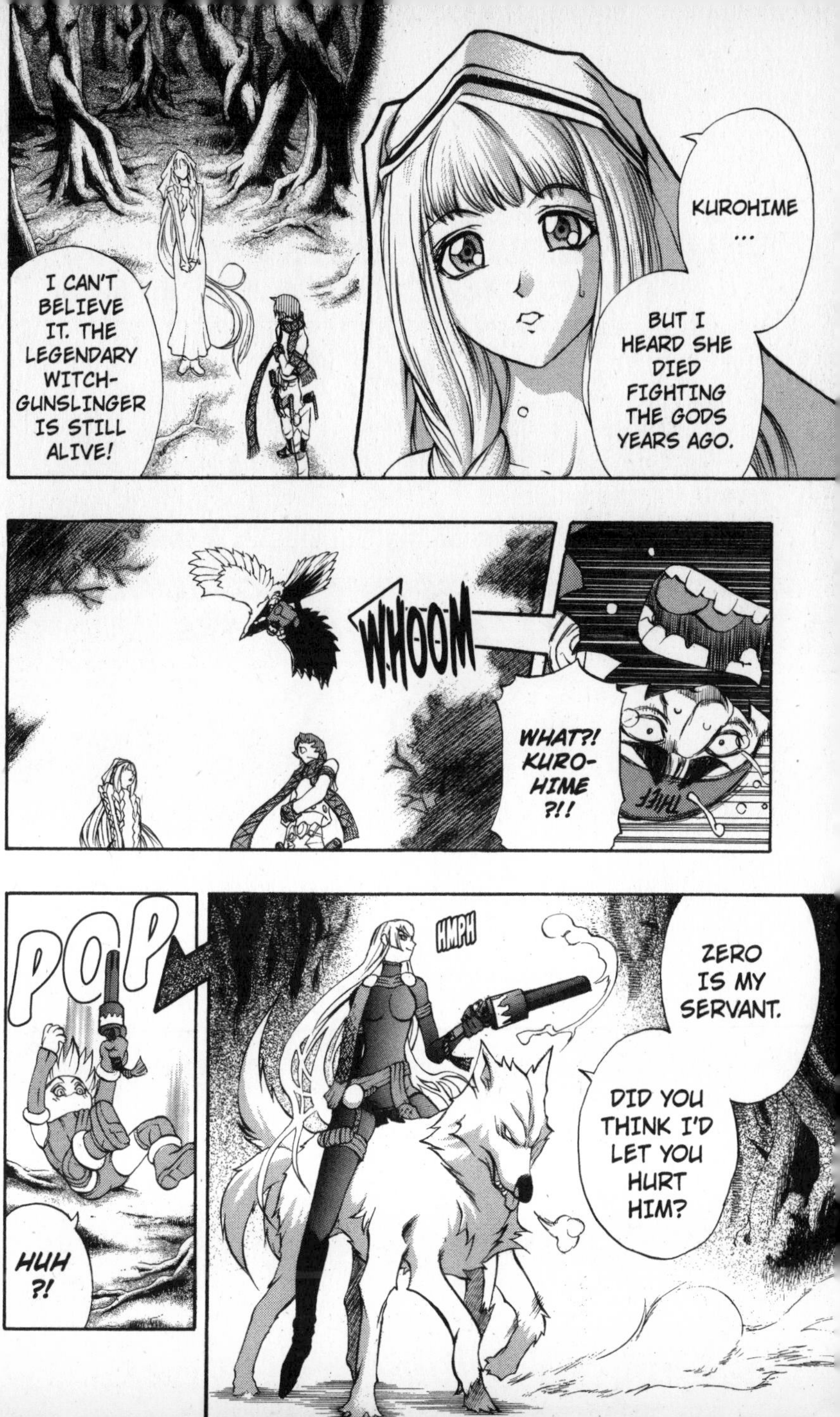
KUROHIME ...
BUT I HEARD SHE DIED FIGHTING THE GODS YEARS AGO.
I CAN'T BELIEVE IT. THE LEGENDARY WITCH-GUNSLINGER IS STILL ALIVE!
WHAT?! KURO-HIME ?!!
THIEF
WHOOM
ZERO IS MY SERVANT.
HMPH
DID YOU THINK I'D LET YOU HURT HIM?
POP
HUH ?!

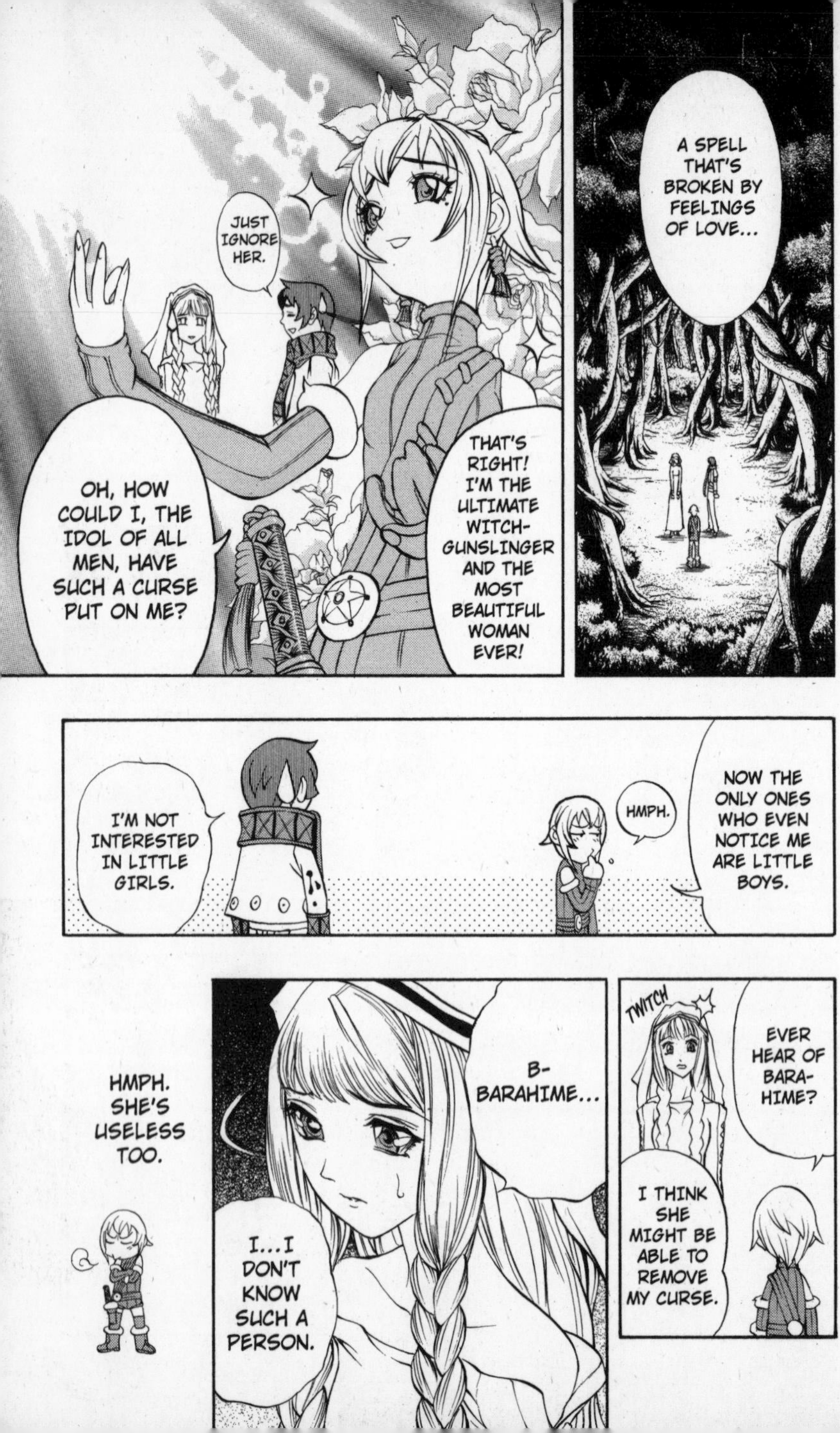
A SPELL THAT'S BROKEN BY FEELINGS OF LOVE...
THAT'S RIGHT! I'M THE ULTIMATE WITCH-GUNSLINGER AND THE MOST BEAUTIFUL WOMAN EVER!
OH, HOW COULD I, THE IDOL OF ALL MEN, HAVE SUCH A CURSE PUT ON ME?
JUST IGNORE HER.
NOW THE ONLY ONES WHO EVEN NOTICE ME ARE LITTLE BOYS.
HMPH.
I'M NOT INTERESTED IN LITTLE GIRLS.
TWITCH
EVER HEAR OF BARAHIME?
I THINK SHE MIGHT BE ABLE TO REMOVE MY CURSE.
B- BARAHIME...
I...I DON'T KNOW SUCH A PERSON.
HMPH. SHE'S USELESS TOO.

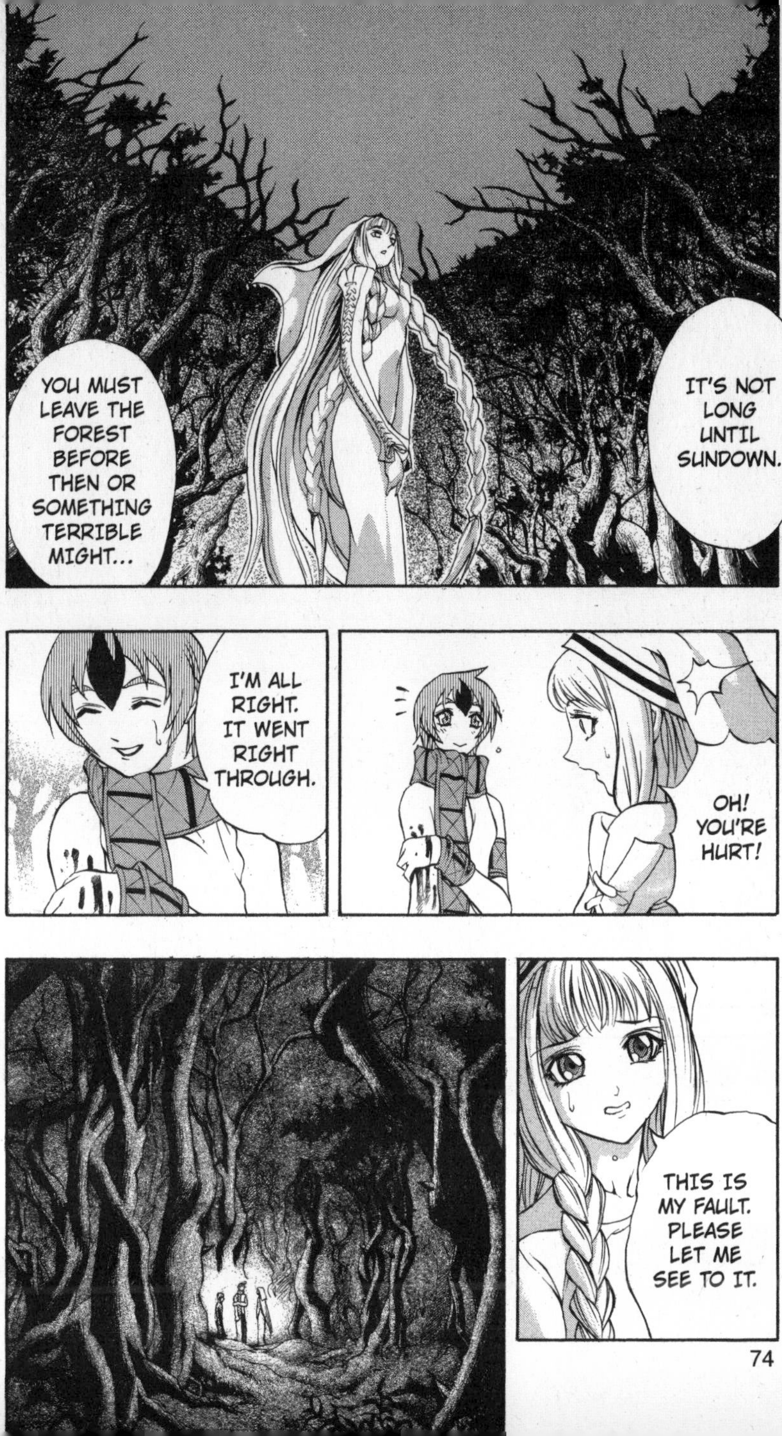
IT'S NOT LONG UNTIL SUNDOWN.
YOU MUST LEAVE THE FOREST BEFORE THEN OR SOMETHING TERRIBLE MIGHT...
OH! YOU'RE HURT!
I'M ALL RIGHT. IT WENT RIGHT THROUGH.
THIS IS MY FAULT. PLEASE LET ME SEE TO IT.

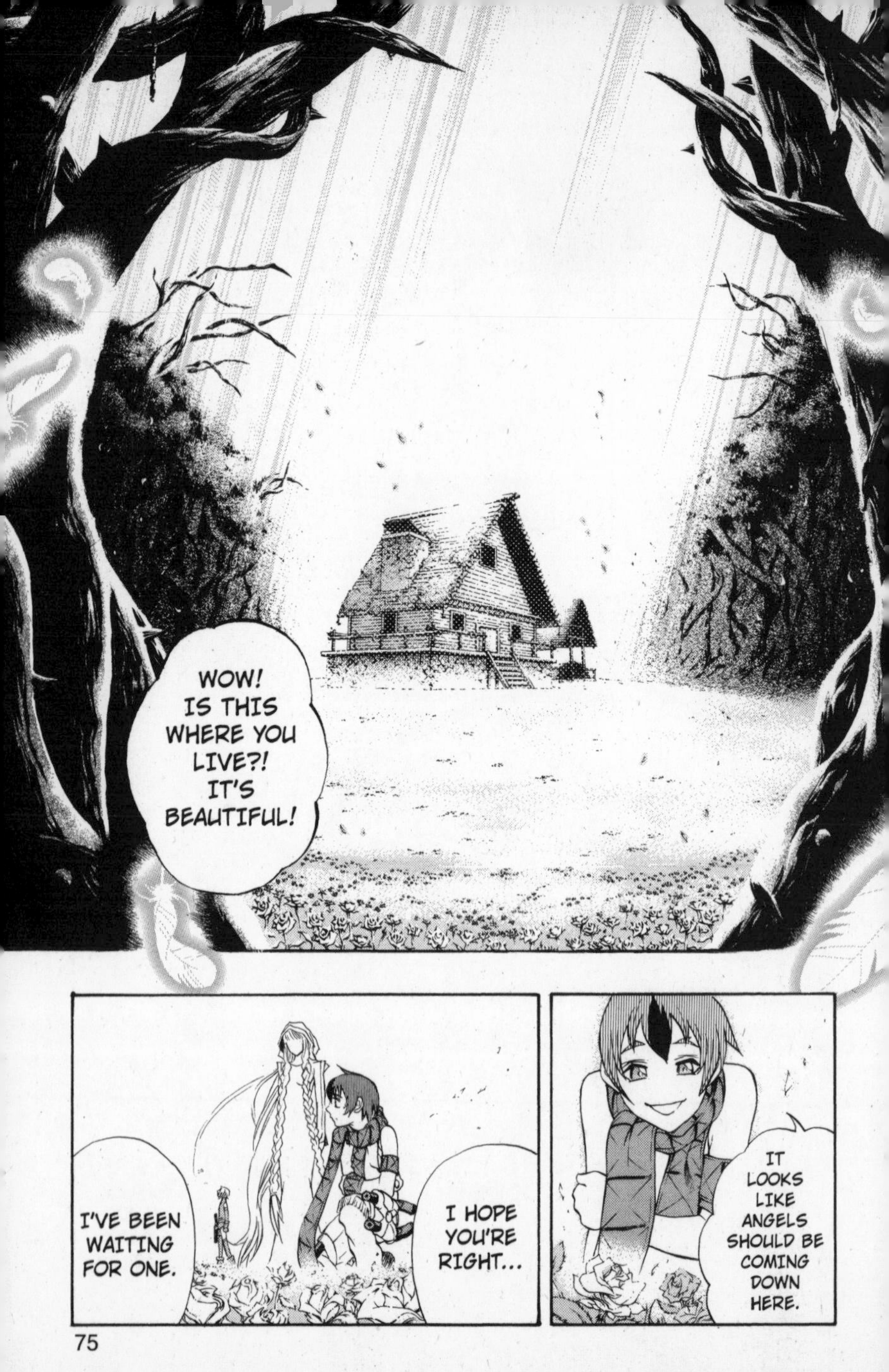
WOW! IS THIS WHERE YOU LIVE?! IT'S BEAUTIFUL!
IT LOOKS LIKE ANGELS SHOULD BE COMING DOWN HERE.
I HOPE YOU'RE RIGHT...
I'VE BEEN WAITING FOR ONE.

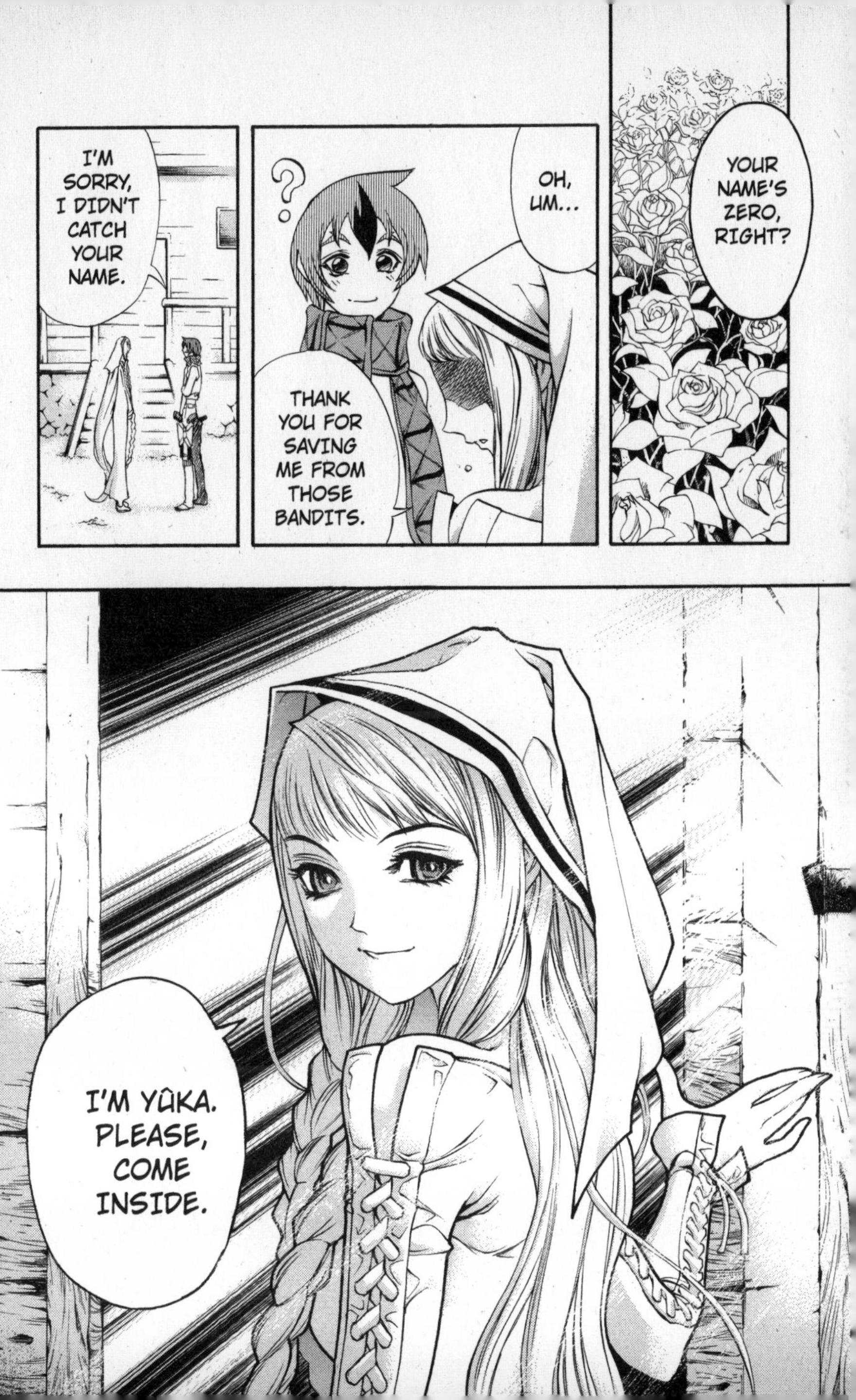
YOUR NAME'S ZERO, RIGHT?
OH, UM...
THANK YOU FOR SAVING ME FROM THOSE BANDITS.
I'M SORRY, I DIDN'T CATCH YOUR NAME.
I'M YÛKA. PLEASE, COME INSIDE.

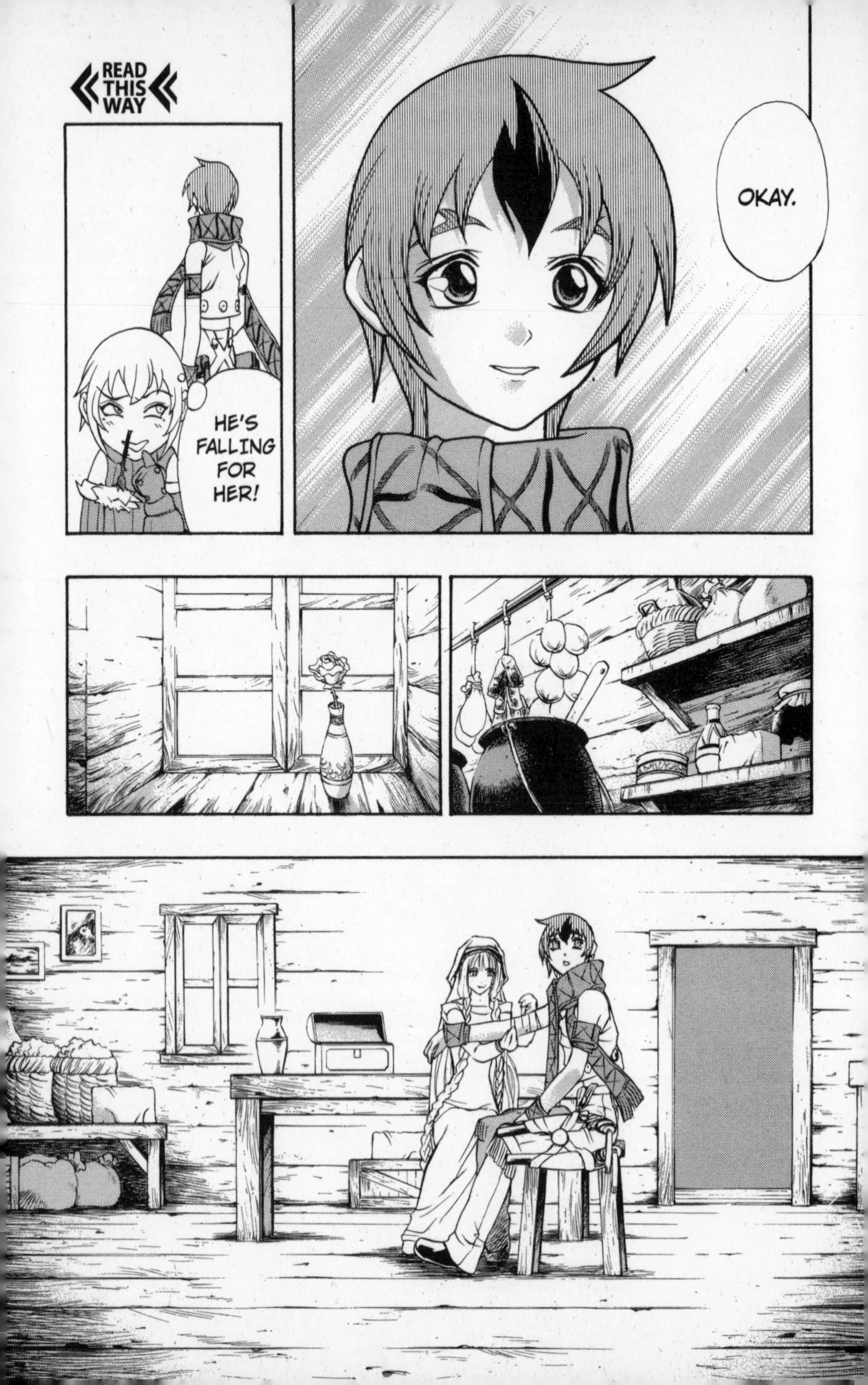
READ THIS WAY
OKAY.
HE'S FALLING FOR HER!

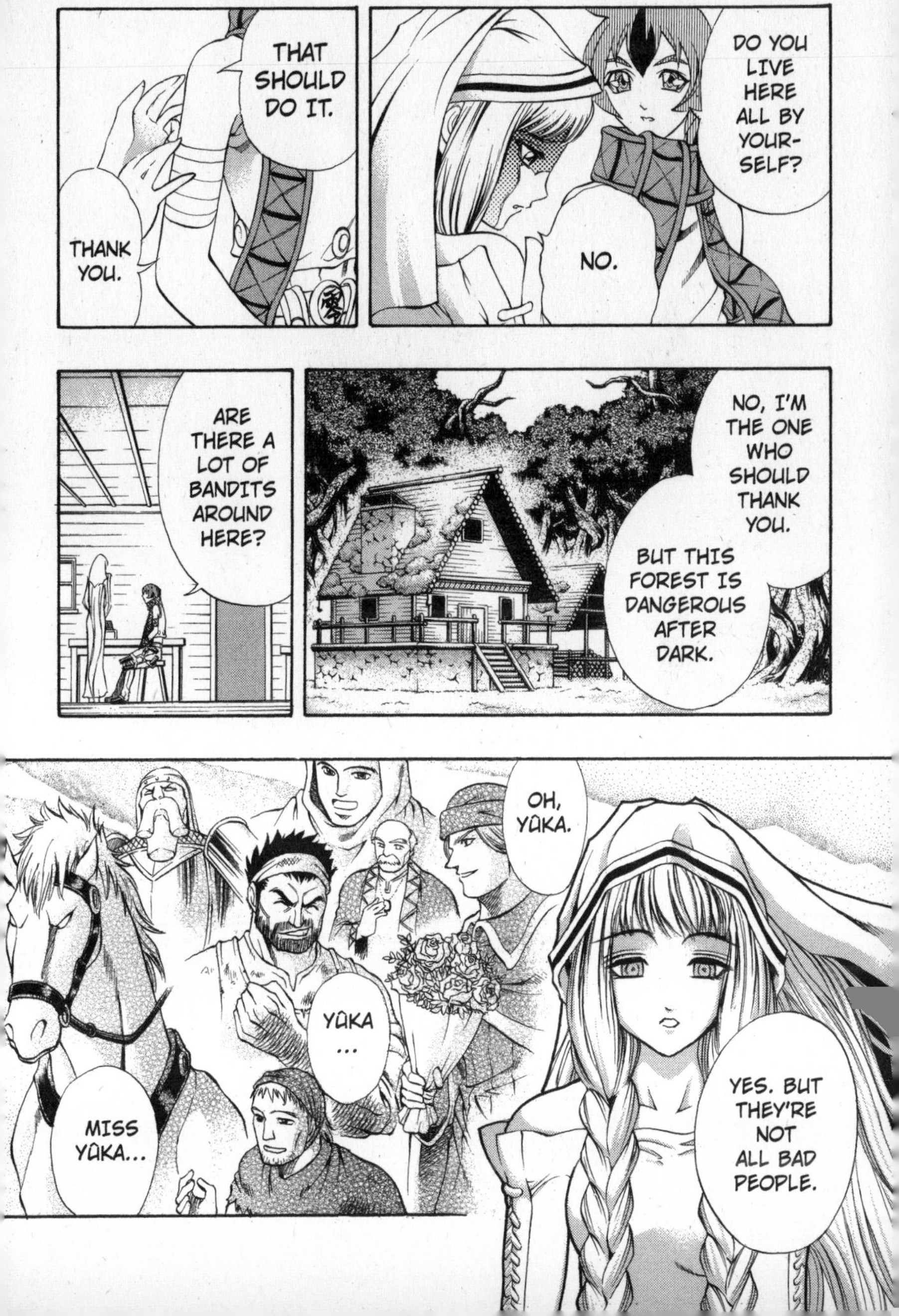
DO YOU LIVE HERE ALL BY YOUR-SELF?
NO.
THAT SHOULD DO IT.
THANK YOU.
NO, I'M THE ONE WHO SHOULD THANK YOU.
BUT THIS FOREST IS DANGEROUS AFTER DARK.
ARE THERE A LOT OF BANDITS AROUND HERE?
YES. BUT THEY'RE NOT ALL BAD PEOPLE.
OH, YÛKA.
YÛKA ...
MISS YÛKA...

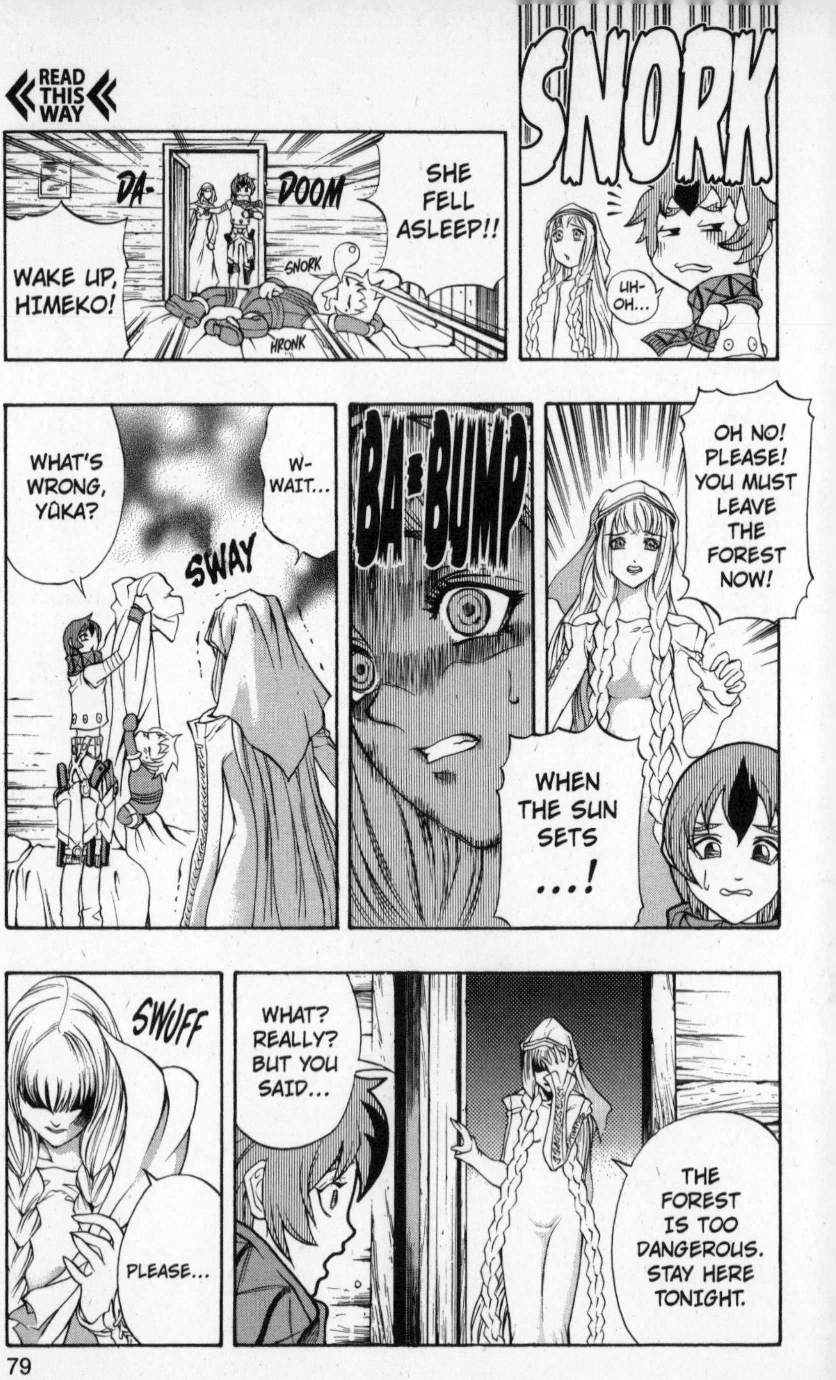

READ THIS WAY
SNORK
UH-OH...
DA-DOOM
SHE FELL ASLEEP!!
SNORK
WAKE UP, HIMEKO!
HRONK
OH NO! PLEASE! YOU MUST LEAVE THE FOREST NOW!
WHEN THE SUN SETS ...!
BA-BUMP
W-WAIT...
SWAY
WHAT'S WRONG, YÛKA?
THE FOREST IS TOO DANGEROUS. STAY HERE TONIGHT.
WHAT? REALLY? BUT YOU SAID...
SWUFF
PLEASE...

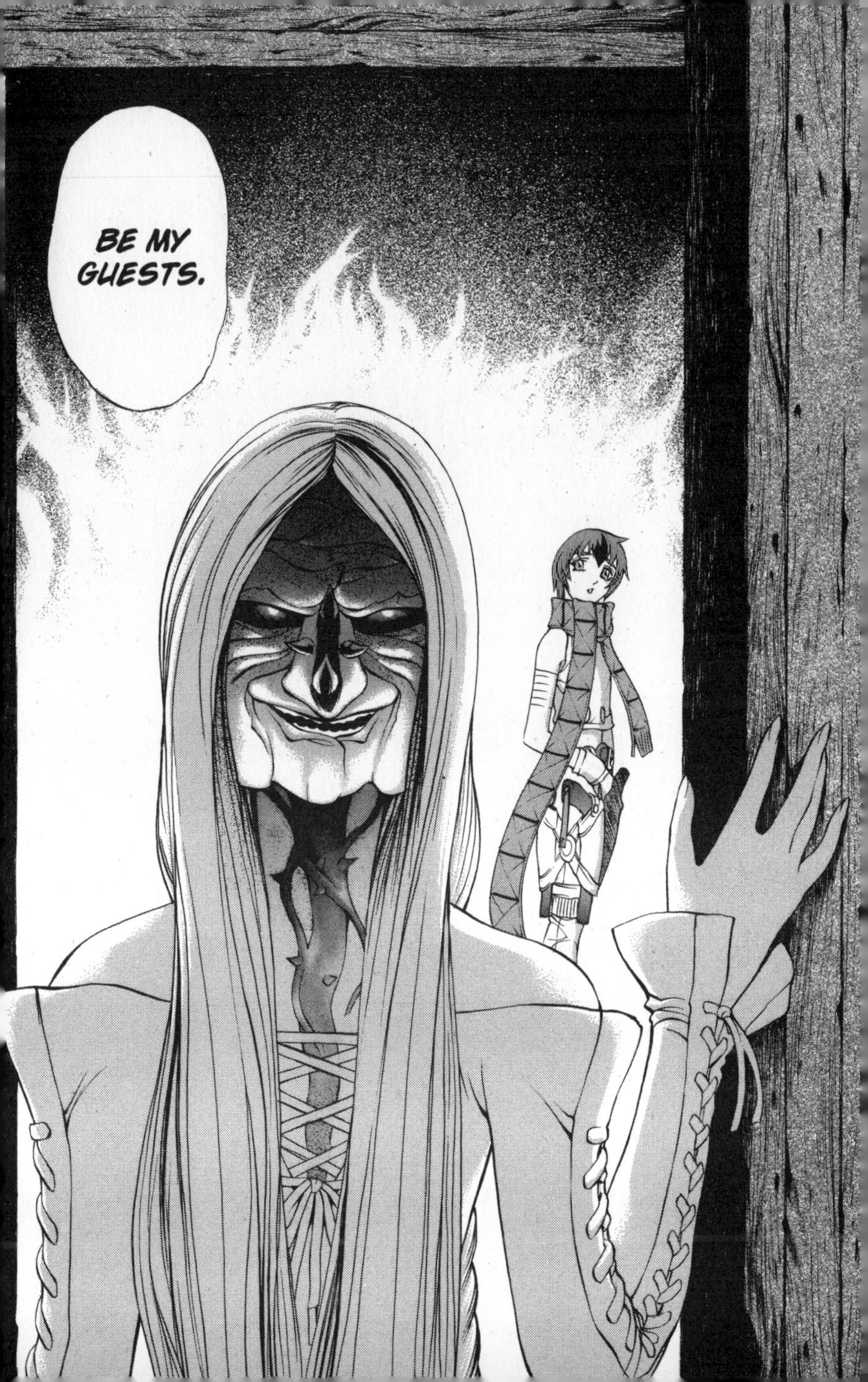
BE MY GUESTS.

READ THIS WAY

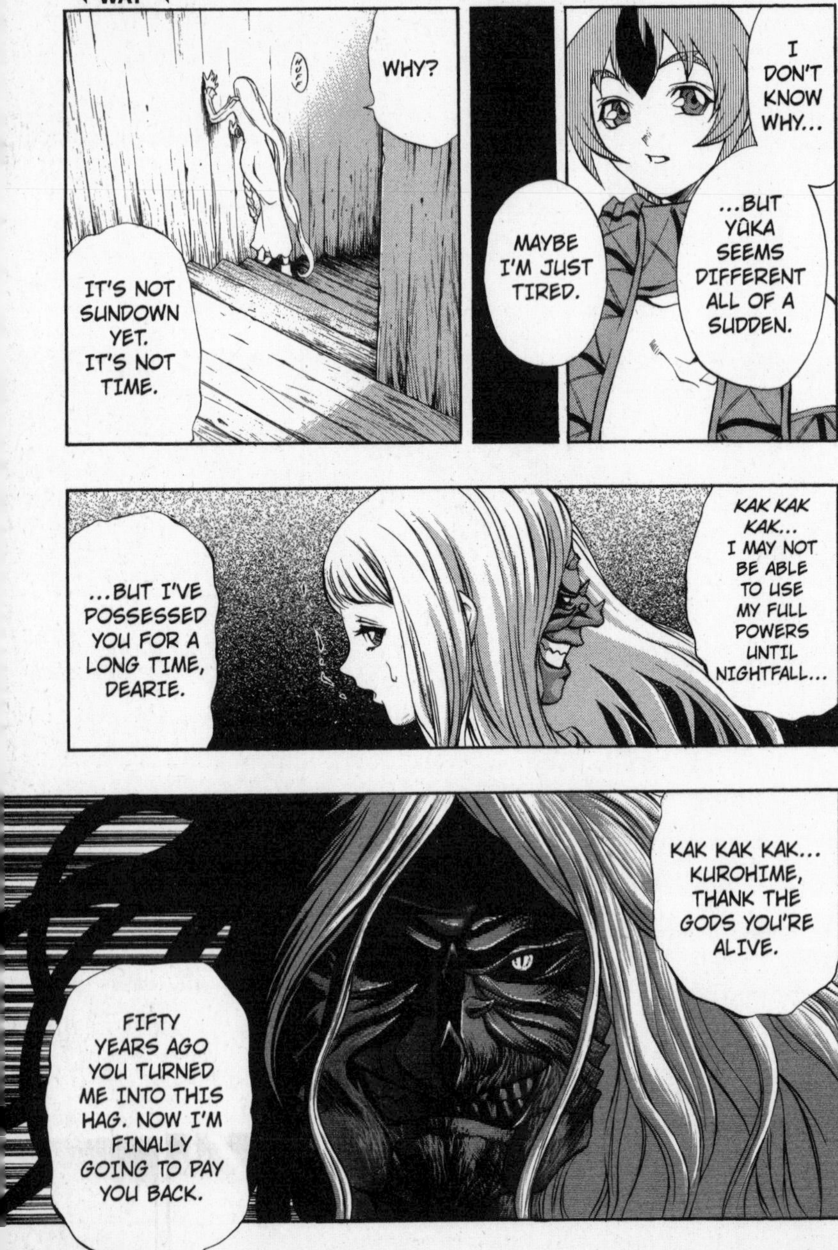
I DON'T KNOW WHY...
...BUT YŪKA SEEMS DIFFERENT ALL OF A SUDDEN.
MAYBE I'M JUST TIRED.
WHY?
HUFF
IT'S NOT SUNDOWN YET. IT'S NOT TIME.
KAK KAK KAK... I MAY NOT BE ABLE TO USE MY FULL POWERS UNTIL NIGHTFALL...
...BUT I'VE POSSESSED YOU FOR A LONG TIME, DEARIE.
KAK KAK KAK... KUROHIME, THANK THE GODS YOU'RE ALIVE.
FIFTY YEARS AGO YOU TURNED ME INTO THIS HAG. NOW I'M FINALLY GOING TO PAY YOU BACK.

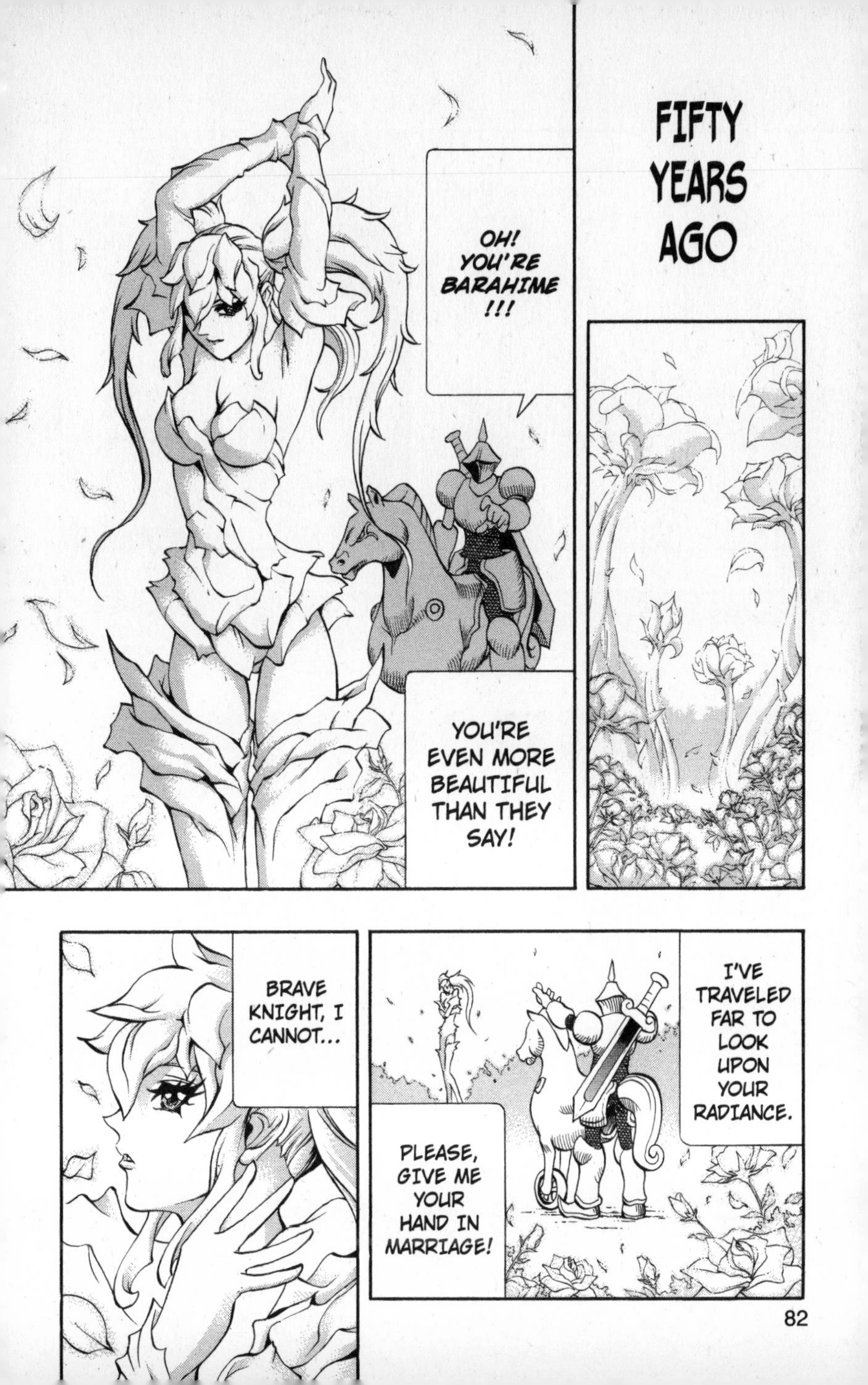
FIFTY YEARS AGO
OH! YOU'RE BARAHIME!!!
YOU'RE EVEN MORE BEAUTIFUL THAN THEY SAY!
I'VE TRAVELED FAR TO LOOK UPON YOUR RADIANCE.
PLEASE, GIVE ME YOUR HAND IN MARRIAGE!
BRAVE KNIGHT, I CANNOT...

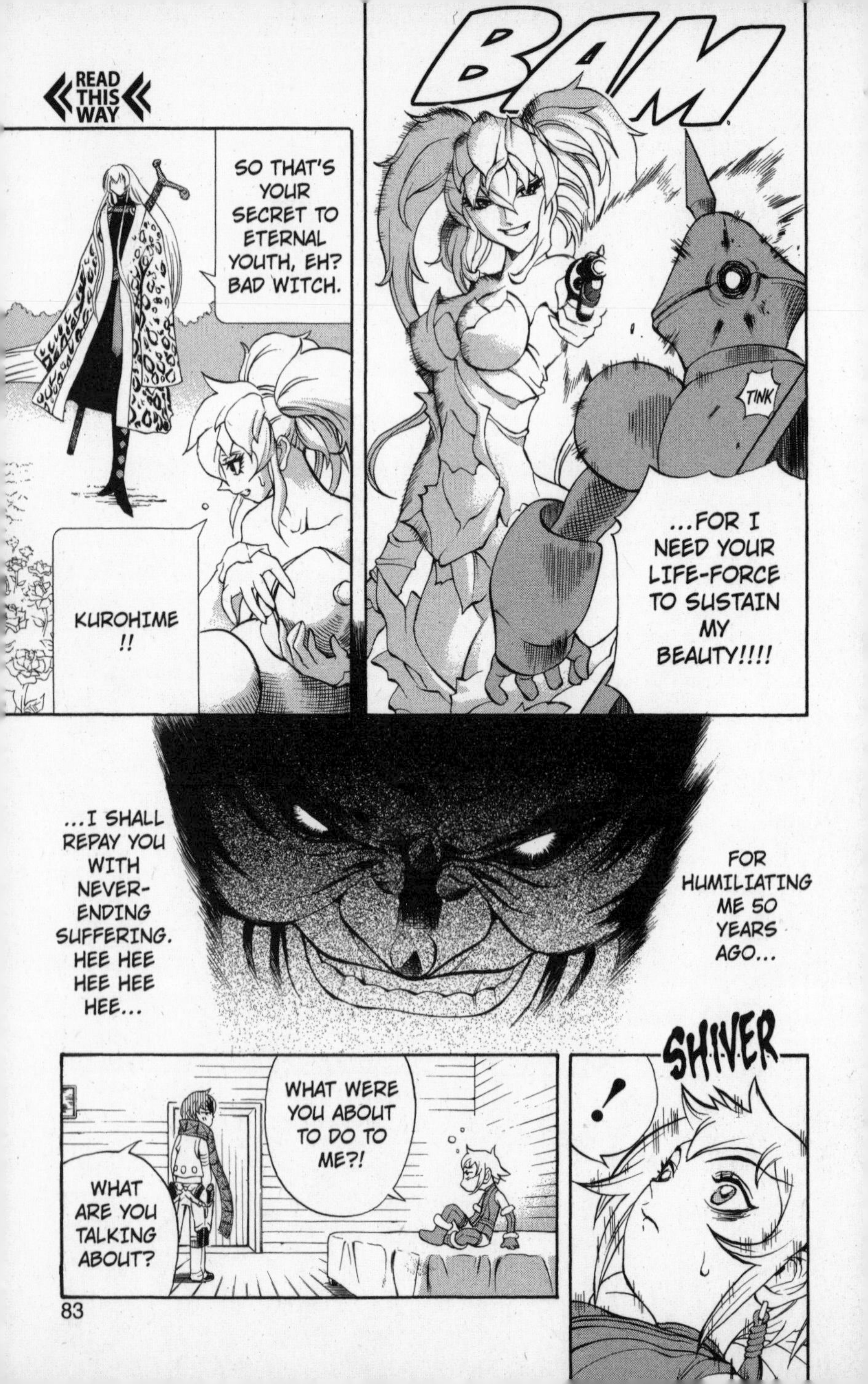
READ THIS WAY
BAM
TINK
...FOR I NEED YOUR LIFE-FORCE TO SUSTAIN MY BEAUTY!!!!
SO THAT'S YOUR SECRET TO ETERNAL YOUTH, EH? BAD WITCH.
KUROHIME !!
FOR HUMILIATING ME 50 YEARS AGO...
...I SHALL REPAY YOU WITH NEVER-ENDING SUFFERING. HEE HEE HEE HEE HEE...
SHIVER
!
WHAT WERE YOU ABOUT TO DO TO ME?!
WHAT ARE YOU TALKING ABOUT?

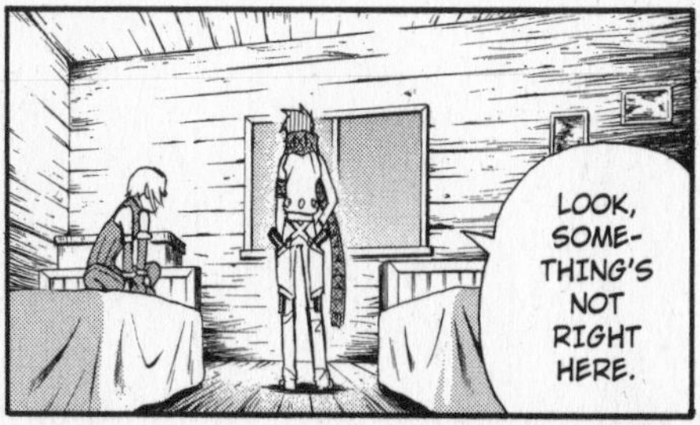
LOOK, SOME-THING'S NOT RIGHT HERE.

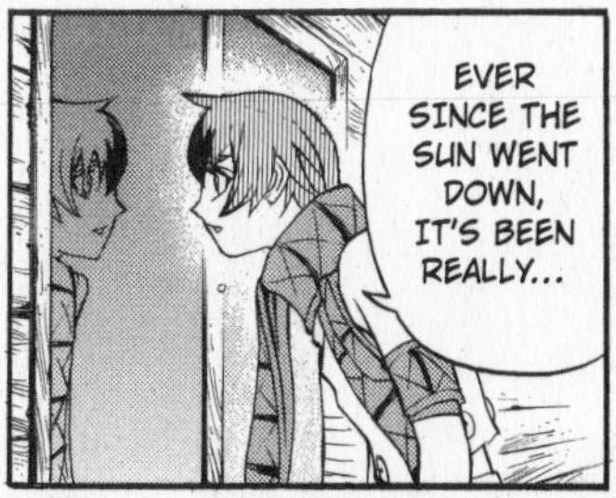
EVER SINCE THE SUN WENT DOWN, IT'S BEEN REALLY...

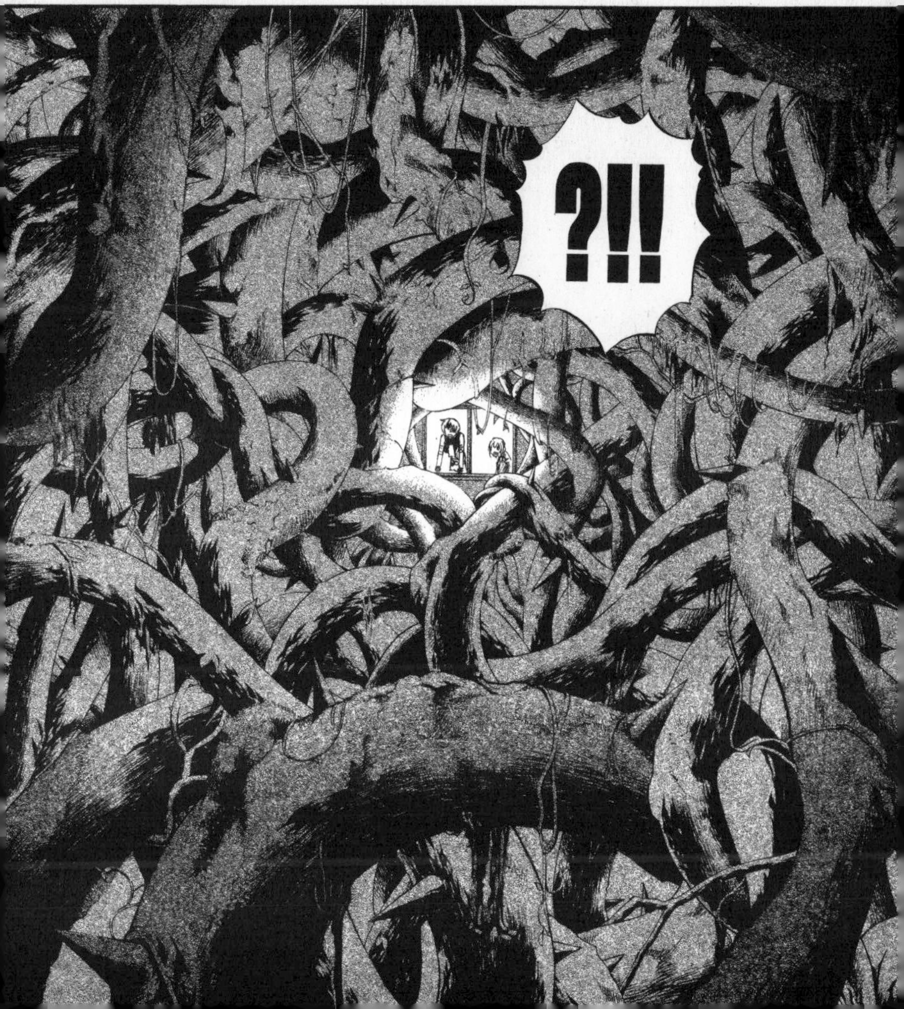
?!!

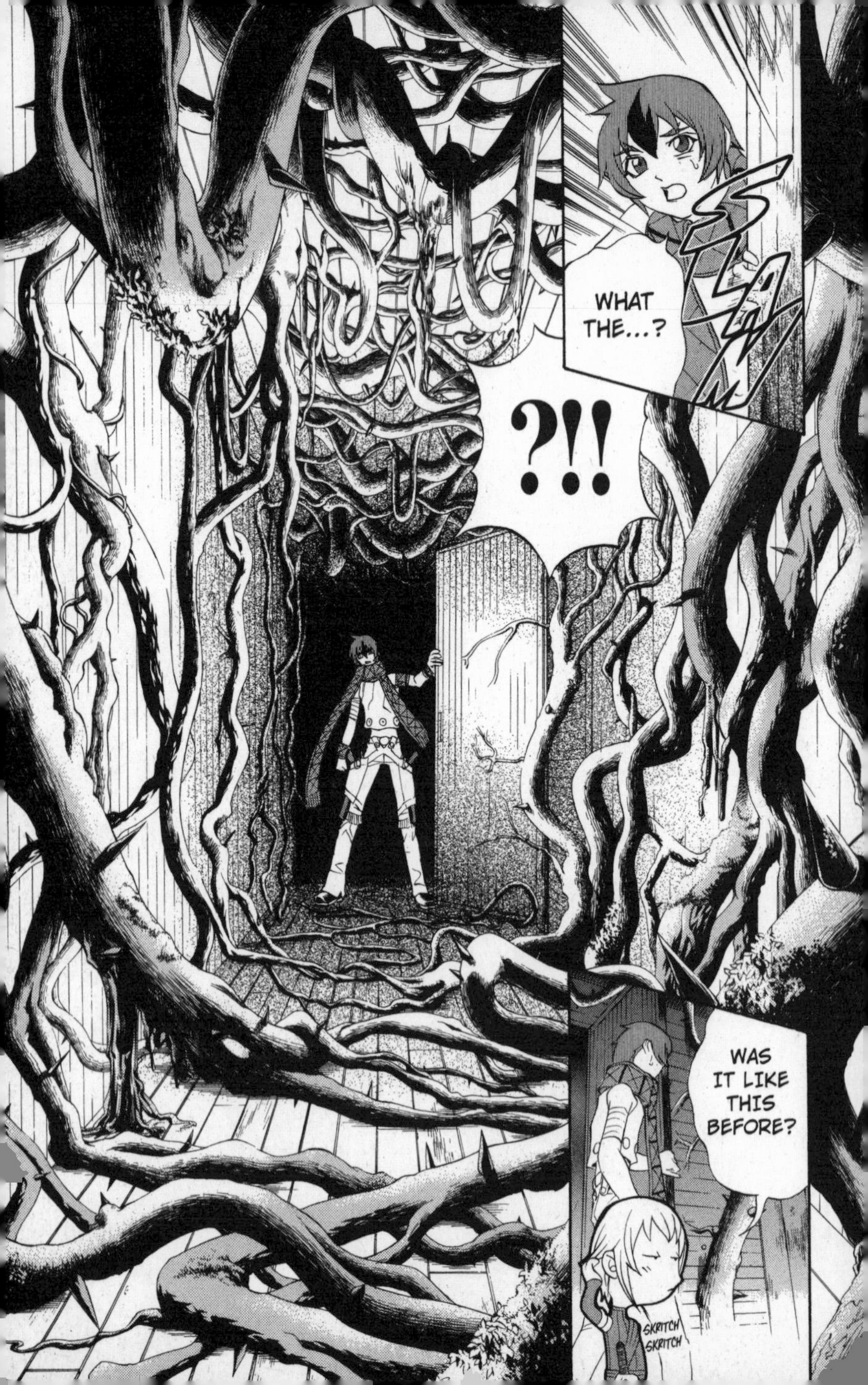
WHAT THE...?
WAS IT LIKE THIS BEFORE?
SKRITCH SKRITCH
?!!

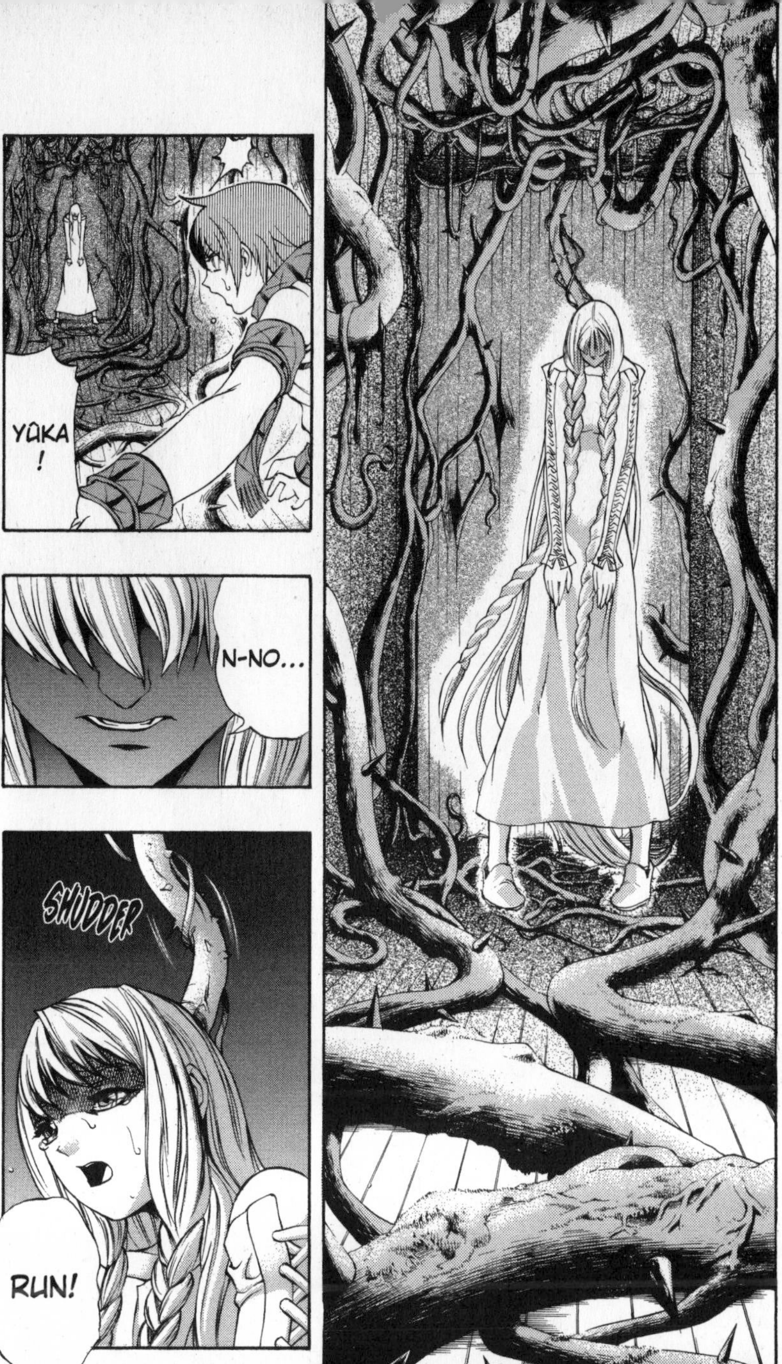
YŪKA!
N-NO...
SHUDDER
RUN!

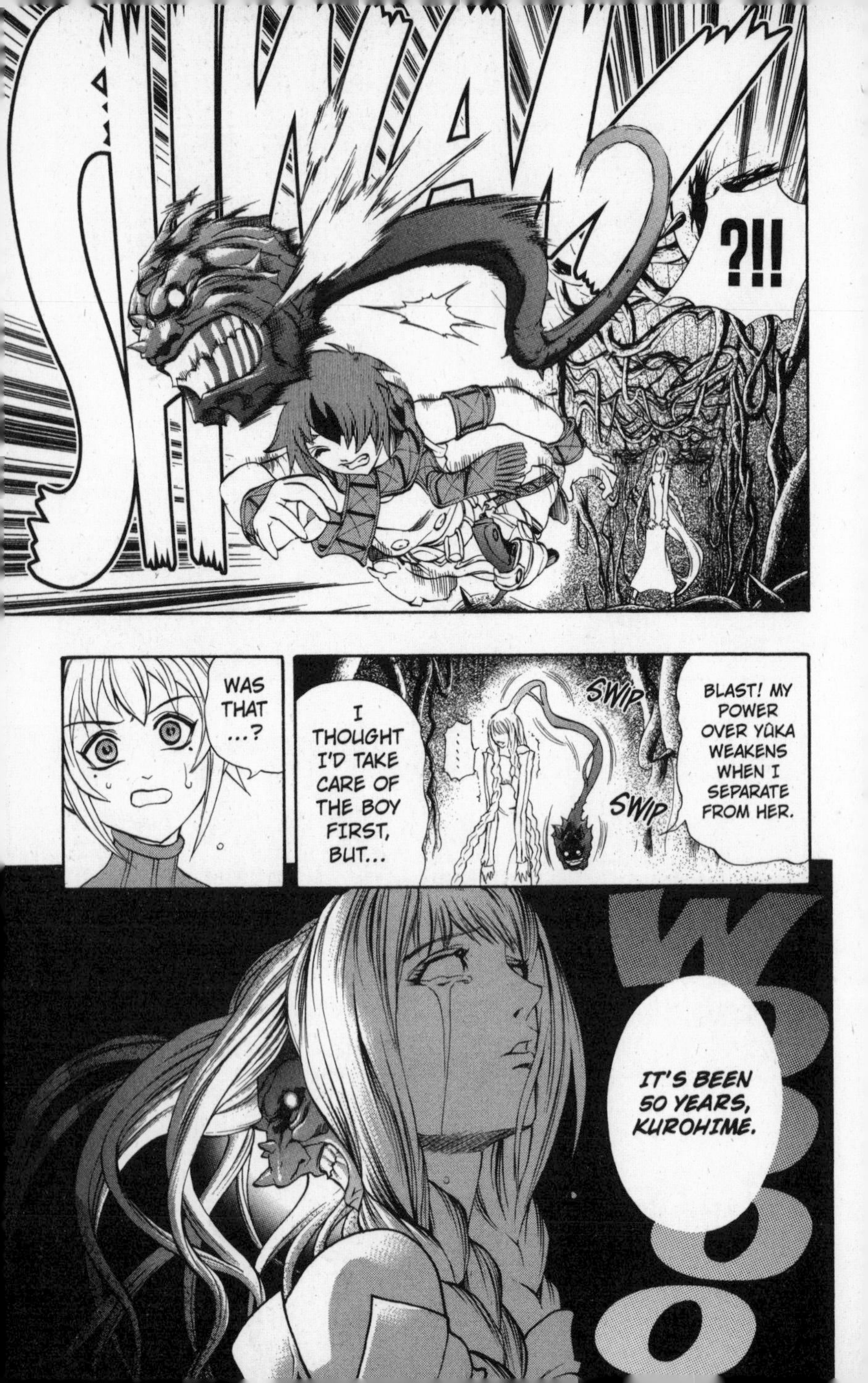
?!!
BLAST! MY POWER OVER YŪKA WEAKENS WHEN I SEPARATE FROM HER.
SWIP
SWIP
I THOUGHT I'D TAKE CARE OF THE BOY FIRST, BUT...
WAS THAT ...?
IT'S BEEN 50 YEARS, KUROHIME.

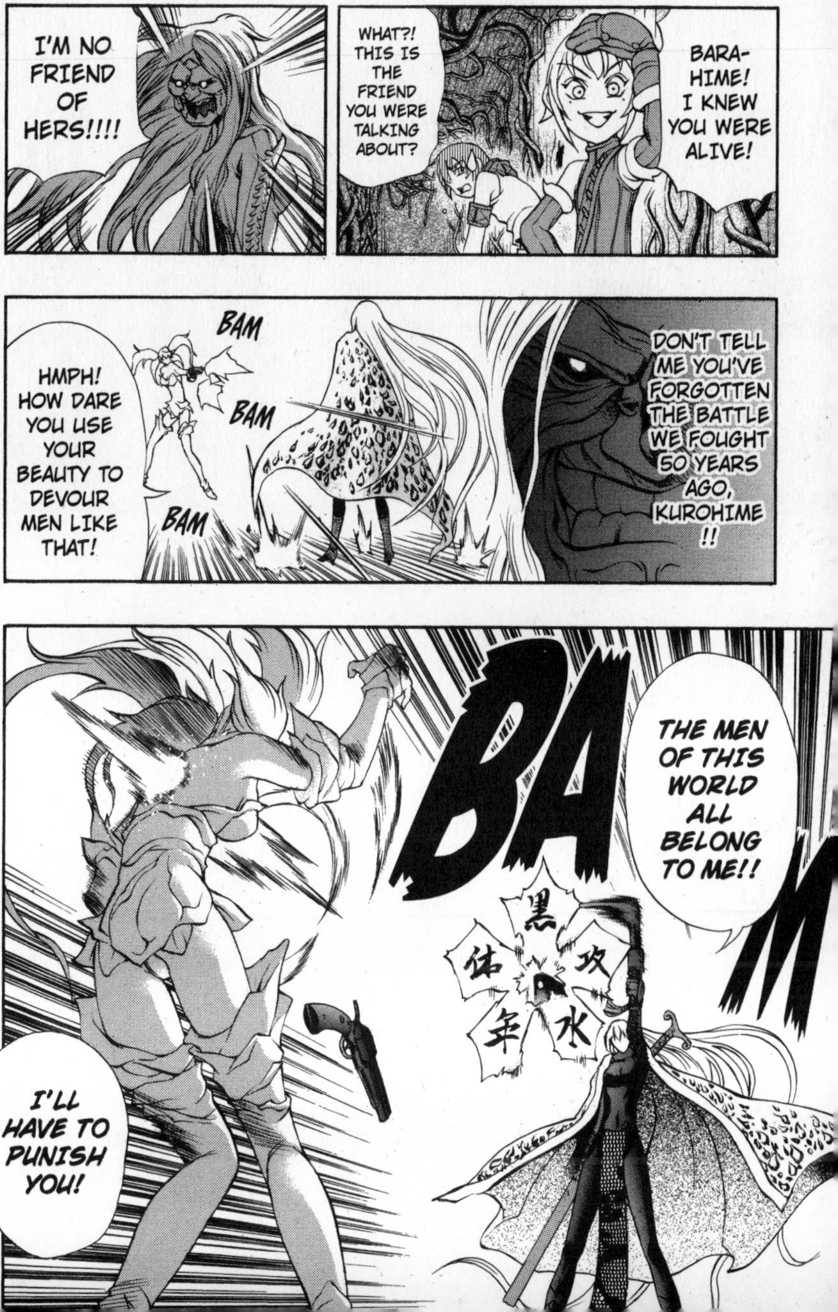
BARA-HIME! I KNEW YOU WERE ALIVE!
WHAT?! THIS IS THE FRIEND YOU WERE TALKING ABOUT?
I'M NO FRIEND OF HERS!!!!
DON'T TELL ME YOU'VE FORGOTTEN THE BATTLE WE FOUGHT 50 YEARS AGO, KUROHIME!!
BAM
BAM
BAM
HMPH! HOW DARE YOU USE YOUR BEAUTY TO DEVOUR MEN LIKE THAT!
BAM
THE MEN OF THIS WORLD ALL BELONG TO ME!!
黒
攻
水
弁
体
I'LL HAVE TO PUNISH YOU!

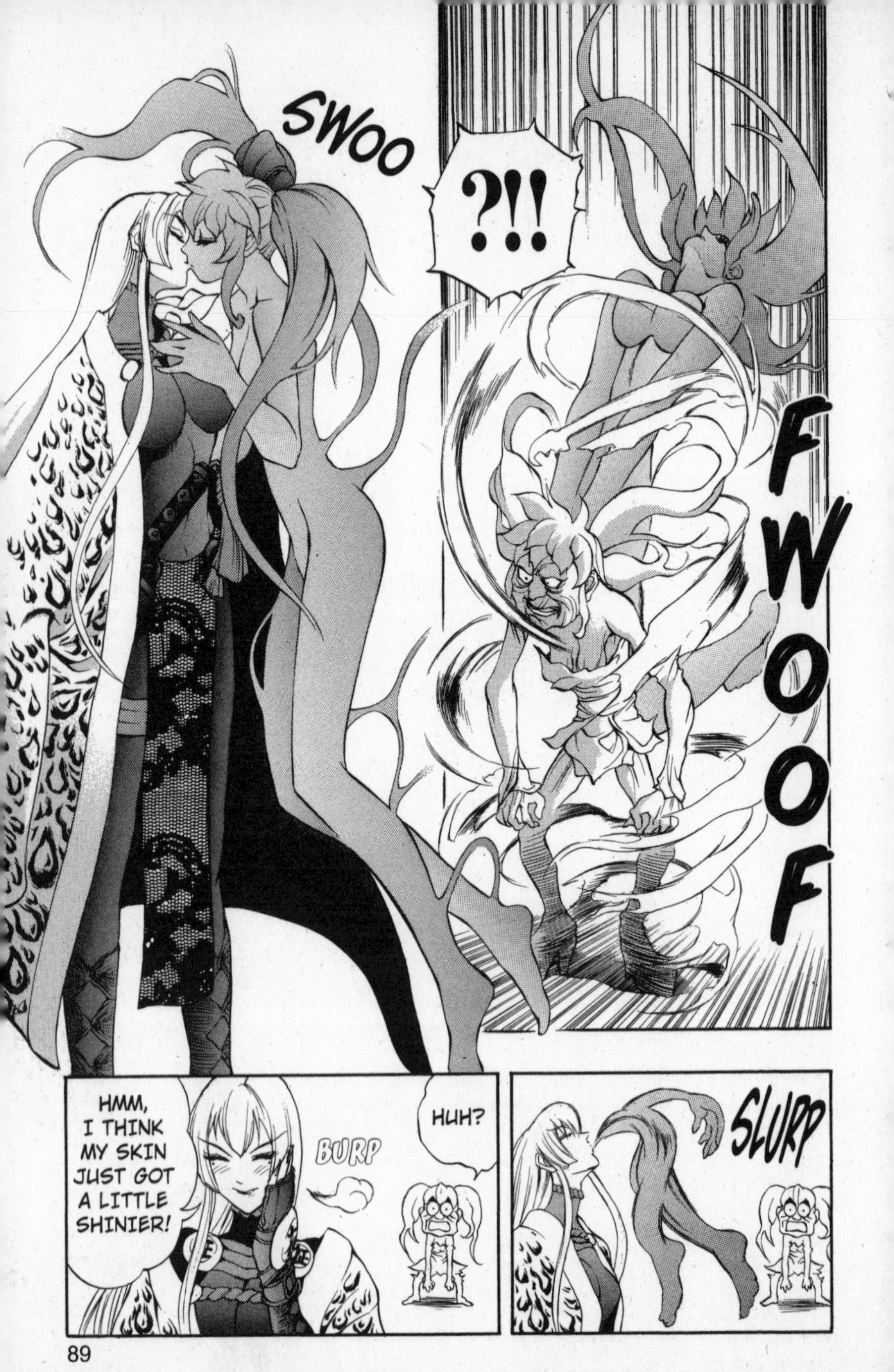
?!!
FWOOF
SWOO
SLURP
HUH?
BURP
HMM, I THINK MY SKIN JUST GOT A LITTLE SHINIER!

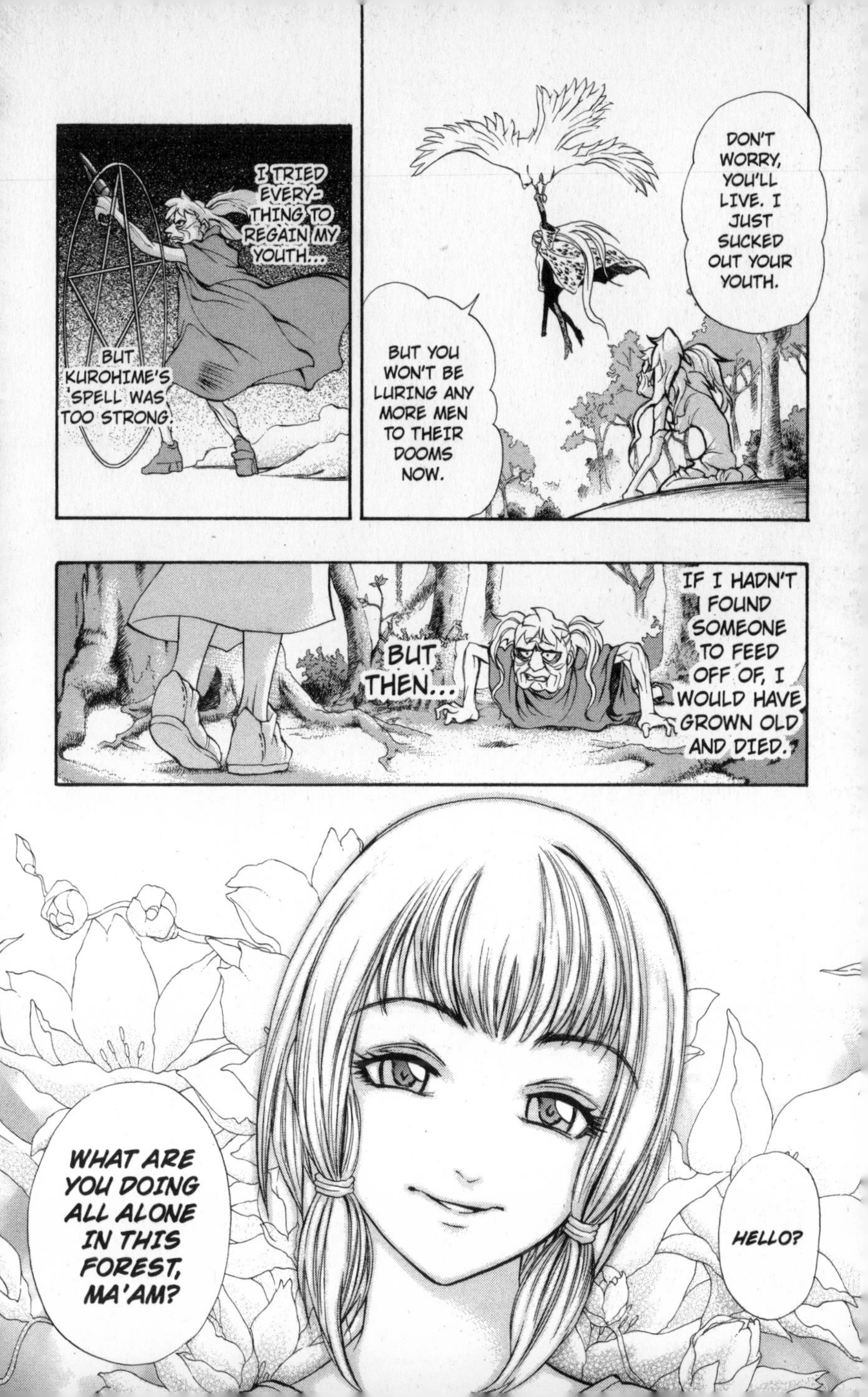
DON'T WORRY, YOU'LL LIVE. I JUST SUCKED OUT YOUR YOUTH.
BUT YOU WON'T BE LURING ANY MORE MEN TO THEIR DOOMS NOW.
I TRIED EVERY-THING TO REGAIN MY YOUTH...
BUT KUROHIME'S SPELL WAS TOO STRONG.
IF I HADN'T FOUND SOMEONE TO FEED OFF OF, I WOULD HAVE GROWN OLD AND DIED.
BUT THEN...
HELLO?
WHAT ARE YOU DOING ALL ALONE IN THIS FOREST, MA'AM?

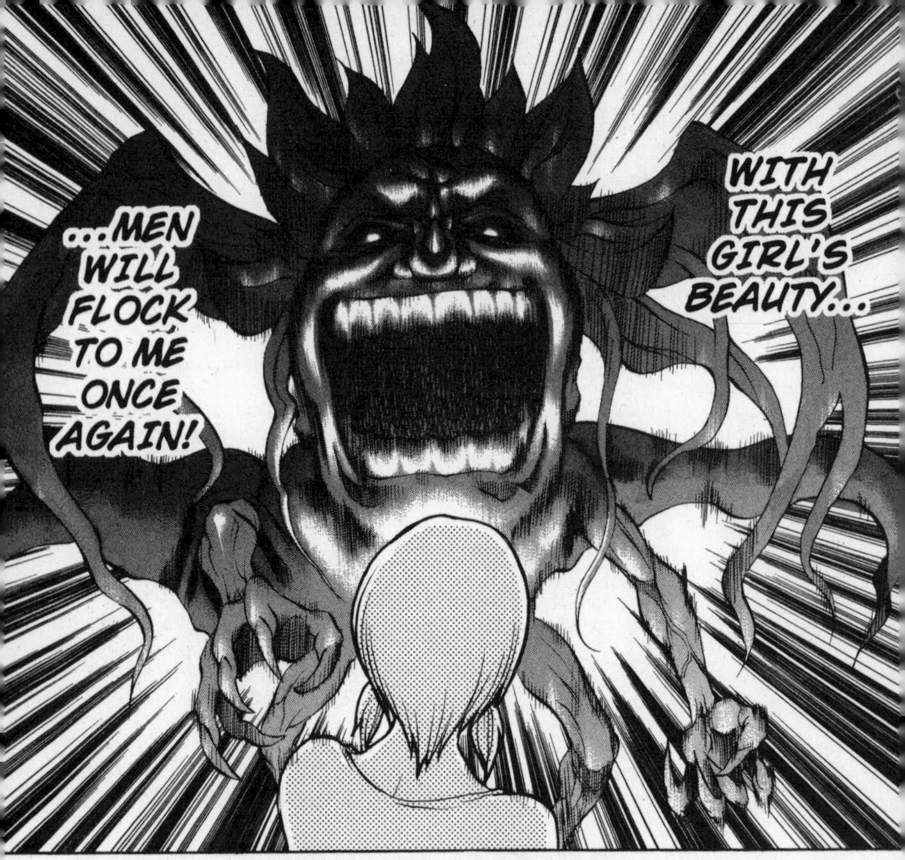
WITH THIS GIRL'S BEAUTY...
...MEN WILL FLOCK TO ME ONCE AGAIN!

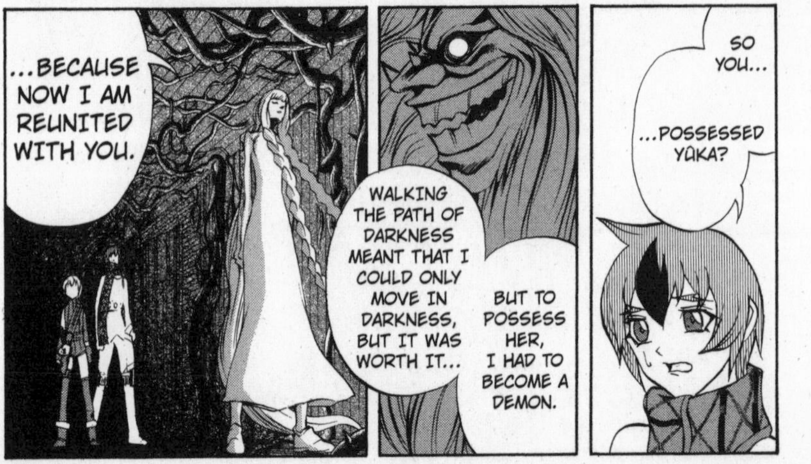
SO YOU...
...POSSESSED YŪKA?
BUT TO POSSESS HER, I HAD TO BECOME A DEMON.
WALKING THE PATH OF DARKNESS MEANT THAT I COULD ONLY MOVE IN DARKNESS, BUT IT WAS WORTH IT...
...BECAUSE NOW I AM REUNITED WITH YOU.

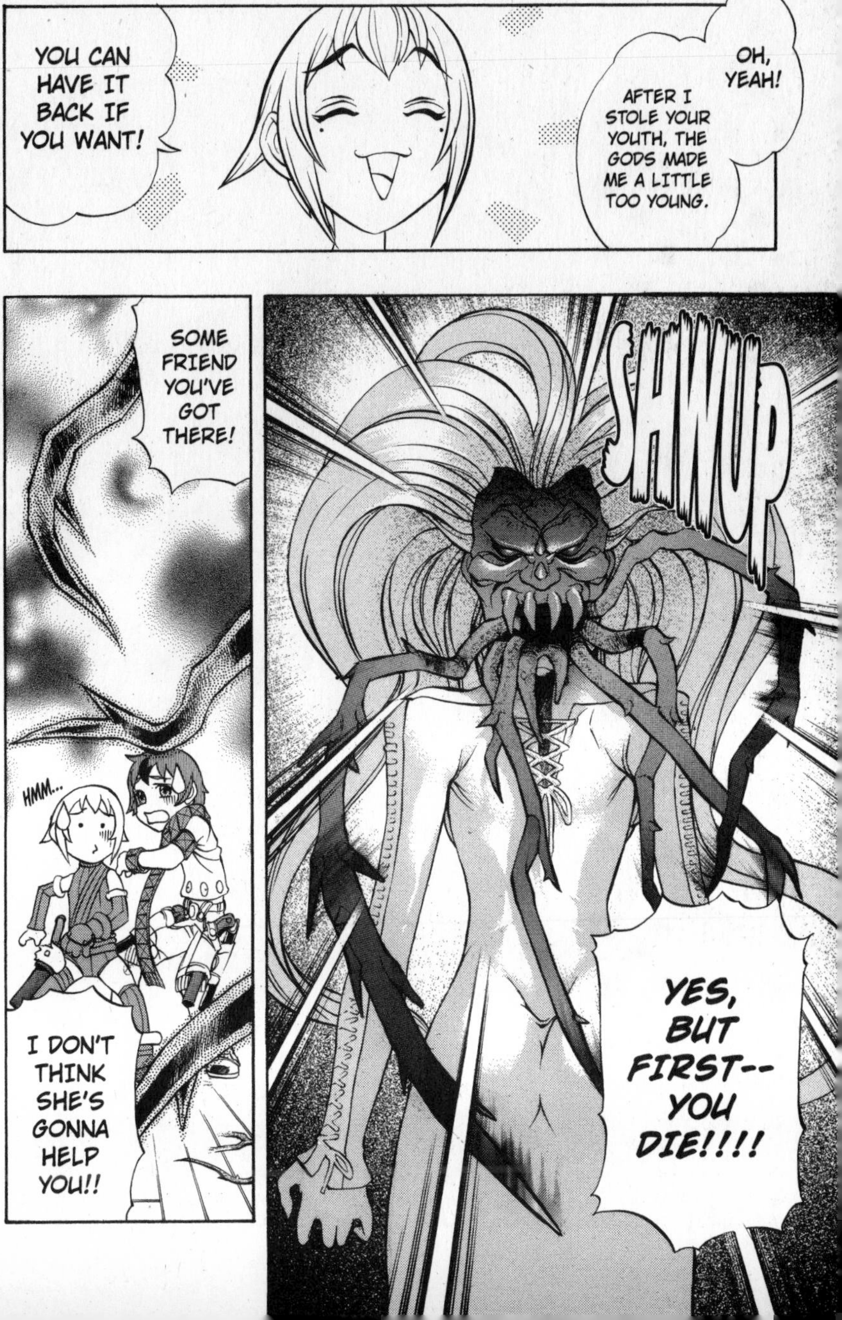
OH, YEAH!
AFTER I STOLE YOUR YOUTH, THE GODS MADE ME A LITTLE TOO YOUNG.
YOU CAN HAVE IT BACK IF YOU WANT!
SHWUP
YES, BUT FIRST-- YOU DIE!!!!
SOME FRIEND YOU'VE GOT THERE!
HMM...
I DON'T THINK SHE'S GONNA HELP YOU!!

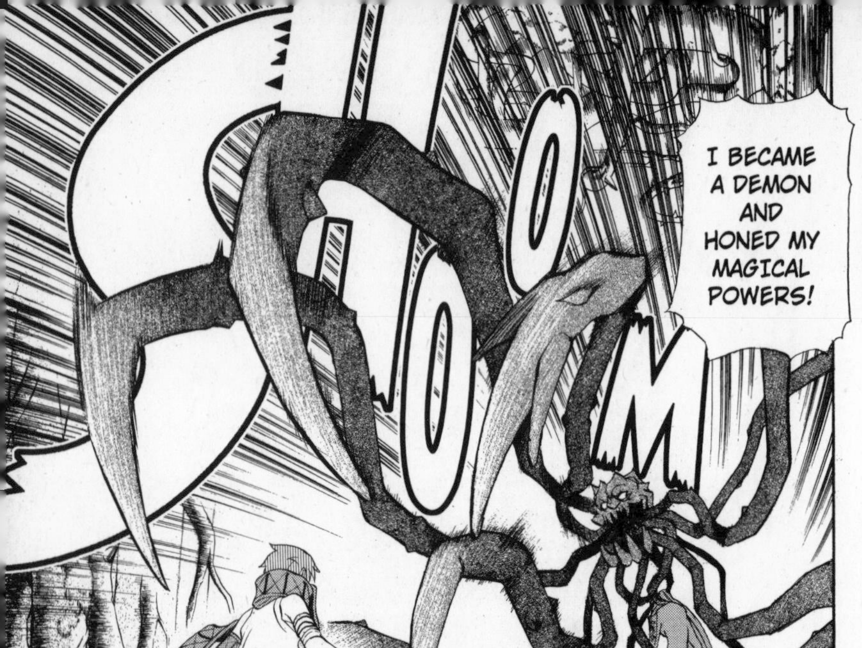
I BECAME A DEMON AND HONED MY MAGICAL POWERS!
I'M NOT THE BARAHIME YOU KNEW, KUROHIME!!!

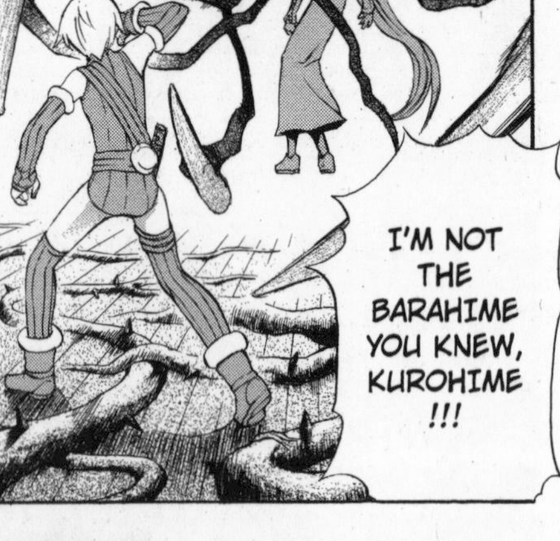
TMP
I CAN'T CREATE WITCH BULLETS IN THIS FORM! RUN, ZERO!

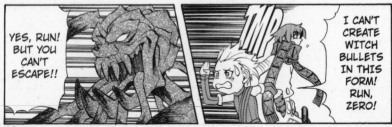

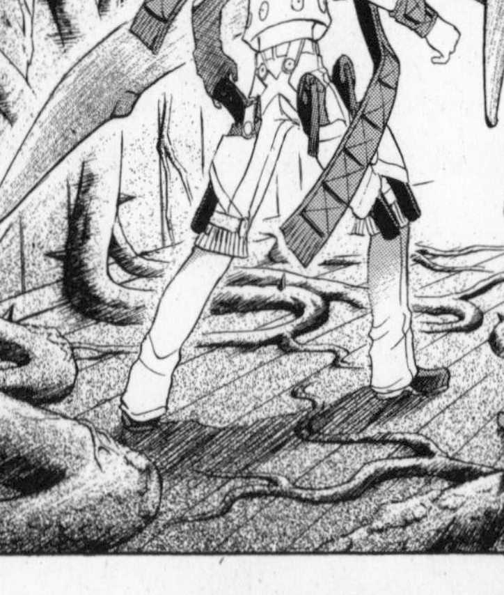
YES, RUN! BUT YOU CAN'T ESCAPE!!

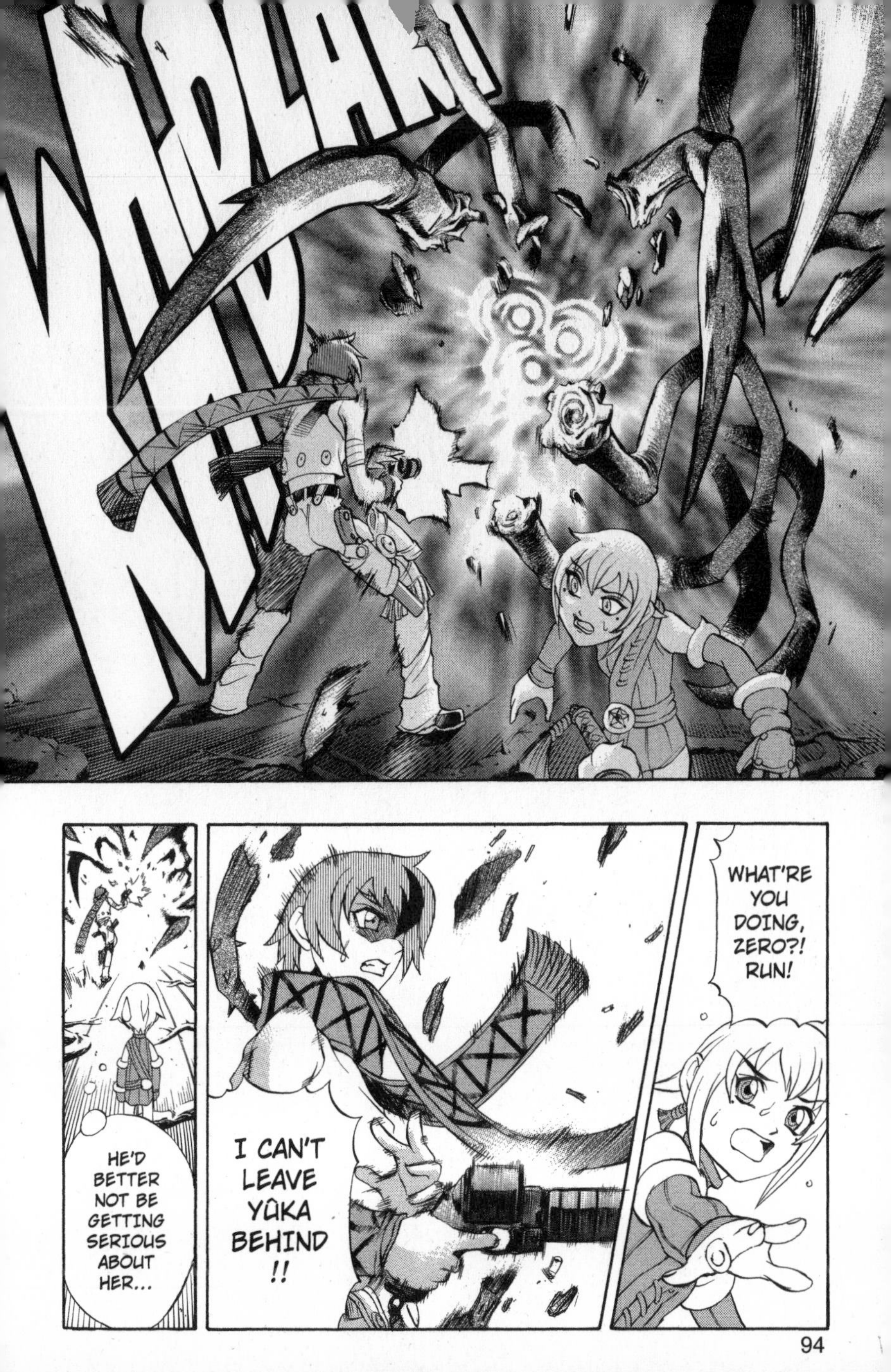
WHAT'RE YOU DOING, ZERO?! RUN!
I CAN'T LEAVE YÛKA BEHIND !!
HE'D BETTER NOT BE GETTING SERIOUS ABOUT HER...

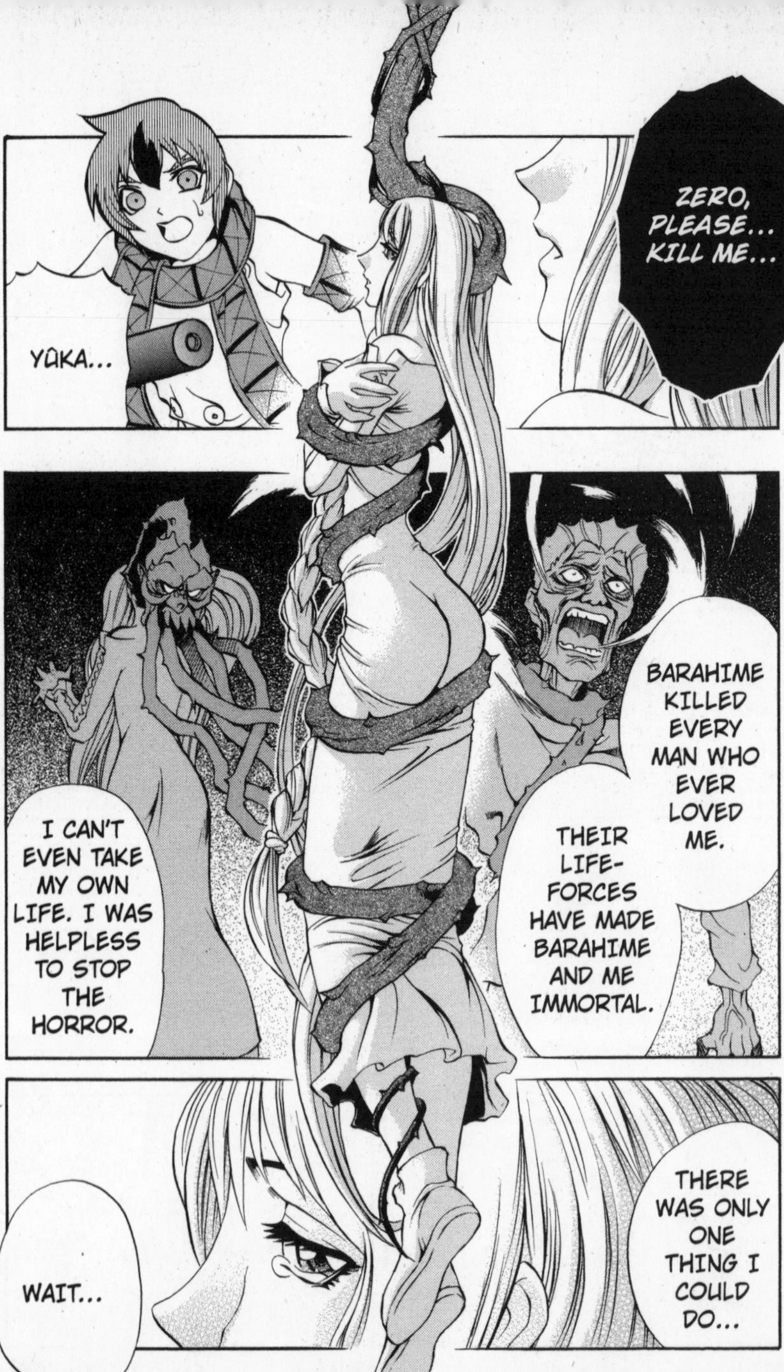
ZERO, PLEASE... KILL ME...
YÛKA...
BARAHIME KILLED EVERY MAN WHO EVER LOVED ME.
THEIR LIFE-FORCES HAVE MADE BARAHIME AND ME IMMORTAL.
I CAN'T EVEN TAKE MY OWN LIFE. I WAS HELPLESS TO STOP THE HORROR.
THERE WAS ONLY ONE THING I COULD DO...
WAIT...

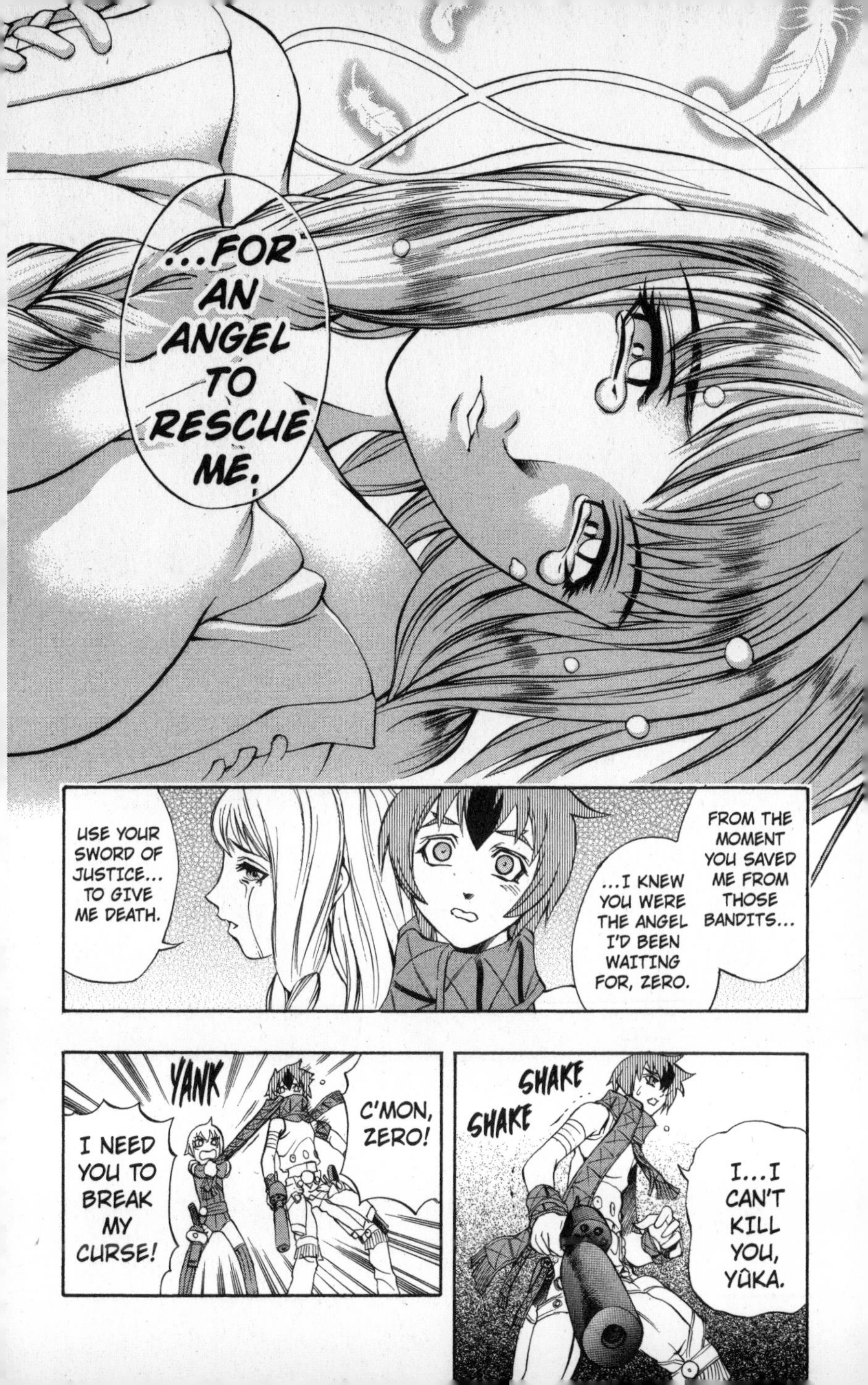
...FOR AN ANGEL TO RESCUE ME.
FROM THE MOMENT YOU SAVED ME FROM THOSE BANDITS...
...I KNEW YOU WERE THE ANGEL I'D BEEN WAITING FOR, ZERO.
USE YOUR SWORD OF JUSTICE... TO GIVE ME DEATH.
SHAKE
SHAKE
I...I CAN'T KILL YOU, YÛKA.
YANK
C'MON, ZERO!
I NEED YOU TO BREAK MY CURSE!

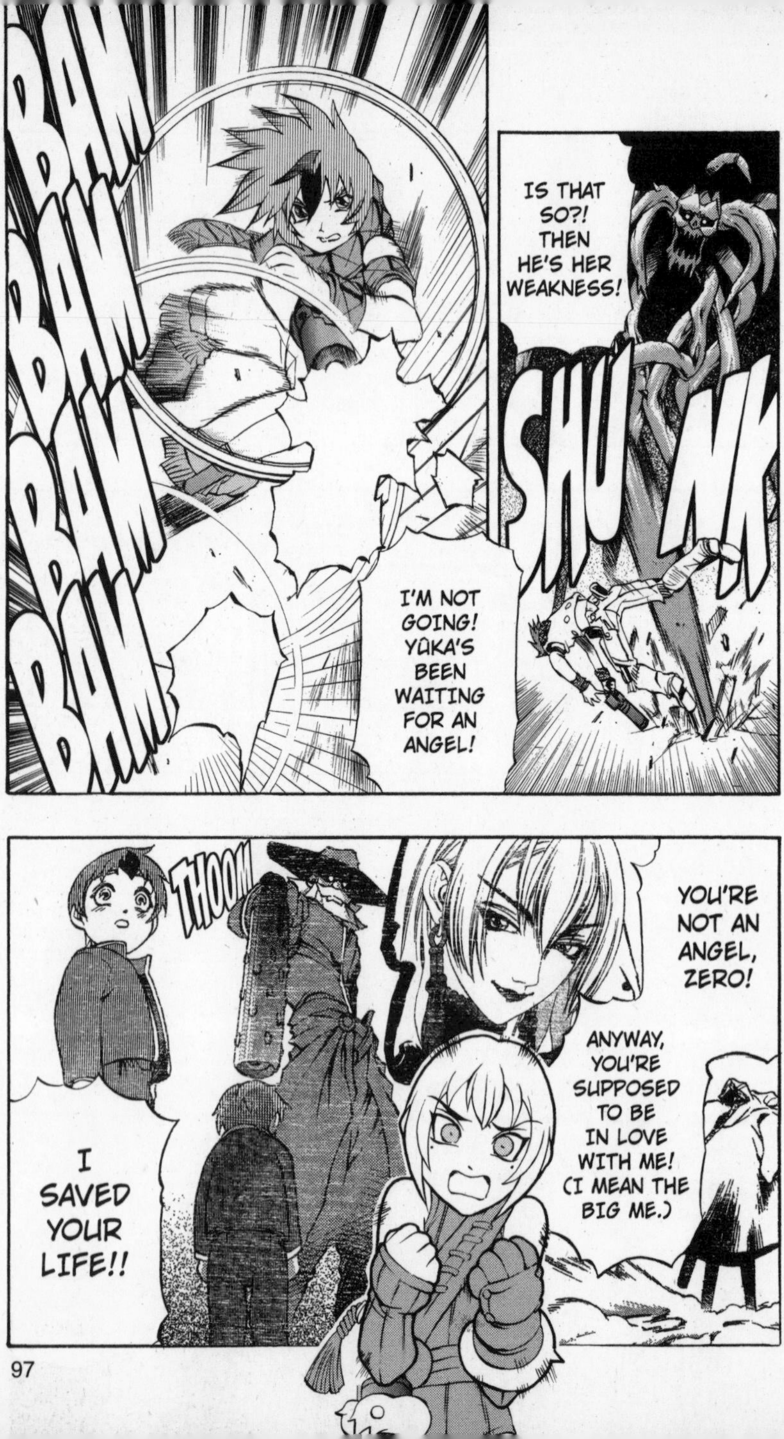
IS THAT SO?! THEN HE'S HER WEAKNESS!
SHUNK
I'M NOT GOING! YŪKA'S BEEN WAITING FOR AN ANGEL!
BAM BAM BAM BAM
YOU'RE NOT AN ANGEL, ZERO!
ANYWAY, YOU'RE SUPPOSED TO BE IN LOVE WITH ME! (I MEAN THE BIG ME.)
THOOM
I SAVED YOUR LIFE!!

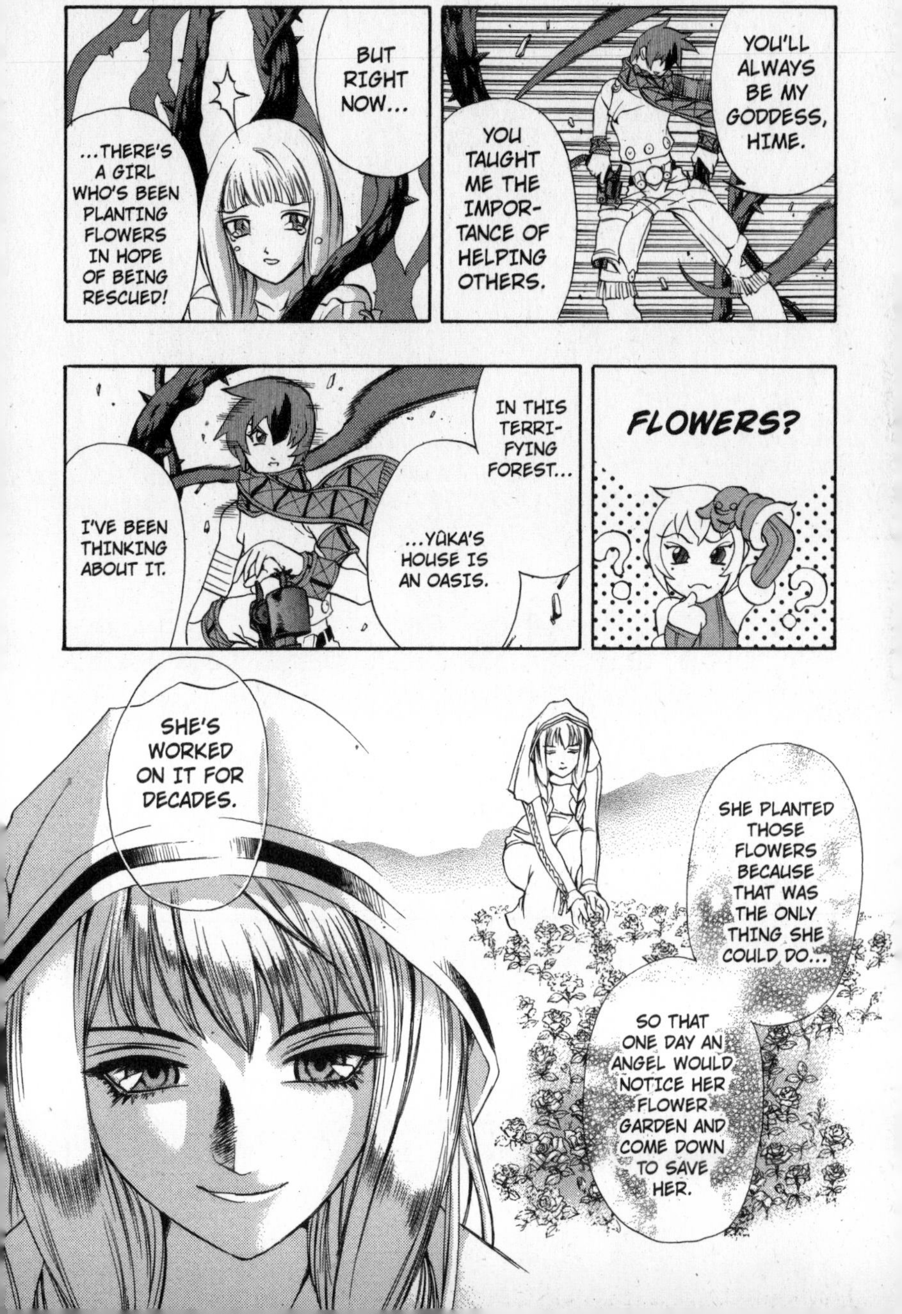
YOU'LL ALWAYS BE MY GODDESS, HIME.
YOU TAUGHT ME THE IMPORTANCE OF HELPING OTHERS.
BUT RIGHT NOW...
...THERE'S A GIRL WHO'S BEEN PLANTING FLOWERS IN HOPE OF BEING RESCUED!
FLOWERS?
IN THIS TERRIFYING FOREST...
...YŪKA'S HOUSE IS AN OASIS.
I'VE BEEN THINKING ABOUT IT.
SHE PLANTED THOSE FLOWERS BECAUSE THAT WAS THE ONLY THING SHE COULD DO...
SO THAT ONE DAY AN ANGEL WOULD NOTICE HER FLOWER GARDEN AND COME DOWN TO SAVE HER.
SHE'S WORKED ON IT FOR DECADES.

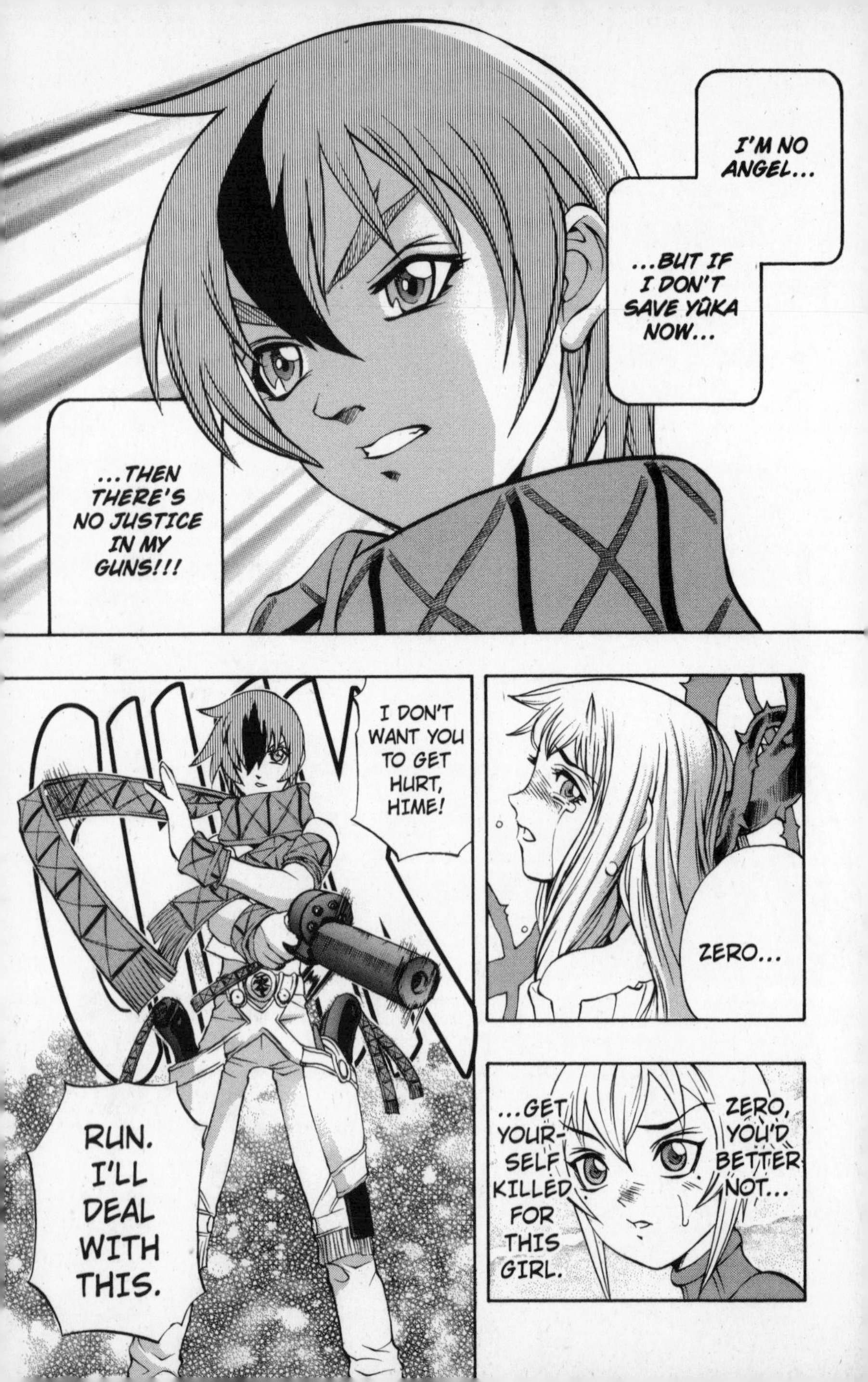
I'M NO ANGEL...
...BUT IF I DON'T SAVE YŪKA NOW...
...THEN THERE'S NO JUSTICE IN MY GUNS!!!
ZERO...
ZERO, YOU'D BETTER NOT...
...GET YOURSELF KILLED FOR THIS GIRL.
I DON'T WANT YOU TO GET HURT, HIME!
RUN. I'LL DEAL WITH THIS.

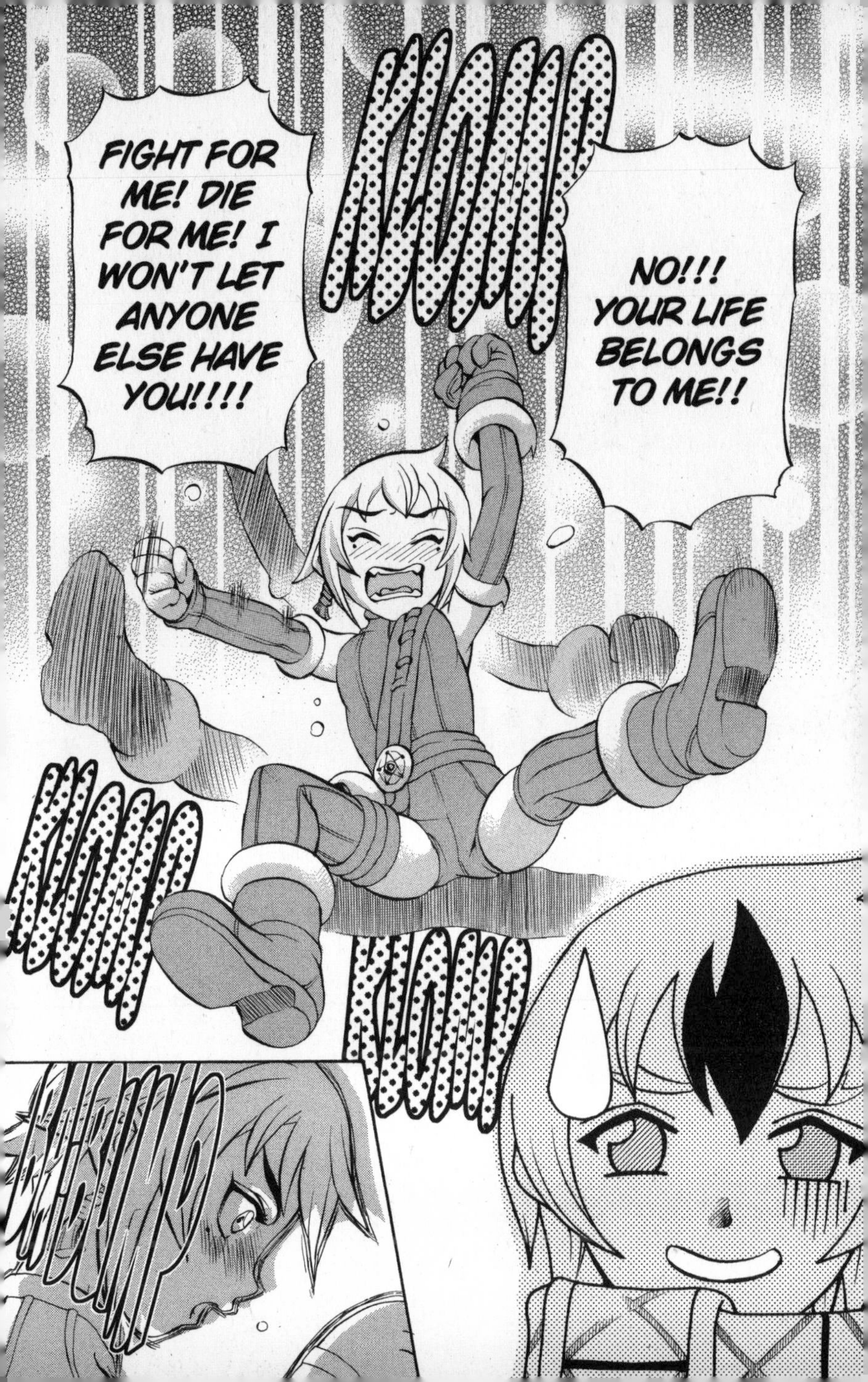
NO!!! YOUR LIFE BELONGS TO ME!!
FIGHT FOR ME! DIE FOR ME! I WON'T LET ANYONE ELSE HAVE YOU!!!!

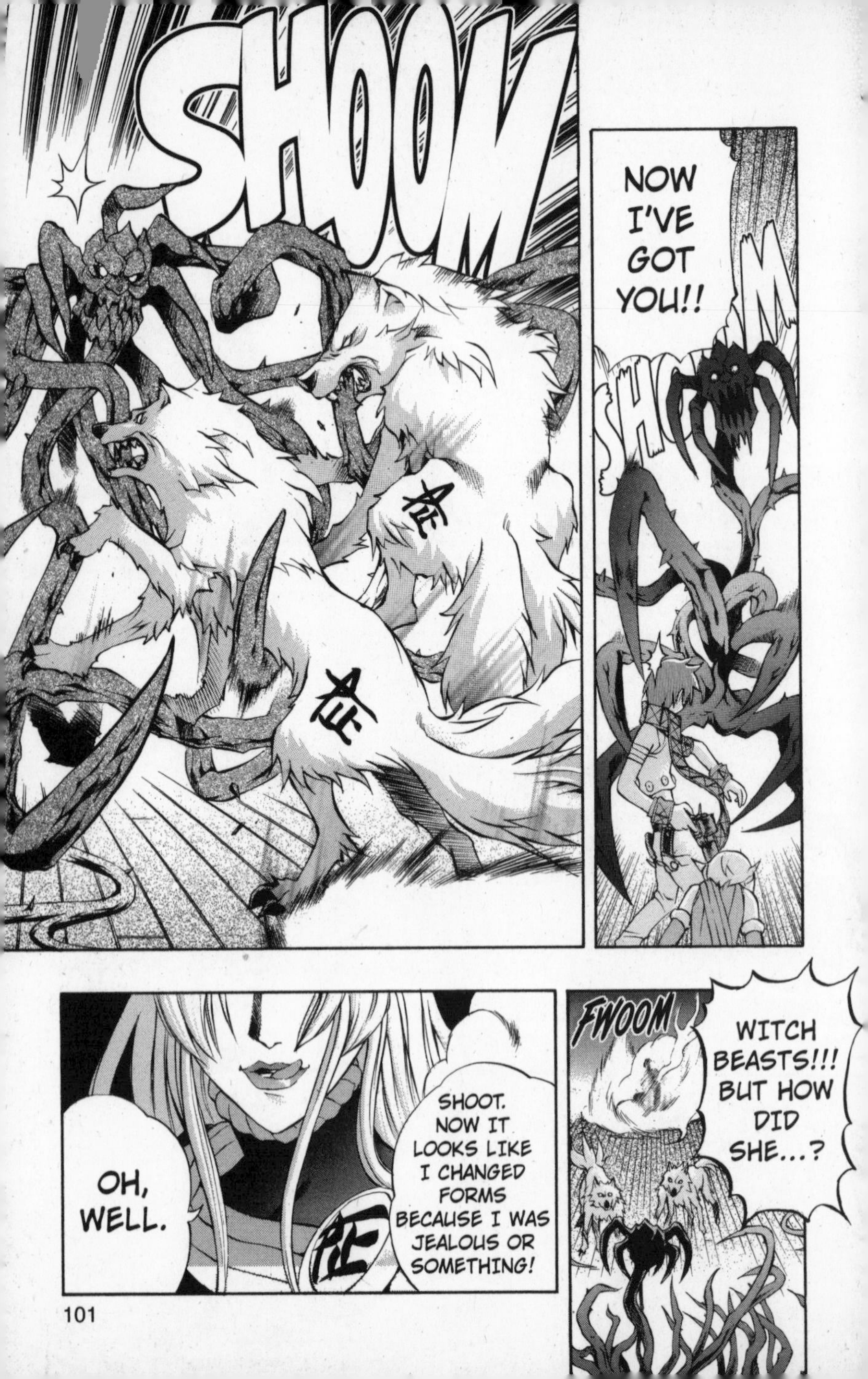
NOW I'VE GOT YOU!!
SHOOM
SHOOM
FWOOM
WITCH BEASTS!!! BUT HOW DID SHE...?
SHOOT. NOW IT LOOKS LIKE I CHANGED FORMS BECAUSE I WAS JEALOUS OR SOMETHING!
OH, WELL.

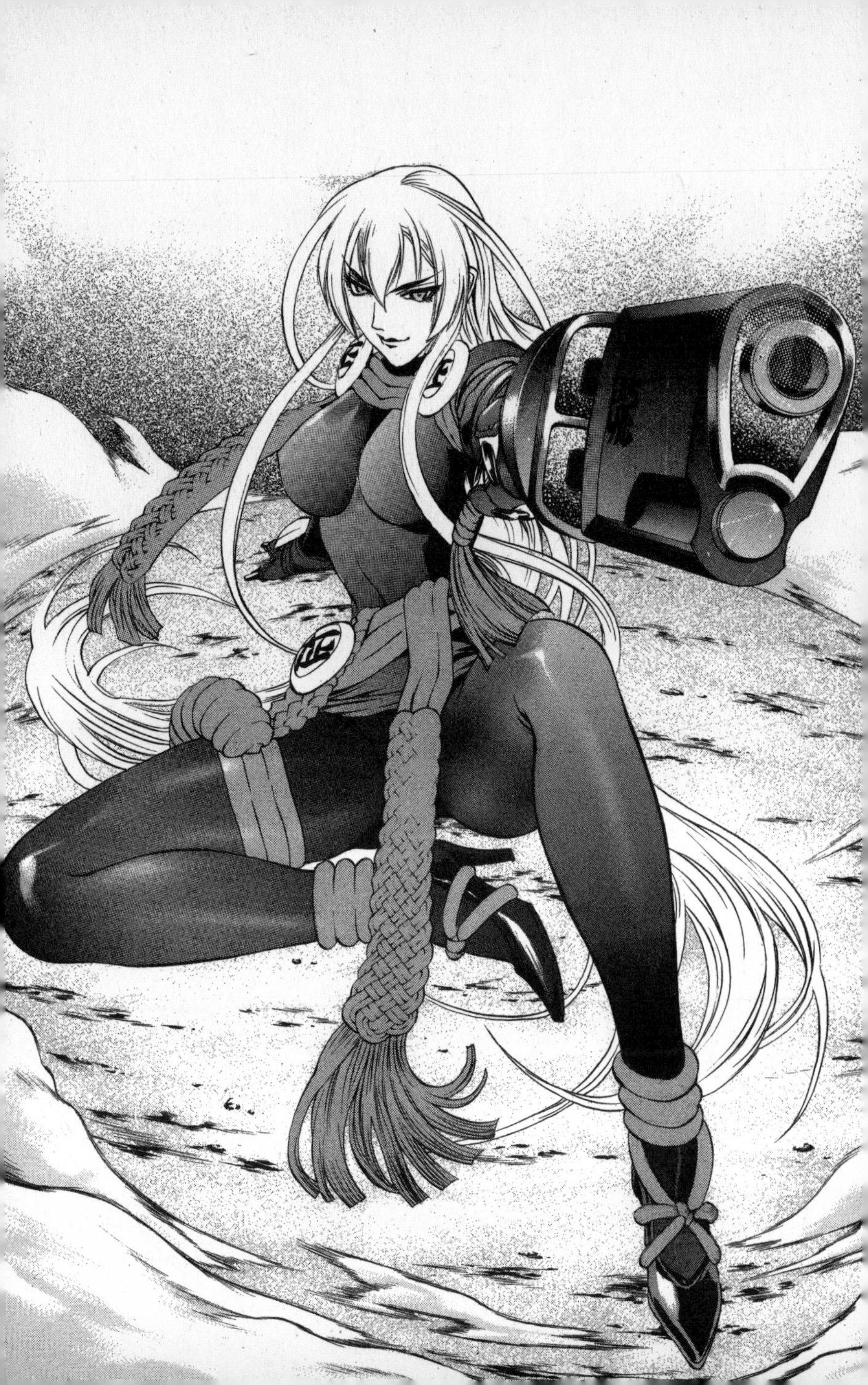

READ THIS WAY

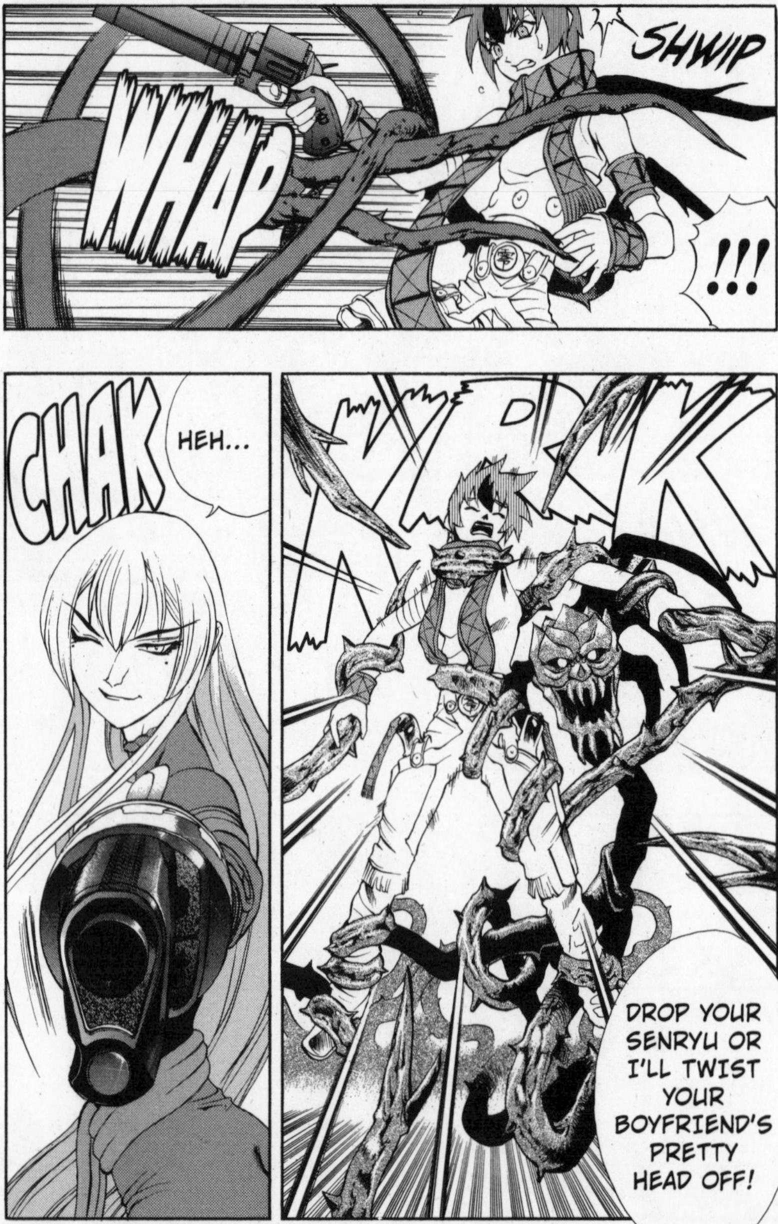
SHWIP
WHAP
!!!
DROP YOUR SENRYU OR I'LL TWIST YOUR BOYFRIEND'S PRETTY HEAD OFF!
HEH...
CHAK

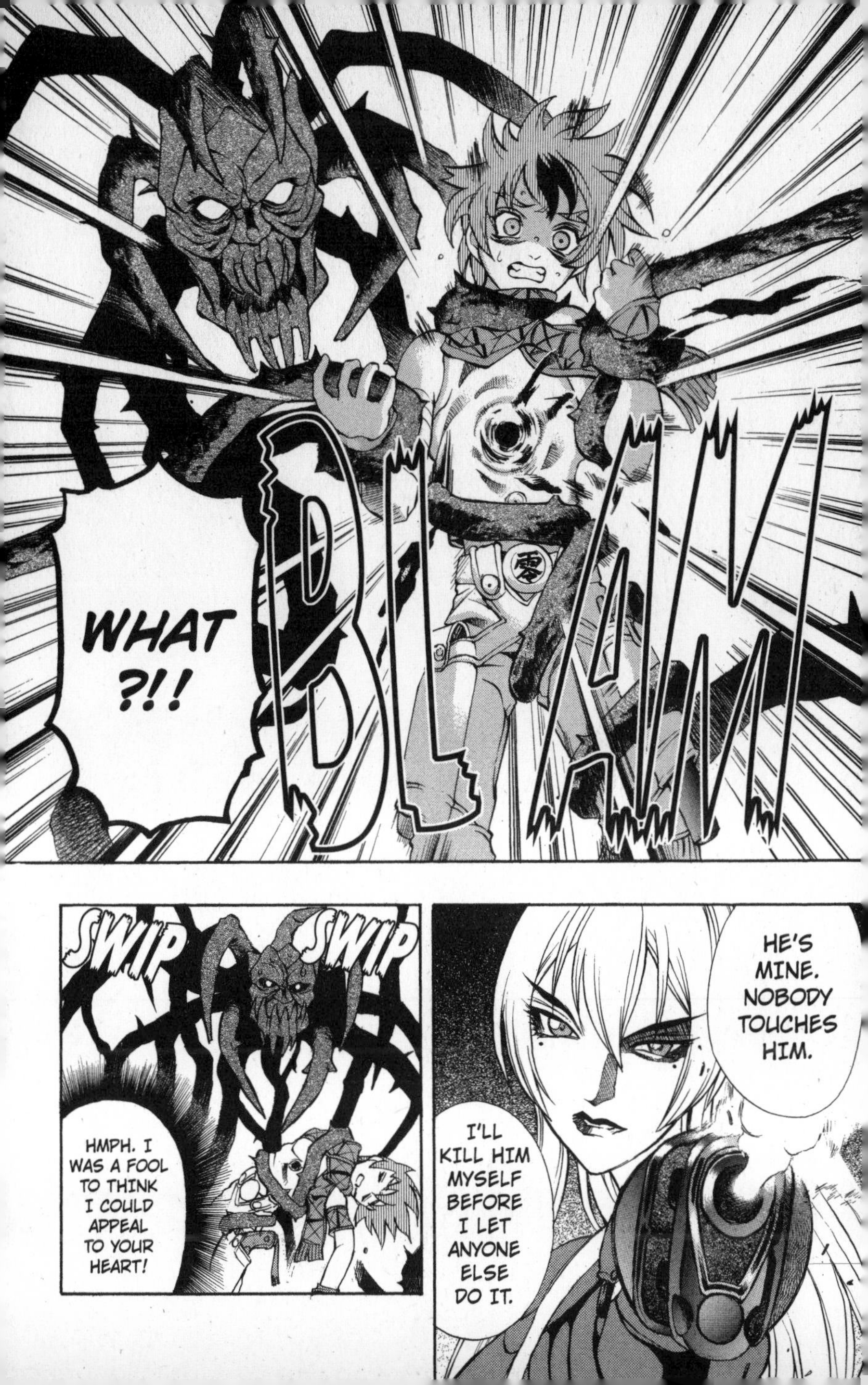
BLAM
WHAT ?!!
HE'S MINE. NOBODY TOUCHES HIM.
I'LL KILL HIM MYSELF BEFORE I LET ANYONE ELSE DO IT.
SWIP SWIP
HMPH. I WAS A FOOL TO THINK I COULD APPEAL TO YOUR HEART!

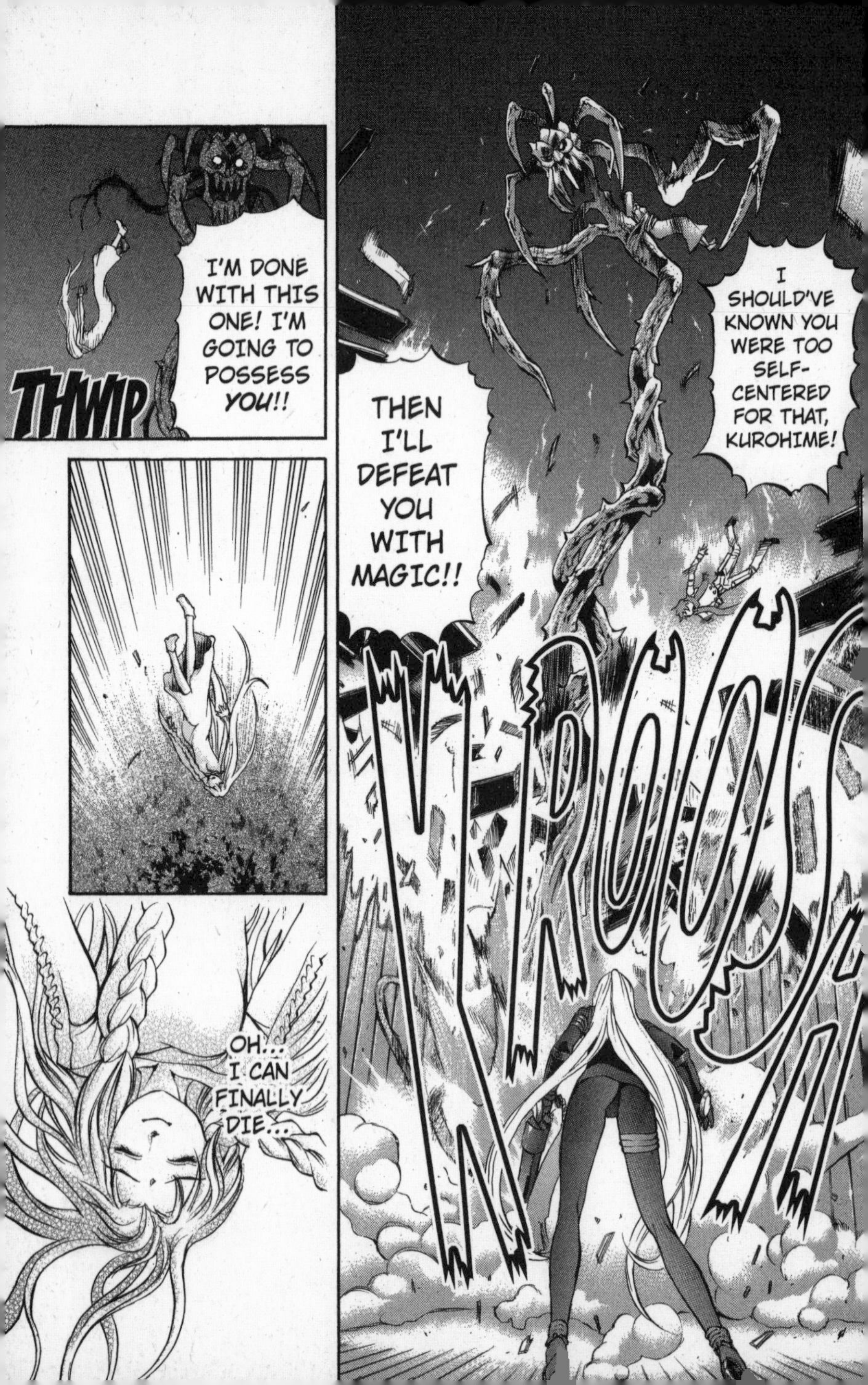
I SHOULD'VE KNOWN YOU WERE TOO SELF-CENTERED FOR THAT, KUROHIME!
THEN I'LL DEFEAT YOU WITH MAGIC!!
I'M DONE WITH THIS ONE! I'M GOING TO POSSESS YOU!!
THWIP
OH... I CAN FINALLY DIE...

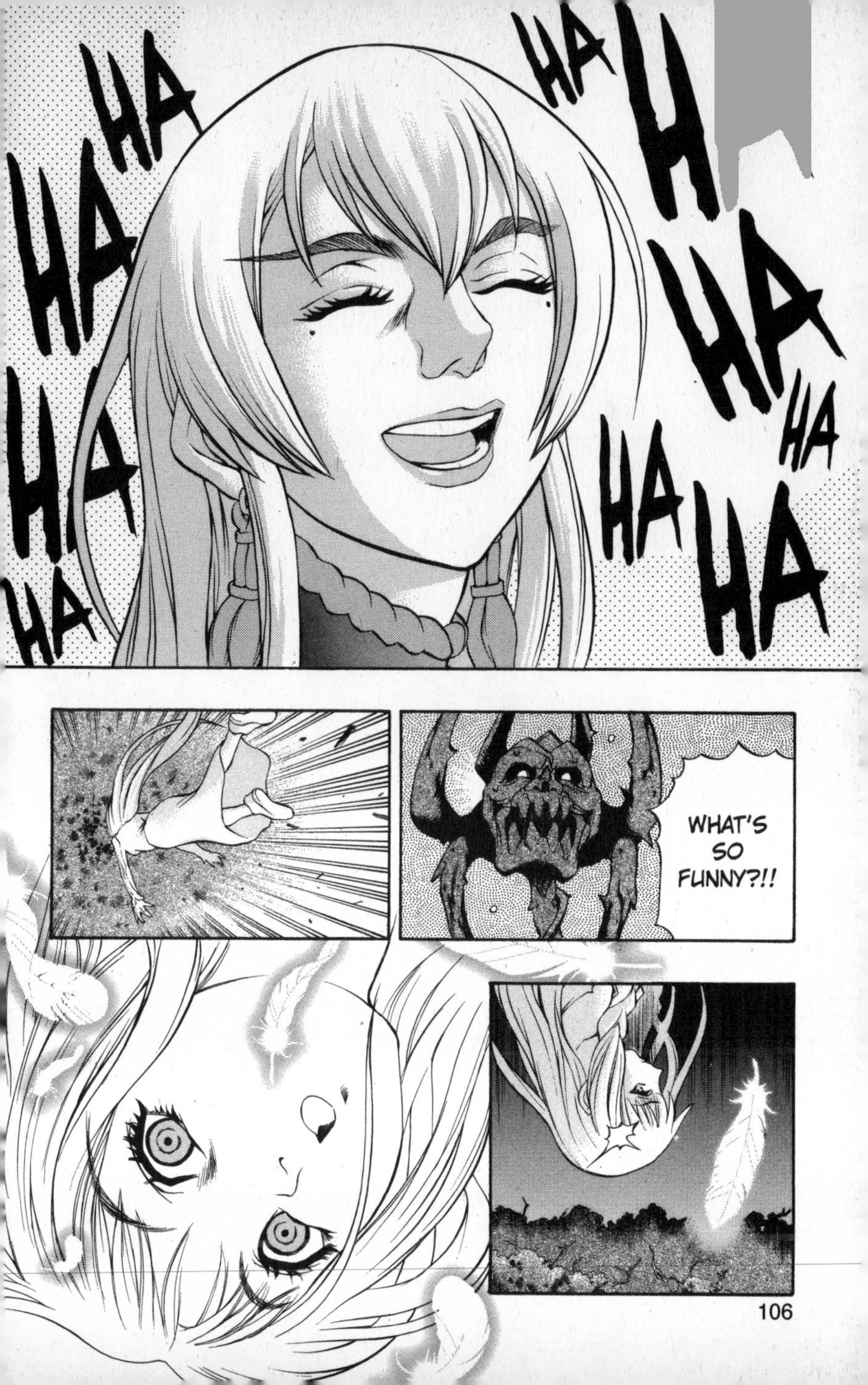
HA HA H HA HA HA HA HA HA
HA HA HA HA HA HA
WHAT'S SO FUNNY?!!

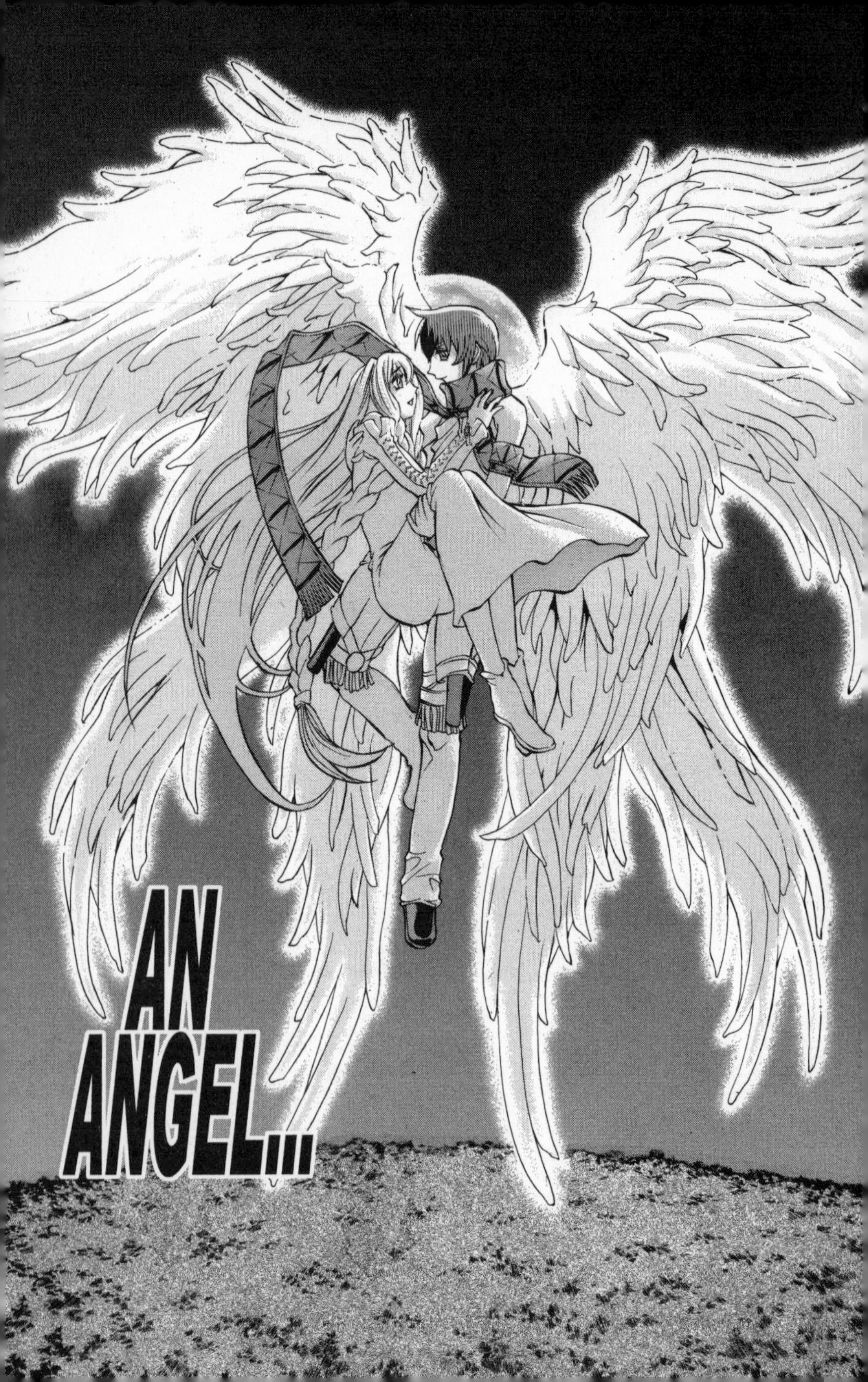
AN ANGEL...

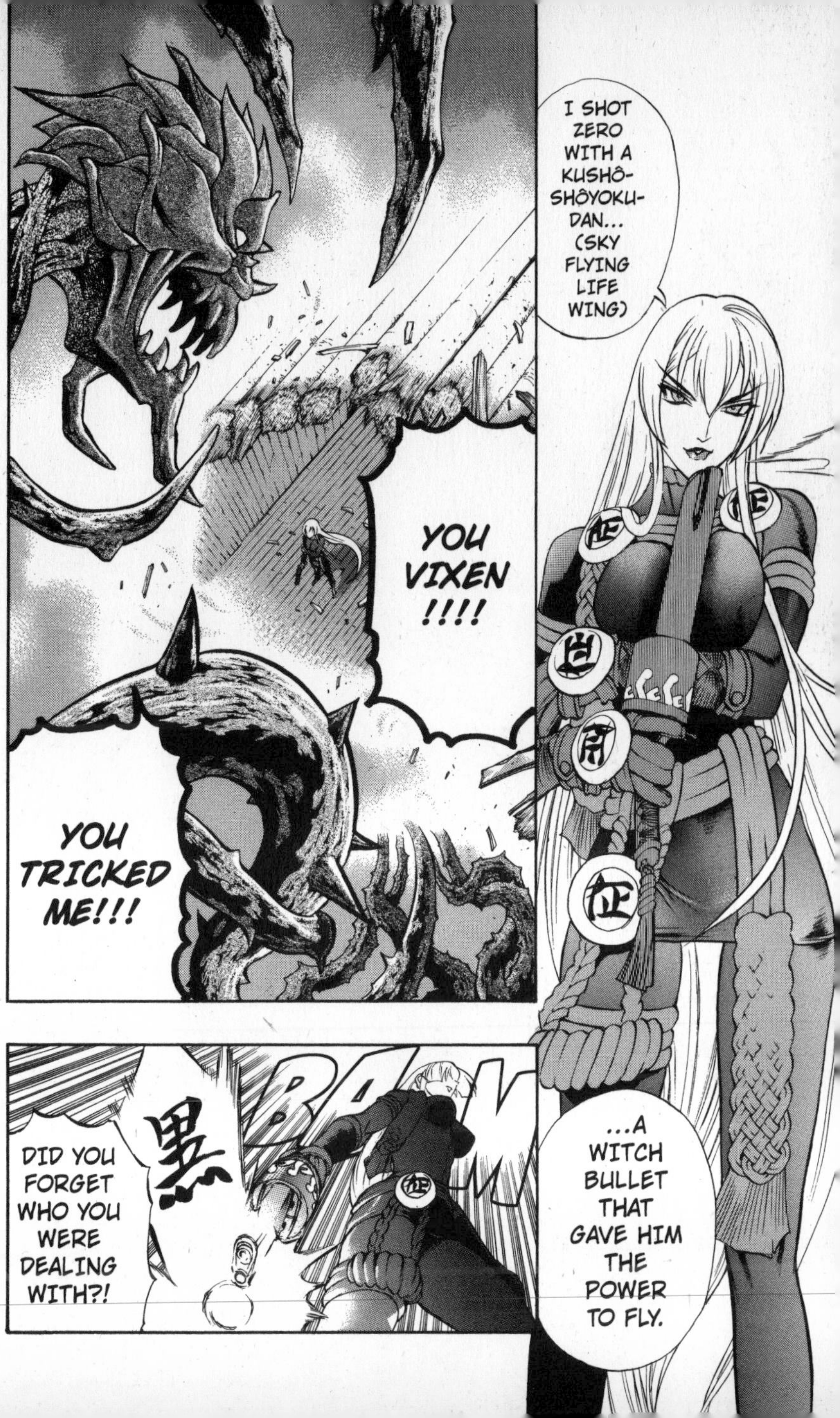
I SHOT ZERO WITH A KUSHÔ-SHÔYOKU-DAN... (SKY FLYING LIFE WING)
...A WITCH BULLET THAT GAVE HIM THE POWER TO FLY.
YOU VIXEN!!!!
YOU TRICKED ME!!!
BAM
黑
DID YOU FORGET WHO YOU WERE DEALING WITH?!

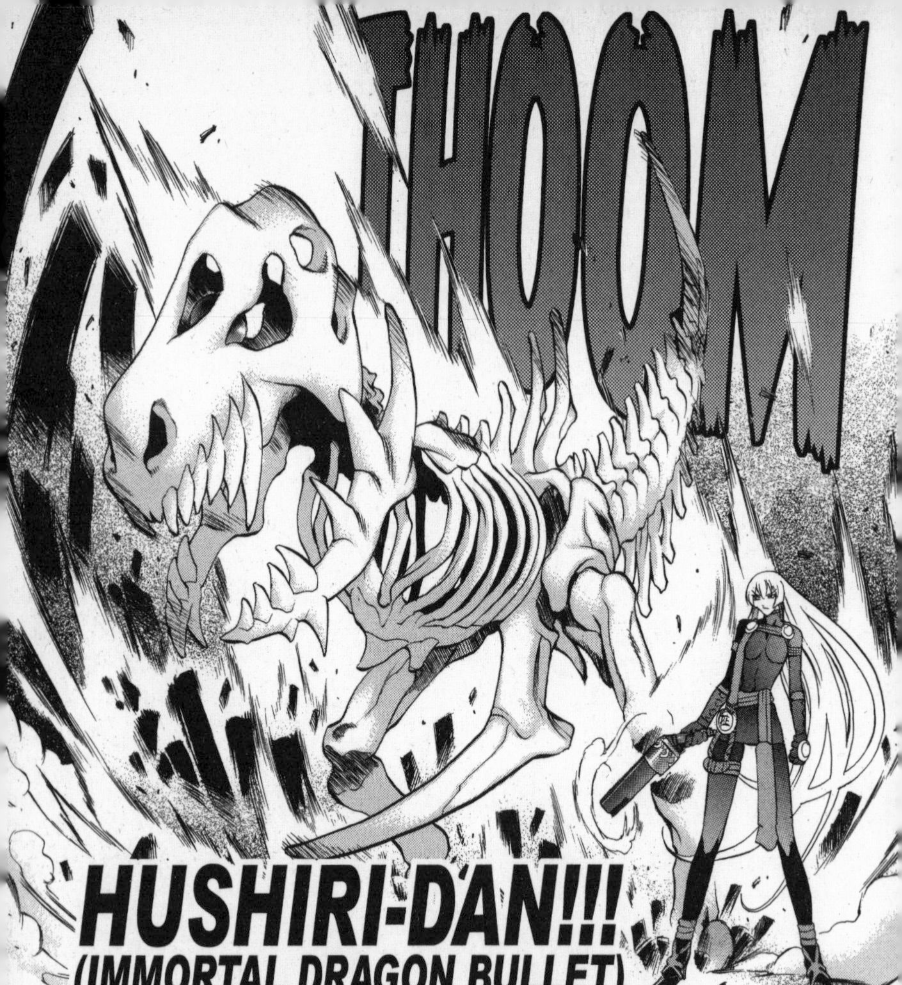
THOOM
HUSHIRI-DĀN!!!
(IMMORTAL DRAGON BULLET)

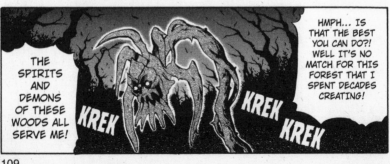

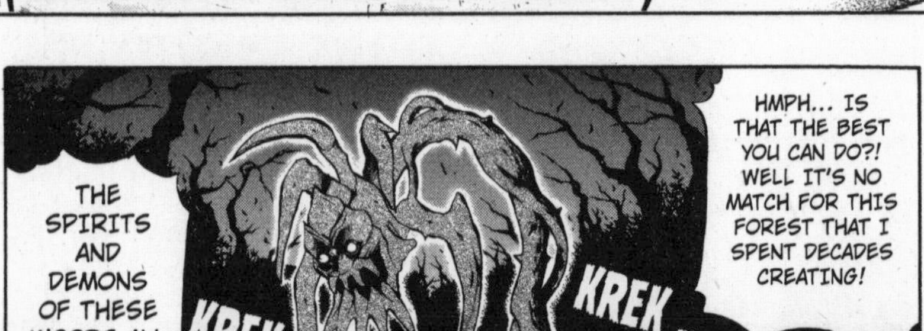
HMPH... IS THAT THE BEST YOU CAN DO?! WELL IT'S NO MATCH FOR THIS FOREST THAT I SPENT DECADES CREATING!
KREK
KREK
KREK
THE SPIRITS AND DEMONS OF THESE WOODS ALL SERVE ME!

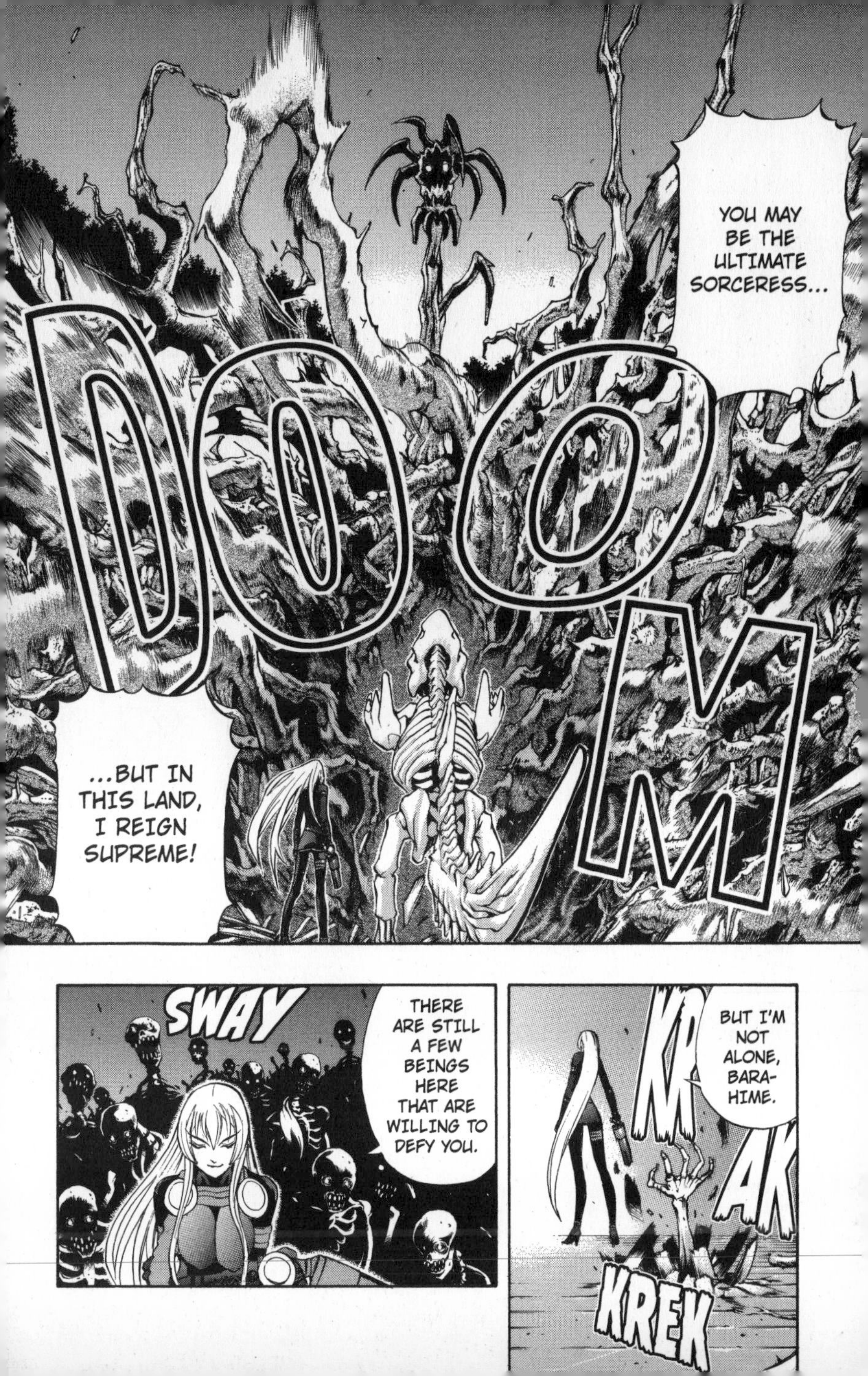
YOU MAY BE THE ULTIMATE SORCERESS...
DOOOM
...BUT IN THIS LAND, I REIGN SUPREME!
KRAK
BUT I'M NOT ALONE, BARA-HIME.
KREK
SWAY
THERE ARE STILL A FEW BEINGS HERE THAT ARE WILLING TO DEFY YOU.

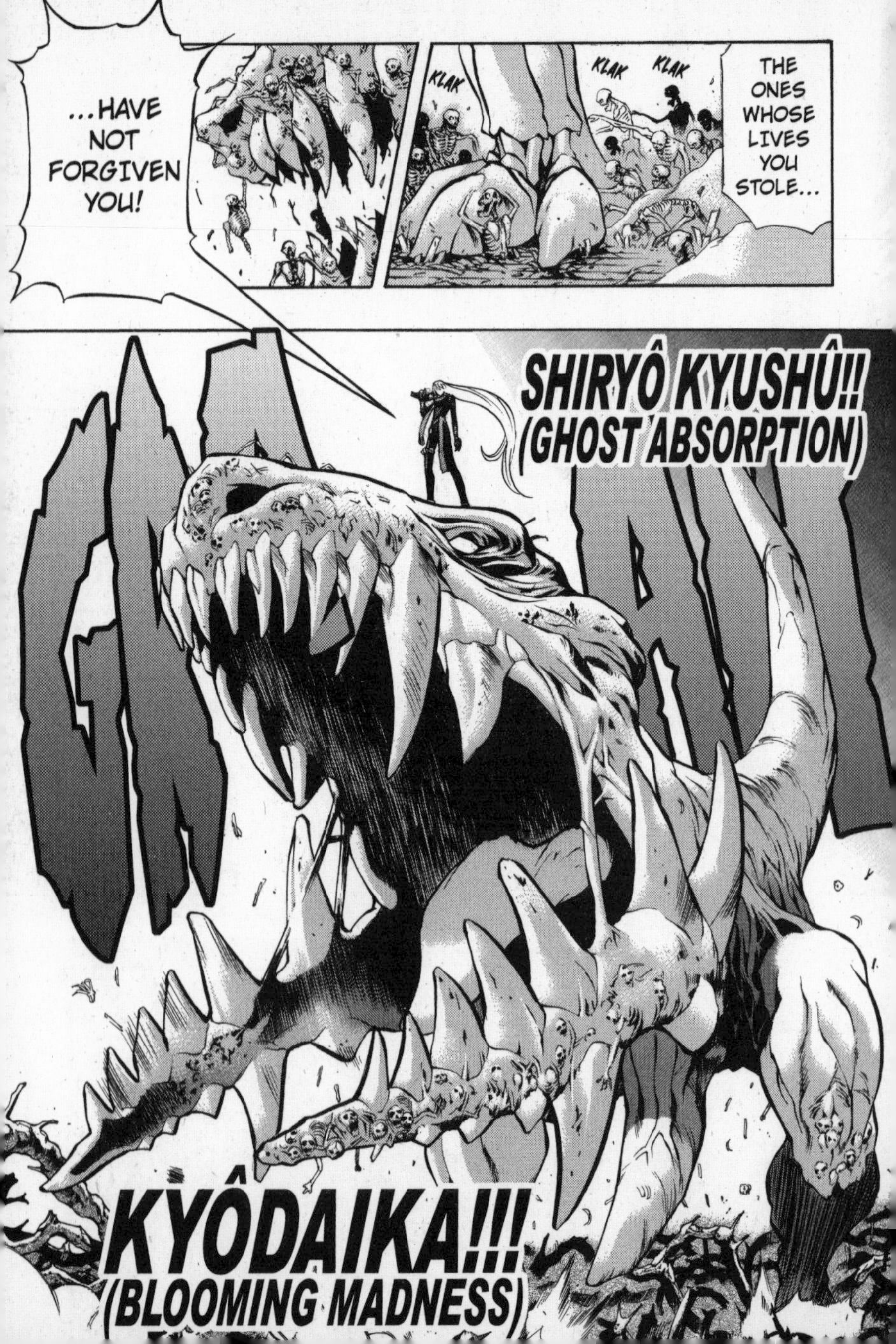
THE ONES WHOSE LIVES YOU STOLE...
KLAK KLAK
KLAK
...HAVE NOT FORGIVEN YOU!
SHIRYÔ KYUSHÛ!! (GHOST ABSORPTION)
KYÔDAIKA!!! (BLOOMING MADNESS)

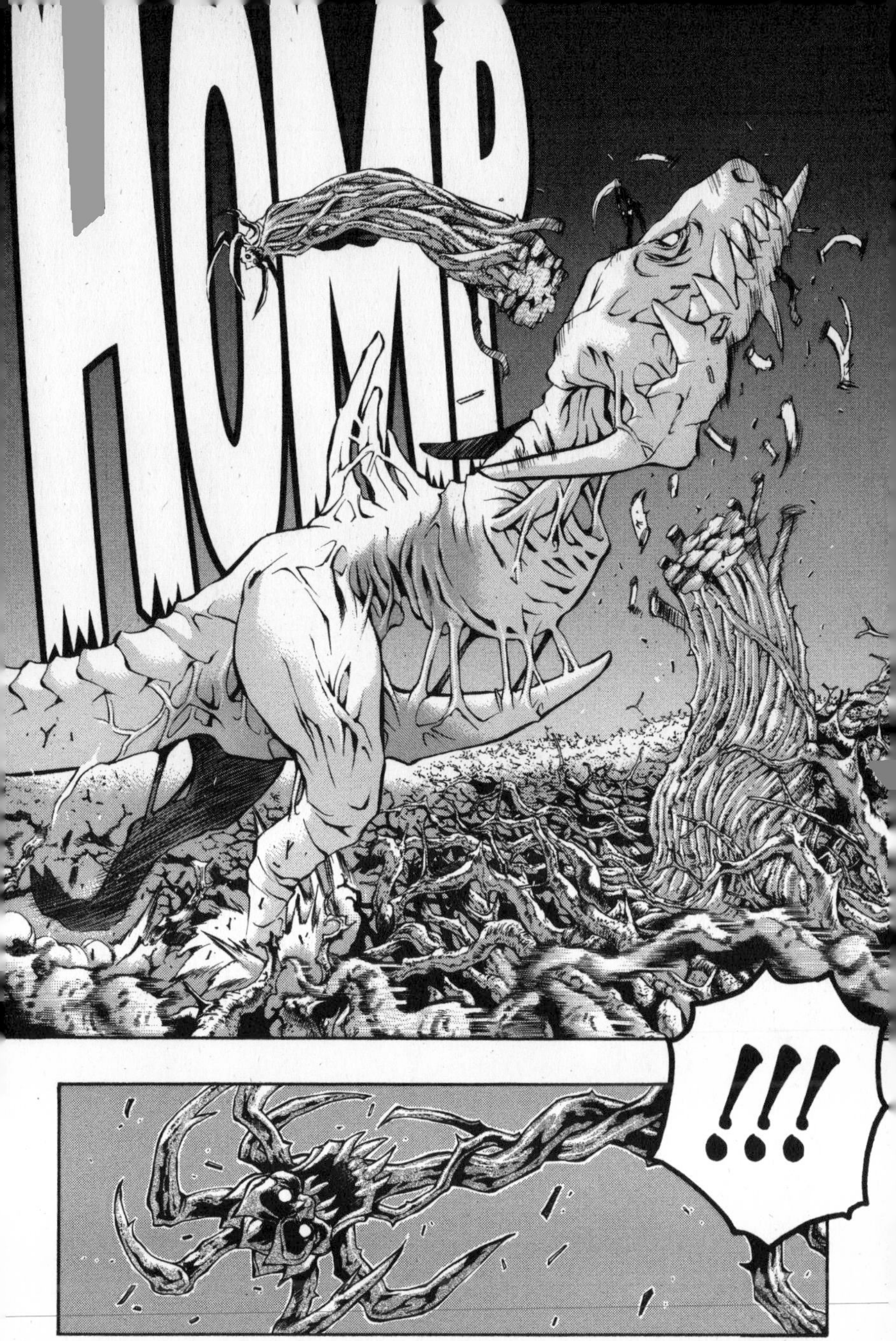
HOMP
!!!

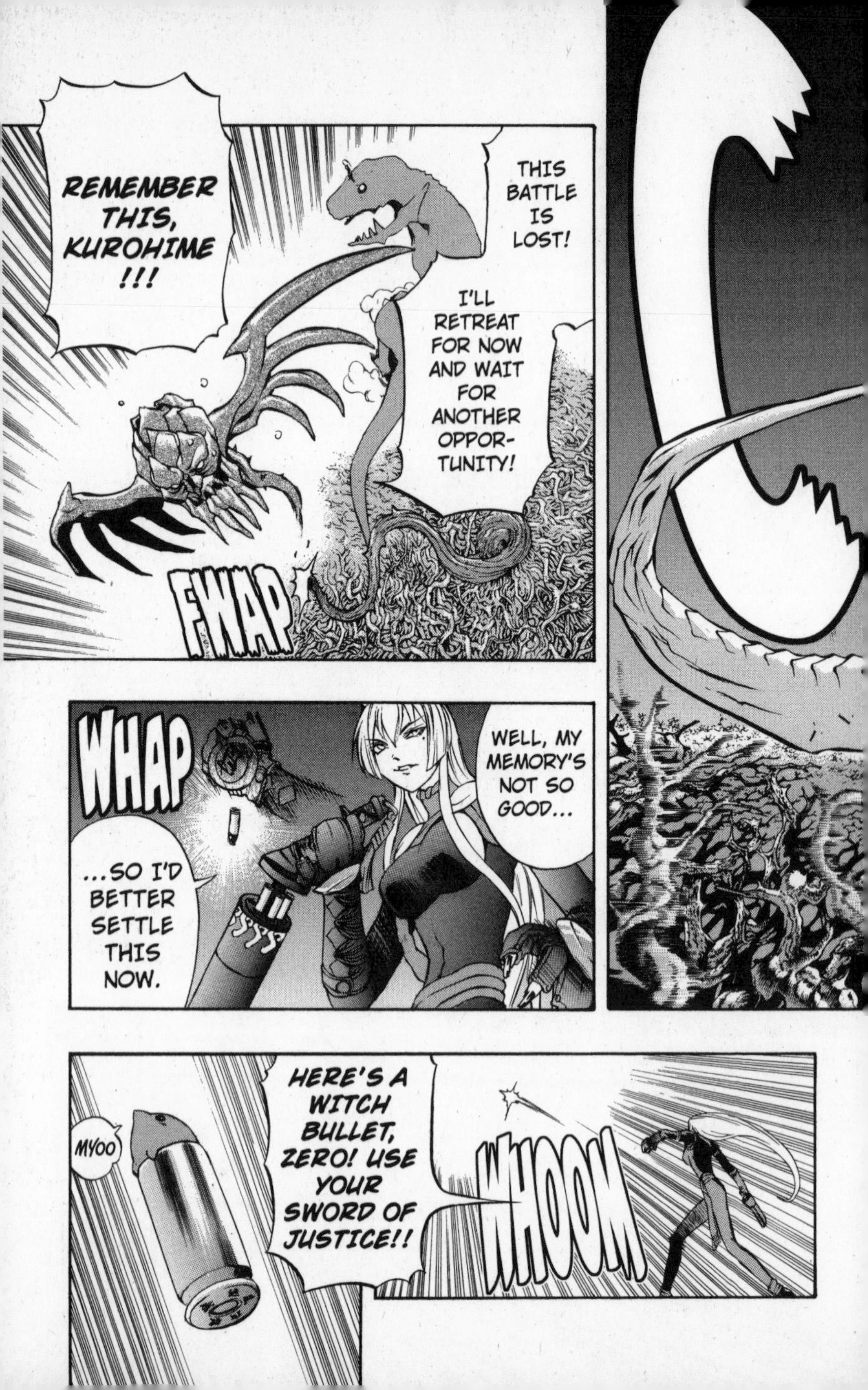
THIS BATTLE IS LOST!
I'LL RETREAT FOR NOW AND WAIT FOR ANOTHER OPPORTUNITY!
REMEMBER THIS, KUROHIME!!!
FWAP
WELL, MY MEMORY'S NOT SO GOOD...
WHAP
...SO I'D BETTER SETTLE THIS NOW.
WHOOM
HERE'S A WITCH BULLET, ZERO! USE YOUR SWORD OF JUSTICE!!
MYOO

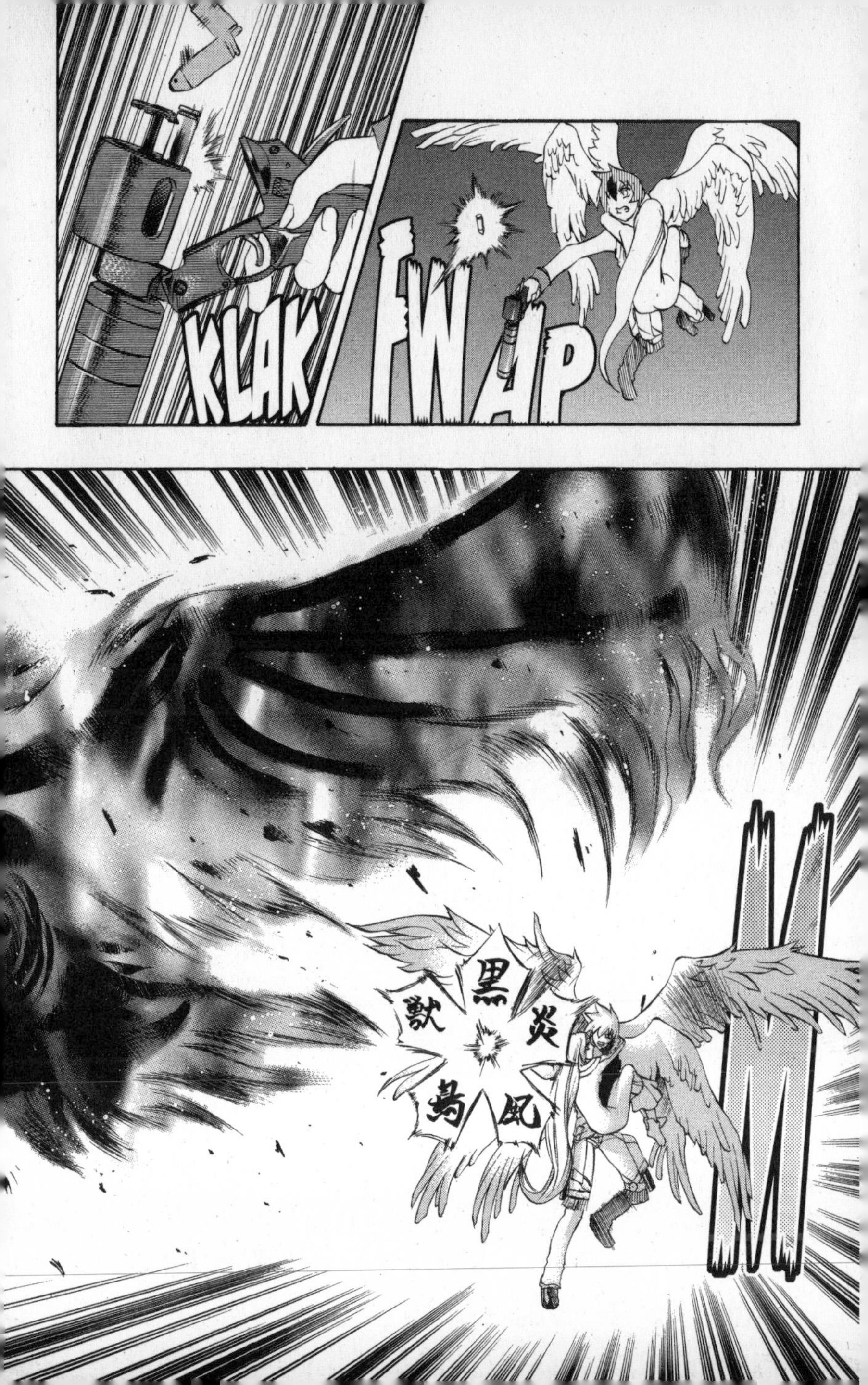
FWAP
KLAK
黒炎風鳥獣
M

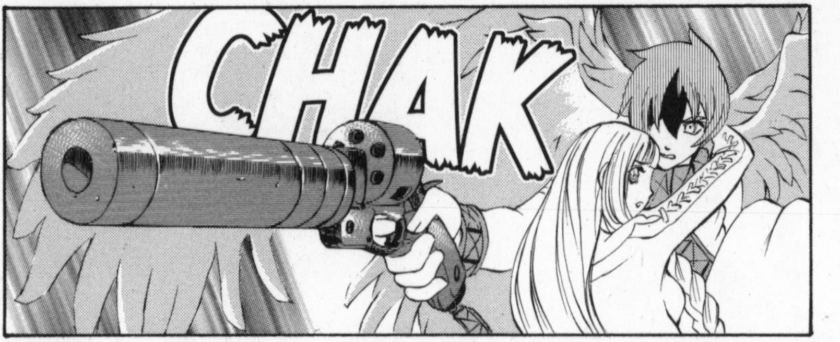
CHAK

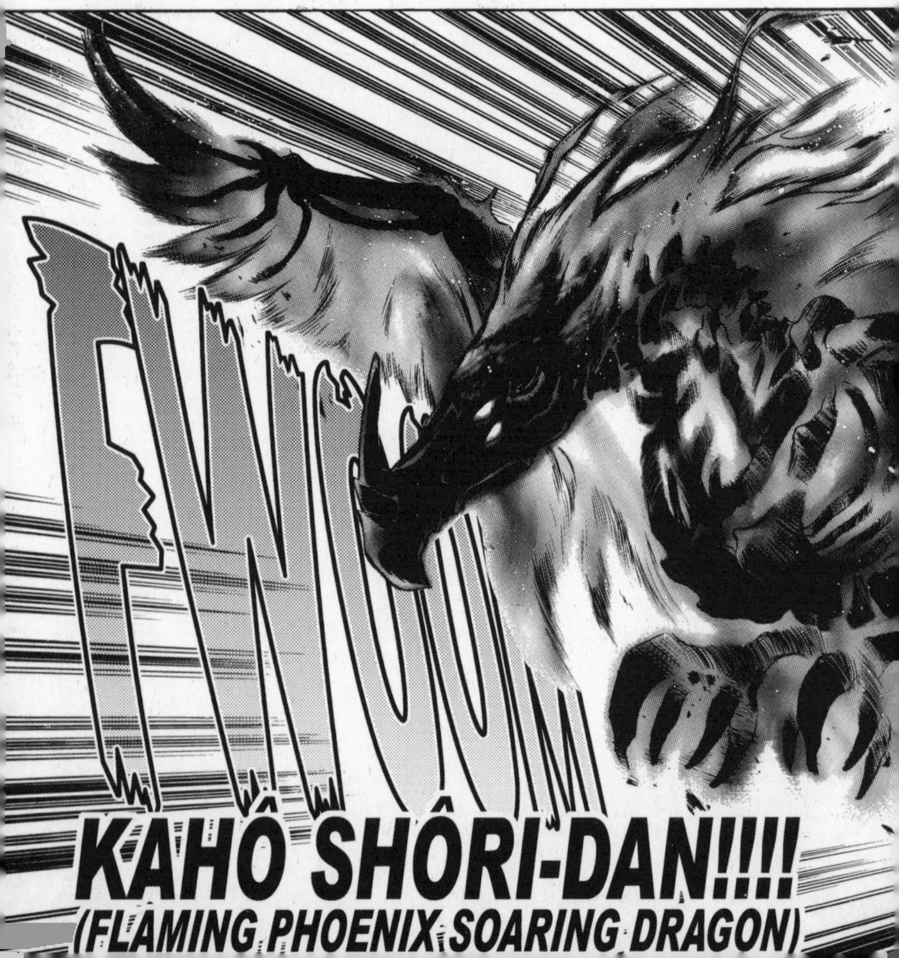
FWOOM
KAHÔ SHÔRI-DAN!!!!
(FLAMING PHOENIX SOARING DRAGON)

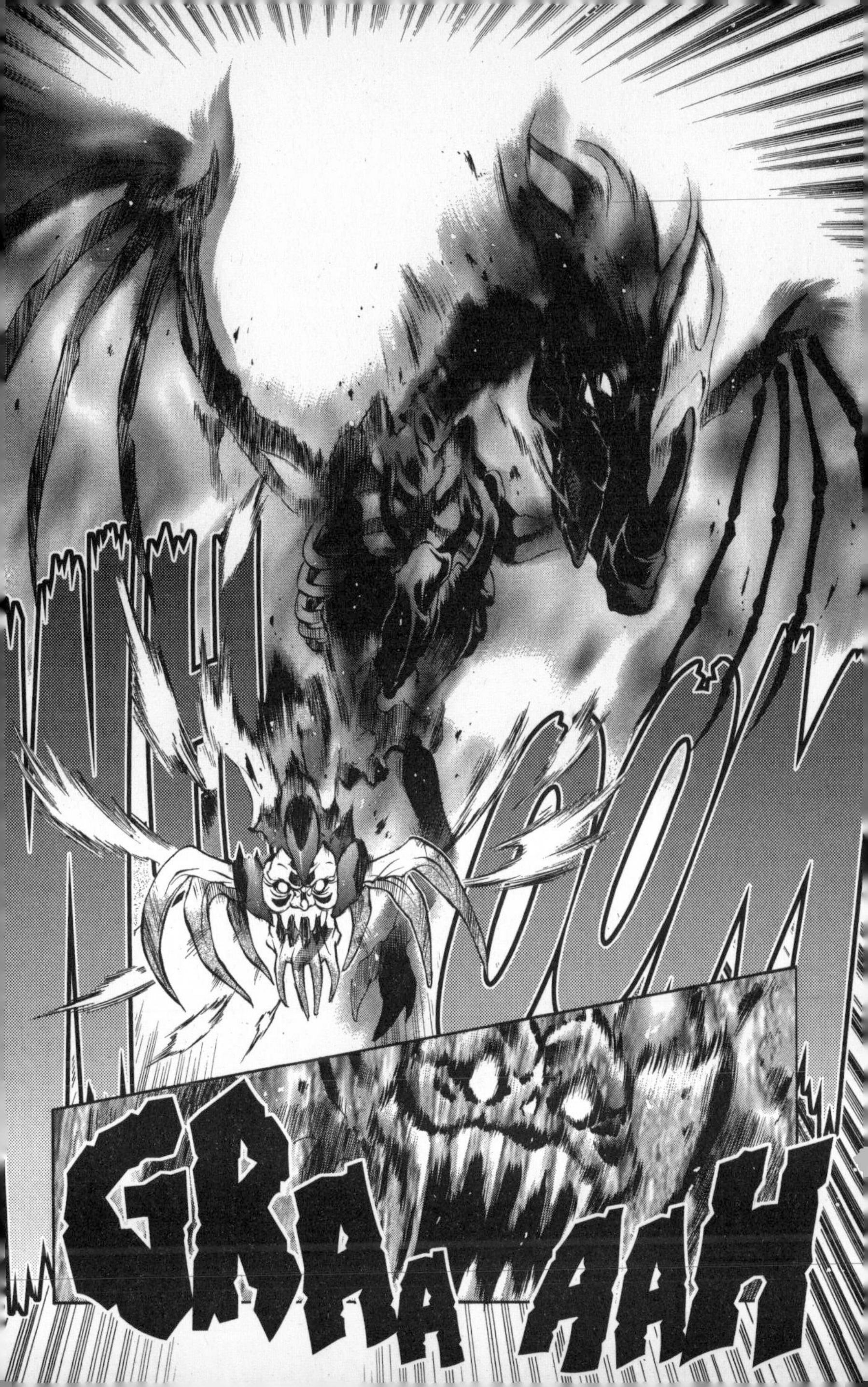
GRAAAAH

READ THIS WAY

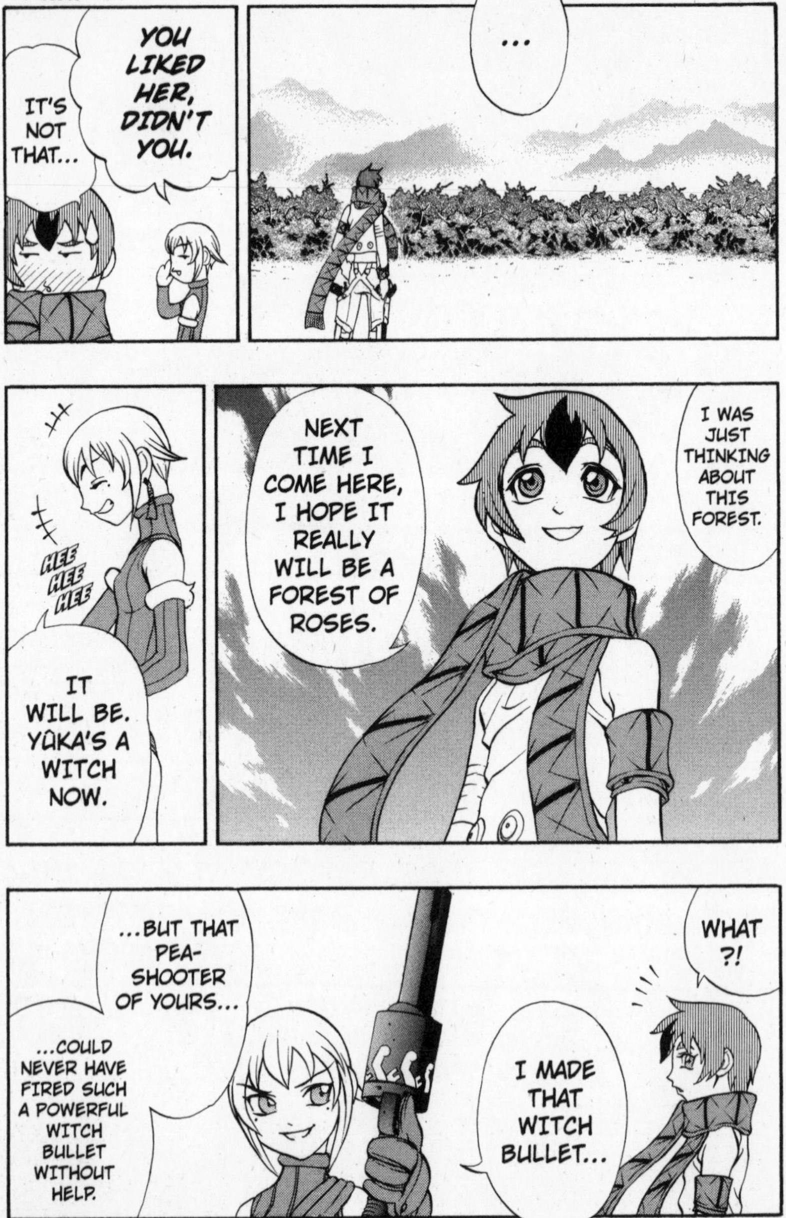
...
YOU LIKED HER, DIDN'T YOU.
IT'S NOT THAT...
I WAS JUST THINKING ABOUT THIS FOREST.
NEXT TIME I COME HERE, I HOPE IT REALLY WILL BE A FOREST OF ROSES.
HEE HEE HEE
IT WILL BE. YÛKA'S A WITCH NOW.
WHAT?!
I MADE THAT WITCH BULLET...
...BUT THAT PEA-SHOOTER OF YOURS...
...COULD NEVER HAVE FIRED SUCH A POWERFUL WITCH BULLET WITHOUT HELP.

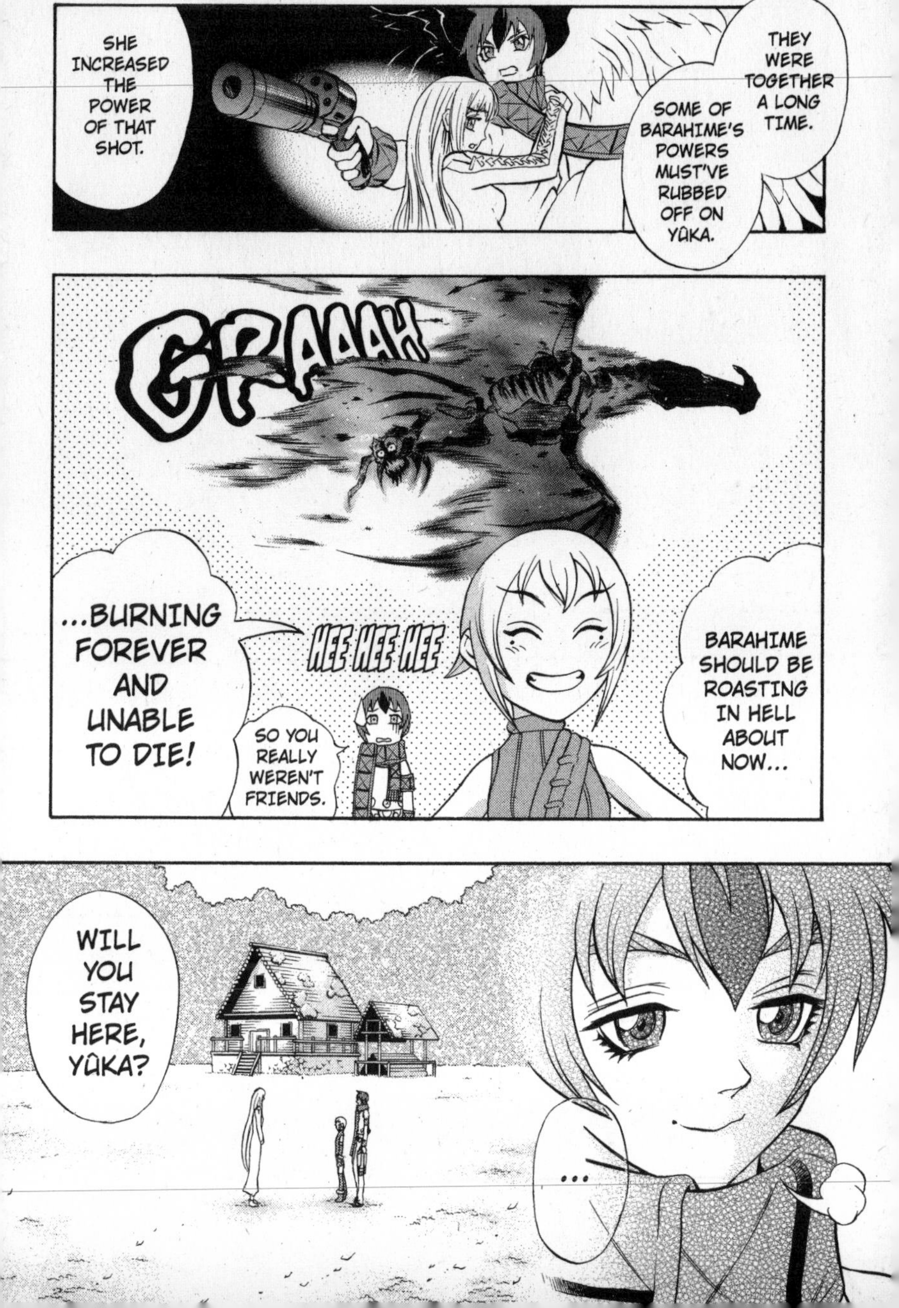
THEY WERE TOGETHER A LONG TIME.
SOME OF BARAHIME'S POWERS MUST'VE RUBBED OFF ON YÛKA.
SHE INCREASED THE POWER OF THAT SHOT.
GRAAAH
BARAHIME SHOULD BE ROASTING IN HELL ABOUT NOW...
HEE HEE HEE
...BURNING FOREVER AND UNABLE TO DIE!
SO YOU REALLY WEREN'T FRIENDS.
WILL YOU STAY HERE, YÛKA?
...

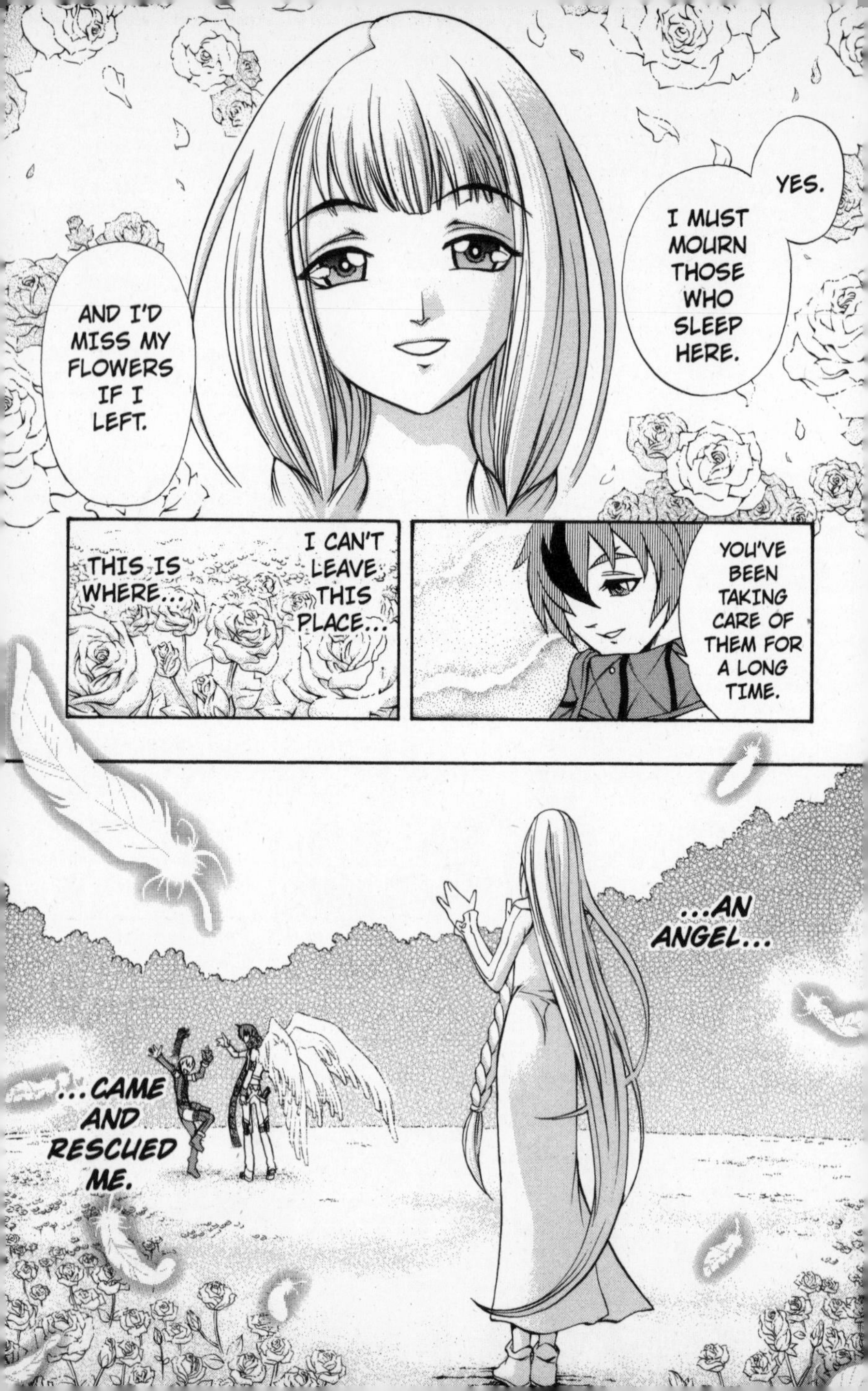
YES.
I MUST MOURN THOSE WHO SLEEP HERE.
AND I'D MISS MY FLOWERS IF I LEFT.
YOU'VE BEEN TAKING CARE OF THEM FOR A LONG TIME.
I CAN'T LEAVE THIS PLACE...
THIS IS WHERE...
...AN ANGEL...
...CAME AND RESCUED ME.

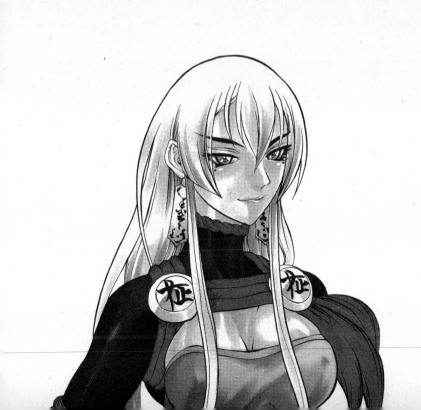

#3 KAON

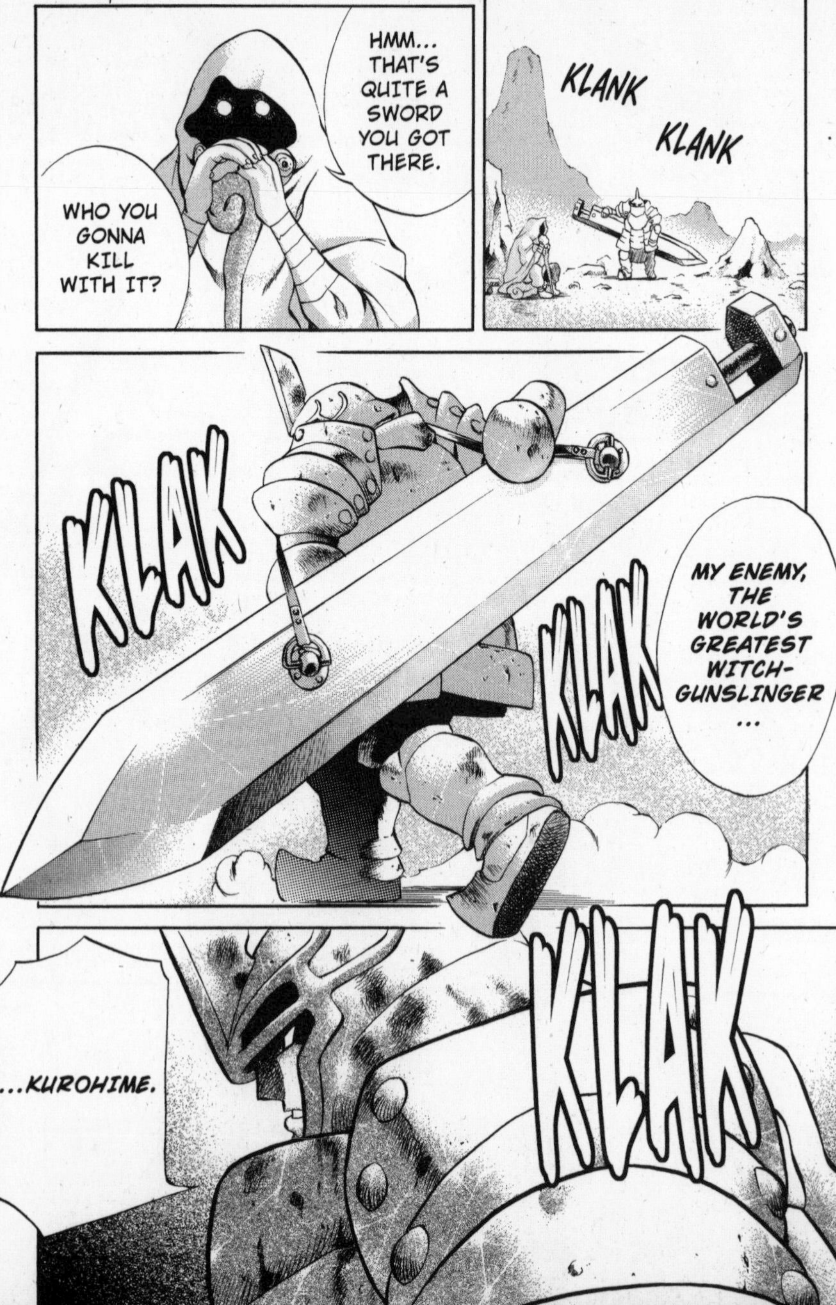
KLANK
KLANK
HMM... THAT'S QUITE A SWORD YOU GOT THERE.
WHO YOU GONNA KILL WITH IT?
MY ENEMY, THE WORLD'S GREATEST WITCH-GUNSLINGER...
KLAK
KLAK
KLAK
...KUROHIME.

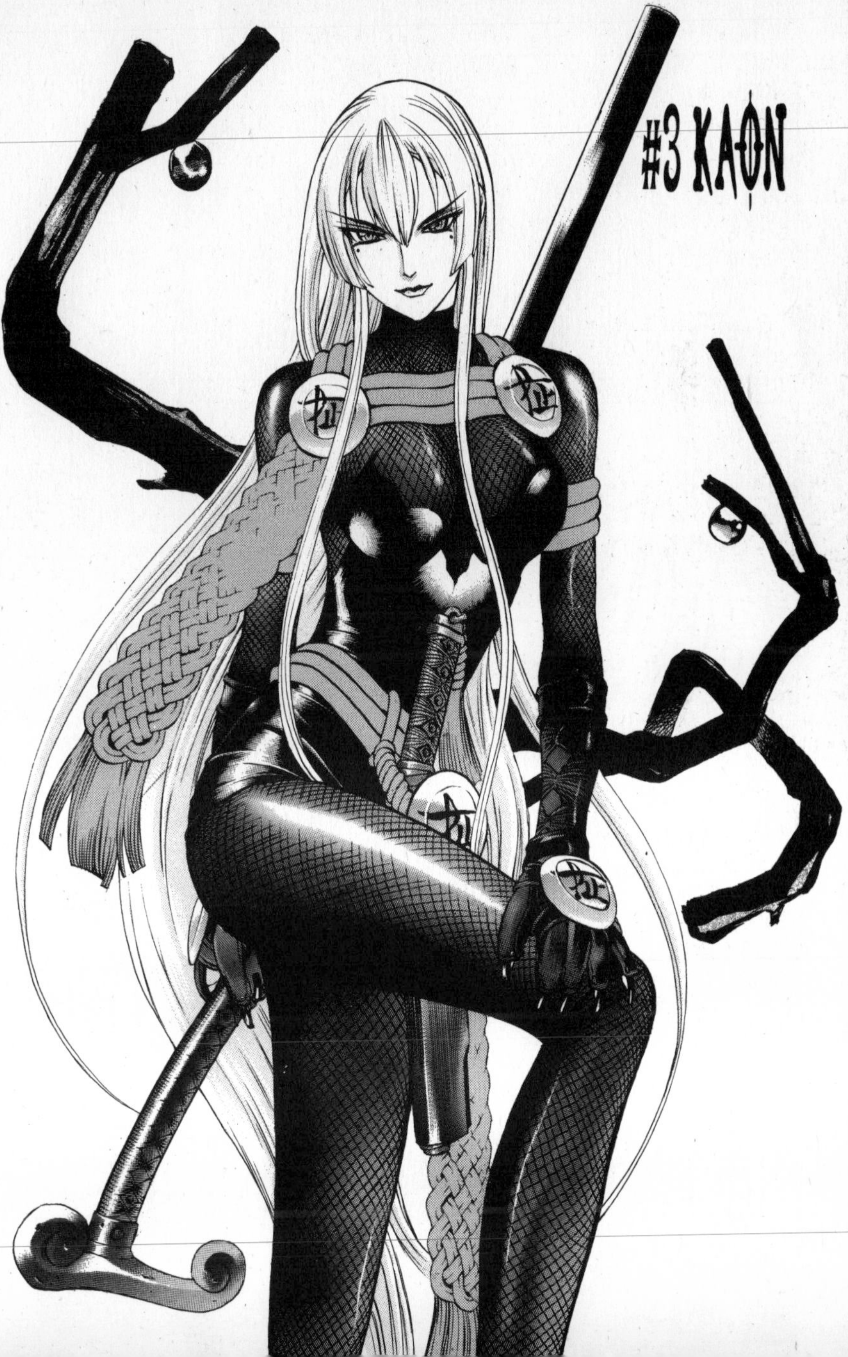
#3 KAON

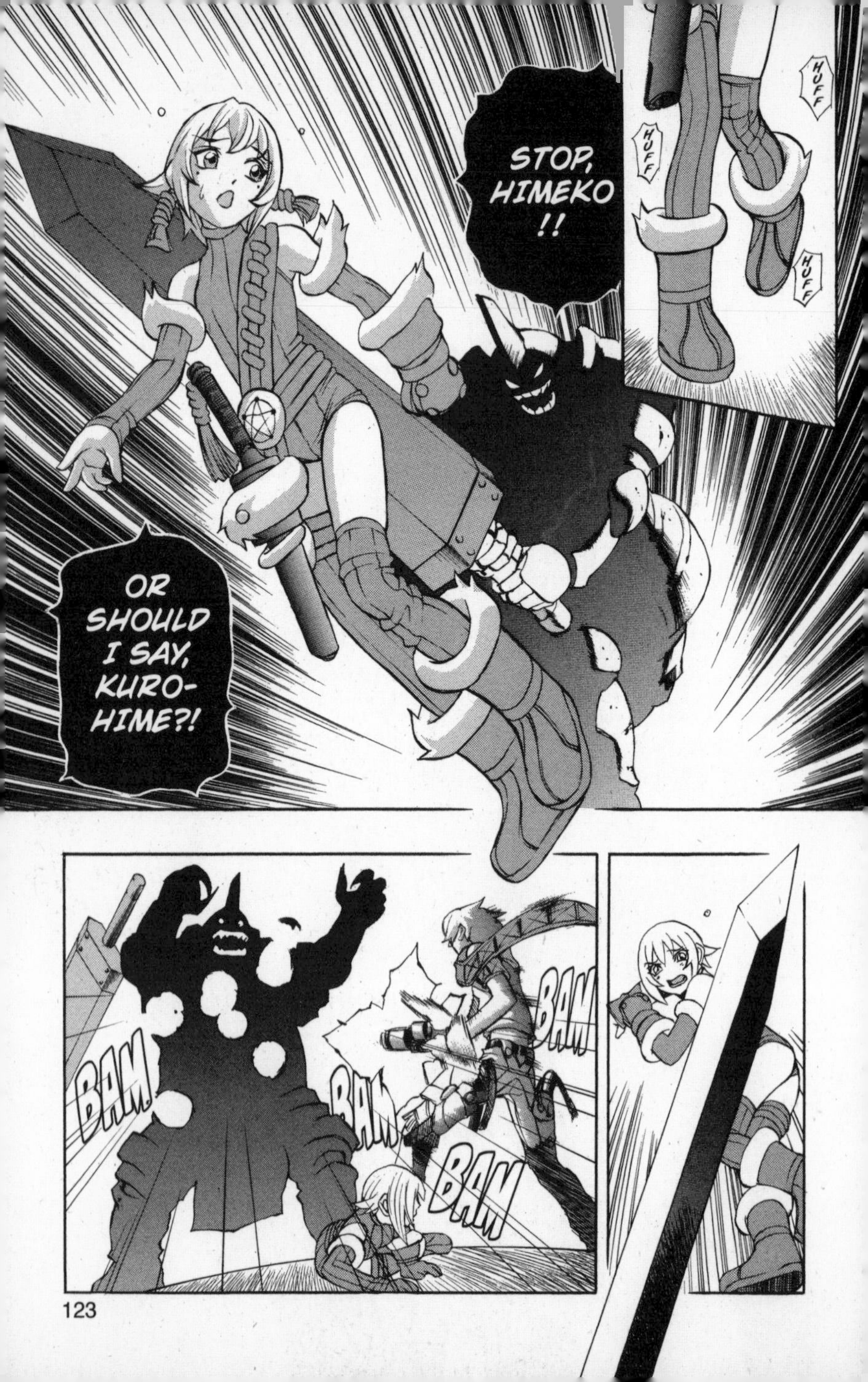
HUFF
HUFF
HUFF
STOP, HIMEKO!!
OR SHOULD I SAY, KURO-HIME?!
BAM
BAM
BAM
BAM

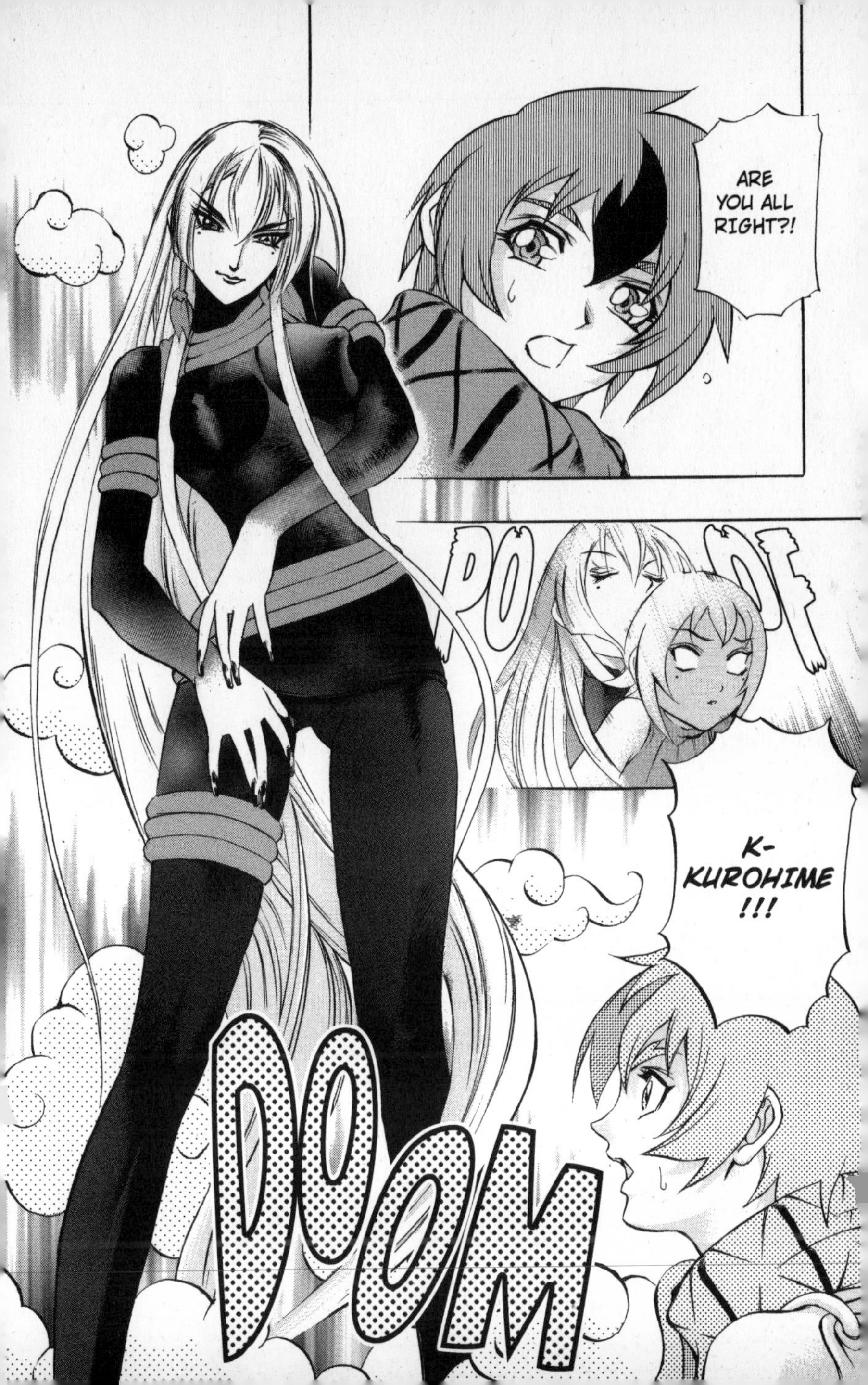
ARE YOU ALL RIGHT?!
POOF
K-KUROHIME!!!
DOOM

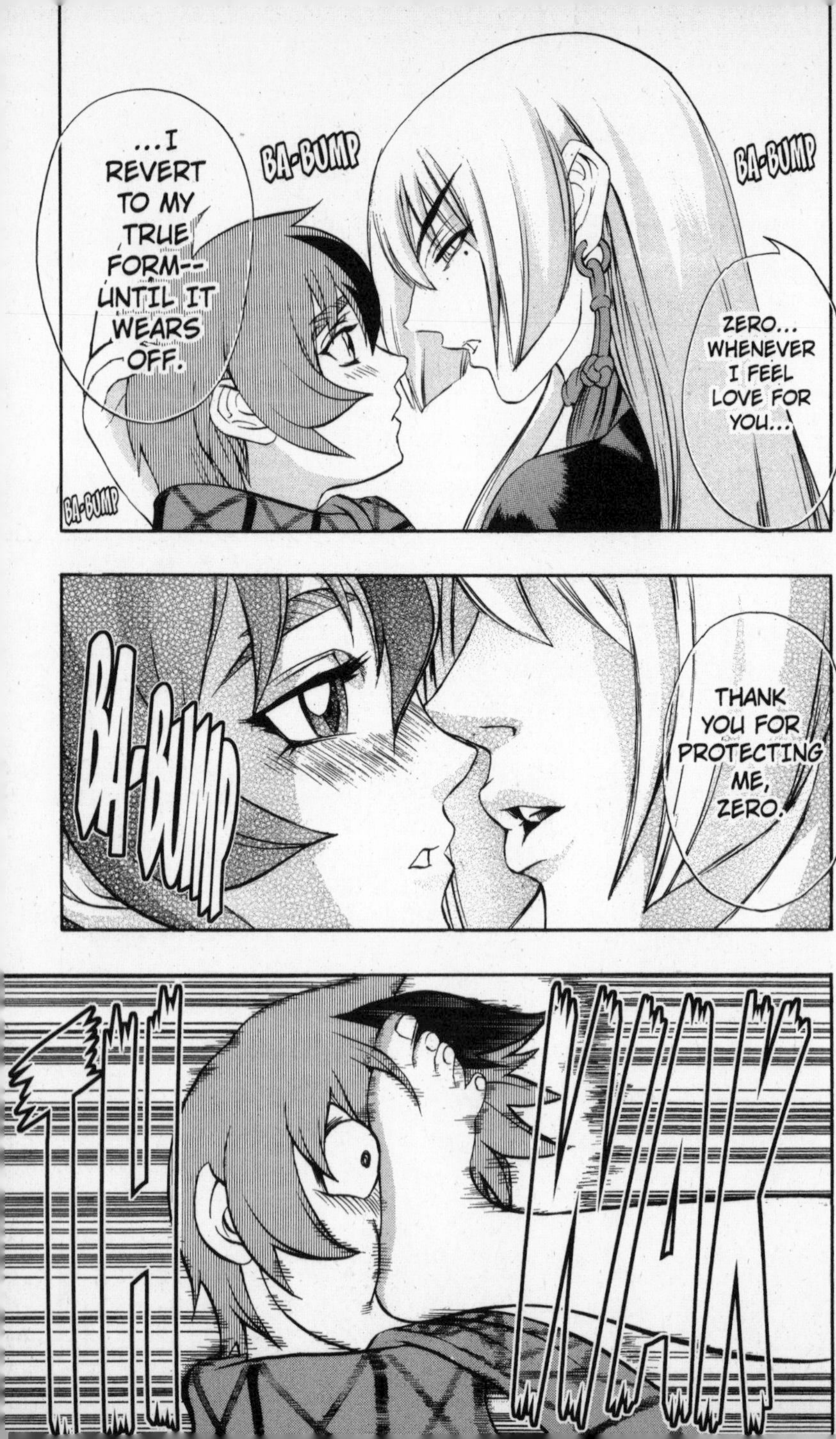
BA-BUMP
ZERO... WHENEVER I FEEL LOVE FOR YOU...
BA-BUMP
...I REVERT TO MY TRUE FORM--UNTIL IT WEARS OFF.
BA-BUMP
THANK YOU FOR PROTECTING ME, ZERO.
BA-BUMP
THWACK

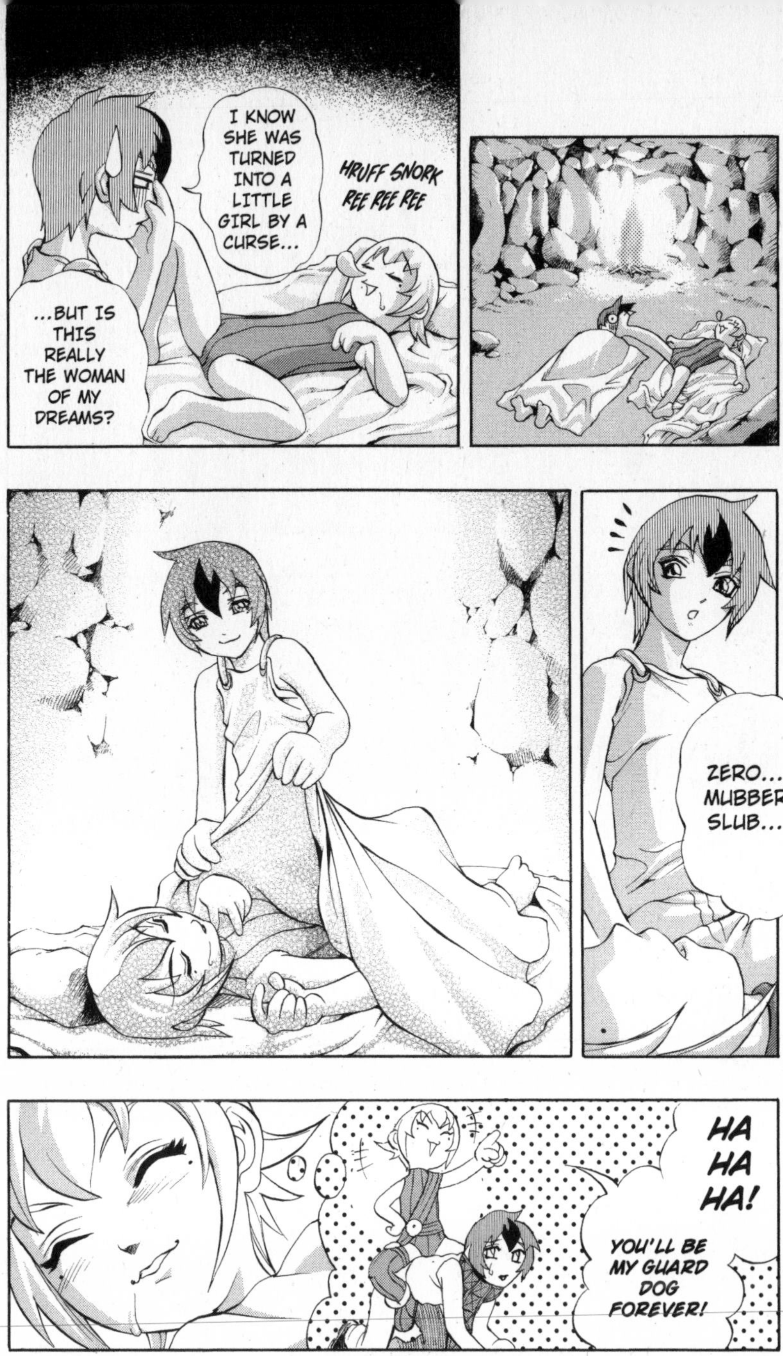
I KNOW SHE WAS TURNED INTO A LITTLE GIRL BY A CURSE...
HRUFF SNORK REE REE REE
...BUT IS THIS REALLY THE WOMAN OF MY DREAMS?
ZERO... MUBBER SLUB...
HA HA HA!
YOU'LL BE MY GUARD DOG FOREVER!

READ THIS WAY

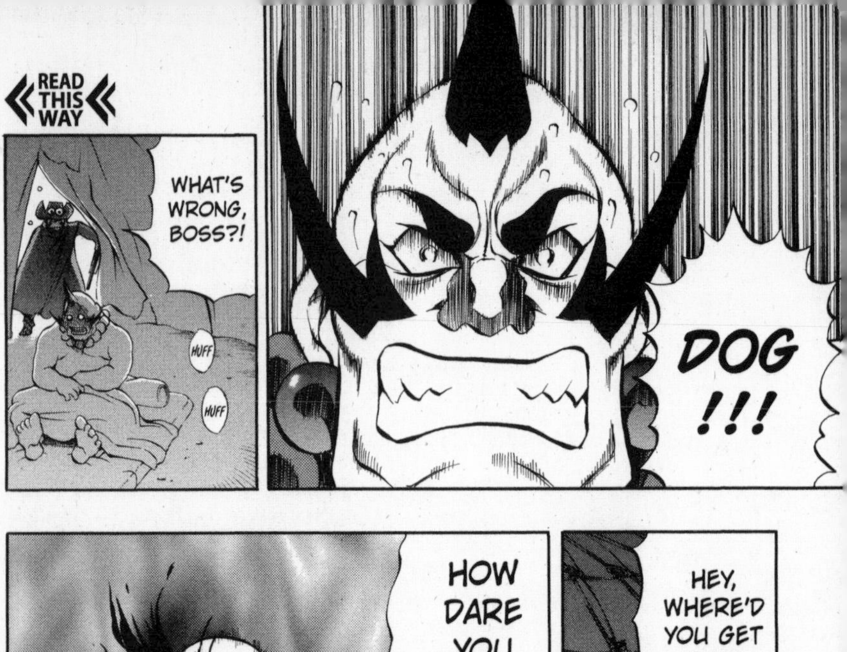
DOG!!!
WHAT'S WRONG, BOSS?!
HUFF
HUFF
HEY, WHERE'D YOU GET THAT BRAND?!
TWITCH
HOW DARE YOU LOOK AT IT!!

* TOP KANJI IN BRAND READS "DOG," BOTTOM READS "KUROHIME."

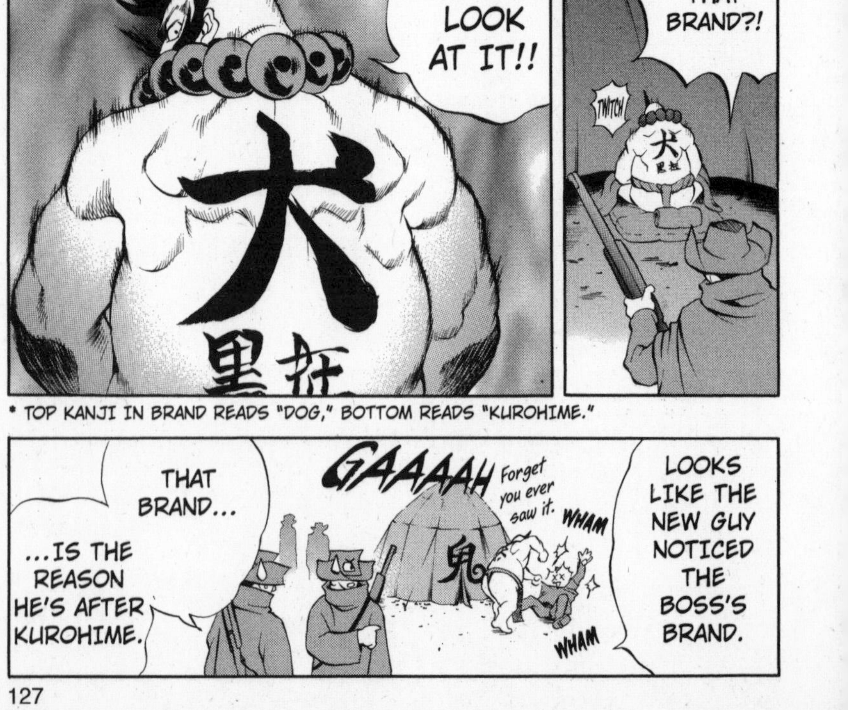
LOOKS LIKE THE NEW GUY NOTICED THE BOSS'S BRAND.
WHAM
Forget you ever saw it.
GAAAAH
WHAM
THAT BRAND...
...IS THE REASON HE'S AFTER KUROHIME.

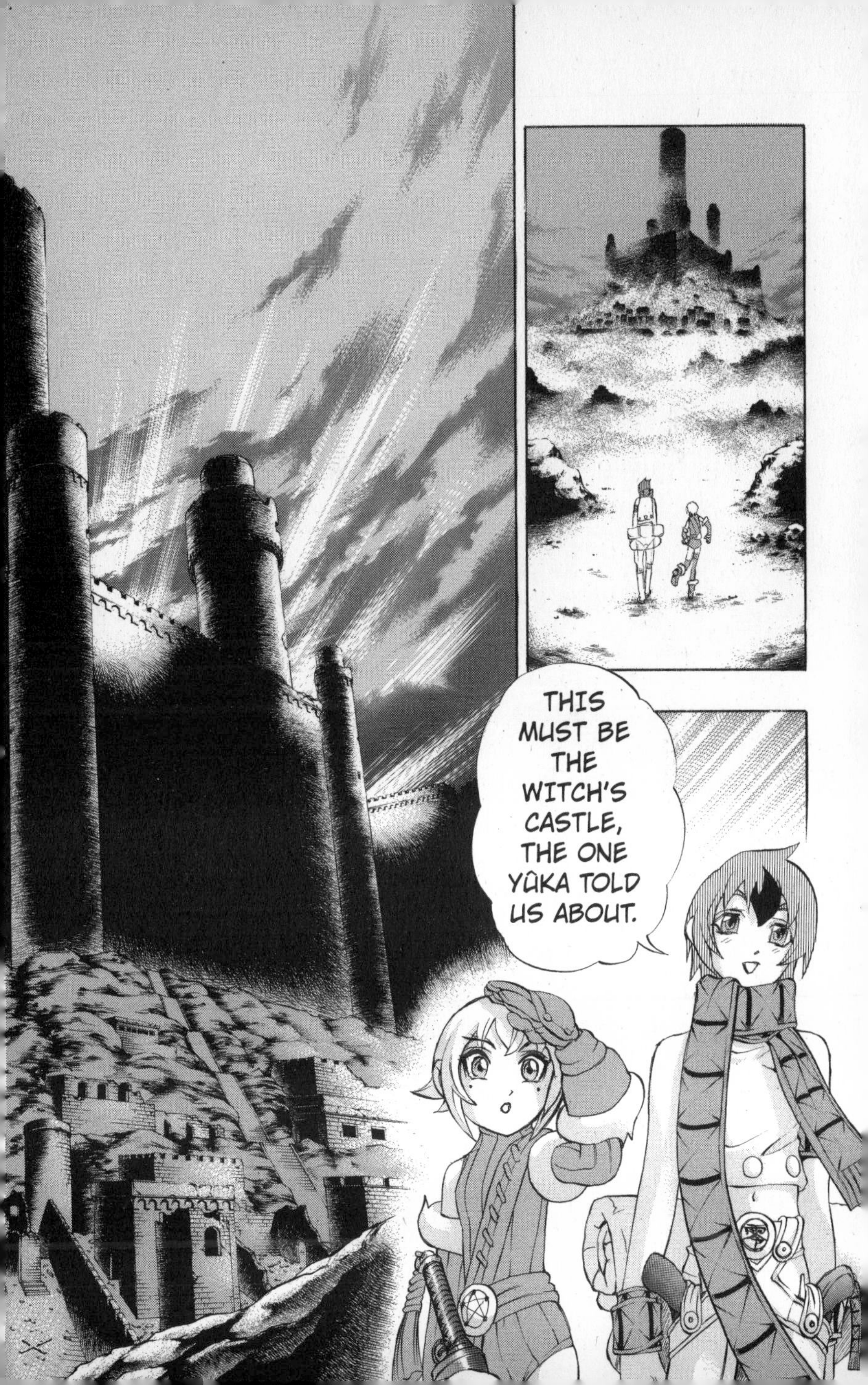
THIS MUST BE THE WITCH'S CASTLE, THE ONE YÛKA TOLD US ABOUT.

READ THIS WAY

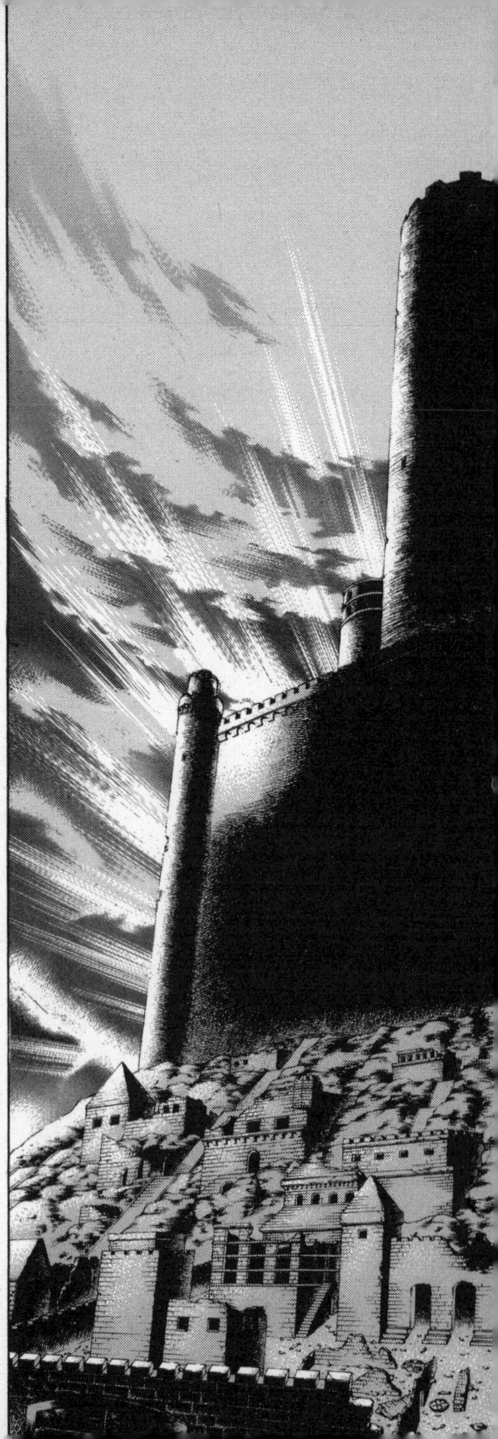

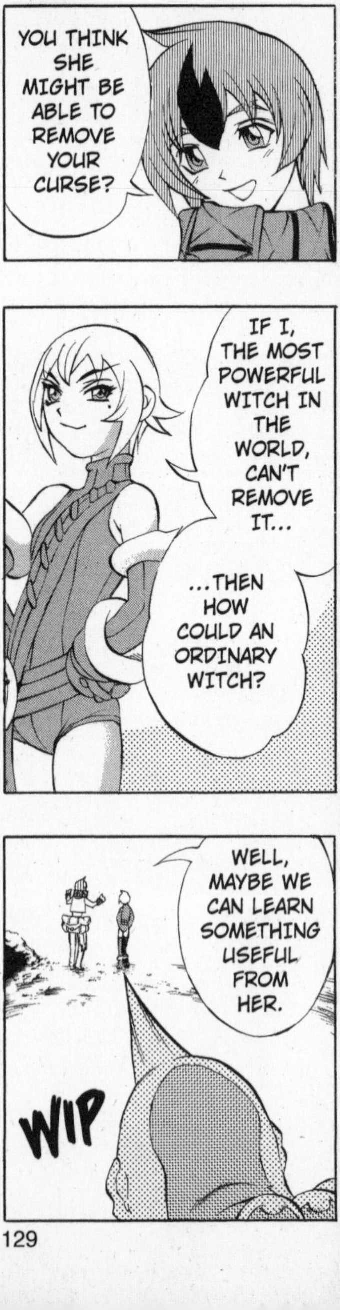
YOU THINK SHE MIGHT BE ABLE TO REMOVE YOUR CURSE?
IF I, THE MOST POWERFUL WITCH IN THE WORLD, CAN'T REMOVE IT...
...THEN HOW COULD AN ORDINARY WITCH?
WELL, MAYBE WE CAN LEARN SOMETHING USEFUL FROM HER.
WIP

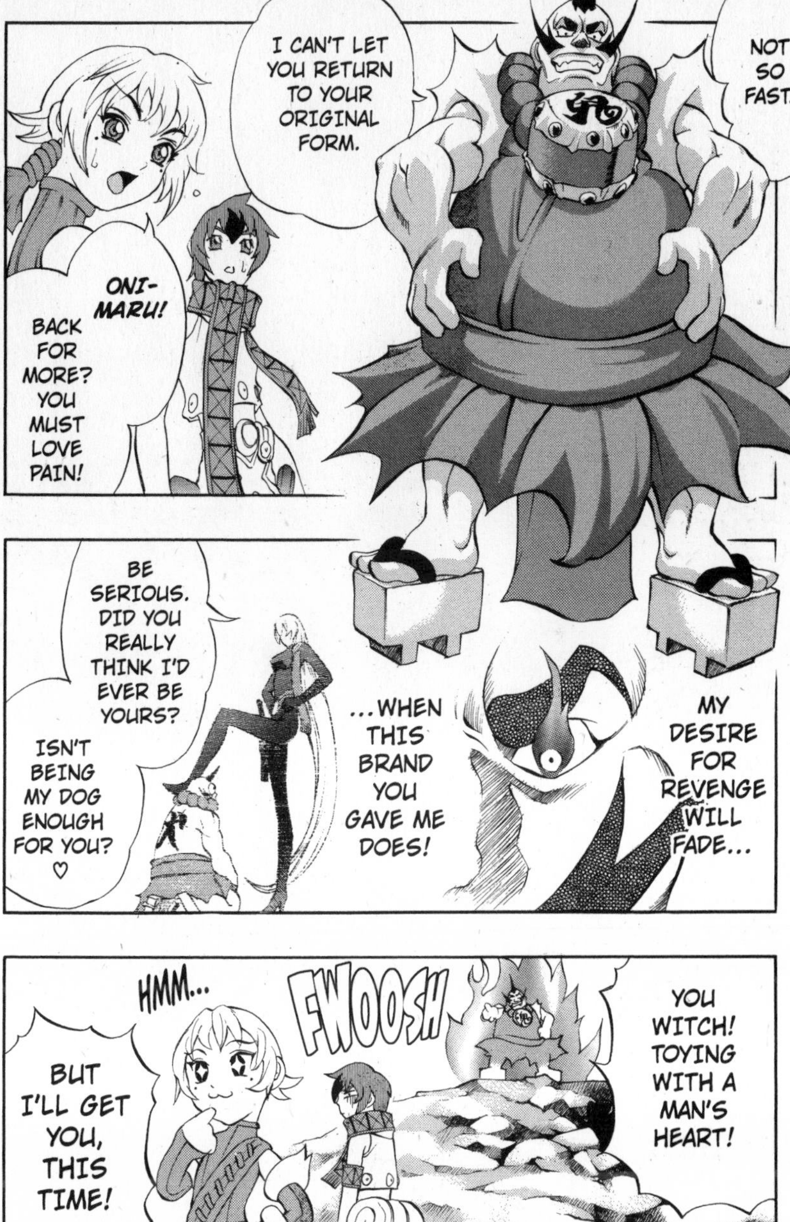
NOT SO FAST.
I CAN'T LET YOU RETURN TO YOUR ORIGINAL FORM.
ONI-MARU!
BACK FOR MORE? YOU MUST LOVE PAIN!
MY DESIRE FOR REVENGE WILL FADE...
...WHEN THIS BRAND YOU GAVE ME DOES!
BE SERIOUS. DID YOU REALLY THINK I'D EVER BE YOURS?
ISN'T BEING MY DOG ENOUGH FOR YOU? ♡
YOU WITCH! TOYING WITH A MAN'S HEART!
FWOOSH
HMM...
BUT I'LL GET YOU, THIS TIME!

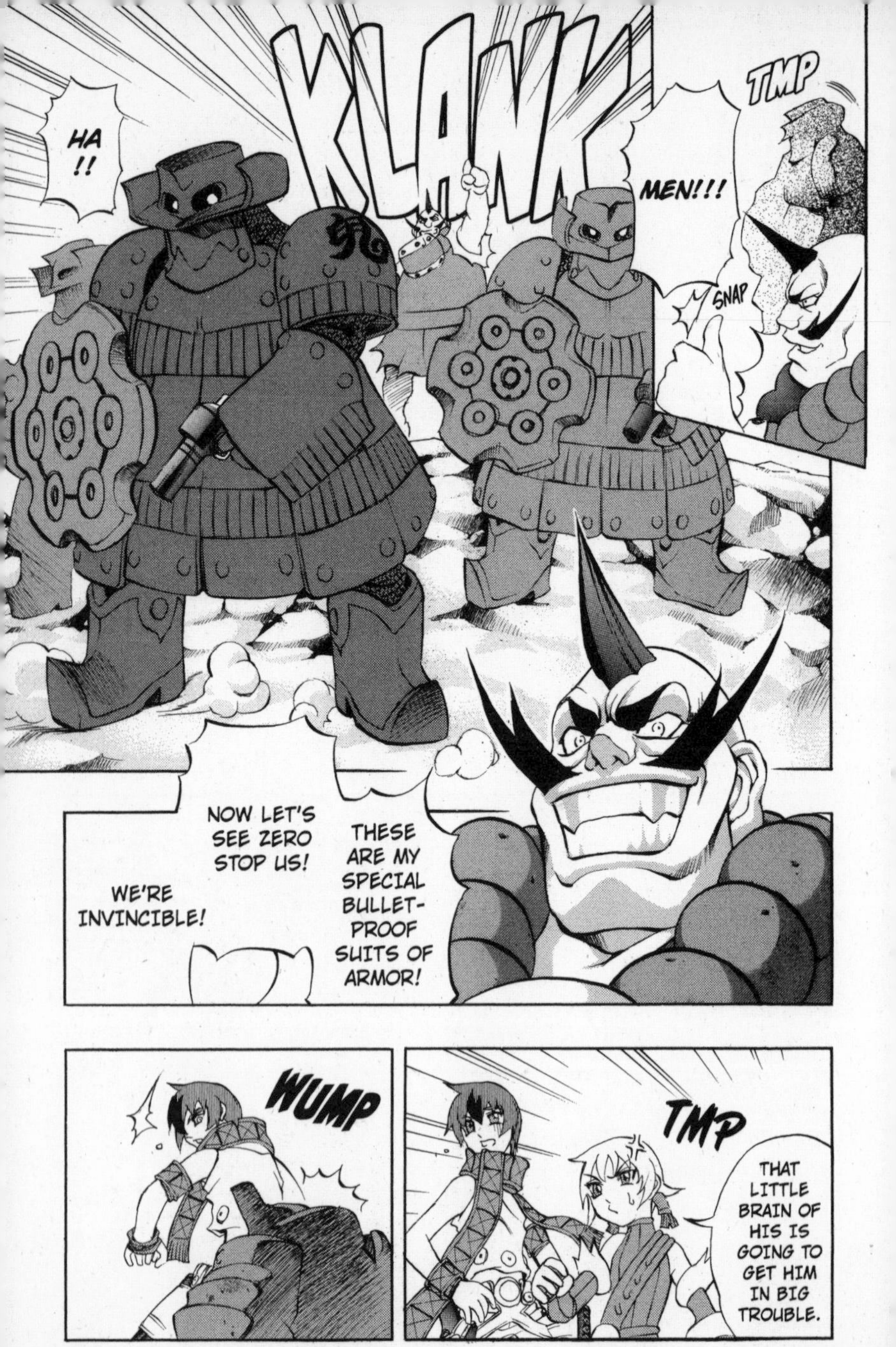
TMP
MEN!!!
SNAP
KLANK
HA!!
THESE ARE MY SPECIAL BULLET-PROOF SUITS OF ARMOR!
NOW LET'S SEE ZERO STOP US!
WE'RE INVINCIBLE!
TMP
THAT LITTLE BRAIN OF HIS IS GOING TO GET HIM IN BIG TROUBLE.
WUMP

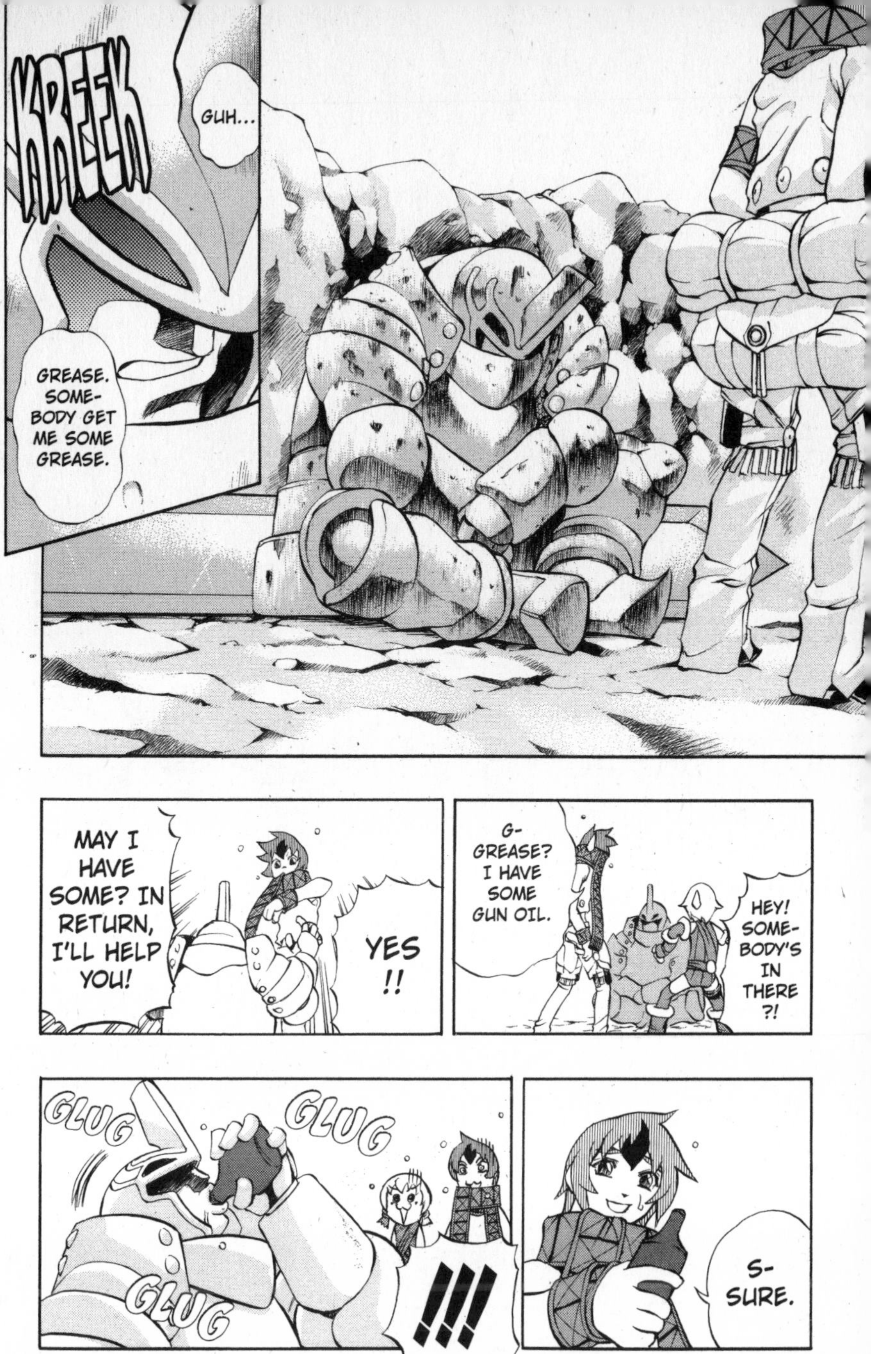
GUH...
KREEK
GREASE. SOME-BODY GET ME SOME GREASE.
HEY! SOME-BODY'S IN THERE?!
G-GREASE? I HAVE SOME GUN OIL.
YES!!
MAY I HAVE SOME? IN RETURN, I'LL HELP YOU!
S-SURE.
!!!
GLUG
GLUG
GLUG

READ THIS WAY

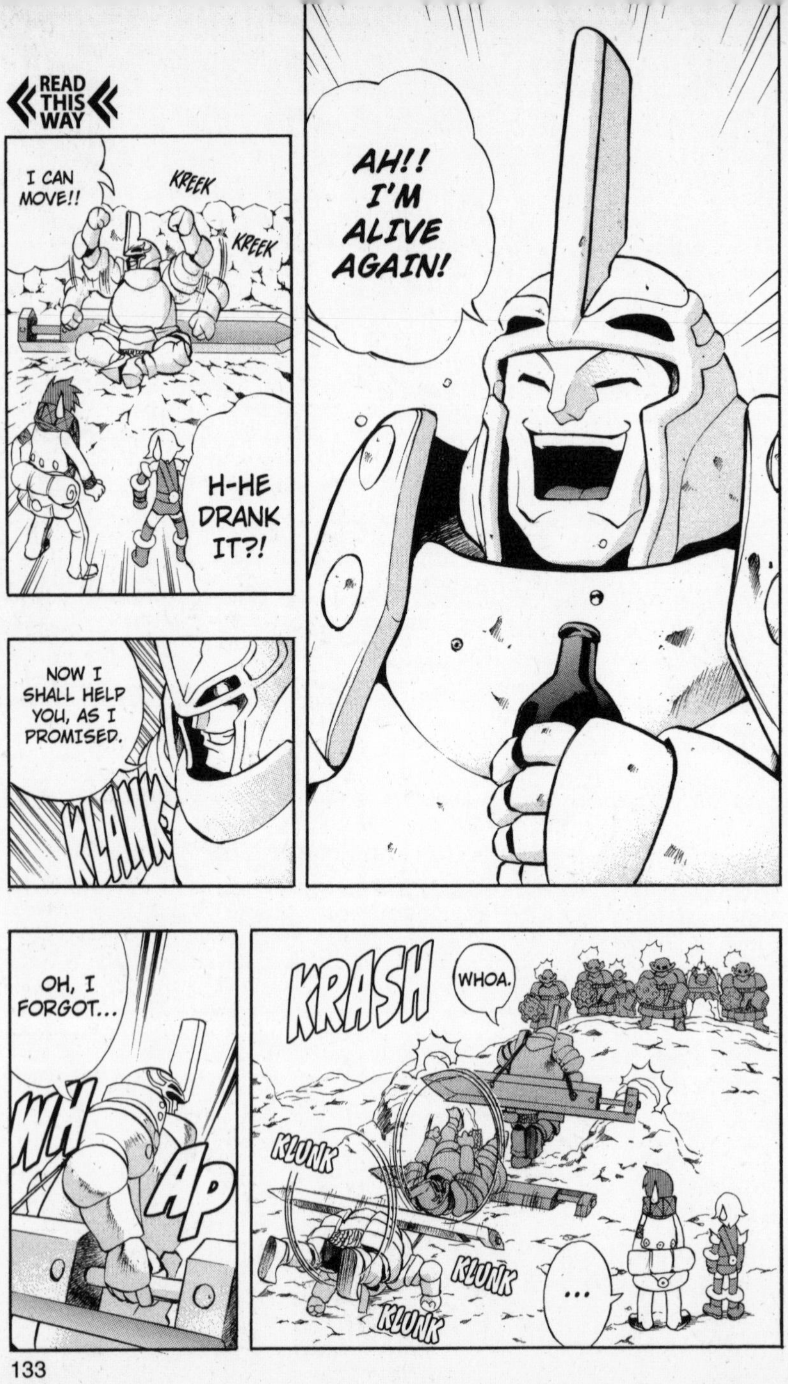
AH!! I'M ALIVE AGAIN!
I CAN MOVE!!
KREEK
KREEK
H-HE DRANK IT?!
NOW I SHALL HELP YOU, AS I PROMISED.
KLANK
KRASH
WHOA.
KLUNK
KLUNK
KLUNK
...
OH, I FORGOT...
WHAP

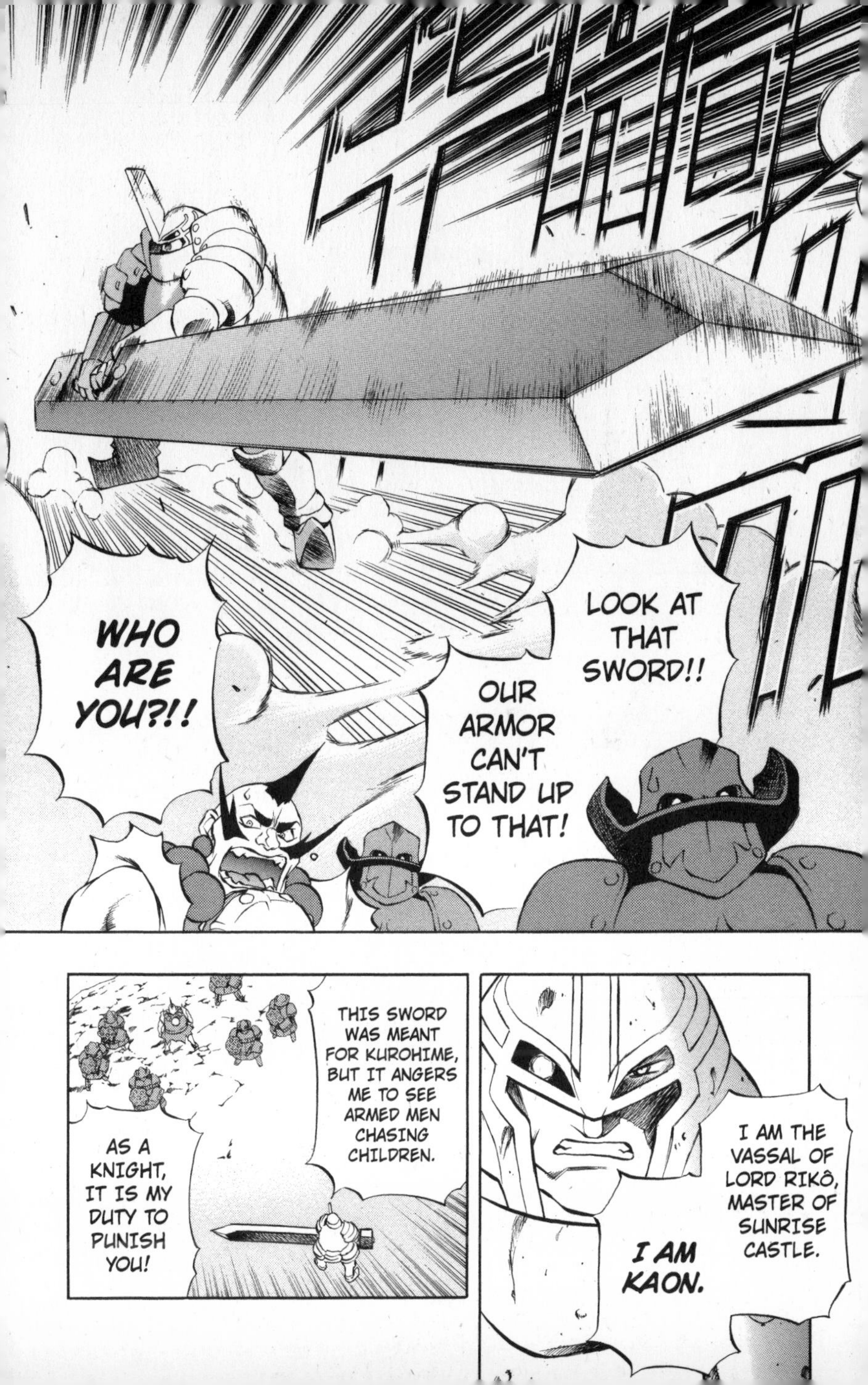
LOOK AT THAT SWORD!!
OUR ARMOR CAN'T STAND UP TO THAT!
WHO ARE YOU?!!
I AM THE VASSAL OF LORD RIKÔ, MASTER OF SUNRISE CASTLE.
I AM KAON.
THIS SWORD WAS MEANT FOR KUROHIME, BUT IT ANGERS ME TO SEE ARMED MEN CHASING CHILDREN.
AS A KNIGHT, IT IS MY DUTY TO PUNISH YOU!

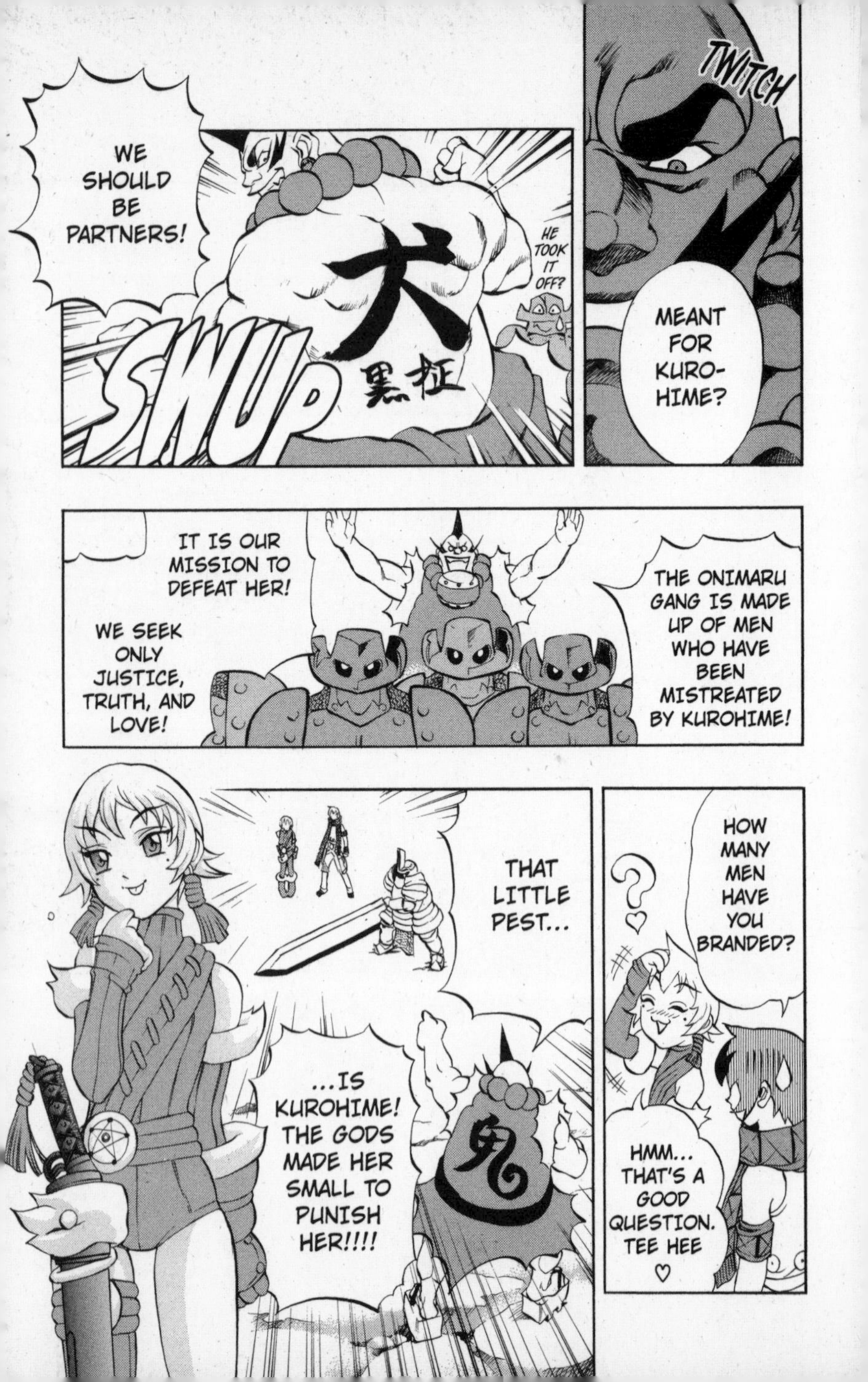
TWITCH
MEANT FOR KURO-HIME?
WE SHOULD BE PARTNERS!
大
SWUP
HE TOOK IT OFF?
THE ONIMARU GANG IS MADE UP OF MEN WHO HAVE BEEN MISTREATED BY KUROHIME!
IT IS OUR MISSION TO DEFEAT HER!
WE SEEK ONLY JUSTICE, TRUTH, AND LOVE!
HOW MANY MEN HAVE YOU BRANDED?
HMM... THAT'S A GOOD QUESTION. TEE HEE ♡
THAT LITTLE PEST...
...IS KUROHIME! THE GODS MADE HER SMALL TO PUNISH HER!!!!
鬼

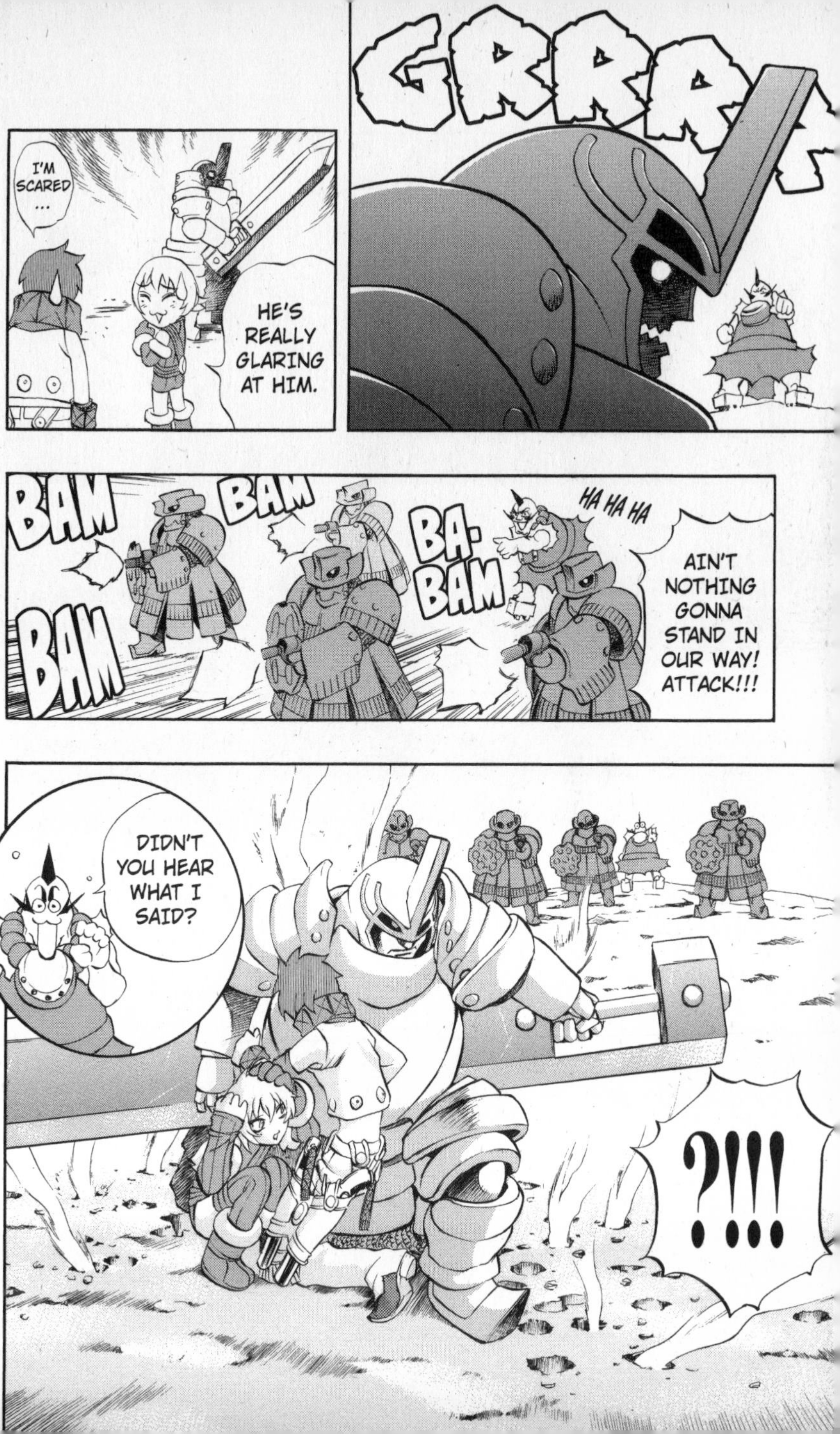
GRR
HE'S REALLY GLARING AT HIM.
I'M SCARED...
HA HA HA
AIN'T NOTHING GONNA STAND IN OUR WAY! ATTACK!!!
BA-BAM
BAM
BAM
BAM
?!!!
DIDN'T YOU HEAR WHAT I SAID?

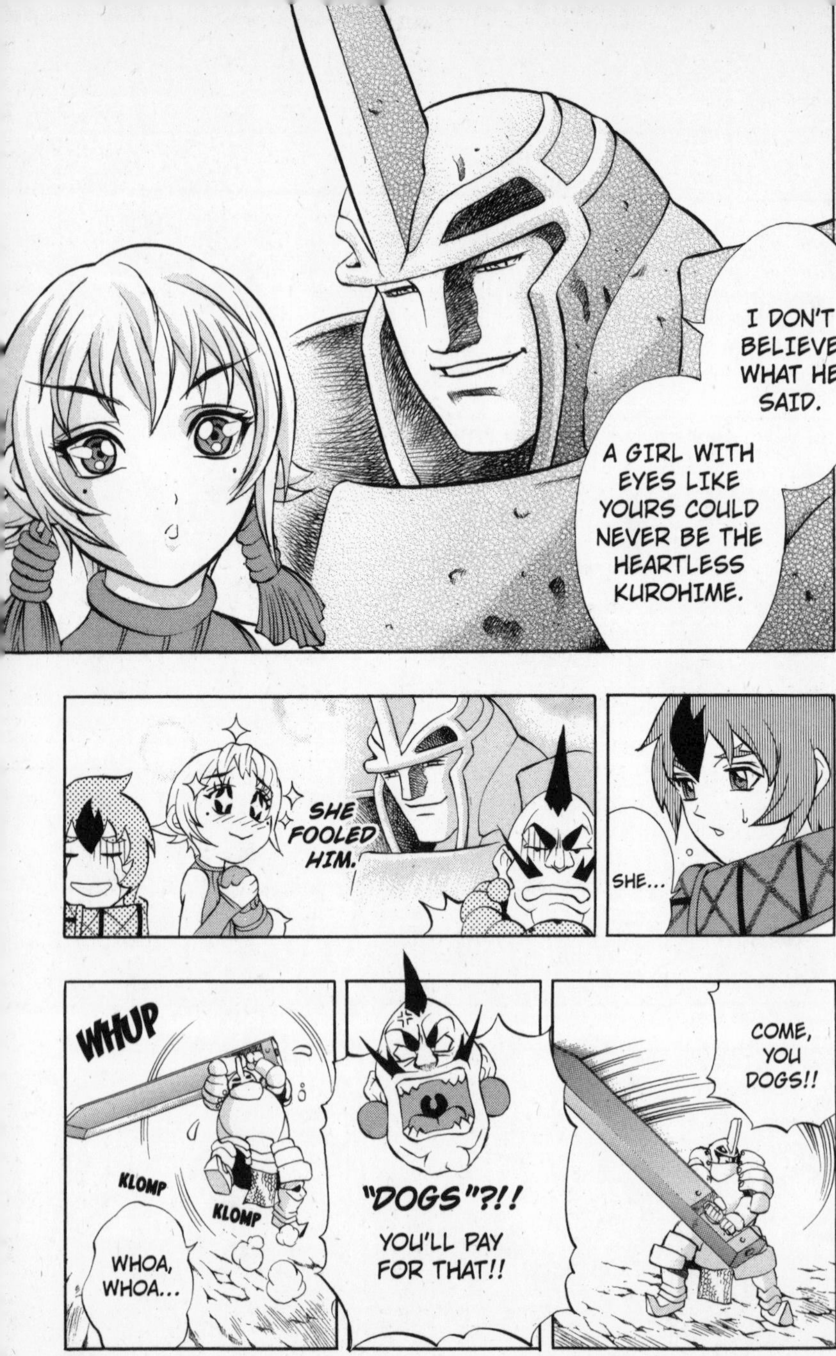
I DON'T BELIEVE WHAT HE SAID.
A GIRL WITH EYES LIKE YOURS COULD NEVER BE THE HEARTLESS KUROHIME.
SHE...
SHE FOOLED HIM.
COME, YOU DOGS!!
"DOGS"?!!
YOU'LL PAY FOR THAT!!
WHUP
KLOMP
KLOMP
WHOA, WHOA...

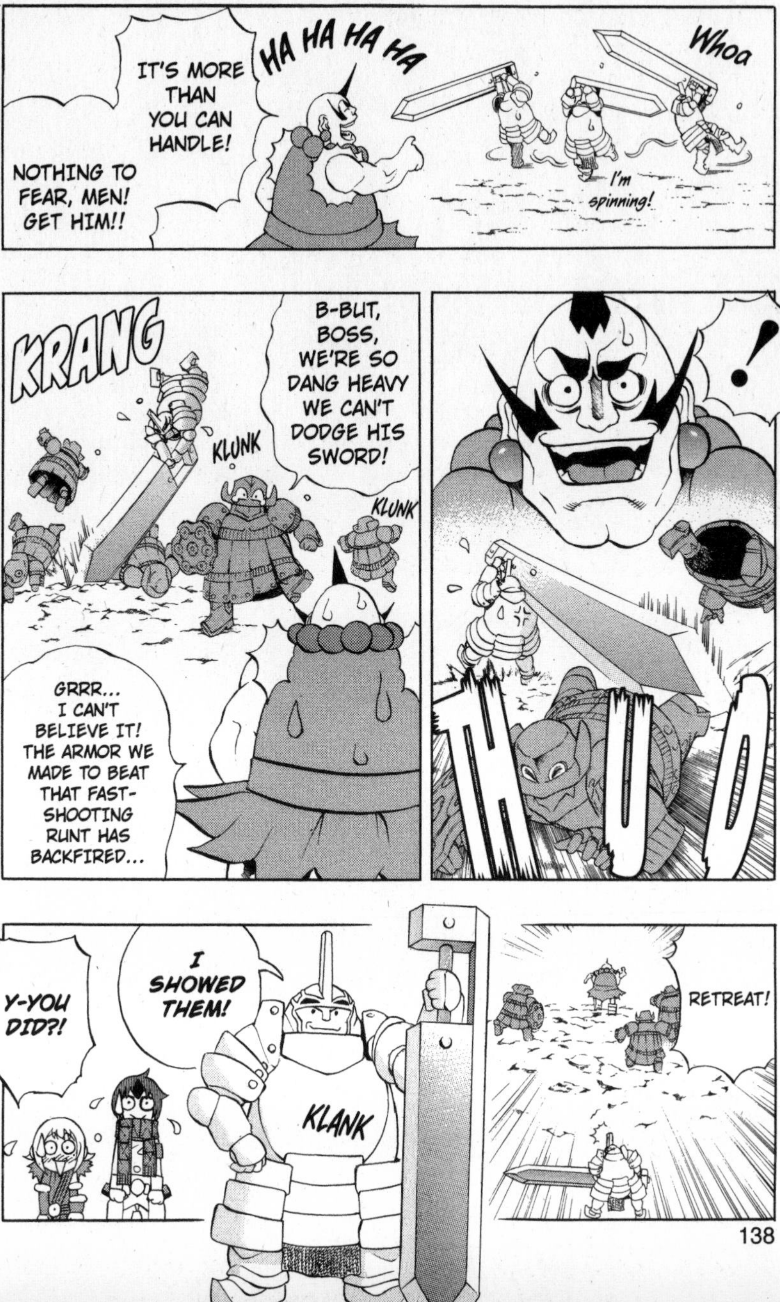
Whoa
HA HA HA HA
IT'S MORE THAN YOU CAN HANDLE!
I'm spinning!
NOTHING TO FEAR, MEN! GET HIM!!
!
THUD
B-BUT, BOSS, WE'RE SO DANG HEAVY WE CAN'T DODGE HIS SWORD!
KRANG
KLUNK
KLUNK
GRRR... I CAN'T BELIEVE IT! THE ARMOR WE MADE TO BEAT THAT FAST-SHOOTING RUNT HAS BACKFIRED...
RETREAT!
I SHOWED THEM!
Y-YOU DID?!
KLANK

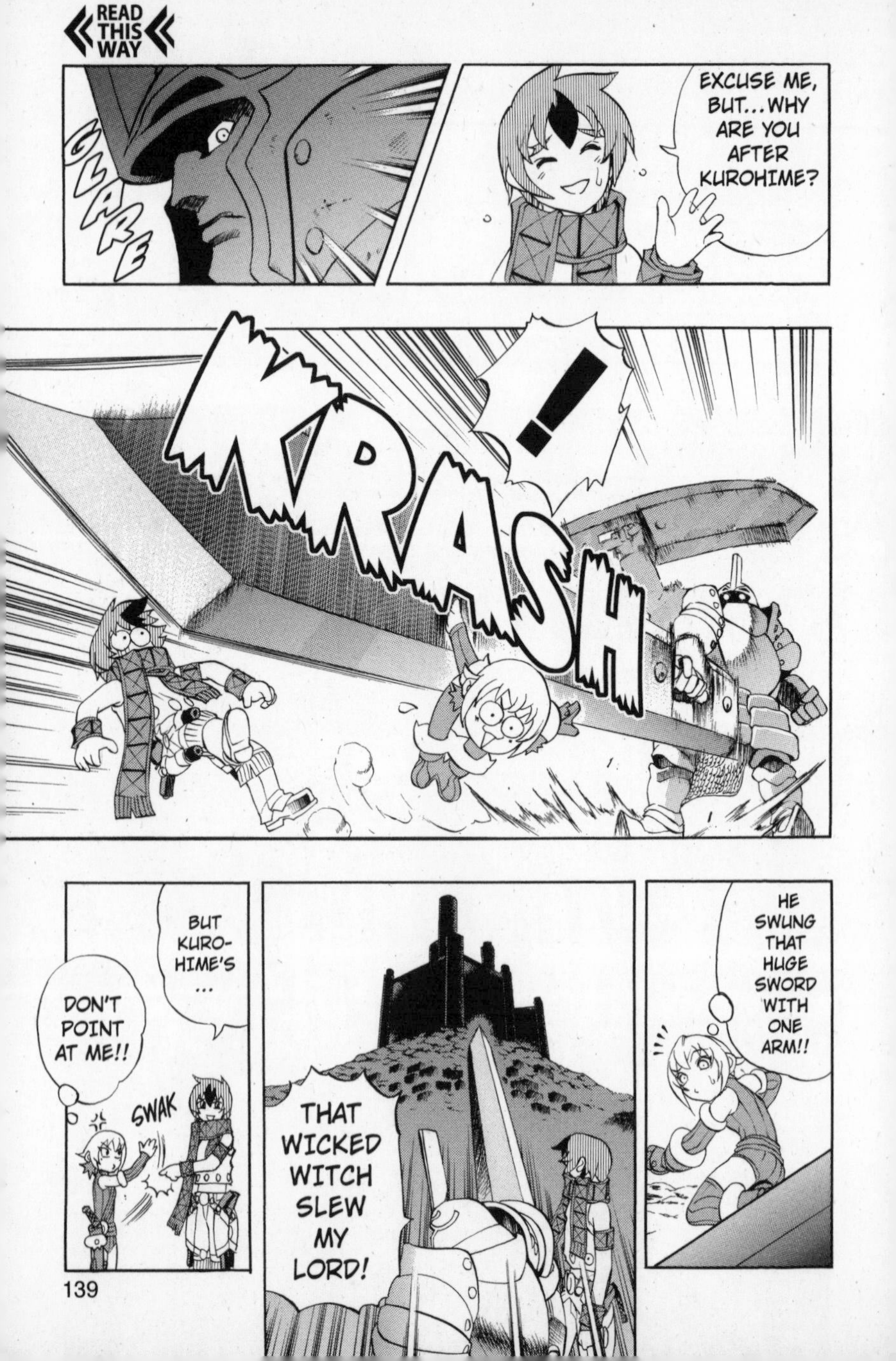
READ THIS WAY
EXCUSE ME, BUT...WHY ARE YOU AFTER KUROHIME?
GLARE
!
KRASH
HE SWUNG THAT HUGE SWORD WITH ONE ARM!!
THAT WICKED WITCH SLEW MY LORD!
BUT KURO-HIME'S ...
DON'T POINT AT ME!!
SWAK

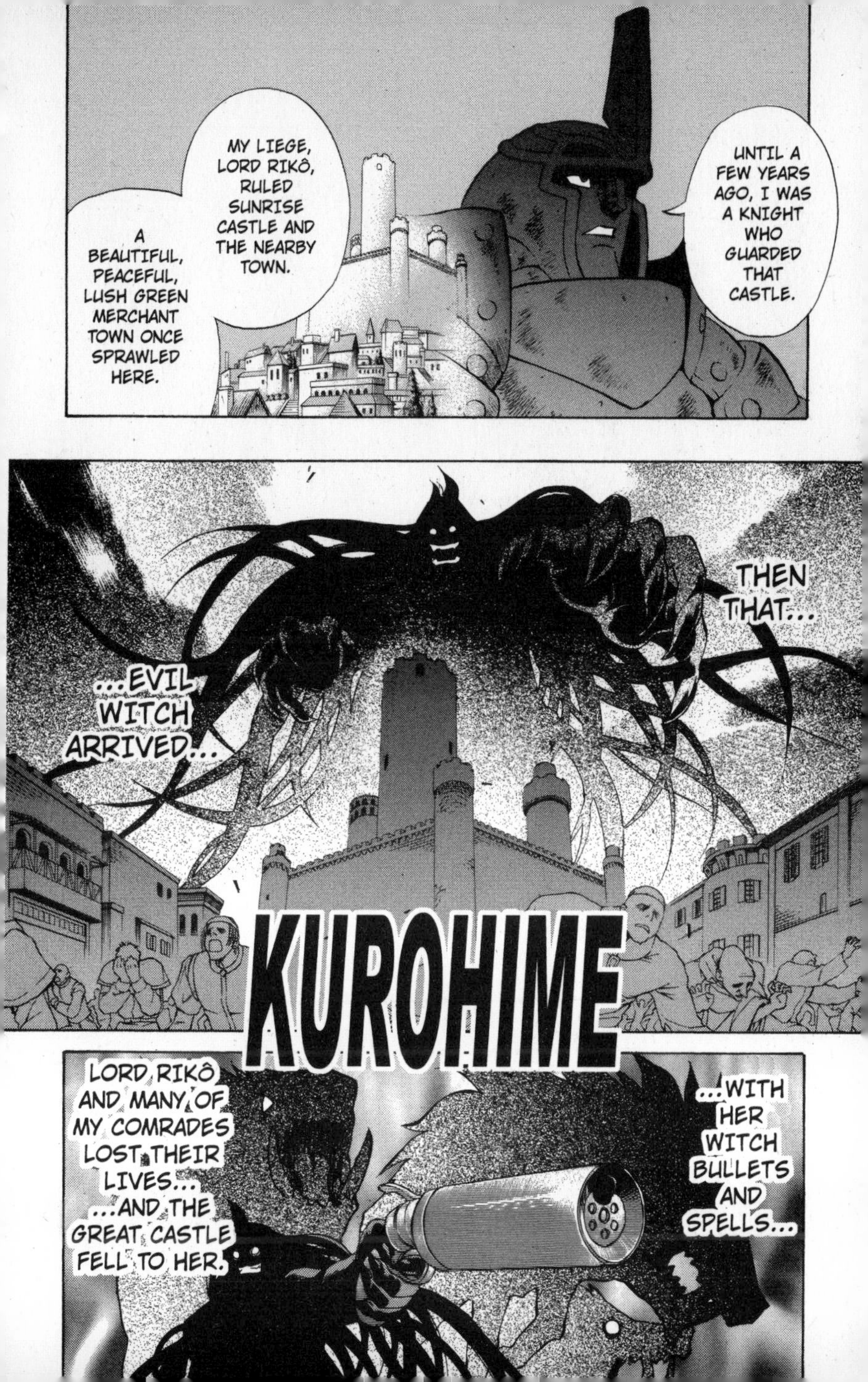
UNTIL A FEW YEARS AGO, I WAS A KNIGHT WHO GUARDED THAT CASTLE.
MY LIEGE, LORD RIKÔ, RULED SUNRISE CASTLE AND THE NEARBY TOWN.
A BEAUTIFUL, PEACEFUL, LUSH GREEN MERCHANT TOWN ONCE SPRAWLED HERE.
THEN THAT...
...EVIL WITCH ARRIVED...
KUROHIME
...WITH HER WITCH BULLETS AND SPELLS...
LORD RIKÔ AND MANY OF MY COMRADES LOST THEIR LIVES...
...AND THE GREAT CASTLE FELL TO HER.

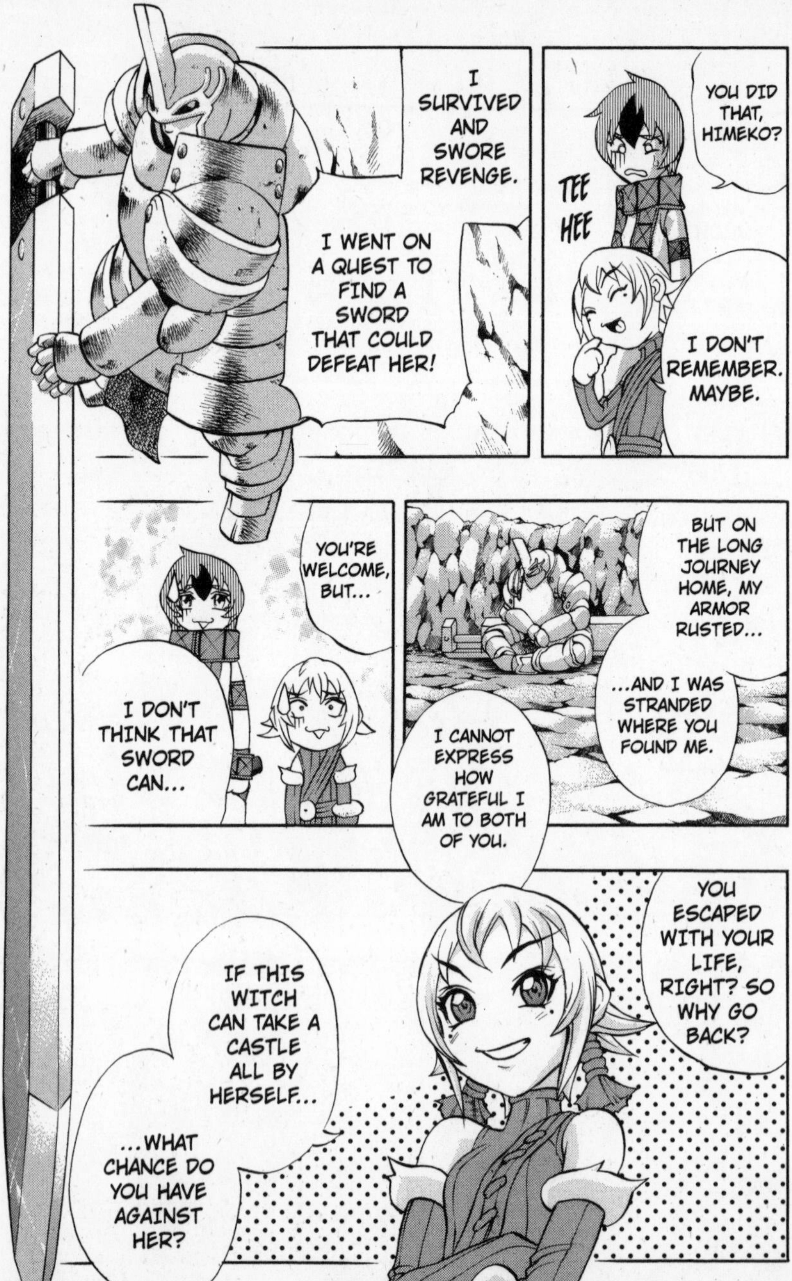
YOU DID THAT, HIMEKO?
TEE HEE
I DON'T REMEMBER. MAYBE.
I SURVIVED AND SWORE REVENGE.
I WENT ON A QUEST TO FIND A SWORD THAT COULD DEFEAT HER!
BUT ON THE LONG JOURNEY HOME, MY ARMOR RUSTED...
...AND I WAS STRANDED WHERE YOU FOUND ME.
I CANNOT EXPRESS HOW GRATEFUL I AM TO BOTH OF YOU.
YOU'RE WELCOME, BUT...
I DON'T THINK THAT SWORD CAN...
YOU ESCAPED WITH YOUR LIFE, RIGHT? SO WHY GO BACK?
IF THIS WITCH CAN TAKE A CASTLE ALL BY HERSELF...
...WHAT CHANCE DO YOU HAVE AGAINST HER?

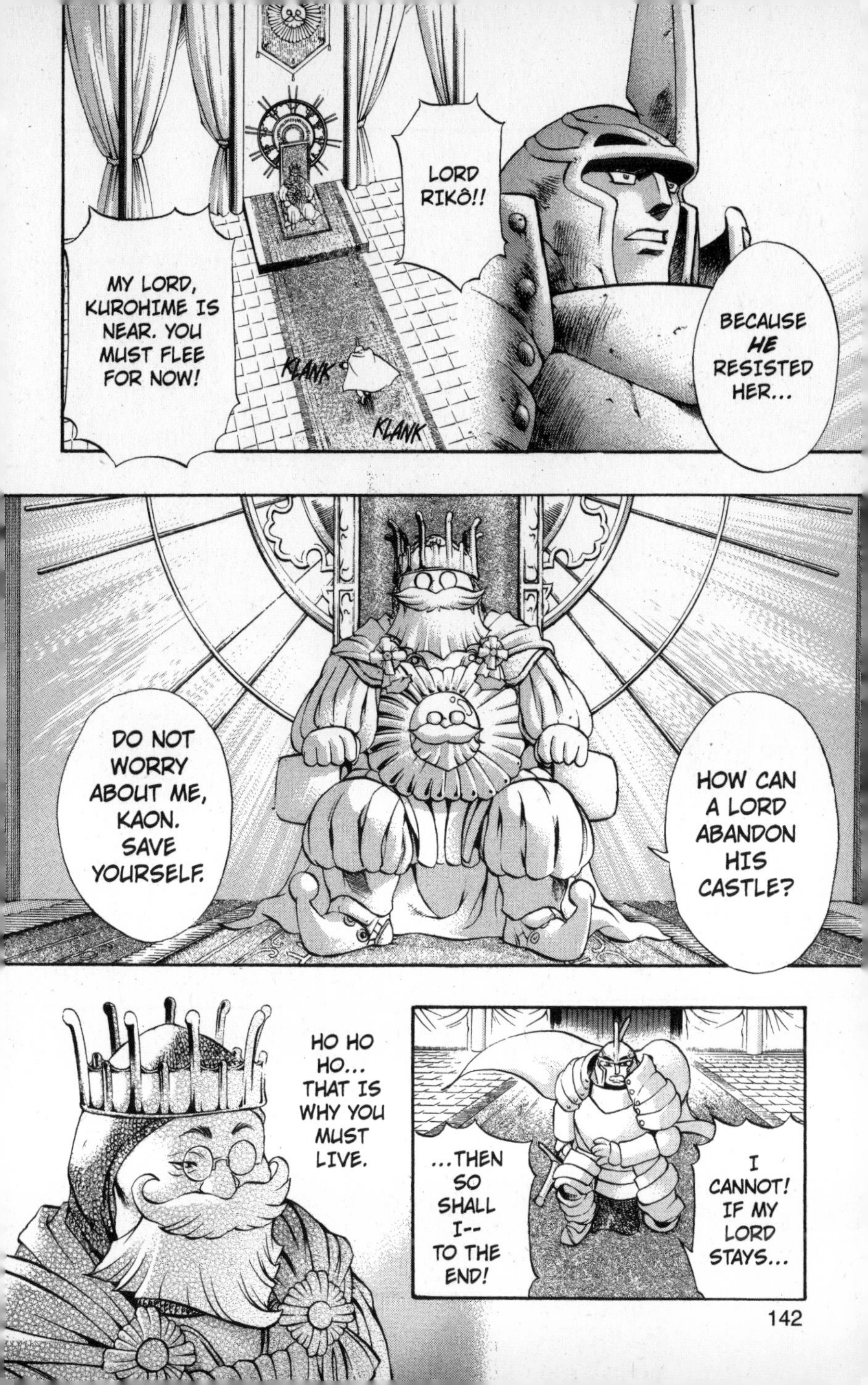
LORD RIKÔ!!
BECAUSE *HE* RESISTED HER...
MY LORD, KUROHIME IS NEAR. YOU MUST FLEE FOR NOW!
KLANK
KLANK
HOW CAN A LORD ABANDON HIS CASTLE?
DO NOT WORRY ABOUT ME, KAON. SAVE YOURSELF.
I CANNOT! IF MY LORD STAYS...
...THEN SO SHALL I-- TO THE END!
HO HO HO... THAT IS WHY YOU MUST LIVE.

READ THIS WAY

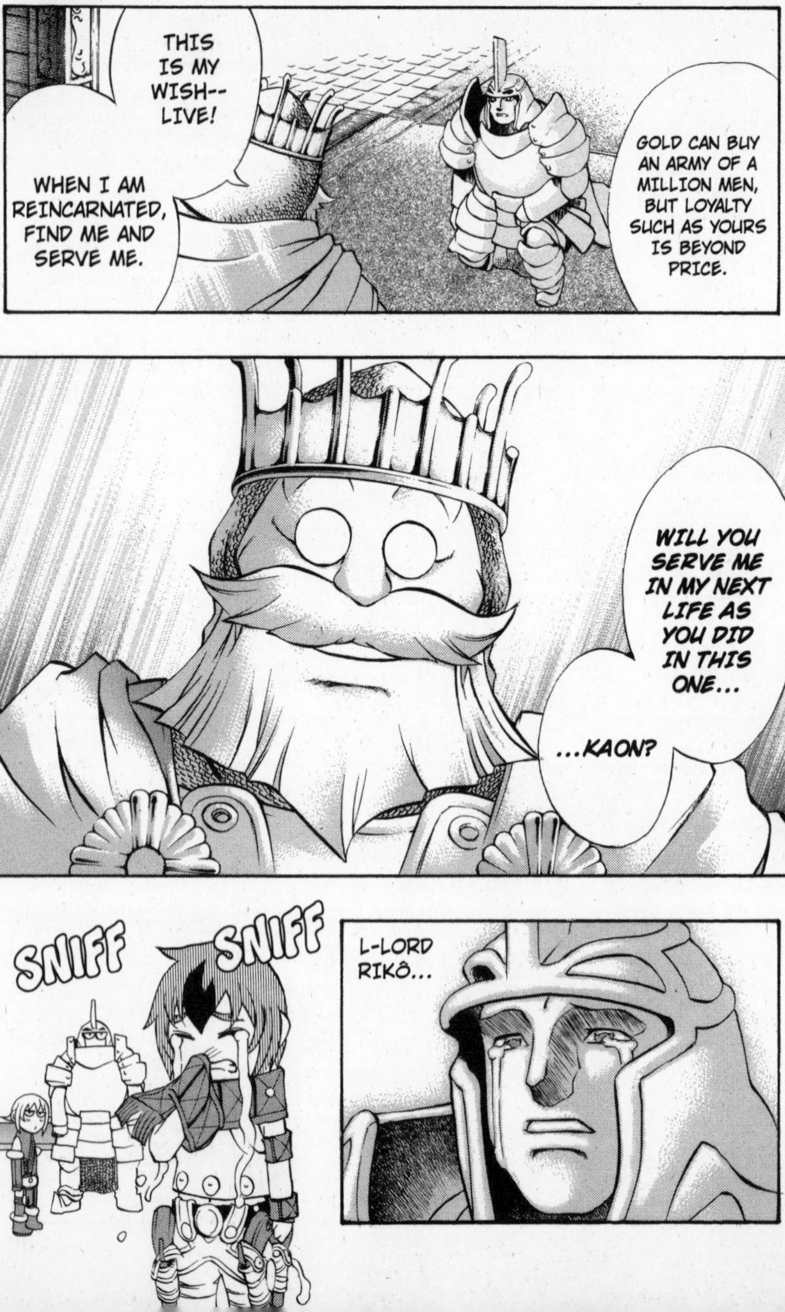
GOLD CAN BUY AN ARMY OF A MILLION MEN, BUT LOYALTY SUCH AS YOURS IS BEYOND PRICE.
THIS IS MY WISH-- LIVE!
WHEN I AM REINCARNATED, FIND ME AND SERVE ME.
WILL YOU SERVE ME IN MY NEXT LIFE AS YOU DID IN THIS ONE...
...KAON?
L-LORD RIKÔ...
SNIFF
SNIFF

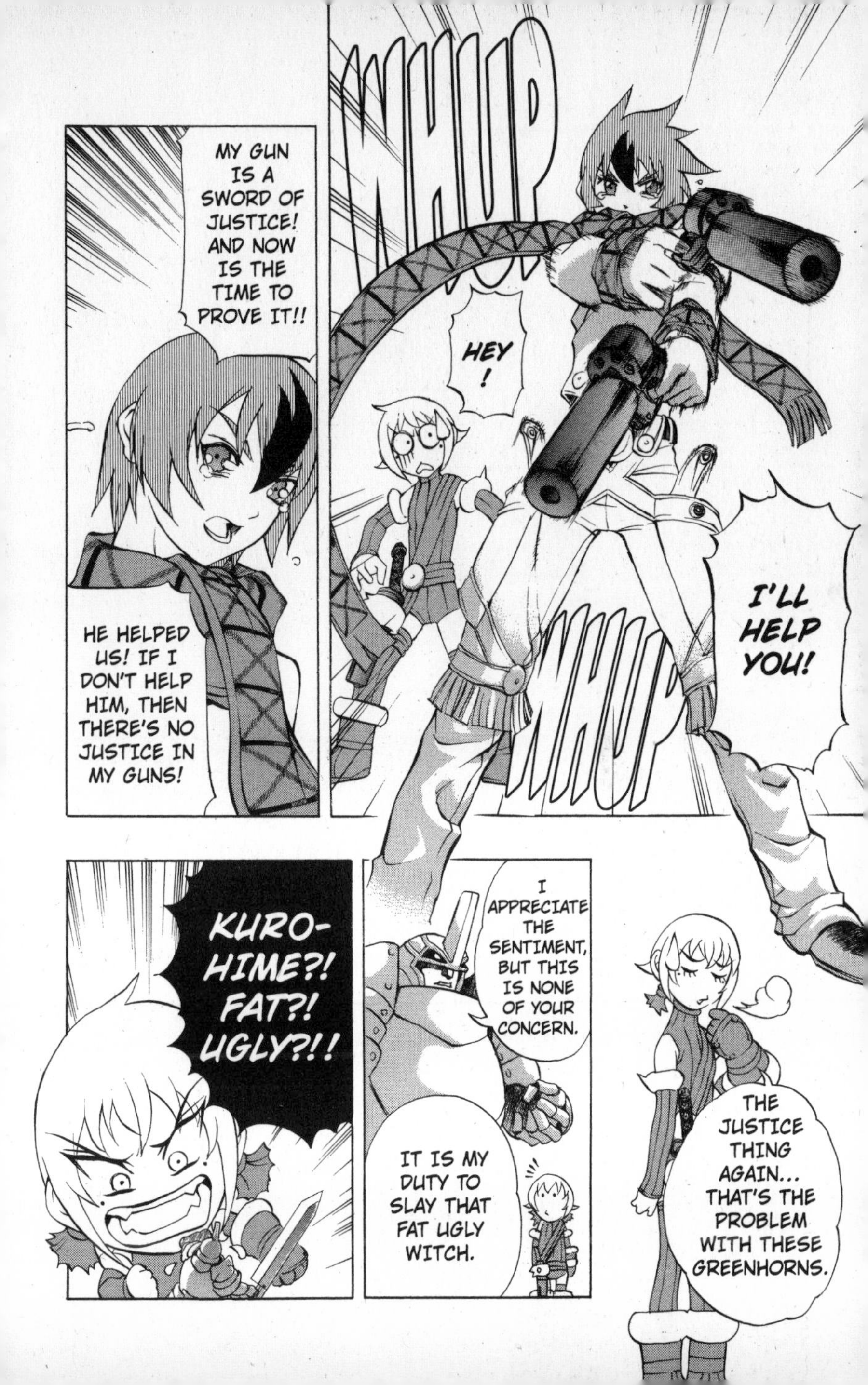
WHUP
HEY!
I'LL HELP YOU!
WHUP
MY GUN IS A SWORD OF JUSTICE! AND NOW IS THE TIME TO PROVE IT!!
HE HELPED US! IF I DON'T HELP HIM, THEN THERE'S NO JUSTICE IN MY GUNS!
THE JUSTICE THING AGAIN... THAT'S THE PROBLEM WITH THESE GREENHORNS.
I APPRECIATE THE SENTIMENT, BUT THIS IS NONE OF YOUR CONCERN.
IT IS MY DUTY TO SLAY THAT FAT UGLY WITCH.
KURO-HIME?! FAT?! UGLY?!!

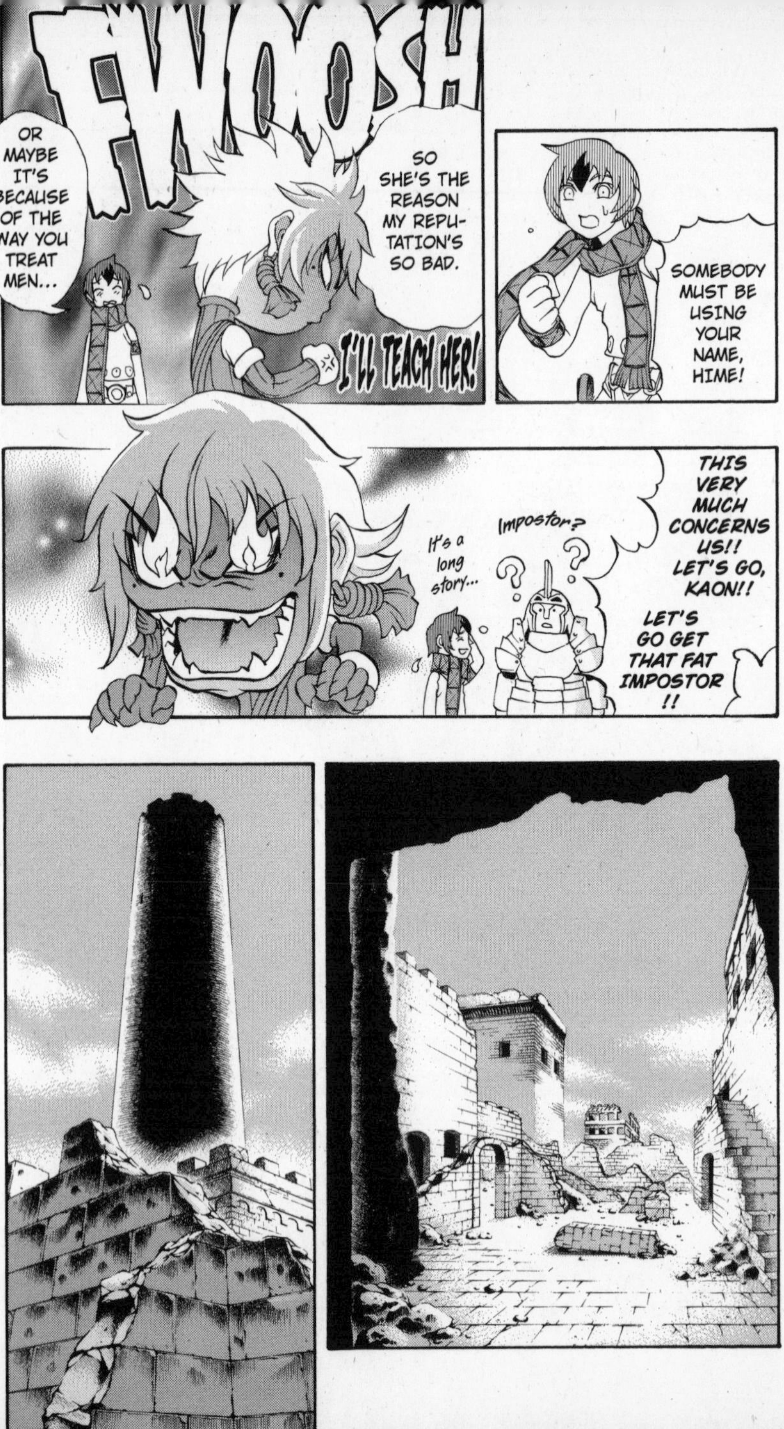
SOMEBODY MUST BE USING YOUR NAME, HIME!
FWOOSH
SO SHE'S THE REASON MY REPUTATION'S SO BAD.
I'LL TEACH HER!
OR MAYBE IT'S BECAUSE OF THE WAY YOU TREAT MEN...
THIS VERY MUCH CONCERNS US!! LET'S GO, KAON!!
LET'S GO GET THAT FAT IMPOSTOR!!
Impostor?
It's a long story...

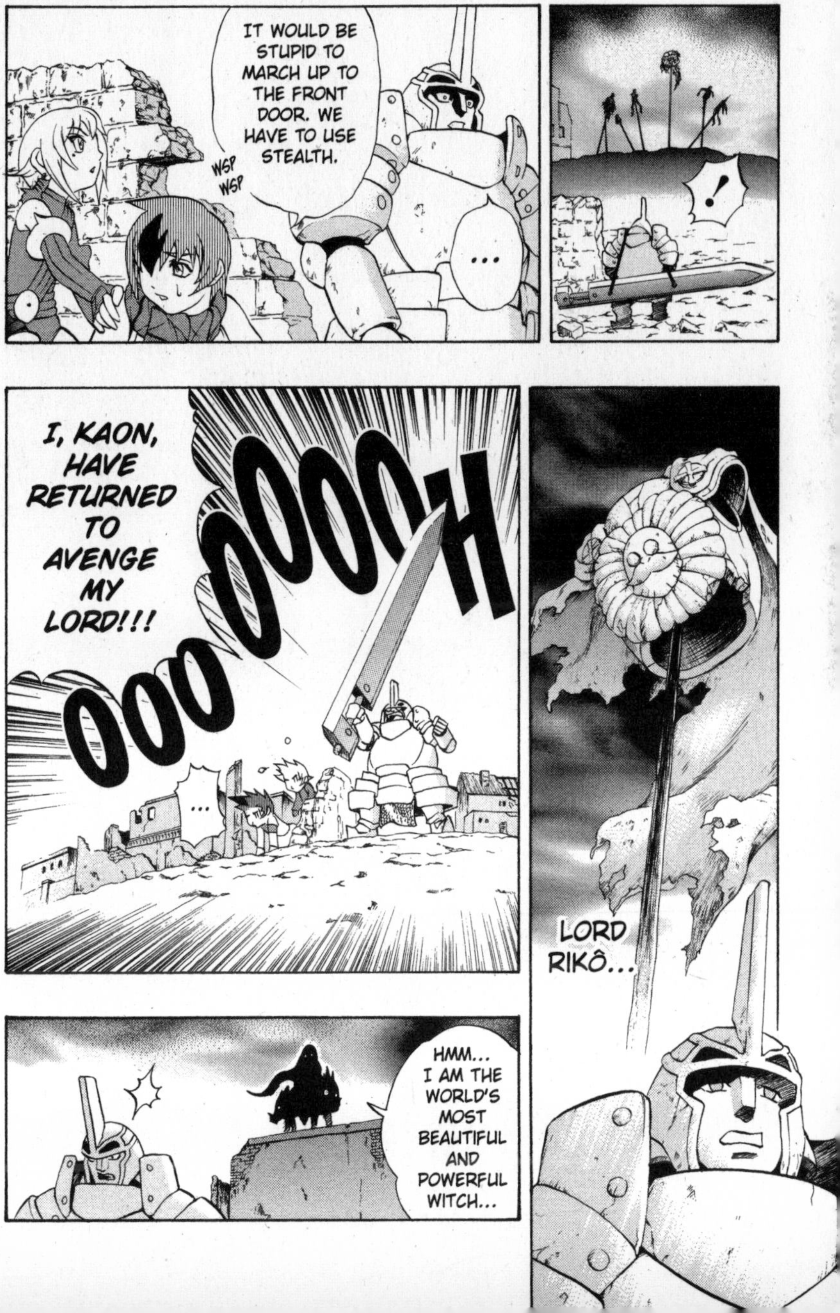
!
IT WOULD BE STUPID TO MARCH UP TO THE FRONT DOOR. WE HAVE TO USE STEALTH.
WSP WSP
...
LORD RIKÔ...
I, KAON, HAVE RETURNED TO AVENGE MY LORD!!!
OOOOOOOOH
...
HMM... I AM THE WORLD'S MOST BEAUTIFUL AND POWERFUL WITCH...

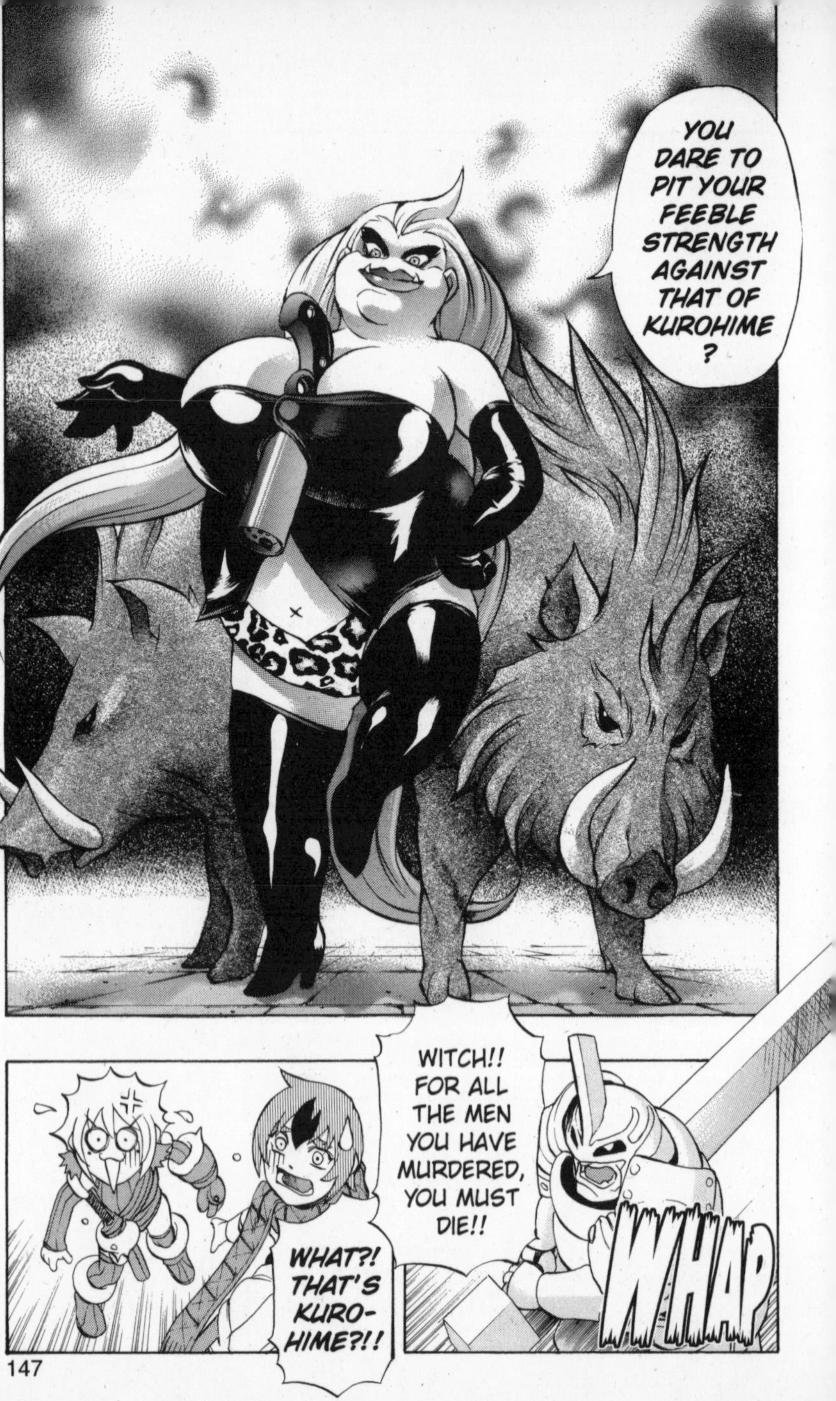
YOU DARE TO PIT YOUR FEEBLE STRENGTH AGAINST THAT OF KUROHIME?
WITCH!! FOR ALL THE MEN YOU HAVE MURDERED, YOU MUST DIE!!
WHAP
WHAT?! THAT'S KURO-HIME?!!

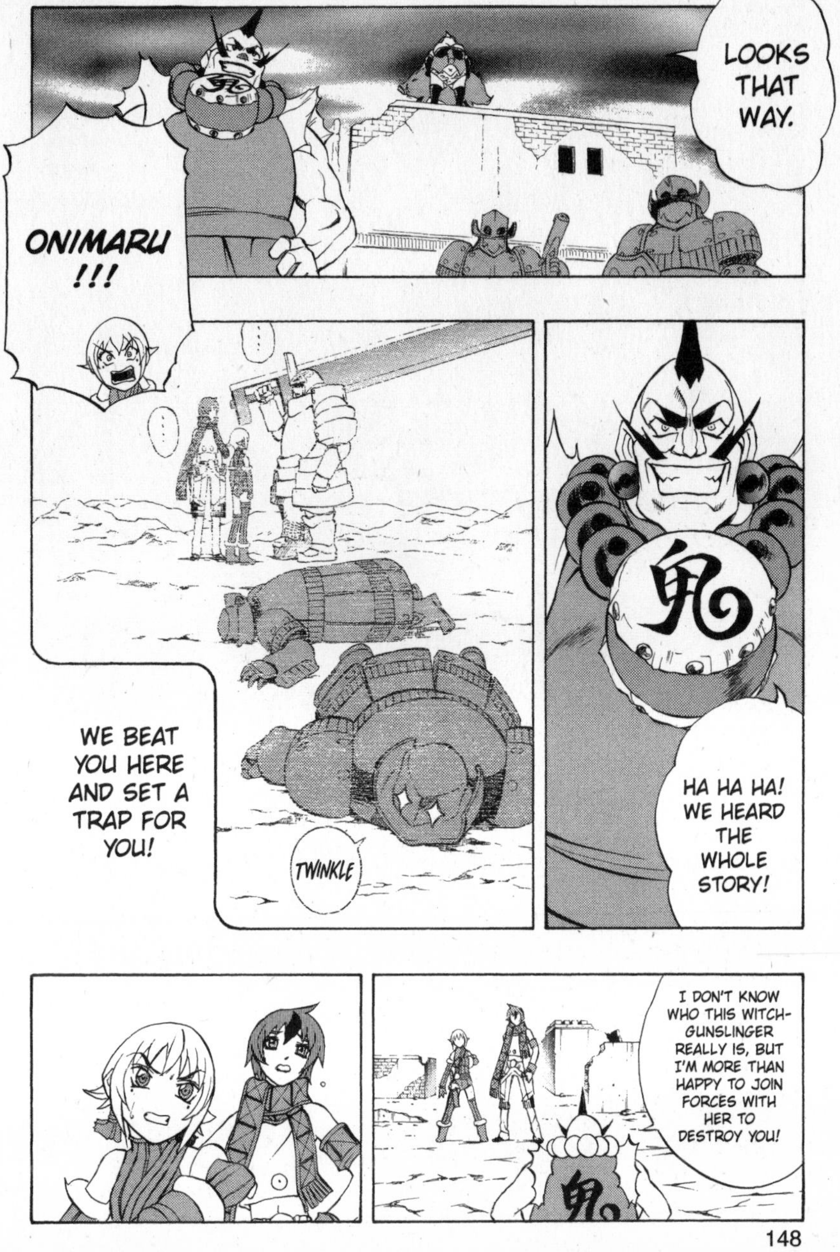
LOOKS THAT WAY.
ONIMARU !!!
HA HA HA! WE HEARD THE WHOLE STORY!
...
...
WE BEAT YOU HERE AND SET A TRAP FOR YOU!
TWINKLE
I DON'T KNOW WHO THIS WITCH-GUNSLINGER REALLY IS, BUT I'M MORE THAN HAPPY TO JOIN FORCES WITH HER TO DESTROY YOU!

READ THIS WAY

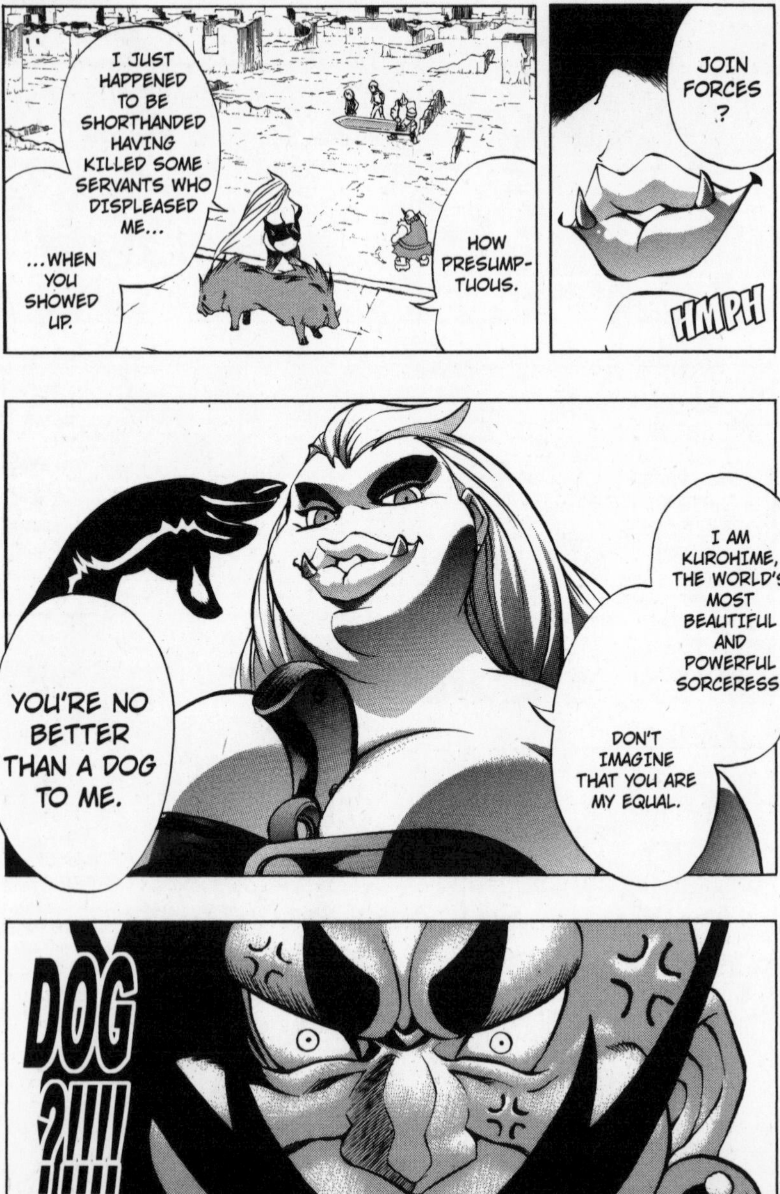
JOIN FORCES ?
HMPH
HOW PRESUMPTUOUS.
I JUST HAPPENED TO BE SHORTHANDED HAVING KILLED SOME SERVANTS WHO DISPLEASED ME...
...WHEN YOU SHOWED UP.
I AM KUROHIME, THE WORLD'S MOST BEAUTIFUL AND POWERFUL SORCERESS.
DON'T IMAGINE THAT YOU ARE MY EQUAL.
YOU'RE NO BETTER THAN A DOG TO ME.
DOG ?!!!!!

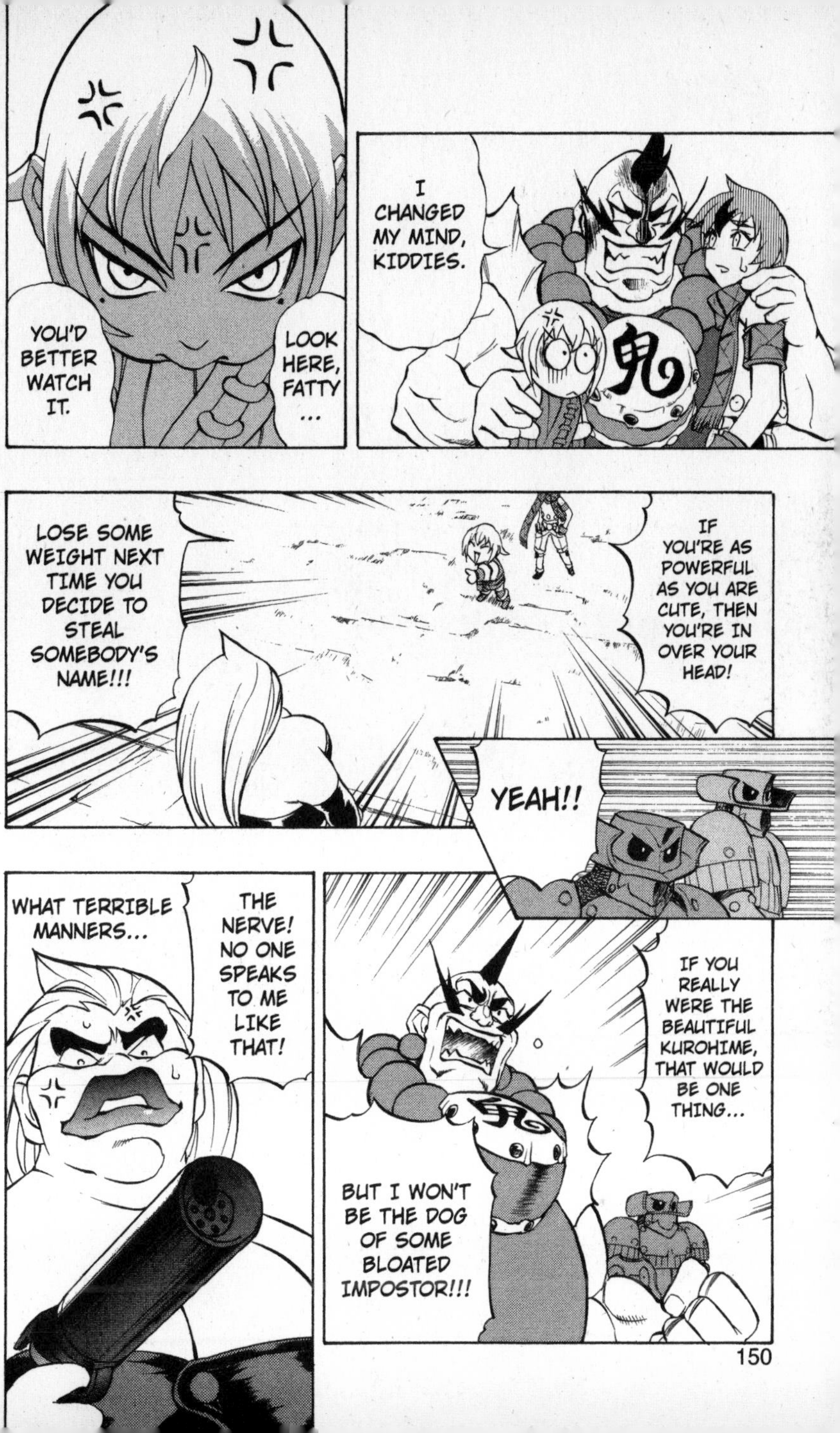
I CHANGED MY MIND, KIDDIES.
LOOK HERE, FATTY...
YOU'D BETTER WATCH IT.
IF YOU'RE AS POWERFUL AS YOU ARE CUTE, THEN YOU'RE IN OVER YOUR HEAD!
LOSE SOME WEIGHT NEXT TIME YOU DECIDE TO STEAL SOMEBODY'S NAME!!!
YEAH!!
IF YOU REALLY WERE THE BEAUTIFUL KUROHIME, THAT WOULD BE ONE THING...
BUT I WON'T BE THE DOG OF SOME BLOATED IMPOSTOR!!!
THE NERVE! NO ONE SPEAKS TO ME LIKE THAT!
WHAT TERRIBLE MANNERS...

READ THIS WAY

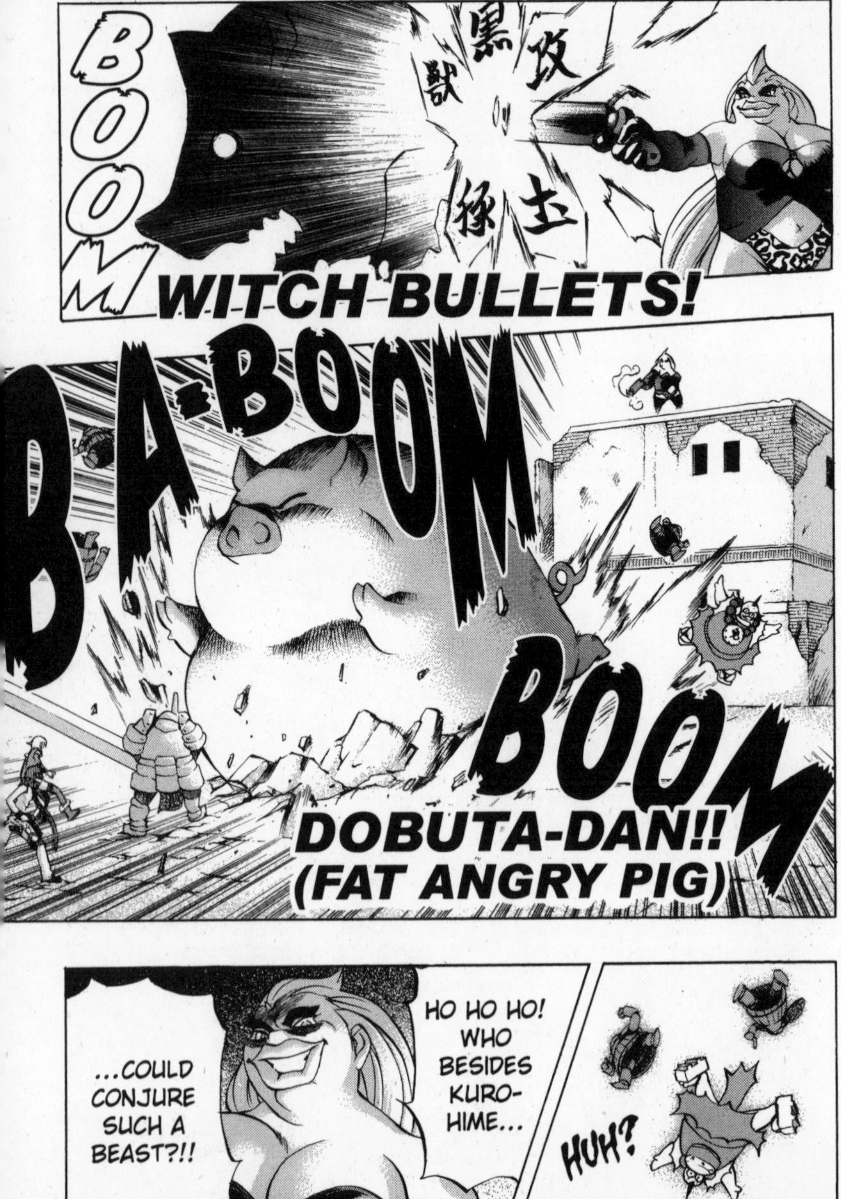
BOOM
WITCH BULLETS!
BA-BOOM
BOOM
DOBUTA-DAN!! (FAT ANGRY PIG)
HUH?
HO HO HO! WHO BESIDES KURO-HIME...
...COULD CONJURE SUCH A BEAST?!!

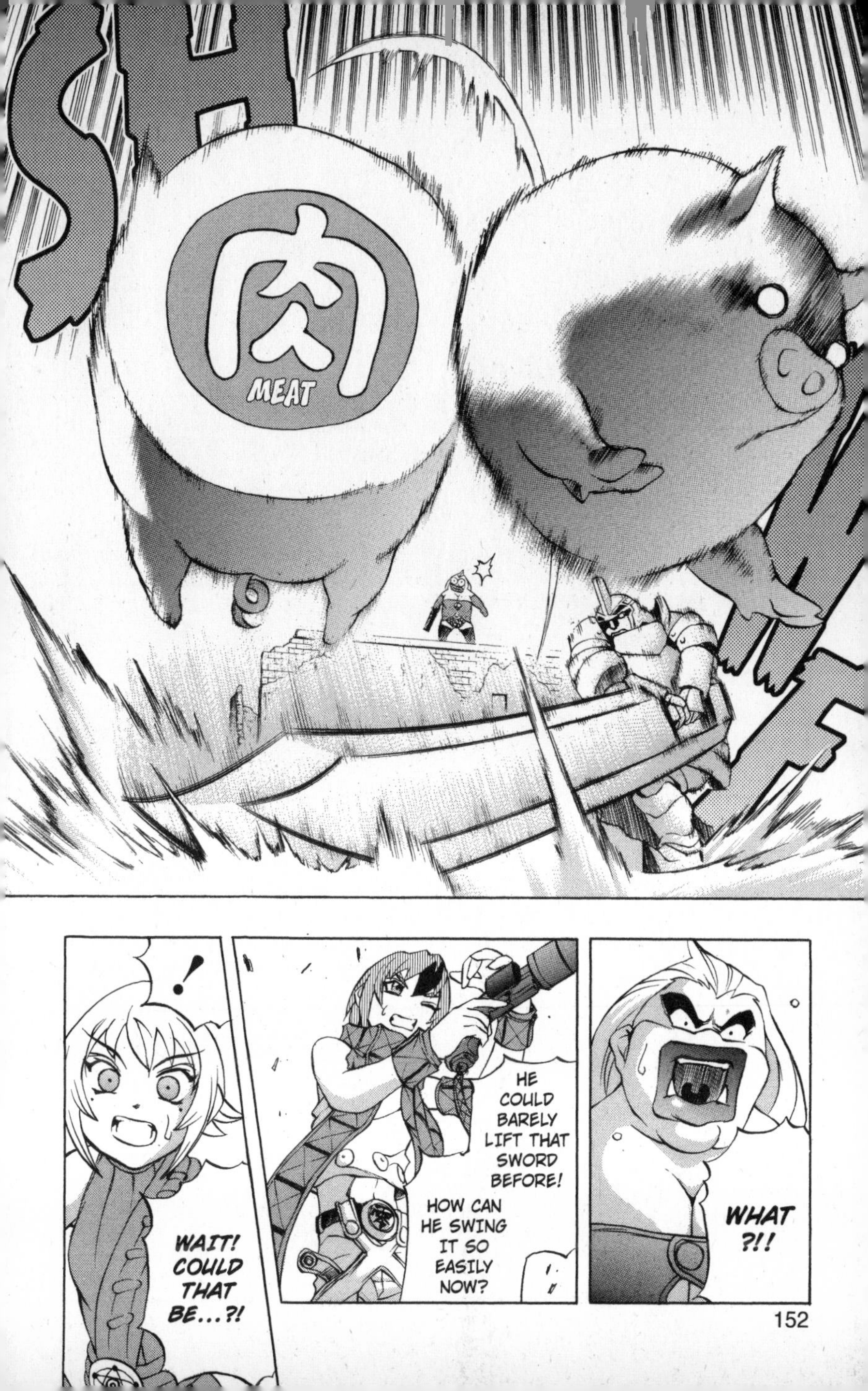
肉
MEAT
WHAT?!!
HE COULD BARELY LIFT THAT SWORD BEFORE!
HOW CAN HE SWING IT SO EASILY NOW?
!
WAIT! COULD THAT BE...?!
152

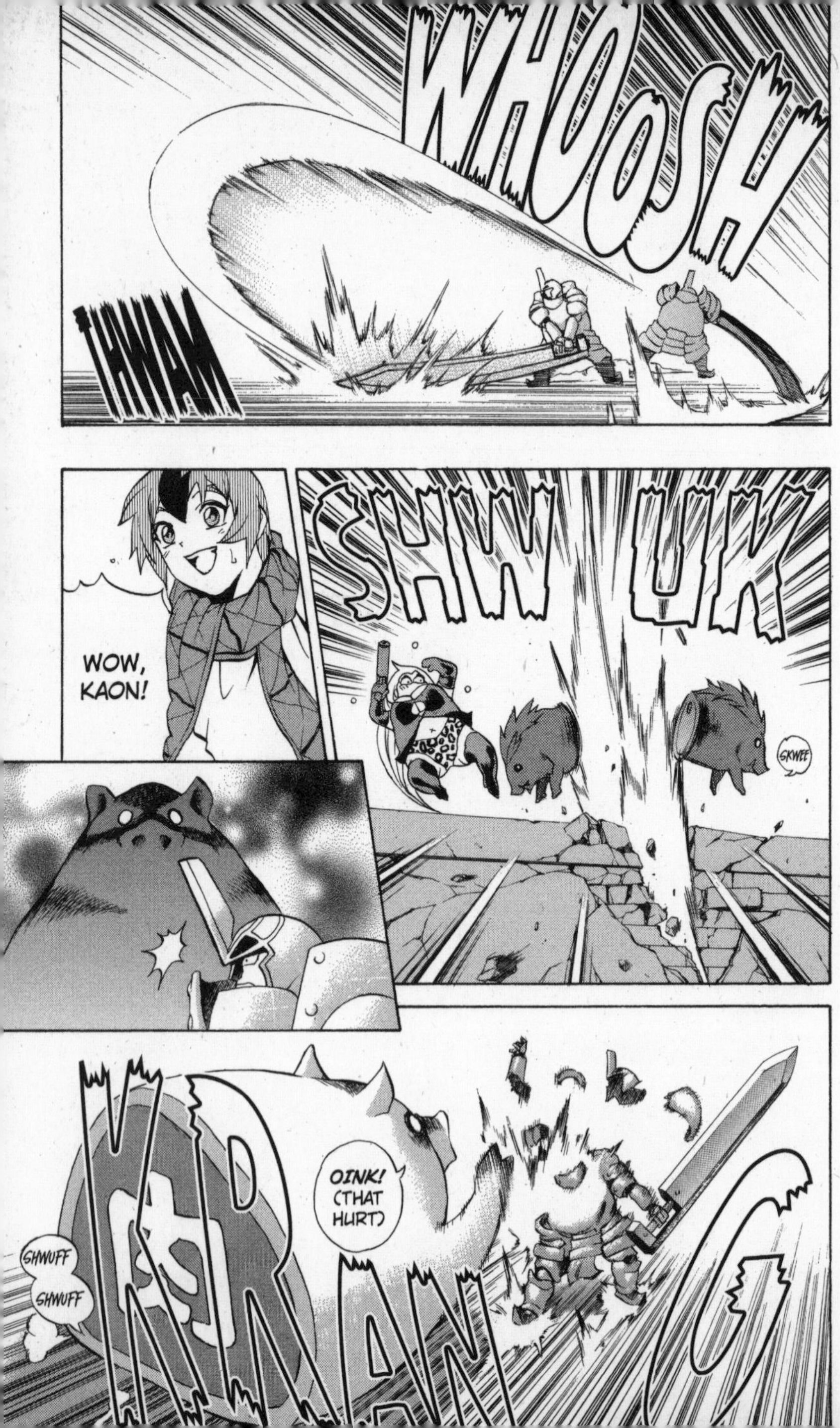
WHOOSH
THWAM
SHWUK
SKWEE
WOW, KAON!
OINK! (THAT HURT)
KRANG
SHWUFF
SHWUFF

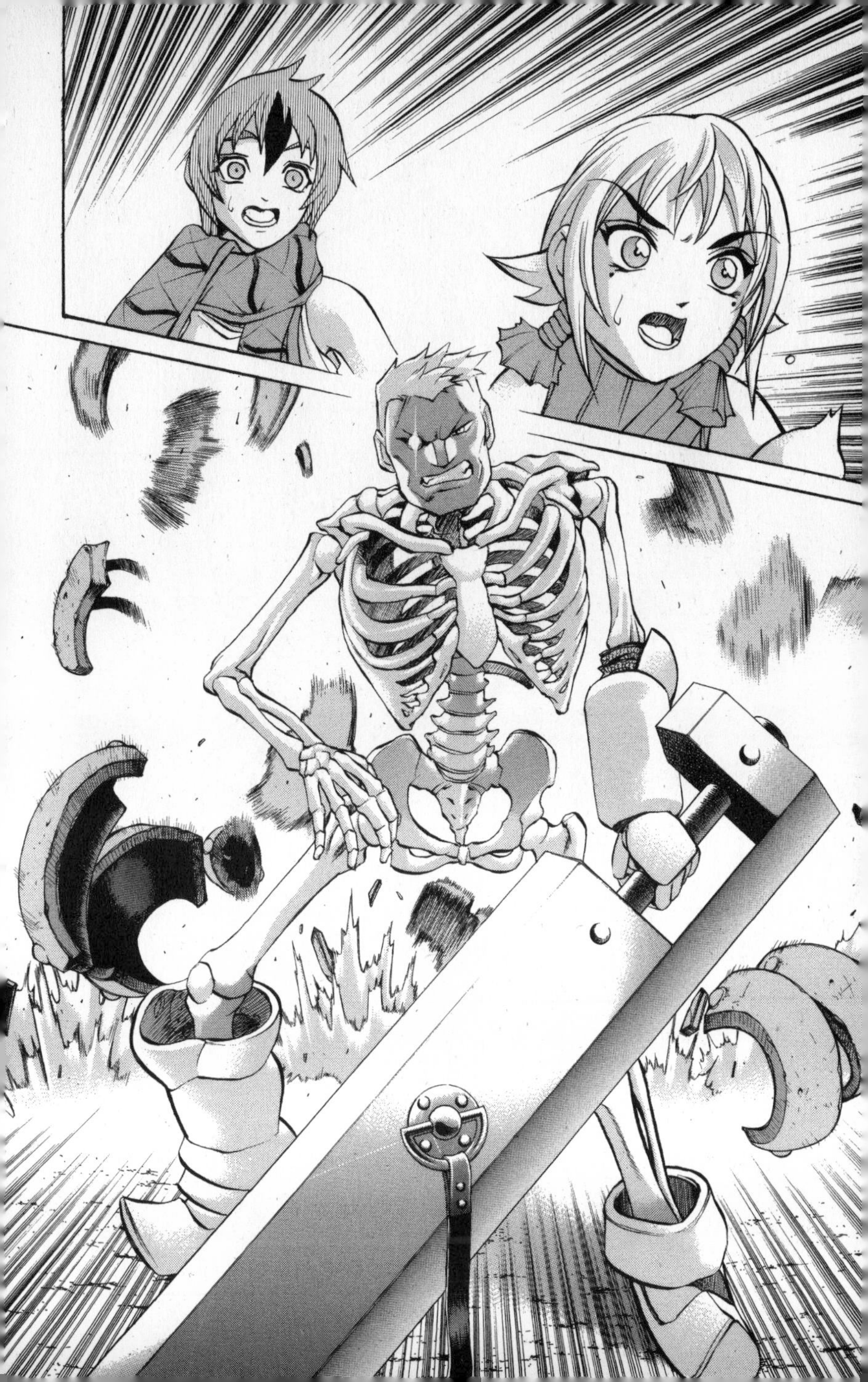

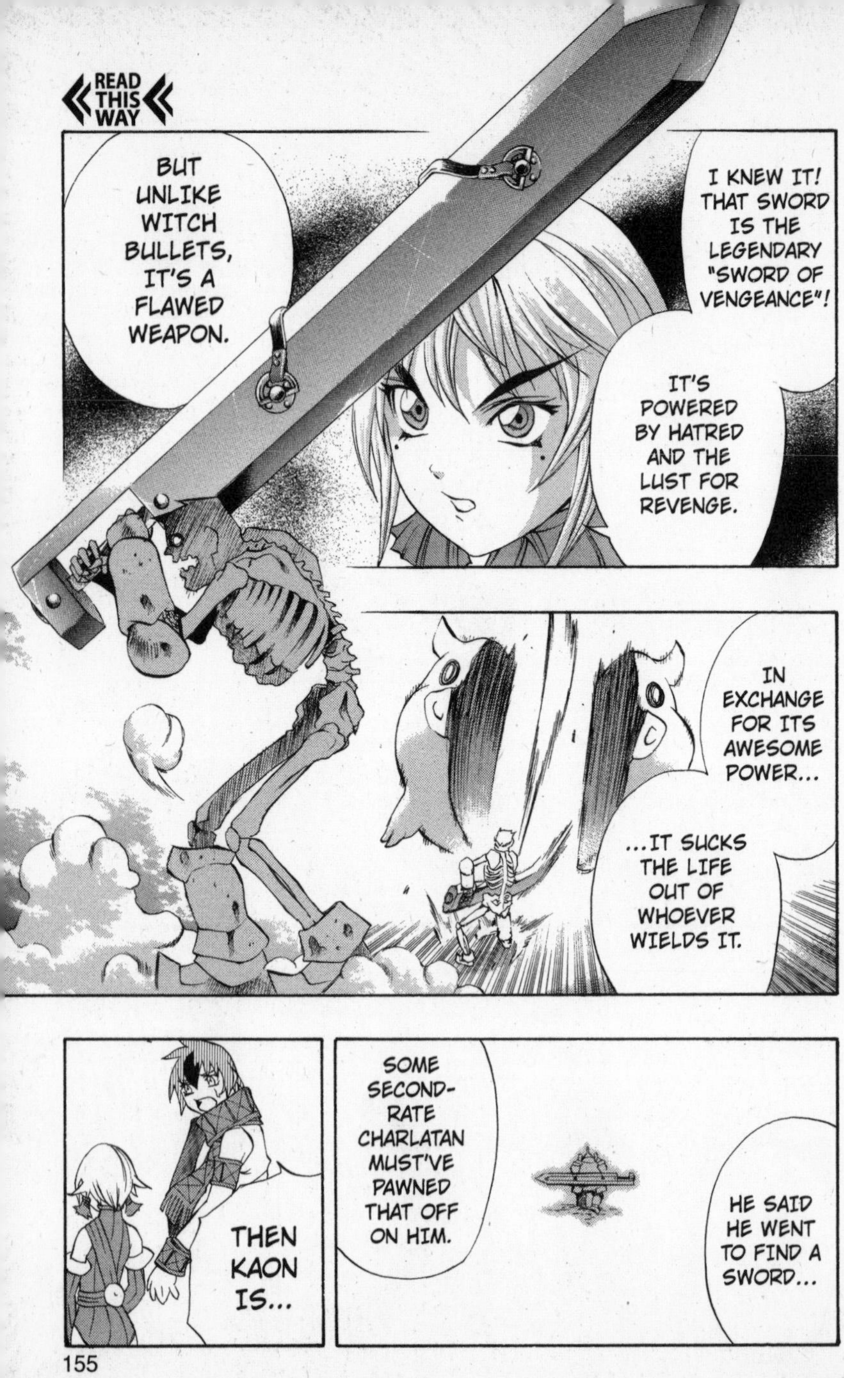
READ THIS WAY
I KNEW IT! THAT SWORD IS THE LEGENDARY "SWORD OF VENGEANCE"!
IT'S POWERED BY HATRED AND THE LUST FOR REVENGE.
BUT UNLIKE WITCH BULLETS, IT'S A FLAWED WEAPON.
IN EXCHANGE FOR ITS AWESOME POWER...
...IT SUCKS THE LIFE OUT OF WHOEVER WIELDS IT.
HE SAID HE WENT TO FIND A SWORD...
SOME SECOND-RATE CHARLATAN MUST'VE PAWNED THAT OFF ON HIM.
THEN KAON IS...

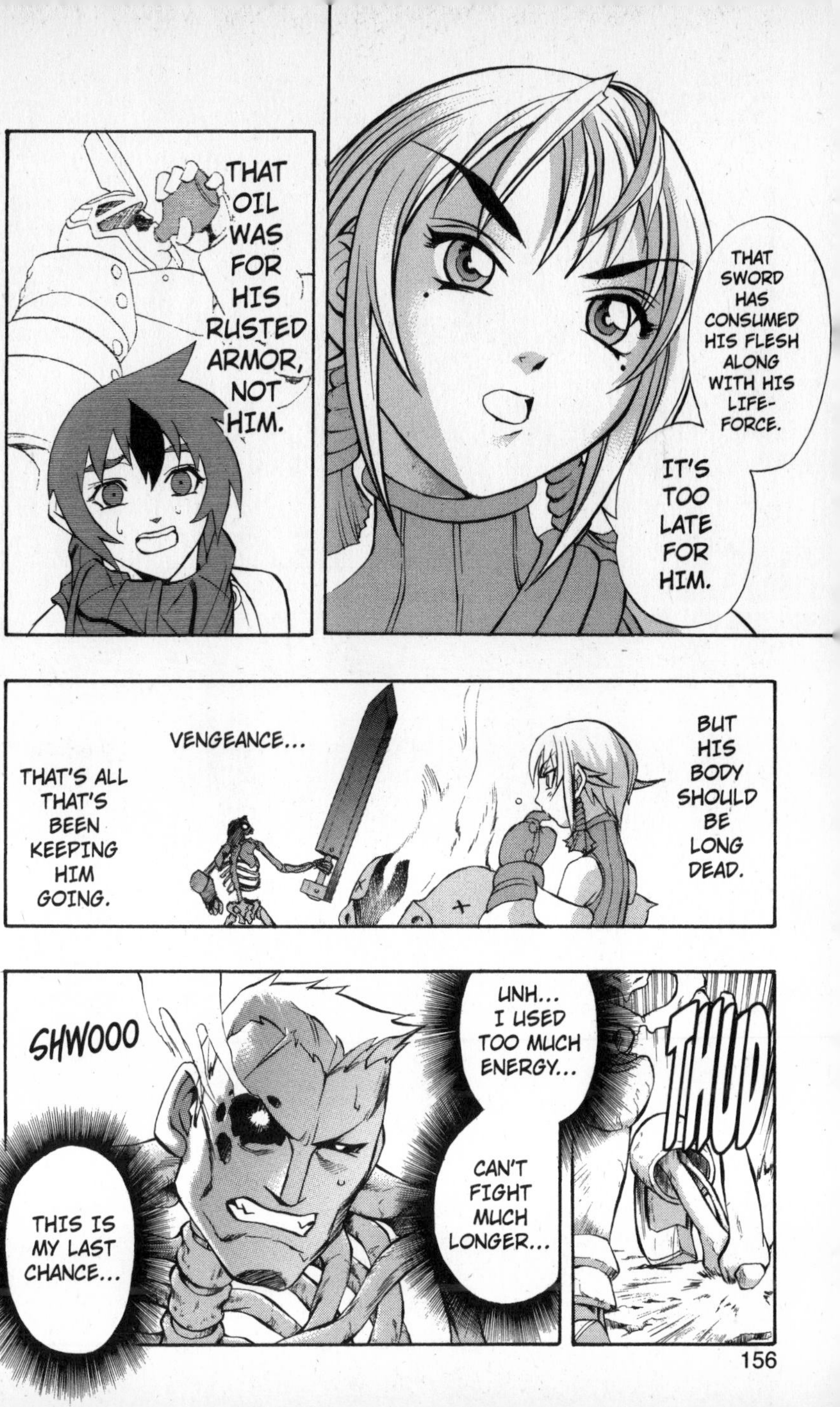
THAT SWORD HAS CONSUMED HIS FLESH ALONG WITH HIS LIFE-FORCE.
IT'S TOO LATE FOR HIM.
THAT OIL WAS FOR HIS RUSTED ARMOR, NOT HIM.
BUT HIS BODY SHOULD BE LONG DEAD.
VENGEANCE...
THAT'S ALL THAT'S BEEN KEEPING HIM GOING.
THUD
UNH... I USED TOO MUCH ENERGY...
CAN'T FIGHT MUCH LONGER...
SHWOOO
THIS IS MY LAST CHANCE...

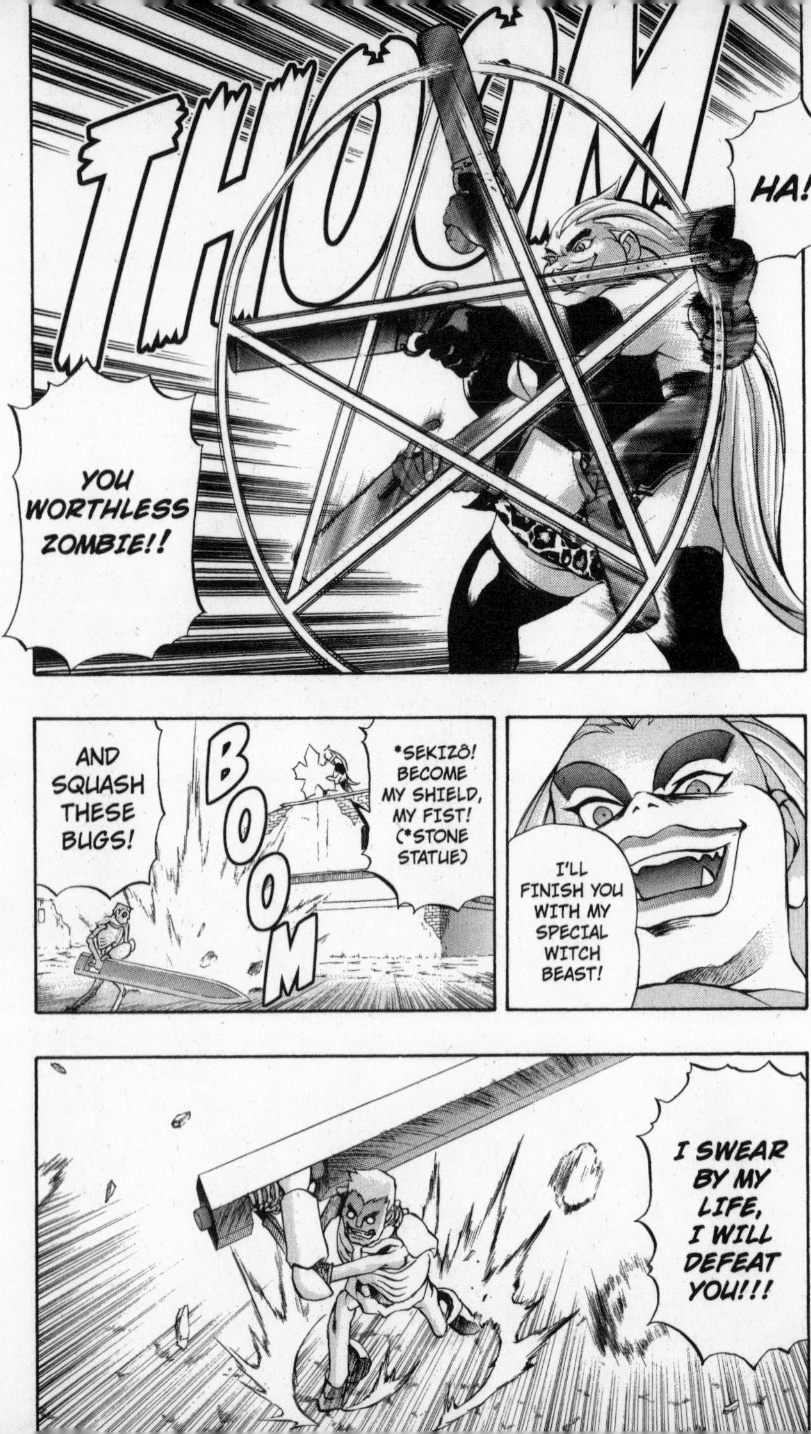
HA!
THOOM
YOU WORTHLESS ZOMBIE!!
I'LL FINISH YOU WITH MY SPECIAL WITCH BEAST!
*SEKIZŌ! BECOME MY SHIELD, MY FIST! (*STONE STATUE)
BOOM
AND SQUASH THESE BUGS!
I SWEAR BY MY LIFE, I WILL DEFEAT YOU!!!

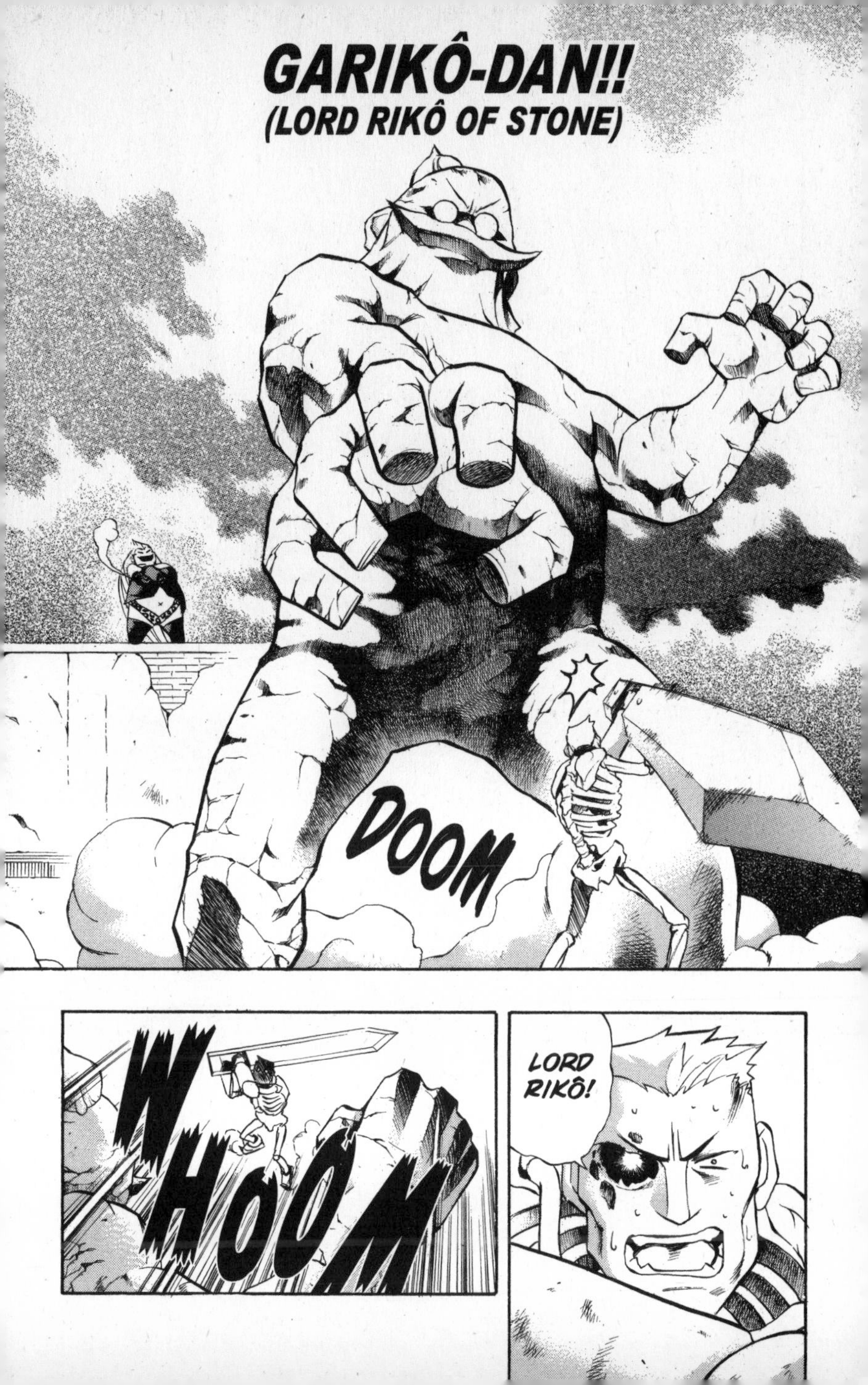
GARIKÔ-DAN!!
(LORD RIKÔ OF STONE)
DOOM
LORD RIKÔ!
WHOOM

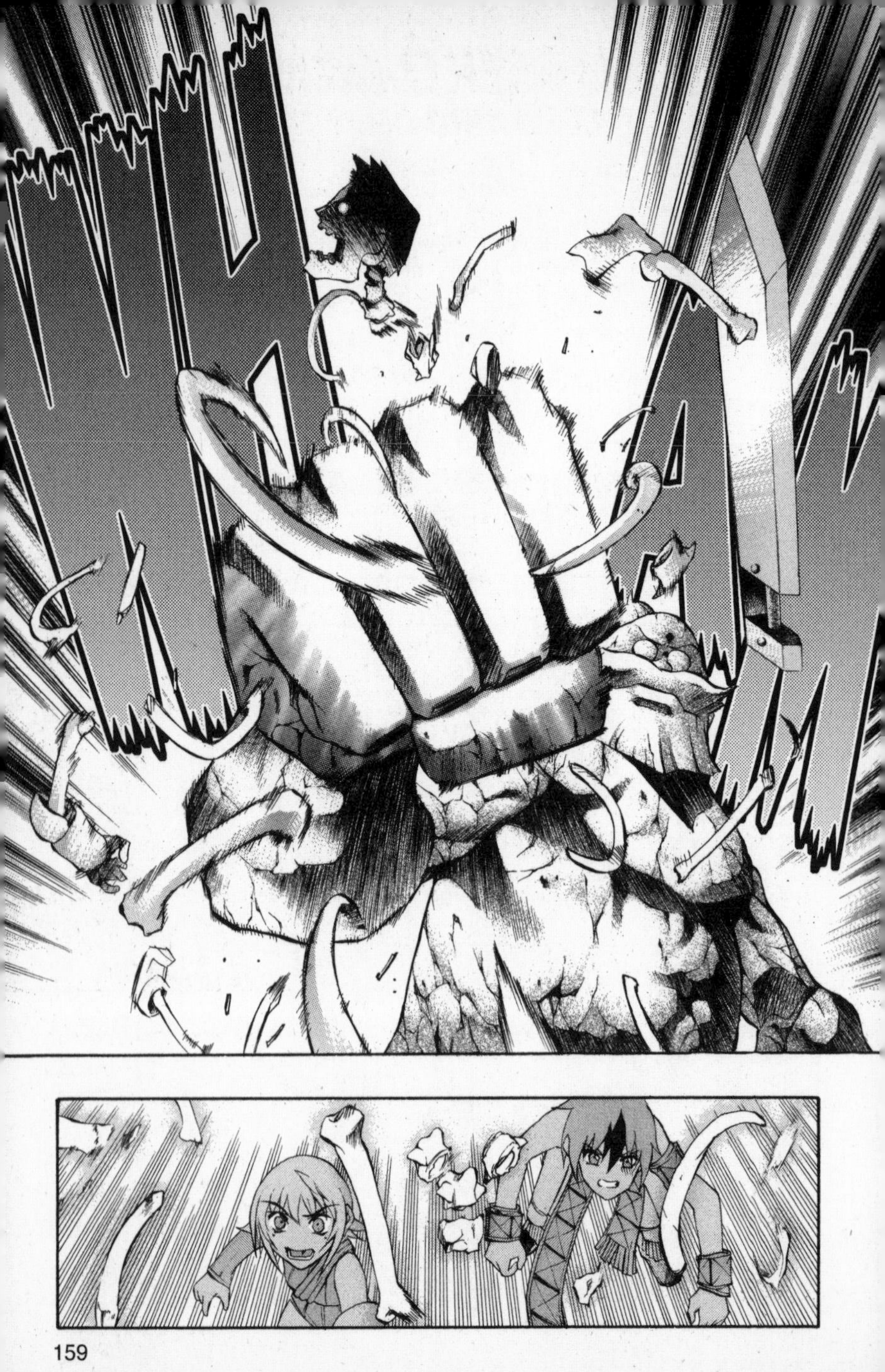

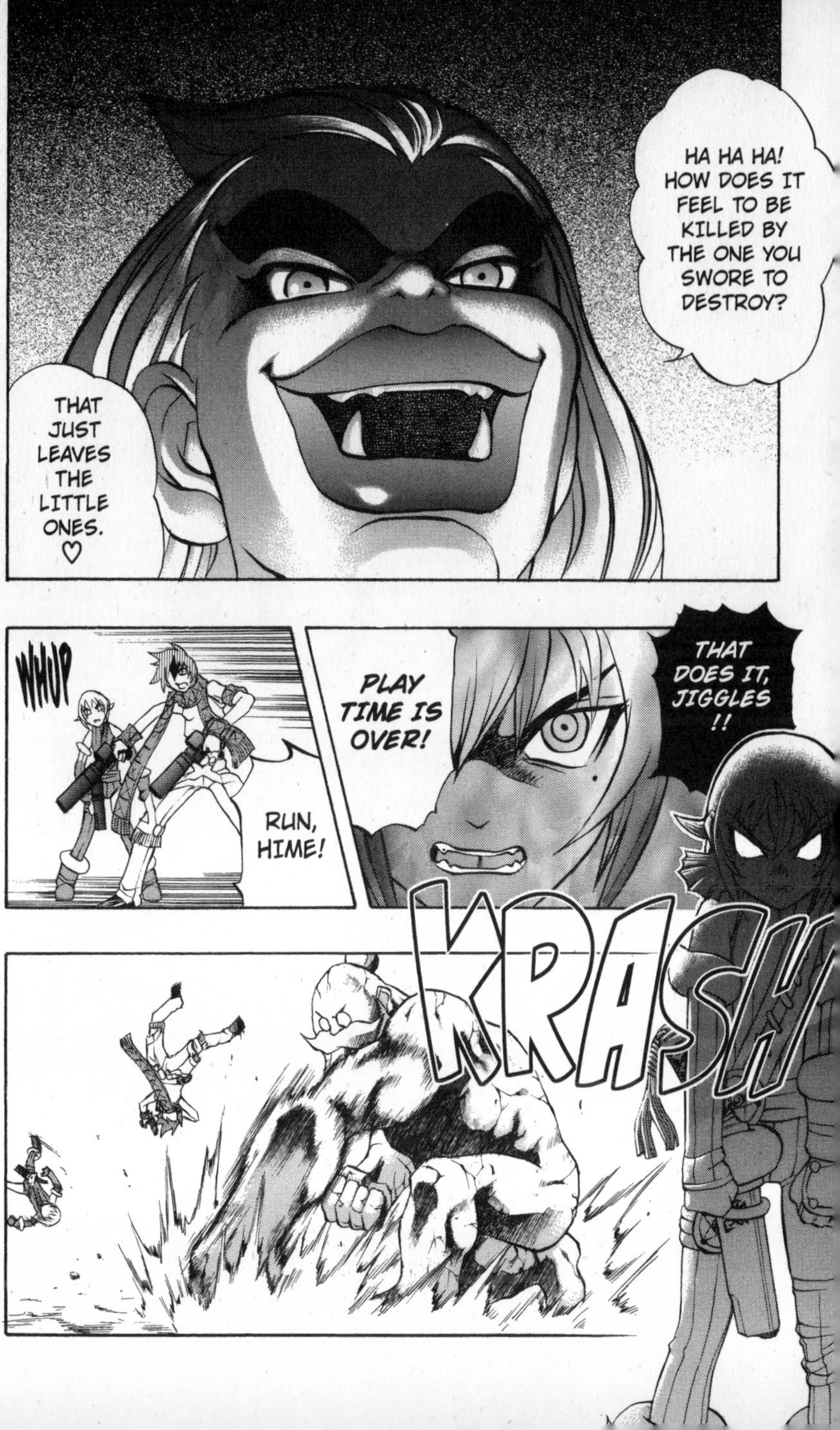
HA HA HA! HOW DOES IT FEEL TO BE KILLED BY THE ONE YOU SWORE TO DESTROY?
THAT JUST LEAVES THE LITTLE ONES. ♡
THAT DOES IT, JIGGLES !!
PLAY TIME IS OVER!
RUN, HIME!
WHUP
KRASH

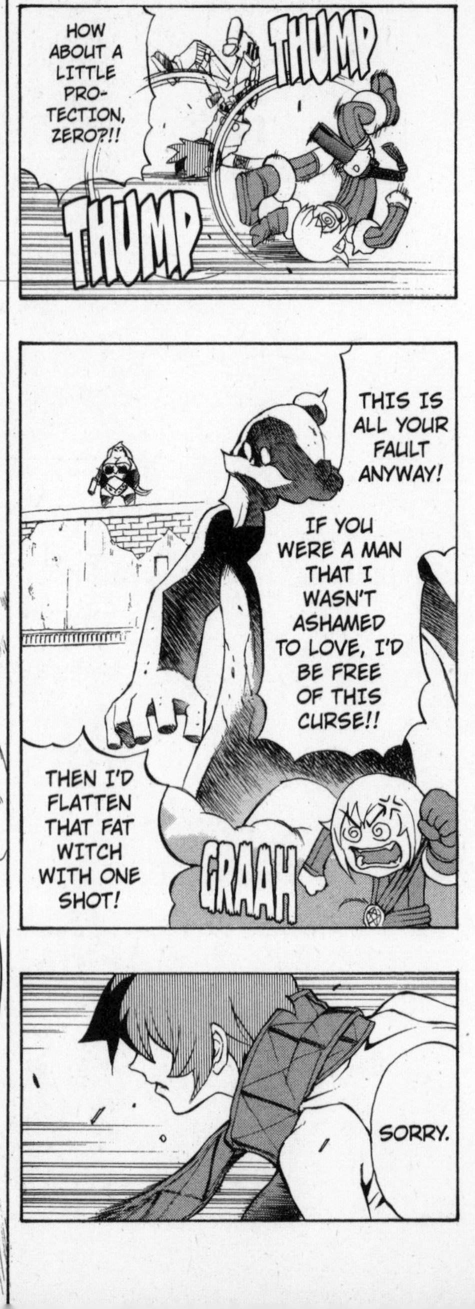
THUMP
HOW ABOUT A LITTLE PRO-TECTION, ZERO?!!
THUMP
THIS IS ALL YOUR FAULT ANYWAY!
IF YOU WERE A MAN THAT I WASN'T ASHAMED TO LOVE, I'D BE FREE OF THIS CURSE!!
THEN I'D FLATTEN THAT FAT WITCH WITH ONE SHOT!
GRAAH
SORRY.
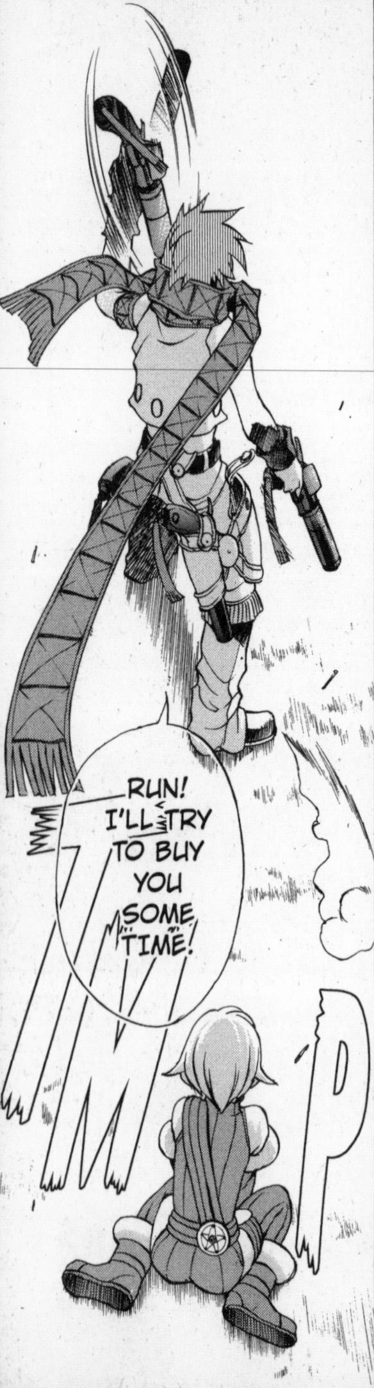
RUN! I'LL TRY TO BUY YOU SOME TIME!

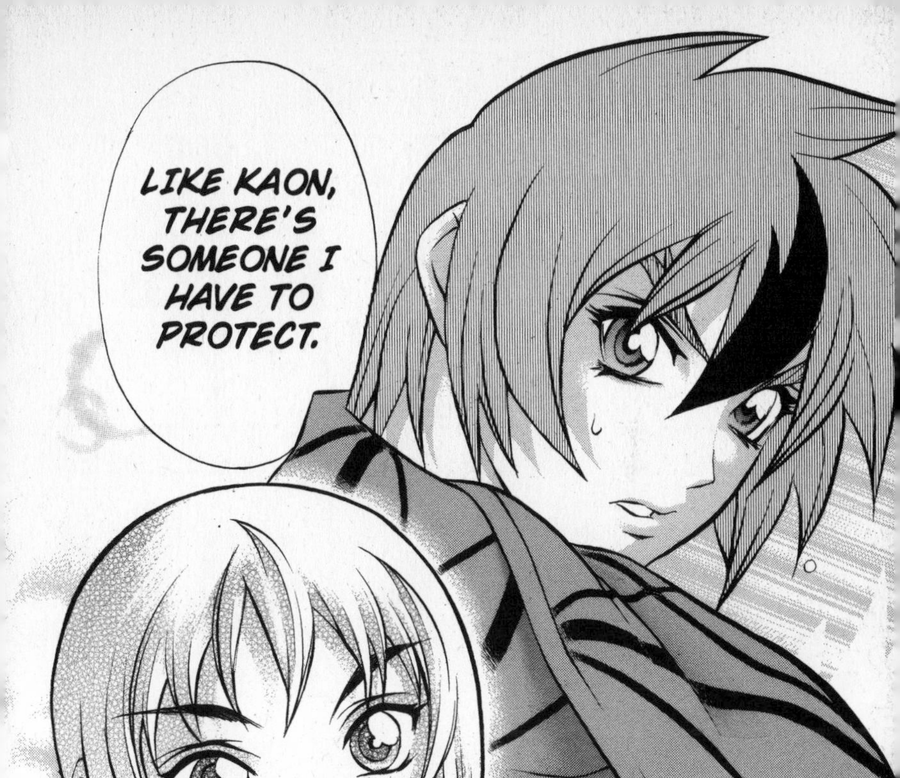
LIKE KAON, THERE'S SOMEONE I HAVE TO PROTECT.

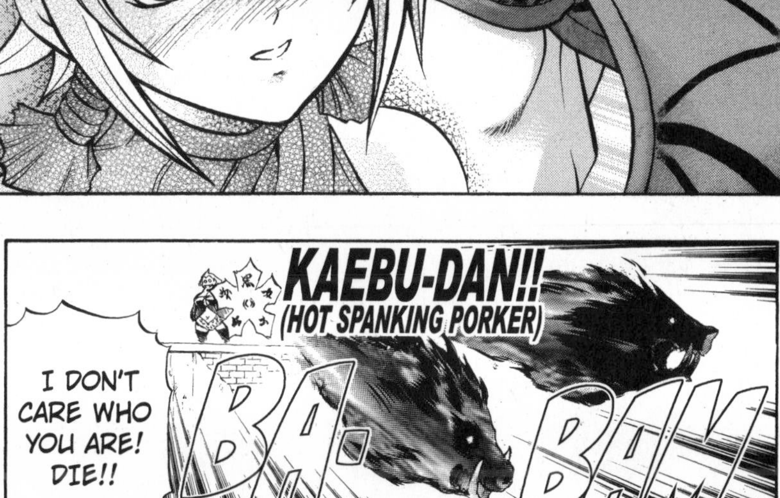
KAEBU-DAN!!
(HOT SPANKING PORKER)
BA-BAM
I DON'T CARE WHO YOU ARE! DIE!!

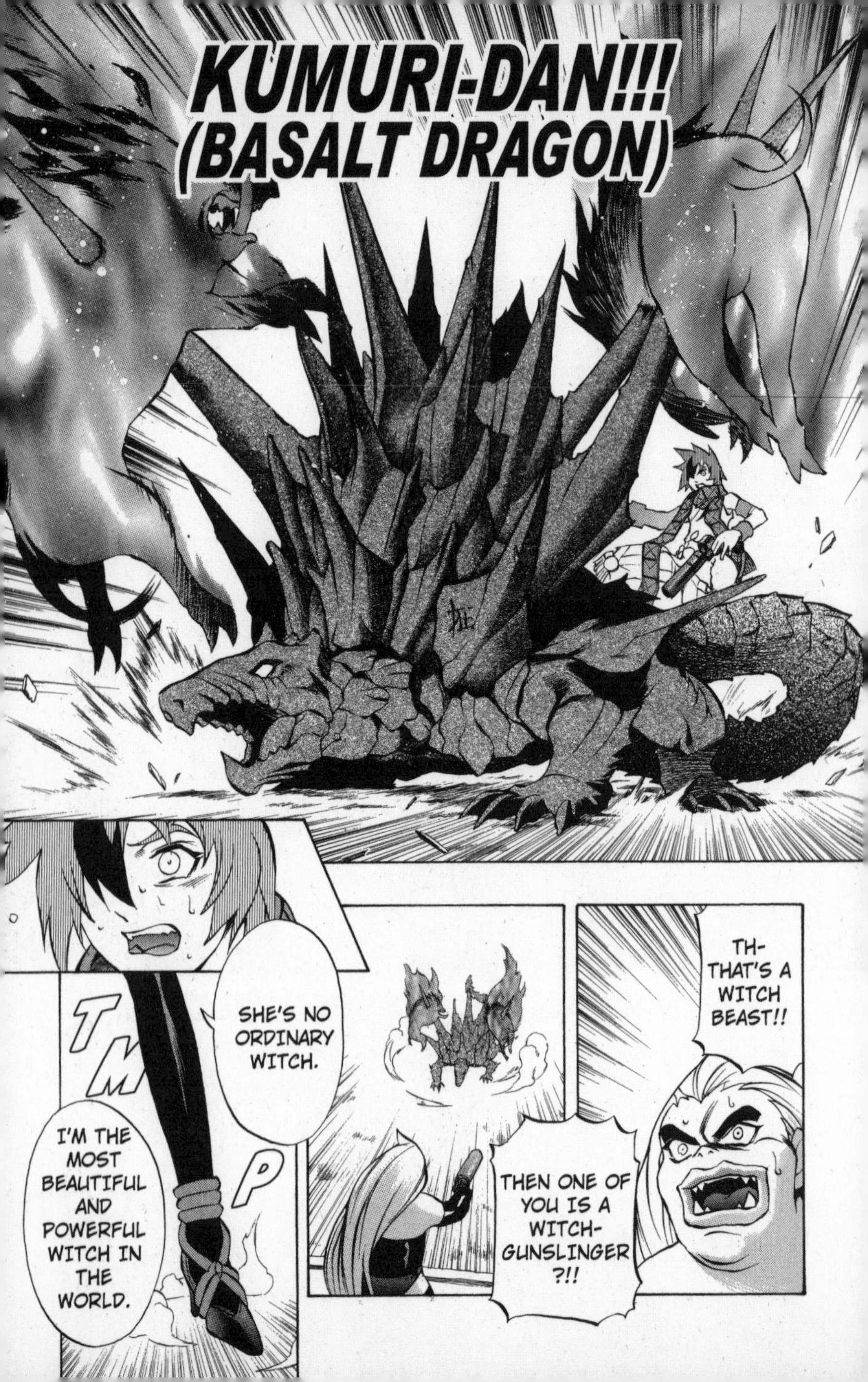
KUMURI-DAN!!!
(BASALT DRAGON)
TH-THAT'S A WITCH BEAST!!
THEN ONE OF YOU IS A WITCH-GUNSLINGER?!!
SHE'S NO ORDINARY WITCH.
I'M THE MOST BEAUTIFUL AND POWERFUL WITCH IN THE WORLD.
TMP

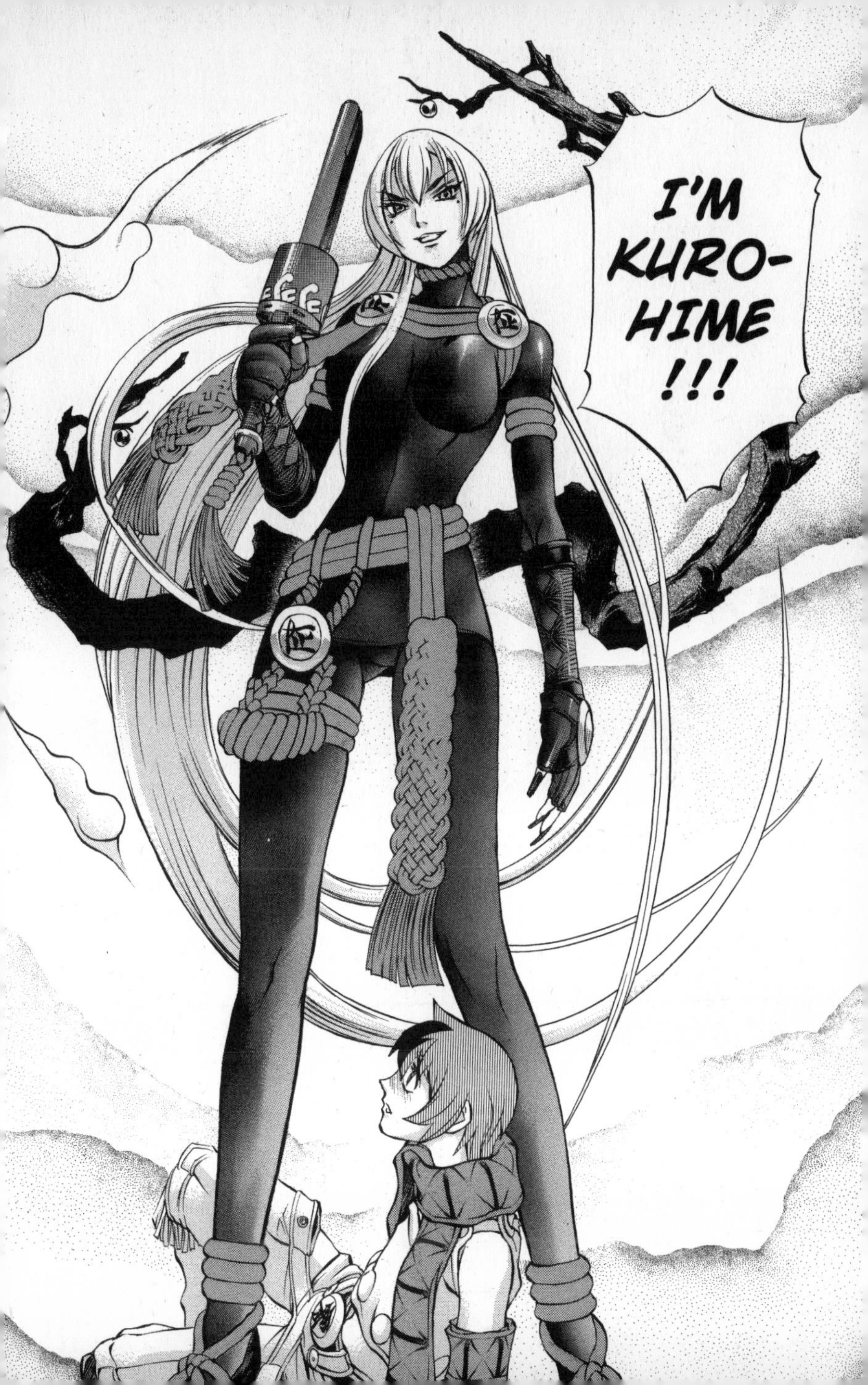
I'M KURO-HIME !!!

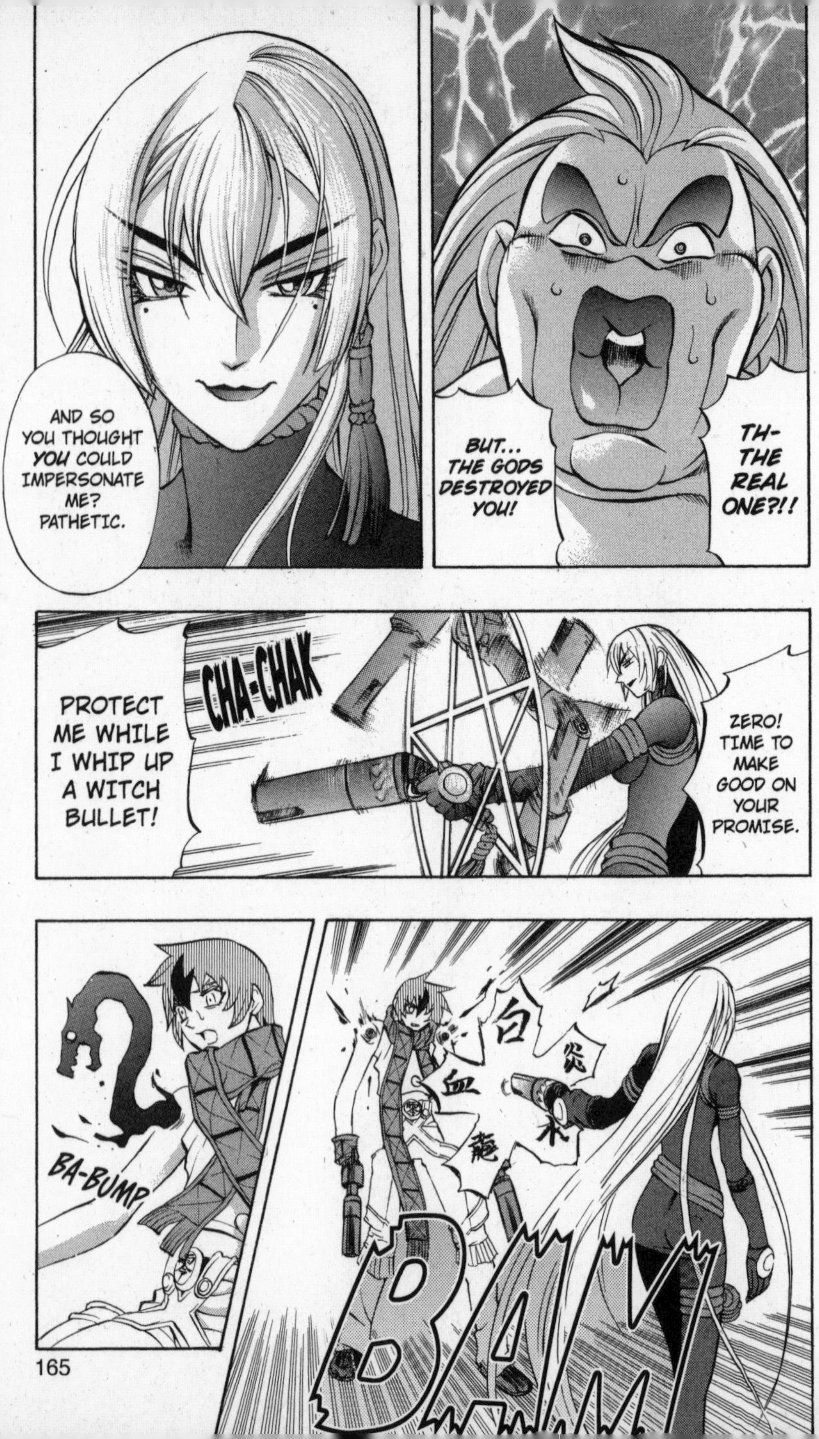
TH- THE REAL ONE?!!
BUT... THE GODS DESTROYED YOU!
AND SO YOU THOUGHT YOU COULD IMPERSONATE ME? PATHETIC.
ZERO! TIME TO MAKE GOOD ON YOUR PROMISE.
CHA-CHAK
PROTECT ME WHILE I WHIP UP A WITCH BULLET!
BAM
BA-BUMP

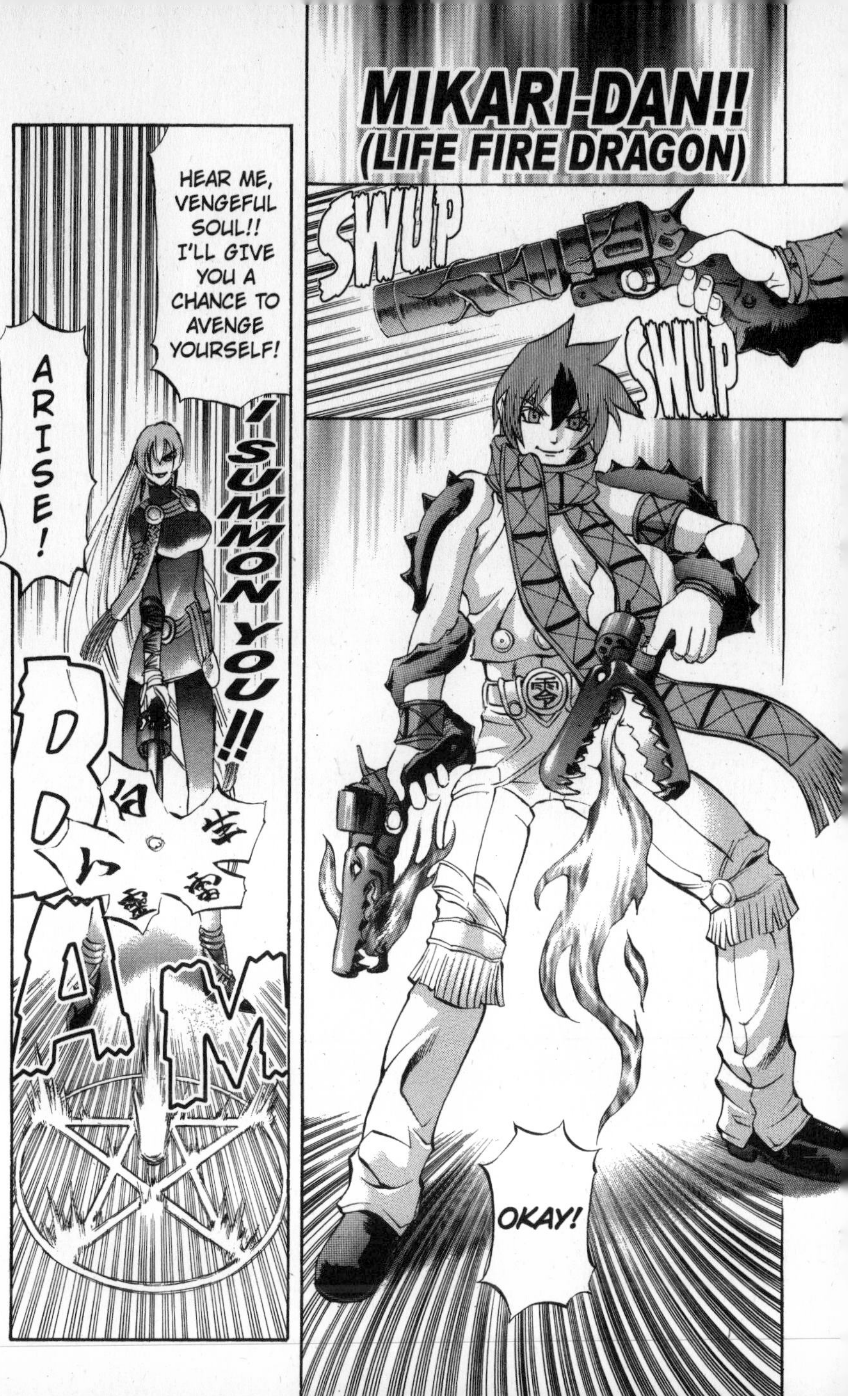
MIKARI-DAN!!
(LIFE FIRE DRAGON)
SWUP
SWUP
OKAY!
HEAR ME, VENGEFUL SOUL!! I'LL GIVE YOU A CHANCE TO AVENGE YOURSELF!
ARISE!
I SUMMON YOU!!

READ THIS WAY

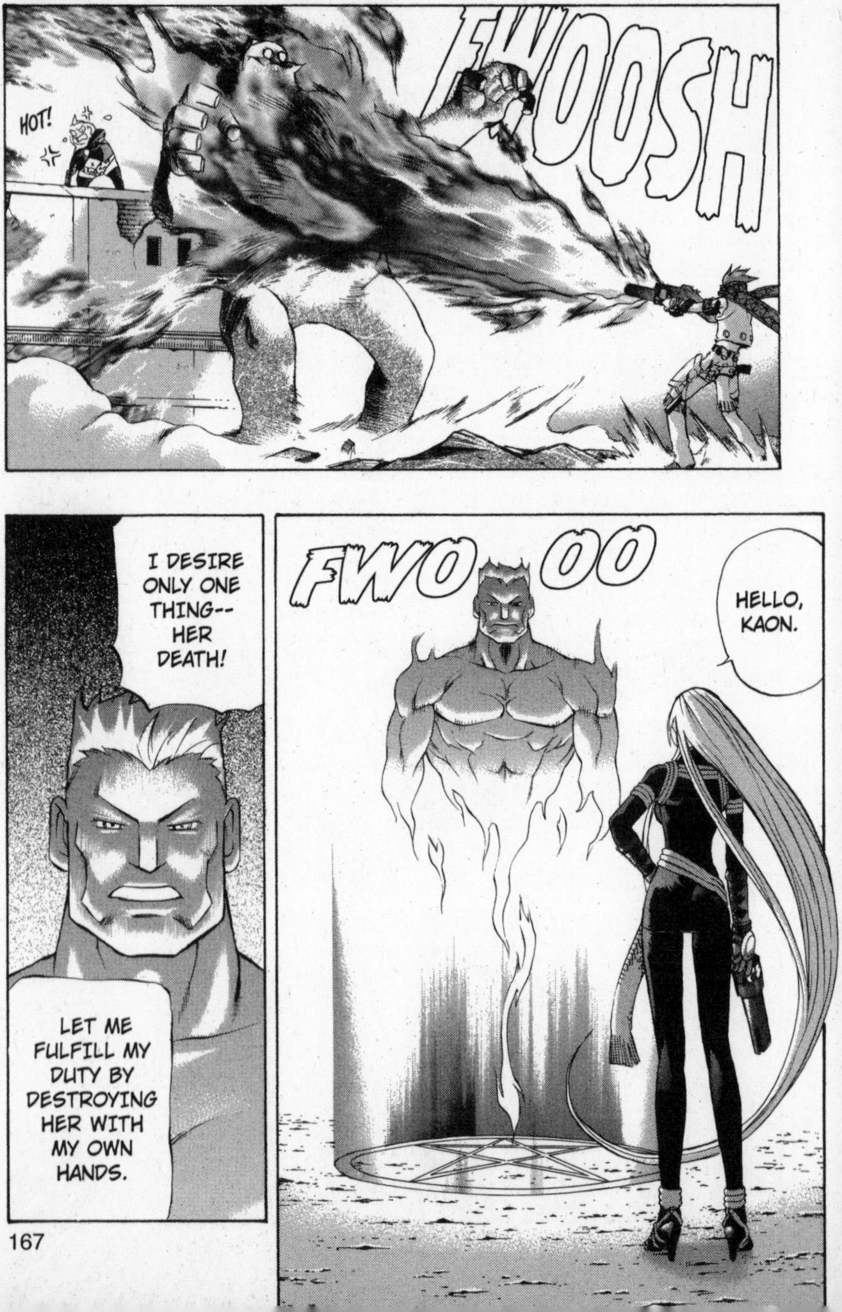
FWOOSH
HOT!
FWO OO
HELLO, KAON.
I DESIRE ONLY ONE THING-- HER DEATH!
LET ME FULFILL MY DUTY BY DESTROYING HER WITH MY OWN HANDS.

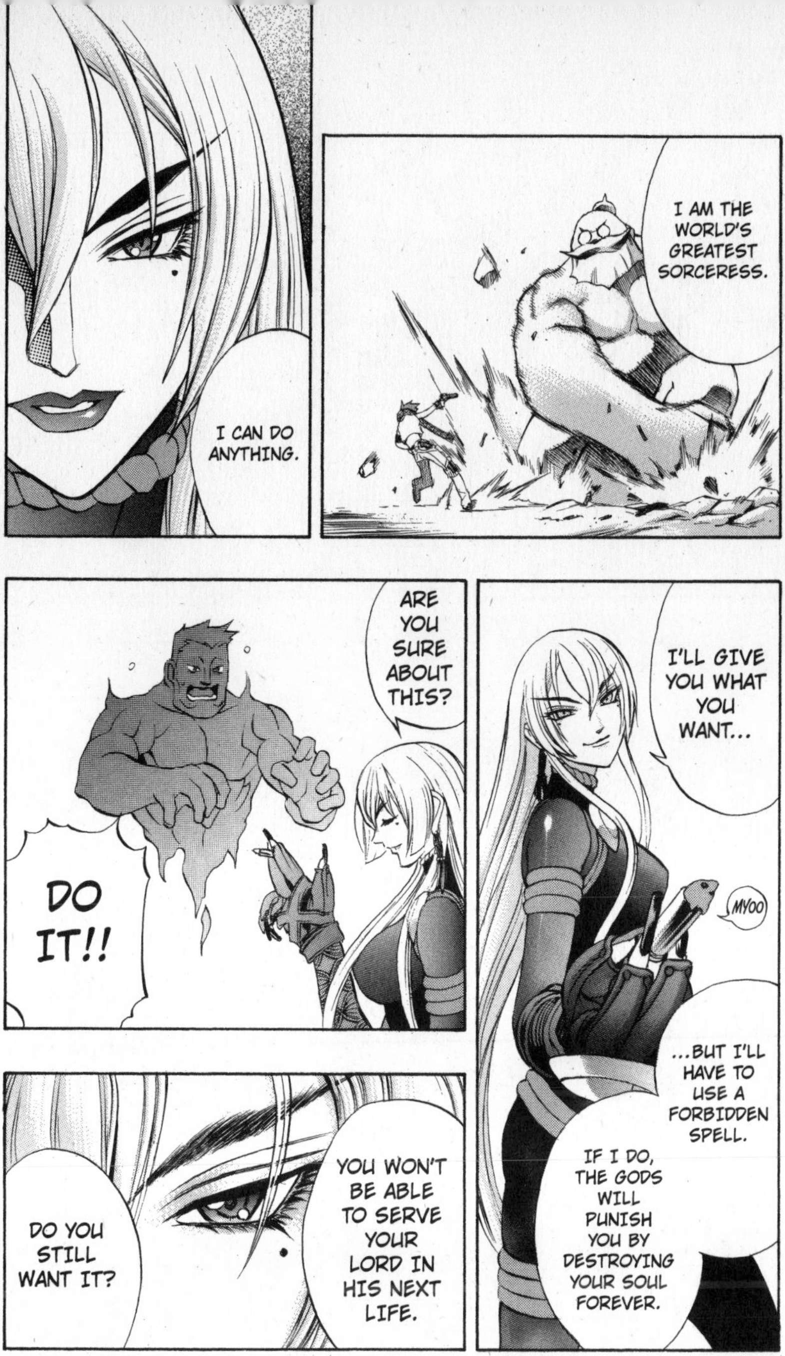
I AM THE WORLD'S GREATEST SORCERESS.
I CAN DO ANYTHING.
I'LL GIVE YOU WHAT YOU WANT...
MYOO
...BUT I'LL HAVE TO USE A FORBIDDEN SPELL.
IF I DO, THE GODS WILL PUNISH YOU BY DESTROYING YOUR SOUL FOREVER.
ARE YOU SURE ABOUT THIS?
DO IT!!
YOU WON'T BE ABLE TO SERVE YOUR LORD IN HIS NEXT LIFE.
DO YOU STILL WANT IT?

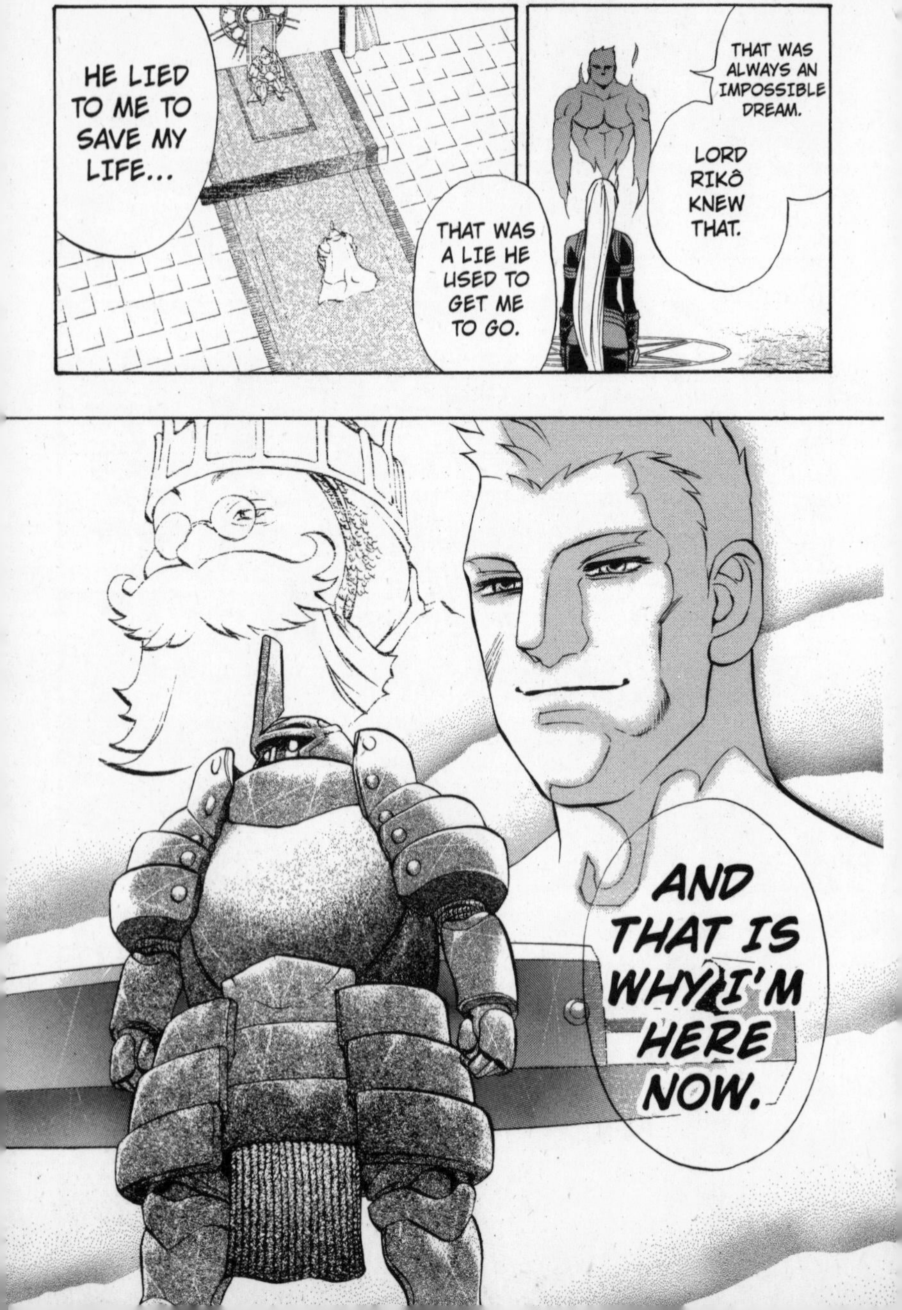
THAT WAS ALWAYS AN IMPOSSIBLE DREAM.
LORD RIKÔ KNEW THAT.
THAT WAS A LIE HE USED TO GET ME TO GO.
HE LIED TO ME TO SAVE MY LIFE...
AND THAT IS WHY I'M HERE NOW.

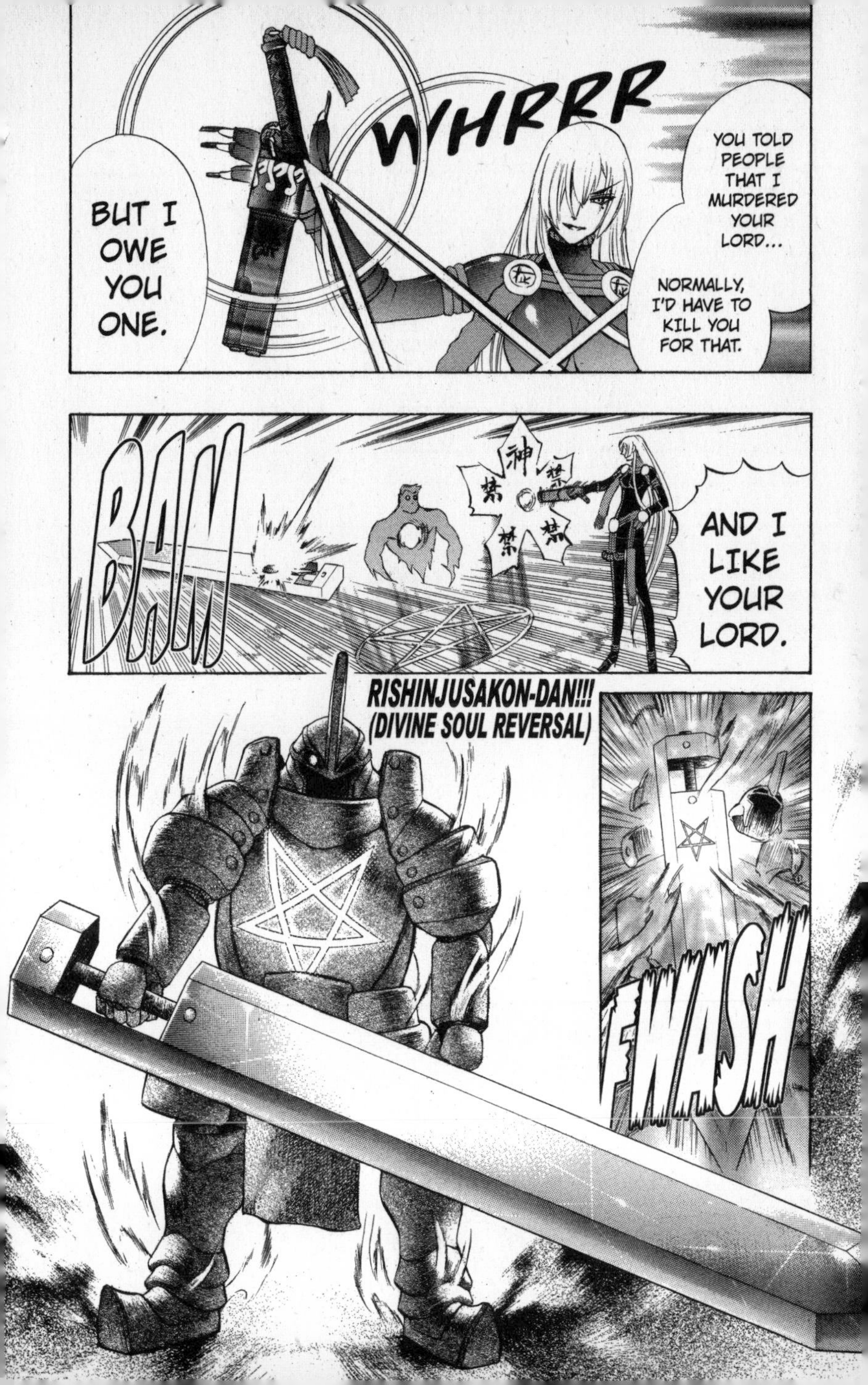
YOU TOLD PEOPLE THAT I MURDERED YOUR LORD...
NORMALLY, I'D HAVE TO KILL YOU FOR THAT.
WHRRR
BUT I OWE YOU ONE.
AND I LIKE YOUR LORD.
BAM
FWASH
RISHINJUSAKON-DAN!!!
(DIVINE SOUL REVERSAL)

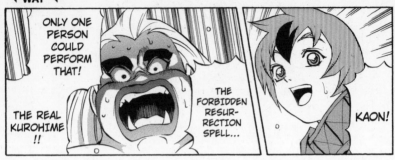

READ THIS WAY

KAON!
THE FORBIDDEN RESUR-RECTION SPELL...
ONLY ONE PERSON COULD PERFORM THAT!
THE REAL KUROHIME !!
PREPARE TO DIE, FALSE KURO-HIME!!!
KLANK
DOOM
!

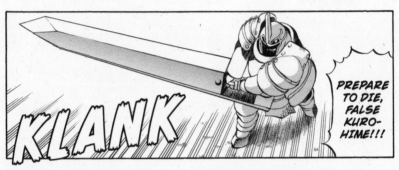

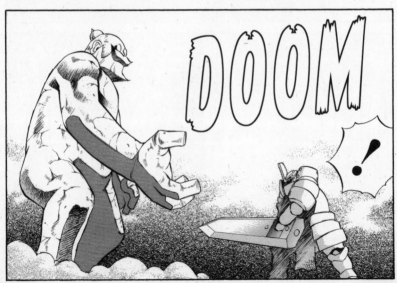

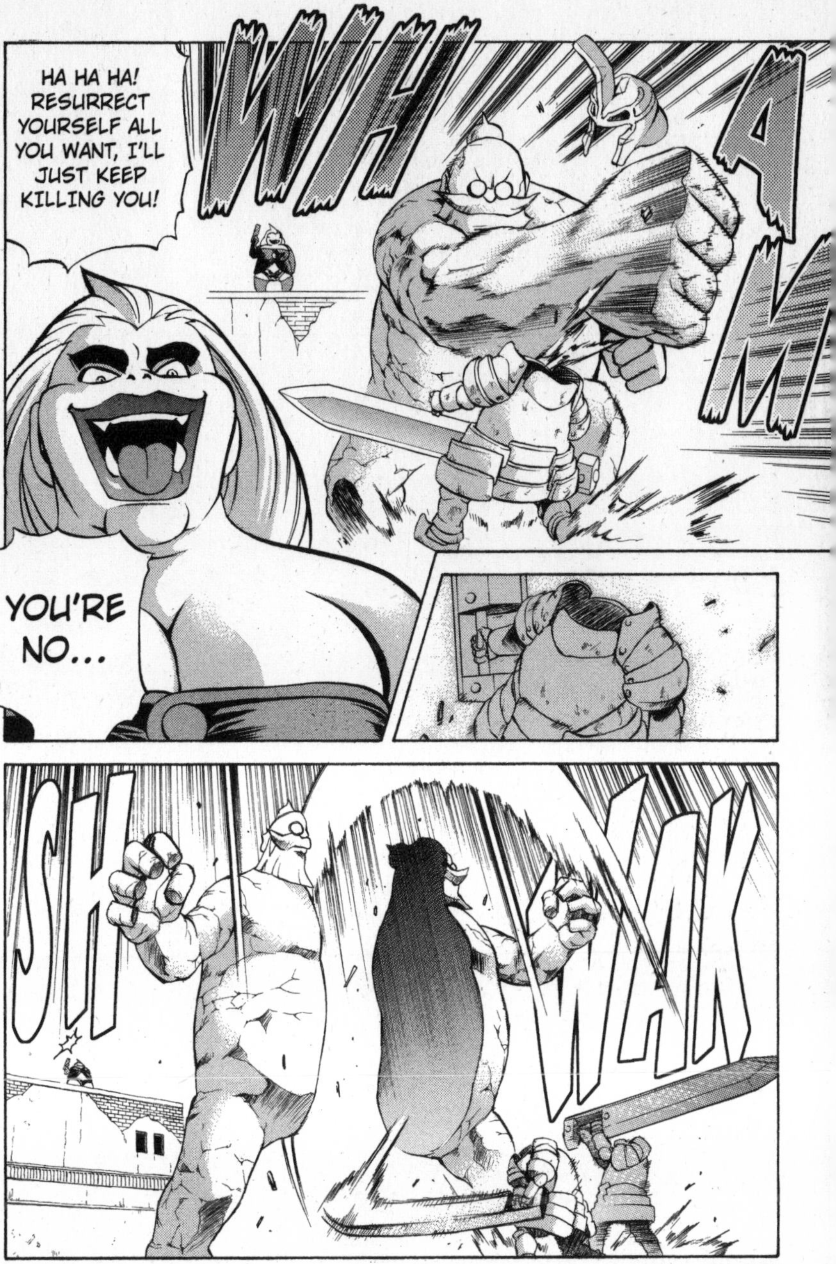
WHAM
HA HA HA! RESURRECT YOURSELF ALL YOU WANT, I'LL JUST KEEP KILLING YOU!
YOU'RE NO...
SHWAK

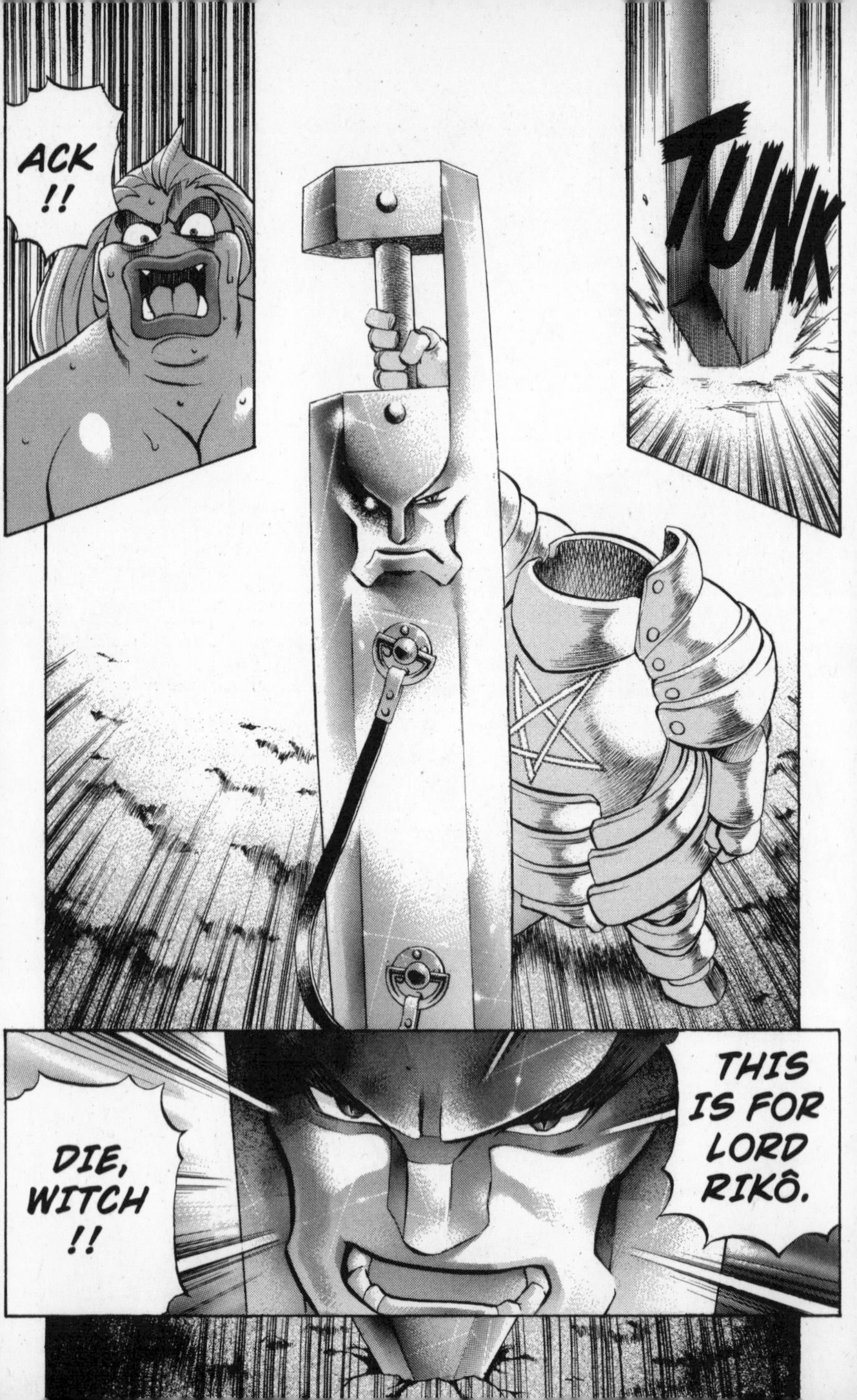
TUNK
ACK !!
THIS IS FOR LORD RIKÔ.
DIE, WITCH !!

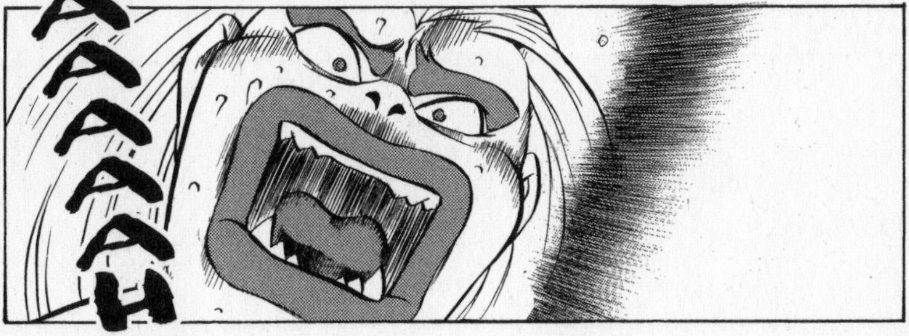
AAAAAH
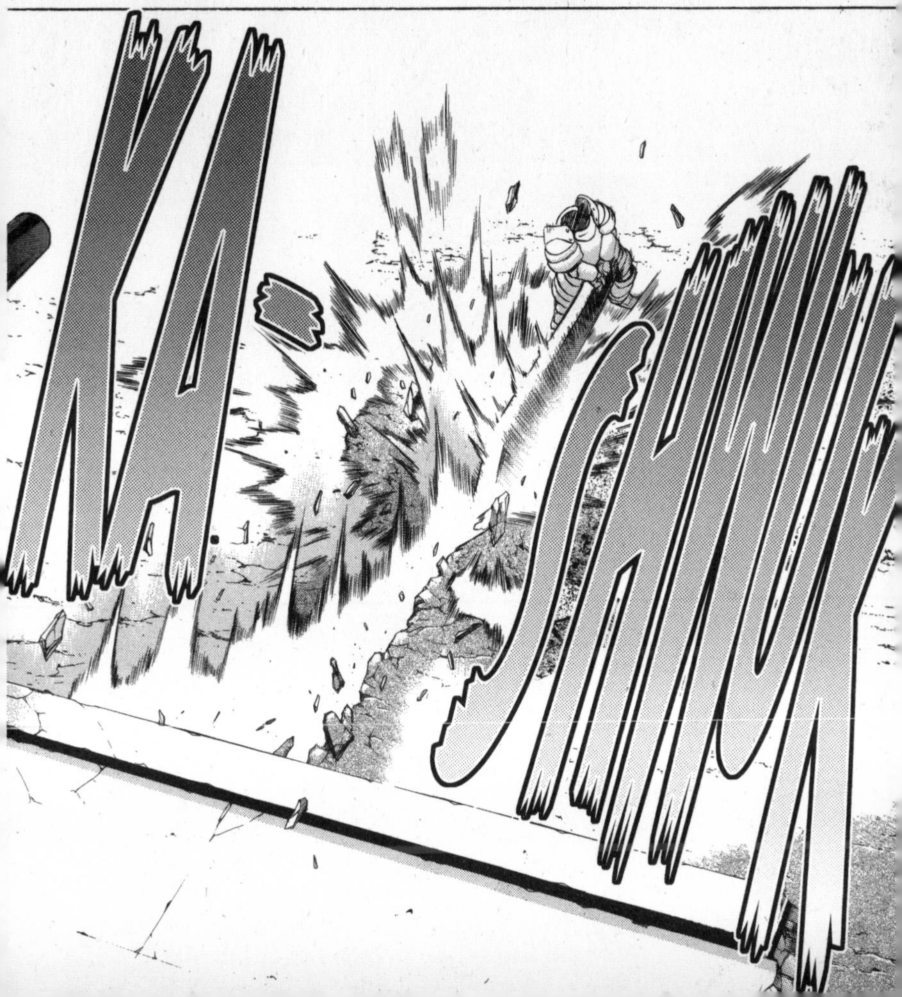
KA-SHUN

READ THIS WAY

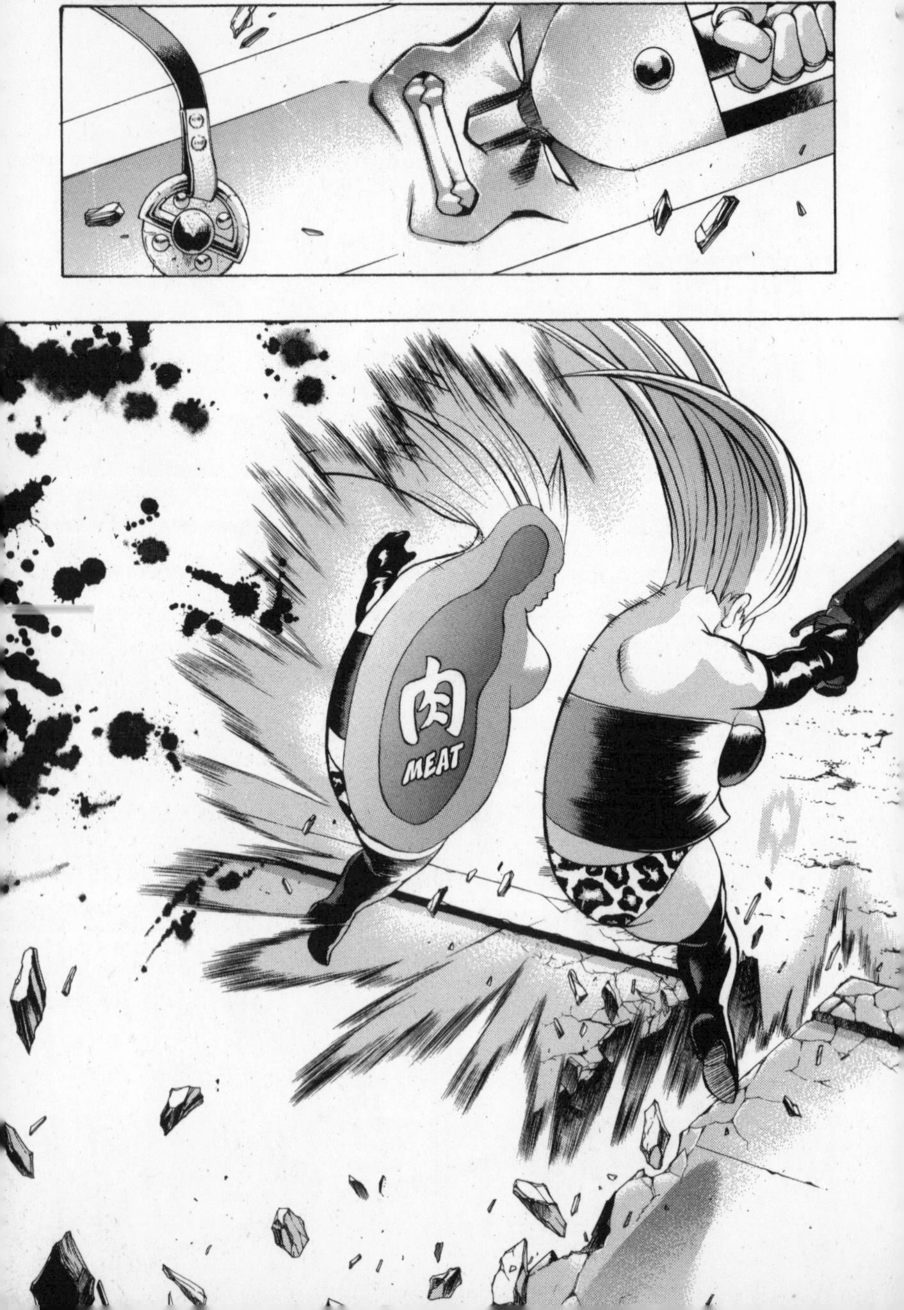
肉
MEAT

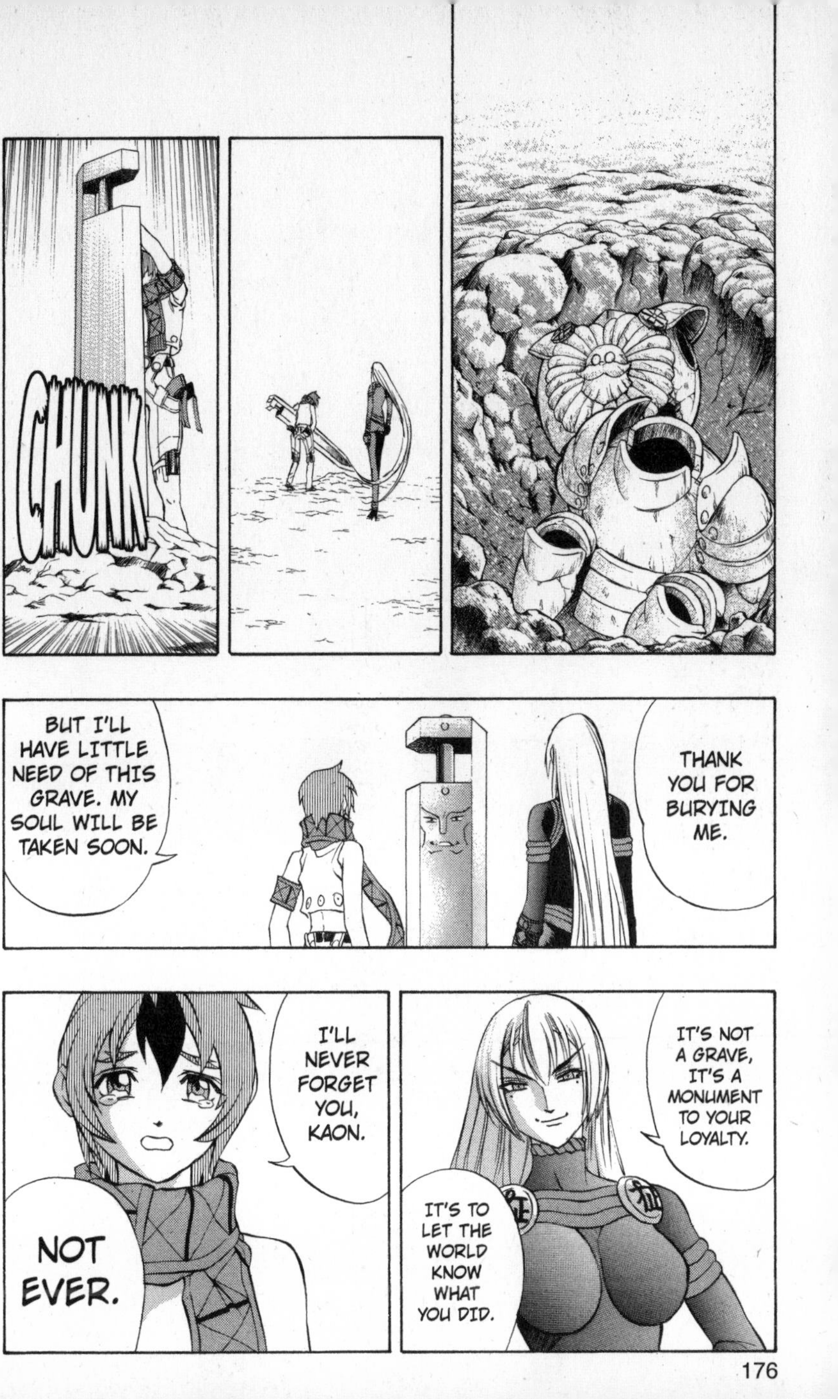
CHUNK
THANK YOU FOR BURYING ME.
BUT I'LL HAVE LITTLE NEED OF THIS GRAVE. MY SOUL WILL BE TAKEN SOON.
IT'S NOT A GRAVE, IT'S A MONUMENT TO YOUR LOYALTY.
IT'S TO LET THE WORLD KNOW WHAT YOU DID.
I'LL NEVER FORGET YOU, KAON.
NOT EVER.

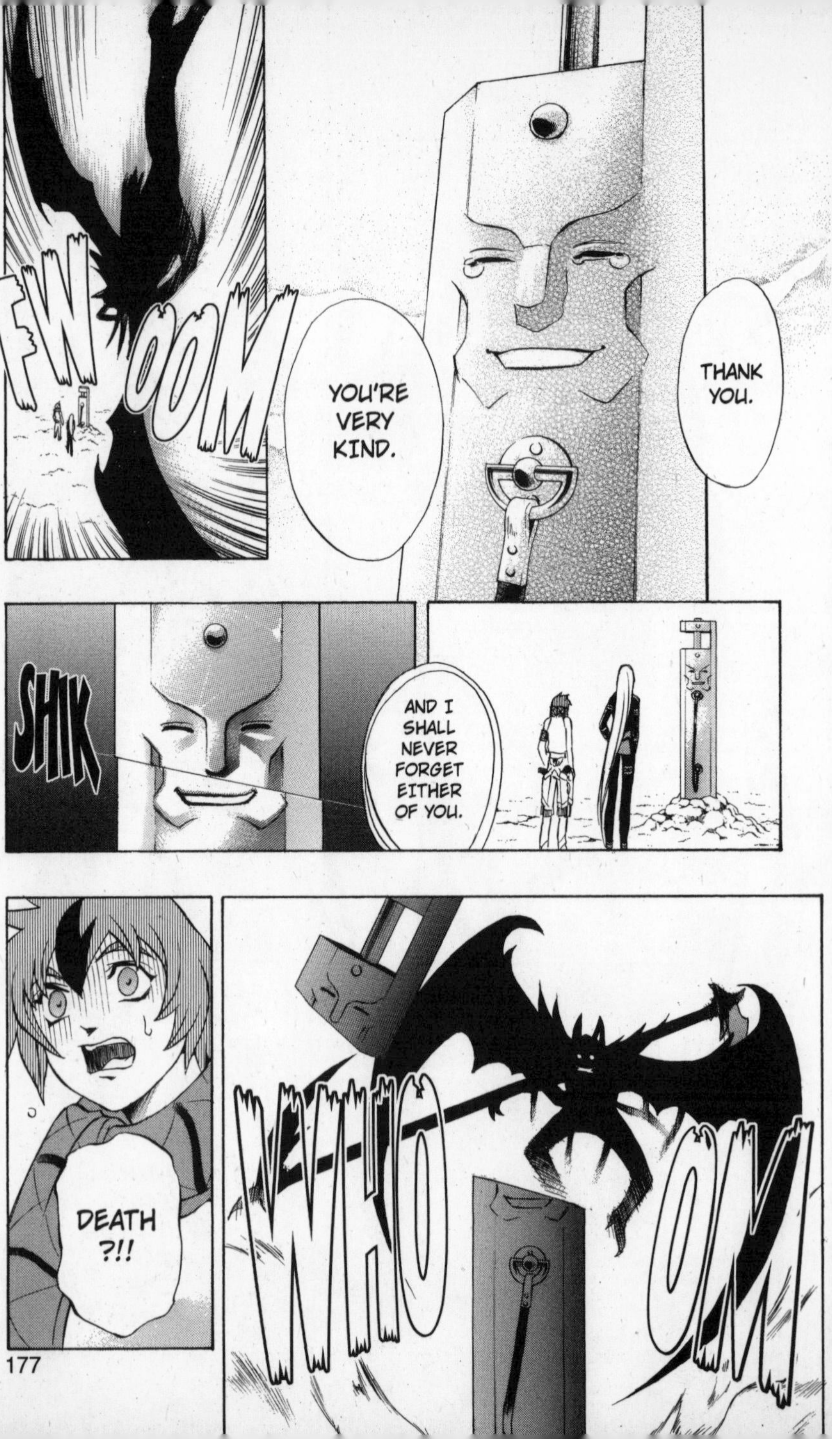
THANK YOU.
YOU'RE VERY KIND.
FWOOOM
AND I SHALL NEVER FORGET EITHER OF YOU.
SHIK
WHOOOM
DEATH ?!!

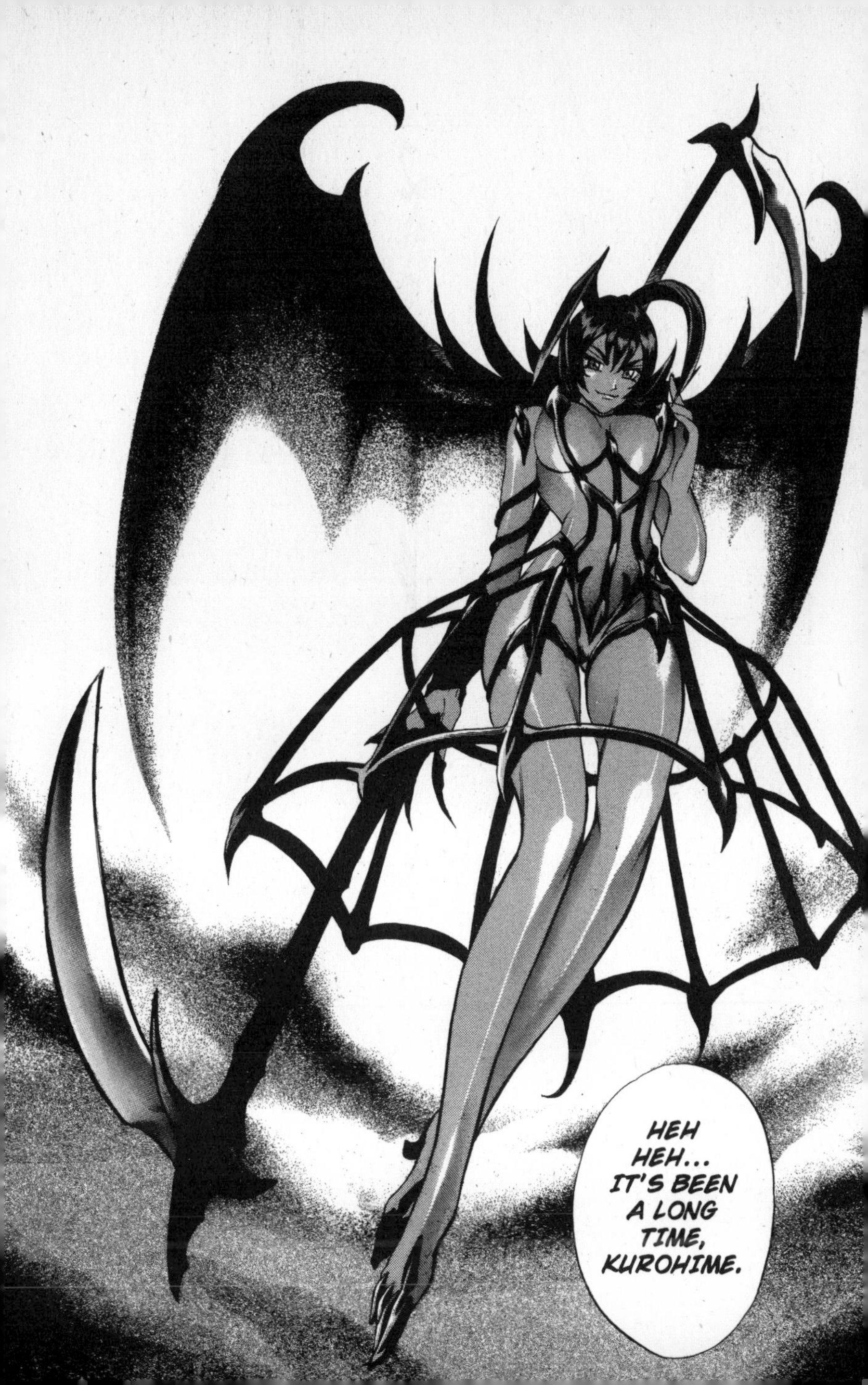
HEH HEH... IT'S BEEN A LONG TIME, KUROHIME.

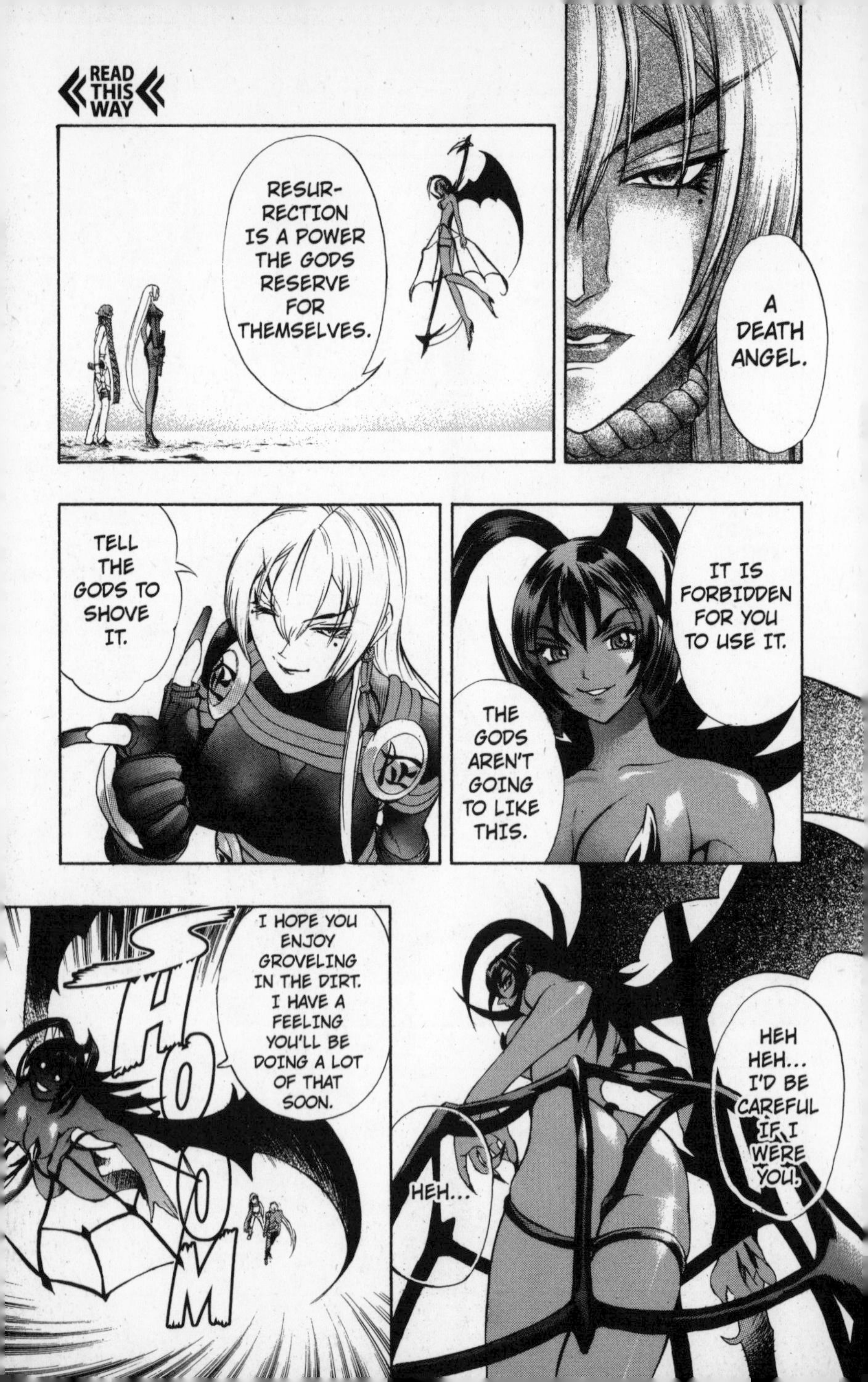
READ THIS WAY
A DEATH ANGEL.
RESURRECTION IS A POWER THE GODS RESERVE FOR THEMSELVES.
IT IS FORBIDDEN FOR YOU TO USE IT.
THE GODS AREN'T GOING TO LIKE THIS.
TELL THE GODS TO SHOVE IT.
HEH HEH... I'D BE CAREFUL IF I WERE YOU.
HEH...
I HOPE YOU ENJOY GROVELING IN THE DIRT. I HAVE A FEELING YOU'LL BE DOING A LOT OF THAT SOON.
SHOOM

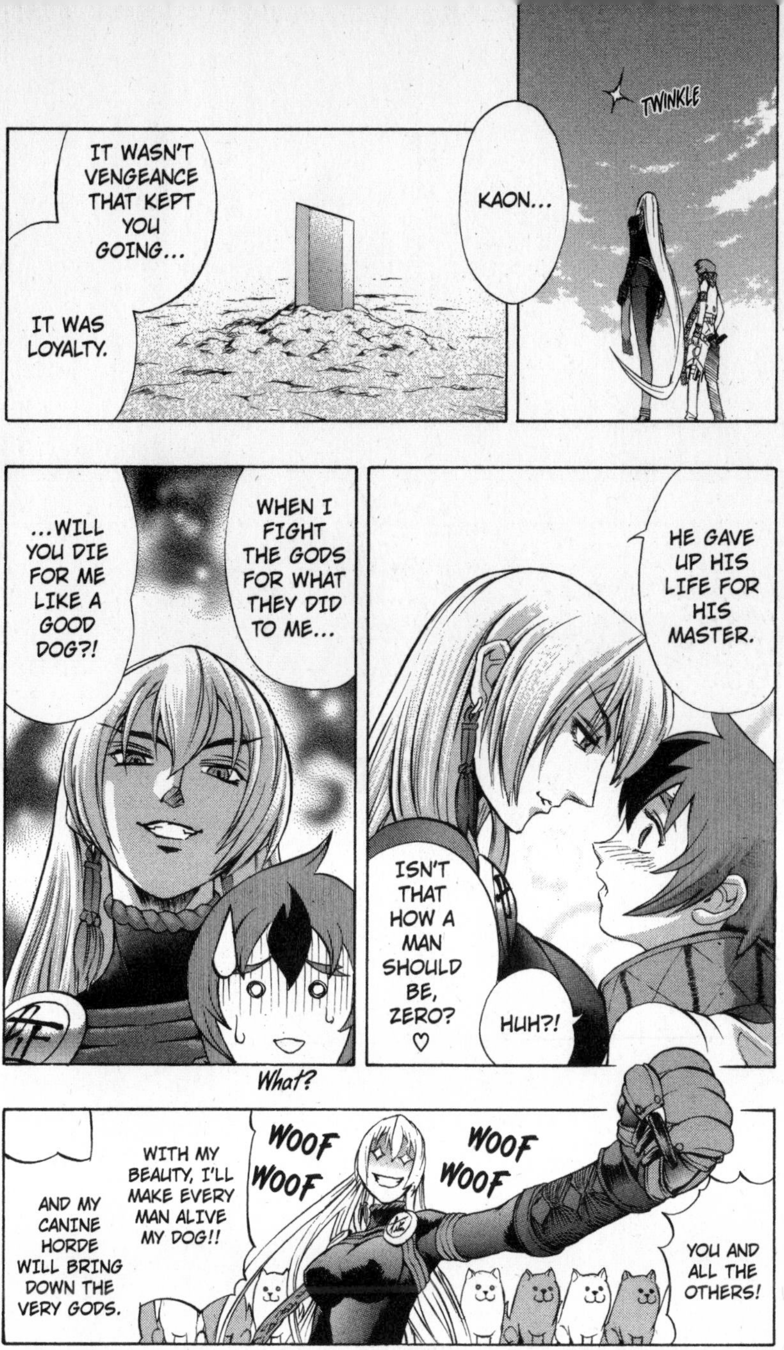
TWINKLE
KAON...
IT WASN'T VENGEANCE THAT KEPT YOU GOING...
IT WAS LOYALTY.
HE GAVE UP HIS LIFE FOR HIS MASTER.
ISN'T THAT HOW A MAN SHOULD BE, ZERO? ♡
HUH?!
WHEN I FIGHT THE GODS FOR WHAT THEY DID TO ME...
...WILL YOU DIE FOR ME LIKE A GOOD DOG?!
What?
YOU AND ALL THE OTHERS!
WOOF WOOF
WOOF WOOF
WITH MY BEAUTY, I'LL MAKE EVERY MAN ALIVE MY DOG!!
AND MY CANINE HORDE WILL BRING DOWN THE VERY GODS.

READ THIS WAY

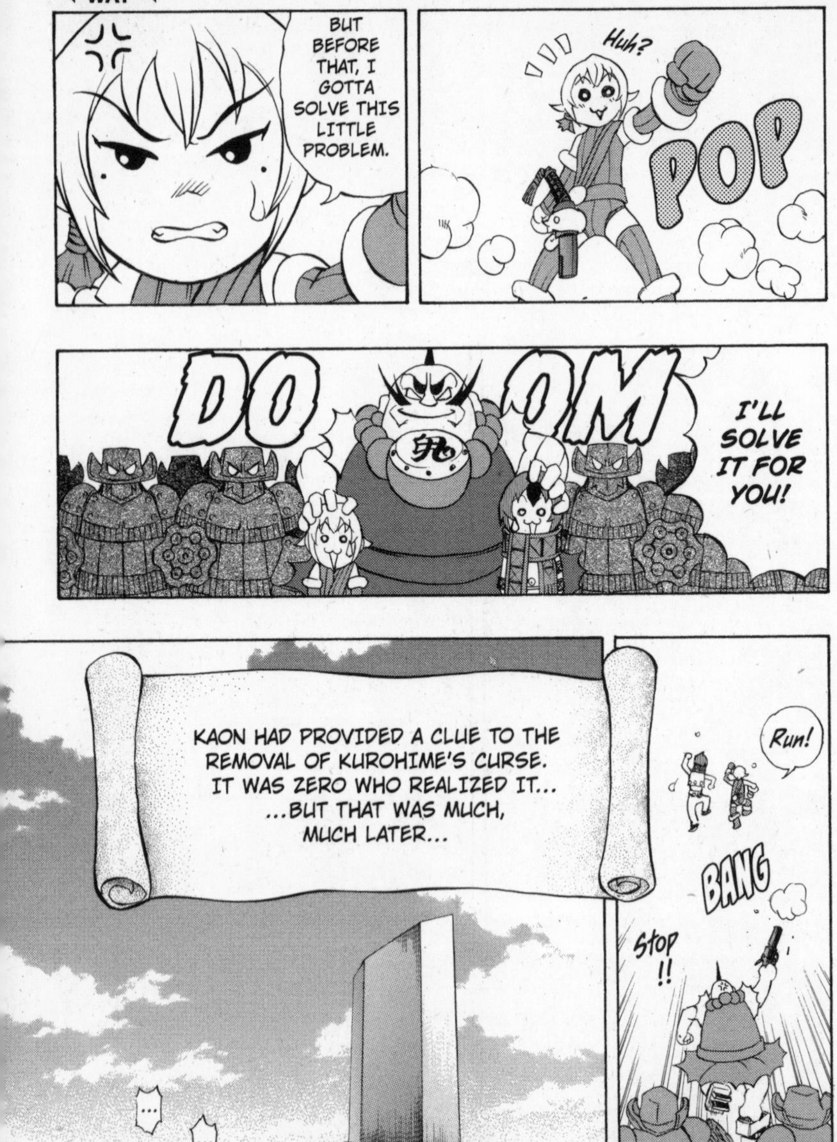
Huh?
POP
BUT BEFORE THAT, I GOTTA SOLVE THIS LITTLE PROBLEM.
DO OM
I'LL SOLVE IT FOR YOU!
Run!
BANG
Stop !!
KAON HAD PROVIDED A CLUE TO THE REMOVAL OF KUROHIME'S CURSE. IT WAS ZERO WHO REALIZED IT... ...BUT THAT WAS MUCH, MUCH LATER...
...
...
...

VOL 1 - THE END

Coming Next Volume

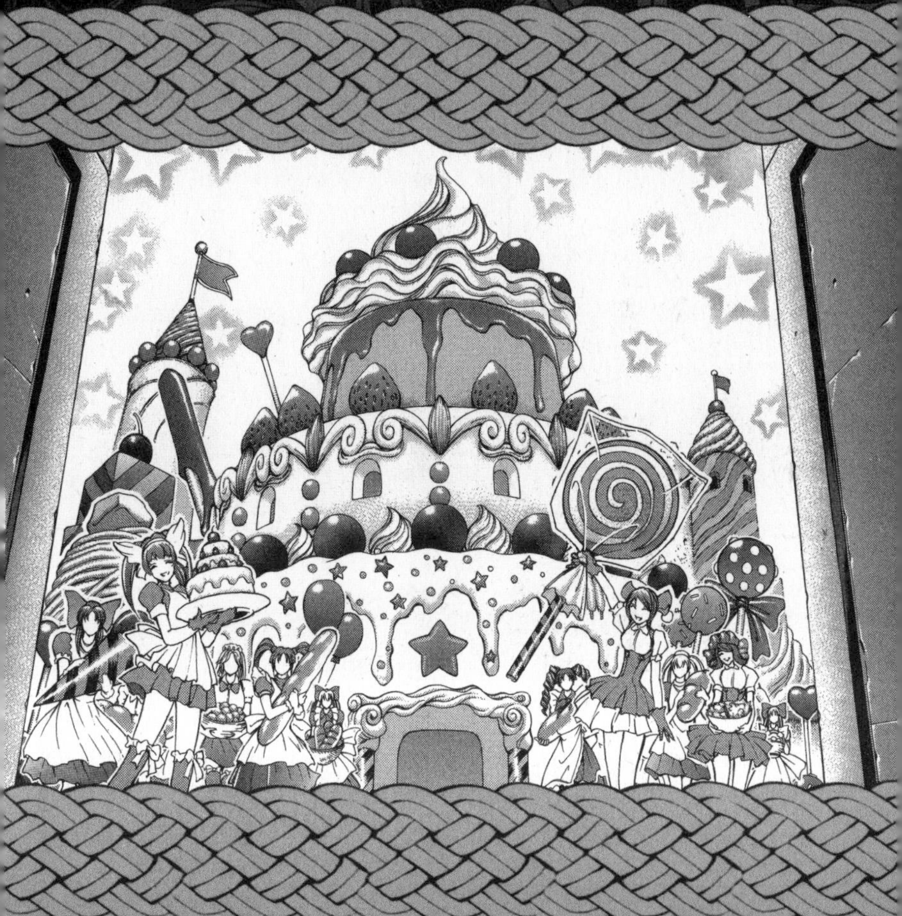

Himeko and Zero stumble upon a castle made of candy only to find themselves trapped by an evil witch, who lures unsuspecting travelers to test her magical bullets on. Luckily Kurohime appears, and it's a battle of the dragon bullets with Zero caught in the middle!

Available Now!

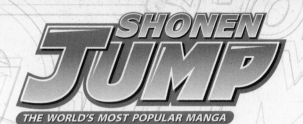
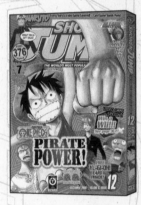
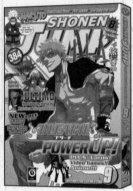
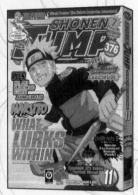